SEARCHING FOR A 'PRINCIPLE OF HUMANITY' IN INTERNATIONAL HUMANITARIAN LAW

The legal norms of international humanitarian law (IHL) are the product of a compromise between humanitarian considerations and the demands of military necessity. In *Searching for a 'Principle of Humanity' in International Humanitarian Law*, international legal scholars consider whether humanitarian considerations have an independent legal impact on IHL beyond the formation of these norms. They ask whether a 'principle of humanity' can be said to have legal force in its own right. Moreover, the book investigates whether regional or national differences are emerging regarding the import and emphasis placed on humanitarian considerations. For instance, do states which are not directly affected by armed conflict attach a greater weight to humanitarian considerations when interpreting and applying IHL than those states which are more directly involved in armed conflicts? Specifically, this book examines whether a particular 'Nordic perspective' can be identified, owing to those states' unique perspective on international conflicts since the Second World War.

KJETIL MUJEZINOVIĆ LARSEN is Associate Professor at the Norwegian Centre for Human Rights, University of Oslo. He is also author of *The Human Rights Treaty Obligations of Peacekeepers*.

CAMILLA GULDAHL COOPER is Legal Adviser and Lecturer at the Norwegian Defence Command and Staff College.

GRO NYSTUEN is Associate Professor at the Norwegian Defence University College and Senior Partner in the International Law and Policy Institute, Oslo. She is also co-editor of *Human Rights, Corporate Complicity and Disinvestment*.

SEARCHING FOR A 'PRINCIPLE OF HUMANITY' IN INTERNATIONAL HUMANITARIAN LAW

Editors

KJETIL MUJEZINOVIĆ LARSEN,

CAMILLA GULDAHL COOPER AND

GRO NYSTUEN

CAMBRIDGE
UNIVERSITY PRESS

CAMBRIDGE
UNIVERSITY PRESS

University Printing House, Cambridge CB2 8BS, United Kingdom

One Liberty Plaza, 20th Floor, New York, NY 10006, USA

477 Williamstown Road, Port Melbourne, VIC 3207, Australia

314-321, 3rd Floor, Plot 3, Splendor Forum, Jasola District Centre, New Delhi - 110025, India

79 Anson Road, #06-04/06, Singapore 079906

Cambridge University Press is part of the University of Cambridge.

It furthers the University's mission by disseminating knowledge in the pursuit of education, learning and research at the highest international levels of excellence.

www.cambridge.org
Information on this title: www.cambridge.org/9781107021846

First published 2013
First paperback edition 2015

A catalogue record for this publication is available from the British Library

Library of Congress Cataloging in Publication data
Searching for a 'principle of humanity' in international humanitarian law / editors Kjetil Mujezinović Larsen, Camilla Guldahl Cooper & Gro Nystuen.
p. cm.
Includes bibliographical references and index.
ISBN 978-1-107-02184-6 (hardback)
1. Humanitarian law. I. Larsen, Kjetil Mujezinović, 1976–
II. Cooper, Camilla Guldahl. III. Nystuen, Gro.
KZ6471.S43 2012
341.6′7–dc23 2012018830

ISBN 978-1-107-02184-6 Hardback
ISBN 978-1-316-50058-3 Paperback

CONTENTS

LIST OF TABLES

NOTES ON CONTRIBUTORS

ARNE WILLY DAHL is Judge Advocate General for the Norwegian armed forces. He has previously worked for the State Pollution Control Authority in Oslo, and as a lecturer in public and military law at the Military Academy. In 1986 he became Judge Advocate and two years later became Judge Advocate General. Since 2006 he has been President of the International Society for Military Law and the Law of War.

YORAM DINSTEIN is Professor Emeritus at Tel-Aviv University. He is a former President of the University (1991–1998), as well as former Rector and former Dean of the Faculty of Law. He served twice as the Charles H. Stockton Professor of International Law at the US Naval War College in Newport, Rhode Island. He was also a Humboldt Fellow at the Max Planck Institute of International Law in Heidelberg, Germany, a Meltzer Visiting Professor of Law at New York University and a Visiting Professor of Law at the University of Toronto. He is a Member of the Institute of International Law.

OLA ENGDAHL is Associate Professor at the Swedish National Defence College. His main research areas are international humanitarian law and human rights law, including international law aspects on peace operations. He has served as Legal Adviser in the SFOR operation in Bosnia-Herzegovina and as an adviser on international law at the Ministry of Foreign Affairs. He is also a Member of the Delegation for International Humanitarian Law Monitoring of Arms Projects, and Legal Adviser on the Army Tactical Staff. His previous publications include *Protection of Personnel in Peace Operations.*

CAMILLA GULDAHL COOPER is Legal Adviser and Lecturer at the Norwegian Defence Command and Staff College, where she works on the development of a Norwegian Manual of the Law of Armed Conflict. She teaches operational law at all levels in the Armed Forces, including soldiers, at the Army War College and at the Command and Staff College.

Camilla has also taught several specialised courses, such as the US Navy ILOMO course in Newport, Rhode Island, in 2010, and the Vienna Course on International Law for Military Legal Advisers in 2011 and 2012. In 2011, she deployed as a military legal adviser to ISAF.

LAURI HANNIKAINEN is Professor Emeritus of International Law at the University of Turku, Finland. He is a member of the European Commission against Racism and Intolerance (ECRI) at the Council of Europe. He has written extensively on human rights and humanitarian law, and previous publications include *Peremptory Norms (Jus Cogens) in International Law: History, Criteria, Present Status*.

CECILIE HELLESTVEIT is a special adviser with the International Law and Policy Institute (ILPI), Oslo. She is also affiliated with the University of Oslo, where she is finalising a dissertation on humanitarian law in non-international armed conflict. In 2009, Cecilie served as international rapporteur to the International Society for Military Law and the Law of War, co-editing the XVIII Recueil. She has previously worked at the Norwegian Centre for Human Rights, and the Peace Research Institute, Oslo (PRIO).

RIKKE ISHØY works as a legal adviser, coordinator of protection activities and deputy head of delegation for the International Committee of the Red Cross with whom she has worked in Israel and the Occupied Territories, Afghanistan, Lebanon, Ethiopia and Liberia. Whilst writing her chapter, Rikke worked for a period for the Copenhagen Police as a prosecutor.

ROBERT KOLB is Professor of Public International Law at the University of Geneva. He has worked as legal adviser at the International Committee of the Red Cross from 1998 to 1999 and occasionally for the International Law Directorate of the Swiss Federal Department of Foreign Affairs.

KJETIL MUJEZINOVIĆ LARSEN is Associate Professor at the Norwegian Centre for Human Rights, University of Oslo, where he teaches human rights law and international humanitarian law. His research experience includes human rights law, international humanitarian law, and general international law (particularly the responsibility of international organisations). Kjetil's previous publications include *The Human Rights Treaty Obligations of Peacekeepers*. He is a former member of the Council of Europe's Working Group on Missing Persons, and of the Advisory Committee on International Humanitarian Law in the Norwegian Red Cross.

KATARINA MÅNSSON is Associate Officer at the Executive Office of the Secretary-General. From 2008 to 2012 she worked for the Office of the High Commissioner for Human Rights, based in Uganda and Geneva. She has published widely on human rights, peace and security and conflict resolution. Katarina has previously worked at the Raoul Wallenberg Institute for Human Rights and Humanitarian Law in Sweden, at diplomatic missions to the United Nations in Geneva and New York, and as a journalist. The views expressed in her chapter are those of the author and do not necessarily reflect the views of the United Nations.

GRO NYSTUEN is Associate Professor of International Humanitarian Law at the University of Oslo, and Associate Professor at the Norwegian Defence University College. Between 1991 and 2005, she worked for the Norwegian Ministry for Foreign Affairs. She has written extensively on international humanitarian law, peace agreements, human rights, international terrorism, corporate social responsibility and *jus ad bellum* issues. Gro is also Chair of the Council on Ethics for the Norwegian Government Pension Fund and founding partner of the International Law and Policy Institute in Oslo.

SIGRID REDSE JOHANSEN is a lecturer in international and military law at the Norwegian Defence University College.

PETER VEDEL KESSING is a senior researcher at the Danish Institute for Human Rights and a lecturer at the Faculty of Law at Copenhagen where he specialises in armed conflict, security, counter-terrorism and human rights. He has worked in the field of international human rights law for many years, and has previously been head of the International Law Department at the Danish Red Cross. Additionally, he has been a judge in a Danish district court and worked with the Danish Ministry of the Interior and the UNHCR on international refugee law.

ABBREVIATIONS

AP	Additional Protocol
CCW	Convention on Prohibitions or Restrictions on the Use of Certain Conventional Weapons
CRC	Convention on the Rights of the Child
CRC-OPAC	Optional Protocol to the CRC on the Involvement of Children in Armed Conflict
CWC	Convention on the Prohibitions of the Development, Production, Stockpiling and Use of Chemical Weapons
DPH	direct participation in hostilities
DRC	Democratic Republic of the Congo
ECHR	European Convention on Human Rights
ECtHR	European Court of Human Rights
GC	Geneva Convention
HRC	Human Rights Committee
HRL	human rights law
IAC	international armed conflict
ICC	International Criminal Court
ICCPR	International Covenant on Civil and Political Rights
ICERD	International Covenant on the Elimination of All Forms of Racial Discrimination
ICESCR	International Covenant on Economic, Social and Cultural Rights
ICJ	International Court of Justice
ICRC	International Committee of the Red Cross
ICTY	International Criminal Tribunal for the Former Yugoslavia
IHL	international humanitarian law
IHRL	international human rights law
ILC	International Law Commission
ISAF	International Security Assistance Force
LOAC	law of armed conflict
MRM	monitoring and reporting mechanism
NIAC	non-international armed conflict
OHCHR	Office of the High Commissioner for Human Rights

OUP	Operation Unified Protector
PCIJ	Permanent Court of International Justice
POW	prisoner of war
RCA	riot control agent
ROE	Rules of Engagement
TCN	troop contributing nation
UDHR	Universal Declaration of Human Rights
UN	United Nations
UNSC	UN Security Council

1

Introduction by the editors: is there a 'principle of humanity' in international humanitarian law?

KJETIL MUJEZINOVIĆ LARSEN,
CAMILLA GULDAHL COOPER AND GRO NYSTUEN

1. Object and purpose of this book

In international humanitarian law (IHL), references are frequently made to a 'principle of humanity' or to 'principles of humanity'. Such terms appear not only in scholarly contributions, but also in legal texts, military manuals and other official documents. But despite the frequent use of these terms, the concept of a 'principle of humanity' is vague in several respects. The primary purpose of the present book is to explore important issues that may contribute to greater clarity concerning the possible emergence, existence, function and significance of the 'principle of humanity' in contemporary IHL. The concept gives rise to a wide range of questions, and at the moment it suffices to introduce three challenges.

First, is it a 'principle' in the same sense as other general principles in IHL? When references are made to general principles, such as the principle of distinction, the principle of proportionality or the principle of unnecessary suffering, the use of the term 'principle' implies a particular legal impact of the concepts.[1] Does the 'principle of humanity' have a similar legal impact? If so, what is this impact? Or is this 'principle' more a form of consideration, as opposed to a legal principle, the violation of which would result in some form of reaction?

Secondly, what is 'humanity'? This is not an easily defined term, and it may be given different meanings and carry different connotations depending both on the user of the term and on the situation in which the term is used. To hint at the possible significance of this question, it should be noted that the 'principle of humanity' in this regard clearly is different from the general principles mentioned above, as 'distinction', 'proportionality' and 'unnecessary suffering' carry a particular, and well-defined, meaning in IHL.[2]

Thirdly, what is the scope of application of such a 'principle'? Is it, for example, relevant when assessing means and methods of combat, or does it apply to the treatment of protected persons under the four Geneva Conventions?

A further introduction to the 'principle of humanity' will be provided in section 2 below, where the focus is to describe the legal basis for the possible principle and to introduce its possible legal impact.

As a consequence of the current lack of clarity with regard to a 'principle of humanity', however, this book also addresses two related issues that bring useful perspectives to the discussion. When combined, these two issues may provide arguments that either support or deny the existence of a 'principle of humanity' in contemporary IHL. Furthermore, if one were to conclude that a 'principle of humanity' does not as such exist in IHL, these issues would also allow for an inquiry to be made as to whether such a principle is, at least, *emerging* in IHL.

The first of these issues is whether there has taken, or is taking, place a shift in the fundamental relationship between humanitarian considerations and considerations of military necessity in IHL. Any textbook on IHL will describe how the IHL legal regime incorporates a delicate balance between these two sets of considerations, but this book inquires as to whether recent developments may arguably have resulted in a generally increased impact of humanitarian considerations in IHL at the cost of considerations of military necessity. This inquiry is addressed further in section 3 below.

The second issue is whether regional or national differences are emerging with regard to the importance and emphasis placed on humanitarian considerations in IHL. The underlying, fundamental hypothesis to be tested is whether states which are not directly affected by armed conflicts attach greater weight to humanitarian considerations when interpreting and applying IHL than those states that are more directly involved in armed conflicts. It follows from this hypothesis that the latter group of states thus places greater emphasis on considerations of military necessity. For practical reasons, the hypothesis will be tested only in a limited manner in this book, through an inquiry as to whether a particular 'Nordic perspective' can be identified under IHL. The Nordic states (Denmark, Finland, Iceland, Norway and Sweden) are typical examples of states which have not been affected by armed conflicts on their own soil since the Second World War, and these states therefore provide useful illustrations in this context. This inquiry is addressed further in section 4 below.

2. Legal basis and the arguable legal impact of a 'principle of humanity'

It is well documented that humanitarian considerations have influenced the law of war in various cultures since ancient times, with the result that some restraints should be observed during armed conflict.[3] Famous examples can be found in the Old Testament, where the prophet Elisha told the king of Israel that he should not slay his prisoners;[4] in the old Indian epic *Mahabharata* and the Code of Manu, which prohibited the killing of those who were incapable of fighting, and further prohibited the use of certain weapons;[5] or in ancient Greece, where the use of poison on weapons or the poisoning of wells were prohibited.[6] Principles of a humanitarian character could also be found, e.g., in the Code of Hammurabi King of Babylon, the teachings of Sun Tzu, the practices of the Roman Empire, or in Islamic tradition, to name but a few sources. In the Middle Ages, concepts of chivalry emerged, and the conduct of hostilities was governed by strict principles.[7] While the end of the Middle Ages saw a decline in the impact of considerations of chivalry and humanity on the conduct of hostilities, the Age of Enlightenment brought with it a reinvigoration of these concepts. It had become generally acknowledged that it was prohibited to kill civilians or persons who had laid down their arms, and such thoughts gradually began to be included in international treaties.[8]

For the purposes of the present book, this cursory account should suffice to provide a background for the first legal text that deserves closer attention, namely the 1863 Lieber Code.[9] The Lieber Code is commonly recognised as the first attempt to codify the laws and customs of war. It consisted of 157 articles and was promulgated as law with binding effect for conduct in the field of the Union Army of the United States during the American Civil War. The Code was described – perhaps somewhat over-enthusiastically – by Root in 1913 as 'an instinctive selection of the best and most humane practice' during armed conflicts.[10] A more realistic description is offered by Meron, who states that the Code's 'balancing of humanitarian concerns with military necessity did not always further the dictates of humanity'[11] (and that a small number of provisions even appear both 'harsh' and 'barbaric'[12] to the modern reader), but that the Code was founded on 'broad humanitarian principles' and contained an 'overall humanitarian spirit'.[13] Several examples may be given of provisions where humanitarian considerations restrict the conduct of hostilities, but in the present context the more relevant issue is the reference made in the Code to a more general 'principle of humanity'. This is particularly evident in Article 4 of the Code, which required those who administered martial law to be 'strictly guided by the principles of justice, honor, and humanity'. While neither the interpretation nor the possible legal impact of these 'principles of … humanity' are clear, the way in which the term is used implies that Lieber *may* have intended this to be a general standard to be respected even in the absence of specific norms.

A few years later, a form of a 'principle of humanity' was invoked for a very specific purpose in the 1868 St. Petersburg Declaration.[14] While the Declaration itself only contains a narrow, specific ban of a particular type of ammunition, it has acquired an importance that significantly exceeds this narrow scope, namely through its codification of the general principle prohibiting the infliction of unnecessary suffering.[15] The relevant parts of the Declaration are found in the Preamble, where it is said that 'the employment of arms which uselessly aggravate the sufferings of disabled men, or render their death inevitable' would be 'contrary to the *laws of humanity*' (emphasis added). While the principle of unnecessary suffering is recognised as a fundamental principle of IHL, the related reference to 'the laws of humanity' has not acquired any independent legal impact. This reference to humanity helped only to justify the creation of the specific norm and to support the more specific principle of unnecessary suffering.

The next step in the development came in the Preamble to the 1899 Hague Convention II and the 1907 Hague Convention IV containing the Regulations on the Laws and Customs of War on Land, namely the well-known Martens Clause. The Clause, in its 1907 version in an English translation, reads:

> Until a more complete code of the laws of war has been issued, the High Contracting Parties deem it expedient to declare that, in cases not included in the Regulations adopted by them, the inhabitants and the belligerents remain under the protection and the rule of the principles of the law of nations, as they result from the usages established among civilized peoples, from the laws of humanity, and the dictates of the public conscience.[16]

The Martens Clause has been interpreted in various ways, and these interpretations will be addressed below. But first it is useful to note (in the words of Cassese) that the Martens Clause 'has been very frequently relied upon in international dealings, restated by states in treaties, cited by international and national courts, invoked by organizations and individuals', and it 'approached the question of the laws of humanity for the first time not as a *moral* issue but from a *positivist* ... perspective'.[17]

Four important examples of restatements of the Martens Clause in later treaties ought to be mentioned before we turn to its possible legal impact. First, it was recalled in the Preamble to Additional Protocol II to the Geneva Conventions in 1977 that 'in cases not covered by the law in force, the human person remains under the protection of the principles of humanity and the dictates of the public conscience'.[18] Secondly, the Preamble to the Convention on Prohibitions or Restrictions on the Use of Certain Conventional Weapons which may be Deemed to be Excessively Injurious or to Have Indiscriminate Effects (CCW) from 1980 contains a similar clause, where the Contracting States confirmed their determination 'that in cases not covered by this Convention and its annexed Protocols or by other international agreements, the civilian population and the combatants shall at all times remain under the protection and authority of the principles of international law derived from established custom, from the principles of humanity and from the dictates of public conscience'.[19] Thirdly, the Convention on the Prohibition of the Use, Stockpiling, Production and Transfer of Anti-Personnel Mines and on their Destruction, in its Preamble, stresses 'the role of public conscience in furthering the principles of humanity as evidenced by the call for a total ban of anti-personnel mines'. Fourthly, it was reaffirmed more recently in the Cluster Munitions Convention in 2008 that 'in cases not covered by this Convention or by other international agreements, civilians and combatants remain under the protection and authority of the principles of international law, derived from established custom, from the principles of humanity and from the dictates of public conscience'.[20]

Finally, it should be recalled that even the four Geneva Conventions of 1949 contain a reference to the 'laws of humanity', as it is provided that a denunciation of the Conventions 'shall in no way impair the obligations which the Parties to the conflict shall remain bound to fulfil by virtue of the principles of the law of nations, as they result from the usages established among civilized peoples, from the laws of humanity and the dictates of the public conscience'.[21] It is also worth recalling that Common Article 3 sets forth the fundamental rule that persons taking no active part in the hostilities shall in all circumstances be 'treated humanely'.

Legal instruments therefore provide ample references to 'principles of humanity' or to 'laws of humanity'. But what is the content of this concept, and what is its legal impact? These questions will be addressed to a varying extent by the different contributions in this book, and this chapter thus only aims to provide some general points of departure for the further discussion.

At the outset, it can be established that no one questions the impact of humanitarian considerations in the *norm-creation* process in IHL. In the creation of binding, positive norms in IHL, humanitarian considerations are always weighed against demands of military necessity, and one may even say that every single norm in IHL represents a compromise between these considerations.[22] Whether one characterises the influential notion as 'humanitarian considerations', a 'principle of humanity' or 'laws of humanity' is then partly a semantic question, and partly a question of how restrictive one is with regard to the use of the term 'principle'.

A more controversial question is whether a 'principle of humanity' exists with a legal impact as an *independent, binding norm* in IHL. Is the legal impact of such a 'principle' limited only to the norm-creation process, or does it have a legal impact as a norm in its own right? This issue is most frequently discussed in relation to the Martens Clause, which has been subject to various interpretations in both legal doctrine and practice. Cassese has identified three main trends.[23]

First, it is contended that the Martens Clause operates only at the level of interpretation of international principles and rules. There are two varieties of this argument. One understanding is that the Clause excludes the *a contrario* argument that when a matter is not covered by the Hague Regulations (or by later conventions where the Clause is reiterated), belligerents would be free to act in whatever manner they wish. Another understanding is that the Clause serves as a general interpretative guideline, in the sense that whenever there are doubts about the interpretation of norms under IHL, the Clause calls for the demands of humanity and public conscience to be taken into account.

Secondly, it is contended that the Clause has had an impact on the sources of international law, and thereby contributed to an expansion of the sources of IHL. The argument is that the Martens Clause has created two new and independent sources of law, namely the 'laws of humanity' and 'the dictates of public conscience'.

Thirdly, it is contended that the Clause is an expression of notions that have motivated and inspired the development of IHL, i.e., that the Clause has had an impact on the norm-creation process.

Cassese also formulates a fourth option, namely to let the Clause have an impact on the assessment of the international customary law status of norms or principles in IHL, in the sense that if a principle or rule reflects the laws of humanity or the dictates of public conscience, the requirements of state practice may be loosened while the requirements of *opinio juris* become more prominent.[24] He formulates this view after having reviewed national and international case law referring to the Martens Clause, from which he draws the conclusion that 'no international or national court has ever found that a principle or rule had emerged in the international community as a result of "the laws of humanity" or the "dictates of public conscience"'.[25] Meron has also expressed the view that the legal significance of the Clause is rather restricted. He also focuses on the impact of the Clause in the formation of customary international law, and states further that the Clause should be taken into consideration in evaluating the legality of weapons and methods of war. Meron is also of the opinion that it provides an argument against a finding of *non liquet*.[26]

In the *Kupreskić* case, the Trial Chamber in the International Criminal Tribunal for the Former Yugoslavia (ICTY) suggested a direct legal impact of the Martens Clause. After expressing that the Clause 'enjoins, as a minimum, reference to those principles and dictates any time a rule of international humanitarian law is not sufficiently rigorous or precise: in those instances the scope and purport of the rule must be defined with reference to those principles and dictates', the Chamber continued:[27]

> As an example of the way in which the Martens Clause may be utilised, regard might be had to considerations such as the cumulative effect of attacks on military objectives causing incidental damage to civilians. In other words, it may happen that single attacks on military objectives causing incidental damage to civilians, although they may raise doubts as to their lawfulness, nevertheless do not appear on their face to fall foul per se of the loose prescriptions of Articles 57 and 58 (or of the corresponding customary rules). However, in case of repeated attacks, all or most of them falling within the grey area between indisputable legality and unlawfulness, it might be warranted to conclude that the cumulative effect of such acts entails that they may not be in keeping with international law. Indeed, this pattern of military conduct may turn out to jeopardise excessively the lives and assets of civilians, contrary to the demands of humanity.

A possible legal impact of a 'principle of humanity' is also discussed in legal literature and other sources without a reference being made to the Martens Clause. For the purposes of the present section, two paragraphs from the UK *Manual of the Law of Armed Conflict* form an appropriate starting point. This manual states first that humanity 'forbids the infliction of suffering, injury or destruction not actually necessary for the accomplishment of legitimate military purposes', and second:

> The principle of humanity is based on the notion that once a military purpose has been achieved, the further infliction of suffering is unnecessary. Thus, if an enemy combatant has been put out of action by being wounded or captured, there is no military purpose to be achieved by continuing to attack him. For the same reason, the principle of humanity confirms the basic immunity of civilian populations and civilian objects from attack because civilians and civilian objects make no contribution to military action.[28]

The wording here suggests that a 'principle of humanity' is understood as having an independent legal impact. On closer examination, however, one may equally well interpret the statement to say either that a 'principle of humanity' is simply the moral justification for the well-established principles of unnecessary suffering and of distinction, or even that these two last principles, when combined, form a wider, overarching principle of humanity.

A more recent reference to a 'principle of humanity' is made in the ICRC's 'Interpretive Guidance on the Notion of Direct Participation in Hostilities under International Humanitarian Law'. Under a heading of 'Restraints on the use of force in direct attack', the Guidance states that 'the kind and degree of force permissible in attacks against legitimate military targets should be determined, first of all, based on the fundamental principles of military necessity and humanity'.[29] Quoting the above-mentioned definition in the UK *Manual of the Law of Armed Conflict*, the Guidance continues to state that the 'principle of humanity' is '[c]omplementing and implicit in the principle of military necessity', and that '[i]n conjunction, the principles of military necessity and of humanity reduce the sum total of permissible military action from that which IHL does not expressly prohibit to that which is actually necessary for the accomplishment of a legitimate military purpose in the prevailing circumstances'.[30] Notwithstanding, the Guidance acknowledges that this is a controversial issue,[31] and the participating experts had differing opinions as to the extent to which the principles of military necessity and humanity impose restraints on the kind and degree of force used.[32] This serves to underline the main point to be made at present, namely that references to a 'principle of humanity' inevitably invite questions as to the exact content, meaning and legal impact of the term.

3. Increased impact of humanitarian considerations *vis-à-vis* other considerations under IHL

As already indicated, this book also inquires as to whether humanitarian considerations are gaining in importance *vis-à-vis* other considerations under IHL, in particular considerations of military necessity. While this is an interesting inquiry in its own right, it should be recalled that the main purpose of including the inquiry in the present book is to provide additional perspectives that may allow for conclusions to be drawn as to the possible existence or emergence of a 'principle of humanity'. The reader should thus not expect to find a complete presentation of this inquiry here.

In the same manner as the inquiry in the previous section, the question of whether humanitarian considerations are gaining in importance must be divided into two parts: first, whether such a shift is taking place in the norm-creation process, and secondly, whether such a shift is taking place in the interpretation and application of specific norms.

With regard to the first issue, it should be recalled that every single norm in IHL represents a balance between humanitarian considerations and considerations of military necessity. This is no less true for norms that have been adopted recently. The inquiry is not, therefore, whether humanitarian considerations now *exclude* considerations of military necessity from having an impact on the norm-creation process, but only whether humanitarian considerations have acquired a relatively stronger impact. The background for raising this issue can be found in the recent adoption of two international conventions: the Mine Ban Convention in 1997,[33] and the Cluster Munitions Convention in 2008.[34] It has been suggested that the Mine Ban Convention was the first time where humanitarian considerations were predominant in the negotiation of treaties prohibiting the use of certain weapons, whereas strategic considerations had played the primary role in previous negotiations.[35] Nevertheless, this observation may be questioned. Already the St Petersburg Declaration of 1868 on exploding ammunition was based primarily on humanitarian and not strategic considerations. The same would appear to apply to a number of treaties dealing with means of warfare, including the Convention on Certain Conventional Weapons of 1980 with its protocols on inhumane weapons such as undetectable fragments and blinding lasers. The significance of the Mine Ban Convention and the Cluster Munitions Conventions was that they went far beyond a prohibition of use of these weapons; they also created a framework for stockpile destruction, clearing of contaminated areas and victim assistance.

At the time when the Mine Ban Convention was being negotiated, it was thought by many experts that the use of anti-personnel mines could create significant military advantages, and that considerations of military necessity supported the use of these weapons,[36] but their use was nevertheless prohibited with no exceptions. Today, it is more commonly recognised that anti-personnel mines are not important as a means of warfare. The same observation also appears to be valid for cluster munitions. They are imprecise and their military utility is in many cases questionable, although many still find that considerations of military necessity indicate that use of the weapons should be permitted.[37] Both anti-personnel mines and cluster munitions represent grave danger to the civilian population, and this danger often remains long after the end of hostilities.[38] Critics of these weapons therefore argue that their use is incompatible with humanitarian considerations, and this view prevailed in the negotiations. In both cases, the outcome can be explained partly by the immense pressure from civil society and the strong public opinion that were displayed.

These factors lead us to the second issue, namely whether humanitarian considerations are also increasingly influential in the interpretation and application of already existing norms. IHL contains a wide range of norms that leave the involved actors with considerable discretion. What is 'excessive' damage to civilian lives or objects? What is 'unnecessary' suffering? What does it mean that a person not taking active part in hostilities is to be treated 'humanely'? And so on. In all assessments of this character, the actor needs to balance humanitarian considerations against other considerations. This is particularly evident with regard to so-called collateral damage, where Article 51.5(b) of the first Additional Protocol[39] explicitly calls for a comparison to be made between the expected incidental damage to civilian lives and objects, and the direct military advantage anticipated.

It is methodically difficult to assess this issue, since it calls for a comparison on two levels of immeasurable values. Not only must humanitarian considerations be balanced against other considerations in a specific case, but one must compare the outcome of this assessment, which is of course based on the facts as the actor saw them at the time, with similar assessments of cases in the past, where the concrete facts and the surrounding circumstances necessarily were different. The best one can do, at least within the boundaries of this book, is to raise the questions and attempt to suggest some trends. One possible trend is that military operations in multilateral enforcement operations are subjected to stronger demands to be guided by humanitarian considerations than other military operations are, especially when these multilateral operations are not involving the survival of the states whose forces are involved, but rather in support of peace in another state. Particularly in the ISAF operation in Afghanistan, there is arguably a tendency that the media, civil society and public opinion consider all civilian casualties unacceptable, without any consideration being made of the anticipated military advantage sought in a particular operation. There are even signs that this may begin to influence the conduct of the involved actors.

A more concrete example for United Nations-authorised peace operations is the fact that the UN Secretary-General's Bulletin on observance by UN forces of international humanitarian law promulgates a clear prohibition against the use of incendiary weapons in peace operations,[40] whereas IHL only contains rules that *restrict* the use of such weapons.[41] This self-commitment to refrain from the use of otherwise lawful weapons is, presumably, based on humanitarian considerations.

It may well be that such a trend to place increased emphasis on humanitarian consideration, if it exists at all, is relevant only for the application of IHL in multilateral (UN-authorised) operations, where there is a range of other factors that imply and maybe even require a strong focus on humanitarian considerations. For example, if there is considerable opposition to a state's involvement in an international operation (as the case is for many troop contributing nations to the ISAF operation) the state is presumably reluctant to engage in conduct that strengthens this opposition. Also a factor is that the troop contributing nations to a large extent are able to 'choose' which conflicts they are willing to become involved in, and the humanitarian consequences of the conflict in the area of deployment may be precisely one of the motivating factors behind such a choice. Further, it is often said that operational success depends on winning the 'hearts and minds' of the local population, which means that great care must be taken to avoid civilian casualties. Yet another factor is that the mandate of the operation in most cases will stress the humanitarian purpose of the operation.

Notwithstanding, strong pressure from international and national media as well as from civil society is also present in other forms of armed conflicts. To the extent that the military actors consider these pressure mechanisms relevant, they may also have influence on the actors' behaviour in these conflicts. In fact, in the modern battle for 'hearts and minds', the avoidance of negative press coverage and international critique has become an important target in itself.[42]

4. A possible 'Nordic perspective' on international humanitarian law?

The question of whether there is a 'Nordic perspective' also raises difficult methodical challenges, and the present book aims only to provide arguments that may support or refute the following hypothesis, without having any realistic ambition to provide definitive conclusions. The hypothesis is that states that are not directly involved in armed conflicts attach relatively more weight to humanitarian considerations, both in the norm-creation process and in the application of existing norms, than those states that are directly involved in armed conflicts.

States may become involved in armed conflicts on a range of different levels. First, a state can become a party to an (international or non-international) armed conflict on its own soil, in a neighbouring state or in a state further away. Secondly, a state can experience a wide range of *consequences* of a conflict, both in neighbouring states and in states further away, such as refugee movements, environmental consequences, trade interruptions, etc. Thirdly, a state can contribute indirectly to the conduct of hostilities, for example through the transfer of weapons and other military equipment, or through financing the efforts of a party to the conflict. Fourthly, a state can become involved in the armed conflict through unilateral or multilateral mediation efforts or through other forms of negotiations to bring about an end to the conflict. Fifthly, a state can become involved in international post-conflict efforts, such as the rebuilding of infrastructure and governmental institutions, or the removal of unexploded remnants of war. Finally, a state can become involved through financial contributions or through the contribution of personnel or equipment to international peace operations. For the purposes of the hypothesis above, the term 'directly involved' refers to those states who become a party to an armed conflict, while the other five categories fall within the term 'not directly involved'.

Three assumptions can be introduced as background to this inquiry. The first assumption is that states that are directly involved in armed conflicts to a greater extent are motivated primarily by the objective of defeating the enemy in the minimum amount of time and with a minimum of own losses. While humanitarian considerations obviously play an important role during the conduct of hostilities, these are secondary to considerations of military necessity.

The second assumption is that states that are not directly involved in armed conflicts do not have the same set of motivations. These states can instead afford to have a more idealistic focus on the alleviation of human suffering in armed conflicts, or they may have an interest in avoiding to the largest possible extent that the consequences of a conflict affect themselves.

The third assumption is that states in the sixth category above, i.e., states that contribute personnel or equipment to international peace operations, and that therefore may become directly engaged in hostilities without being a party to the conflict, have a third set of motivations. These states are motivated by the quickest possible achievement of the operation's purpose with a minimum of own losses, but this motivation must be balanced against the need to satisfy domestic pressure groups. They are, after all, contributing to peace operations to make things better, so any indications that matters are in fact getting worse, even if it is just for a short time, will be politically problematic. Troop contributing nations may also be motivated by the factors described in section 3 above, with the effect that humanitarian considerations play a significant role for the state in general and thus particularly so in operations.

It falls well beyond the scope of this book to analyse the motivations of states that are directly or indirectly involved in armed conflicts in different ways. This perhaps thought-provokingly simplified introduction to some possible motivations is nevertheless sufficient at present to illustrate the inquiry that is being made.

This is a general inquiry that is not limited to a particular region. The reason for nevertheless referring to a 'Nordic perspective' is twofold. First, as mentioned above, the Nordic states are clear examples of states that have not been directly involved in armed conflicts since the Second World War, but that are indirectly involved in armed conflicts in different ways, and that take an active part in norm-creating processes. Secondly, and more pragmatically, a majority of the contributors to this book are from one of these countries, and it is therefore the situation in these countries that is most readily considered in the present book.

A general challenge with regard to this inquiry, however, is that differences between states' practice and position may be caused by either legal considerations or policy considerations, and unfortunately states do not always specify what is influencing their position. It is certainly possible, and not uncommon, that states interpret legal norms differently. The above-mentioned question of whether combatants are permitted to kill a civilian who is directly participating in hostilities, or if the civilian must be captured if this is possible, can serve as an example: a particular state may certainly interpret existing legal norms to say that the use of lethal force is permitted, while another state may interpret the same norms to say that the use of lethal force is prohibited if the civilian can be captured. Nevertheless, different perspectives may (or, in many situations, will) rather be the result of different policy considerations. For example, a state that is engaged in an international peace operation with a humanitarian mandate may be more restrictive in the assessment of permitted means and methods of combat than those states that are directly involved in an armed conflict. The emphasis in current international operations on avoiding virtually any civilian collateral damage and injury to maintain local support is a good example of how policy considerations might impact on an operation without this necessarily indicating any shift in the law.

5. Chapters in the book

The chapters in this book address the overall questions from different perspectives, and the chapters show, in different ways, how the contributors struggle to identify or concretise a 'principle of humanity'. The book is divided into two main parts.

In Part I, which consists of Chapters 2 to 6, the contributors approach the 'principle of humanity' from different theoretical perspectives.

In Chapter 2, Professor Robert Kolb provides a detailed overview of the main phases of evolution of IHL, including its underlying understandings, problems and principles. He draws a picture of how the application and perception of IHL, including considerations of 'humanity', has changed during the different periods considered, in accordance with changing social and legal settings. While the chapter does not directly discuss whether a 'principle of humanity' exists in contemporary IHL, it provides the reader with a basis on which to consider whether or not such a principle is, at least, *emerging* in IHL.

In Chapter 3, Professor Yoram Dinstein denies the very existence a 'principle of humanity', preferring instead to refer to humanitarian considerations. He argues that the principles of humanity should not be viewed as legal norms, but as extra-legal considerations. On this basis, he goes on to argue that the key to the effective protection of civilians is the principle of *proportionality*. The focus of the chapter is thus on the meaning and impact of proportionality in IHL.

In Chapter 4, Cecilie Hellestveit addresses the dichotomy between international and non-international armed conflicts from the perspective of humanitarian protection. She describes the efforts to fill the normative gaps of non-international armed conflicts to improve protection for victims, and offers arguments for and against upholding the dichotomy. She argues that as the normative gap between international and non-international armed conflicts is decreasing, a suppression of this dichotomy will not serve to further the humanitarian purposes of the Geneva Conventions.

In Chapter 5, Kjetil Mujezinović Larsen discusses the relationship between international humanitarian law and human rights law with a view to inquiring whether human rights law now has such an impact on the conduct of hostilities that humanitarian considerations in fact are *emerging* as a legal norm, in the form of a 'principle of humanity' or maybe even a 'principle of human-rightism'. The question is considered from two angles; first, how the European Court of Human Rights assesses alleged human rights violations during armed conflicts, and secondly, whether the Court's case law has an impact on the development of norms and principles of IHL.

In the final chapter of Part I, Chapter 6, Katarina Månsson uses the development of the rights of the child in armed conflicts as a point of departure for demonstrating how human rights law has played a significant role in the development of IHL and *vice versa*. She considers that the convergence of the two legal regimes has gradually led to the development of a set of minimum humanitarian standards for the protection of children, and makes the argument that 'the principle of humanity' has been a driving force behind this cross-fertilisation of child protection provisions in the two bodies of law.

Part II of the book takes a more practical approach, and attempts primarily to test the hypothesis of whether states which are not directly affected by armed conflicts attach greater weight to humanitarian considerations when interpreting and applying IHL. The first two chapters consider the issue from an historical perspective, while the remainder provide more current examples from a Nordic perspective.

In Chapter 7, Professor Lauri Hannikainen addresses legal issues relating to the Finnish occupation of Eastern Karelia from 1941 to 1944. He provides a most sombre presentation of the circumstances and considerations that led to the invasion, and of the goals and intentions behind it. In describing Finnish efforts to create an ethnically clean Eastern Karelia and to annex the area, he shows that the occupying forces' treatment of the civilian population involved inhuman acts contrary both to the 1907 Hague Regulations and the Martens Clause, including humanitarian considerations. He also describes, and criticises, the post-war tendency in Finland to present the occupation in a positive light.

In Chapter 8, Sigrid Redse Johansen also discusses the experiences of the Nordic states in a case of occupation during the Second World War, but this time from the perspective of the *occupied* state. She addresses legal issues relating to the German occupation of Norway from 1940 to 1945, with a particular focus on the occupying state's interference in the internal affairs of the occupied state. Norway had a peculiar arrangement during the war, where the appointed 'national' fascist government supported the occupying force. The author uses the example of Norway to demonstrate how requirements of humanity represent a driving force in the development of international humanitarian law, and that even if an occupying force may try to camouflage its actions by legal terms, considerations of morality or humanity may override the positive law.

In Chapter 9, Ola Engdahl addresses the concept of 'parties' to an armed conflict in a context of multinational peace operations. This issue is of considerable importance in both international and non-international armed conflicts, not least with regard to questions of responsibility. Using the ISAF operation in Afghanistan as a case study, he discusses who the 'parties' to such a conflict are. He shows that even among like-minded states, the position on the conflict differs with regard to the qualification of that conflict and to the status of troop contributing nations in the conflict, and consequently, to the applicability of international humanitarian law. The chapter implies that the above-mentioned suggestion about a possible 'Nordic perspective' on international humanitarian law does not in practice impact on the assessment of the legal regime.

In Chapter 10, Peter Vedel Kessing offers insight into a Nordic perspective by addressing a narrower and more practical issue relating to peace operations, namely the competence of UN forces to detain individuals for security reasons. He describes the legal uncertainties that exist, and attempts to identify minimum detention standards that are applicable in all types of operations. An important premise in the identification of such standards is the humanitarian mandate of UN forces and the corresponding need for a clear legal regime to secure the human rights of detainees.

In Chapter 11, Rikke Ishøy discusses the relationship between what is legal and what is moral. Through case studies on the Danish troop contribution to Afghanistan, a Bosnian war crimes trial before a Danish court, the handling of detainees in Iraq, and the 'Fighters and Lovers' terrorist case, Ishøy presents how Denmark has dealt with questions relating to the application of IHL in recent years. Her conclusion is that there is a tendency to take a legalistic approach to the application of IHL, and that the human dimension of the conflicts has been left unaddressed.

In Chapter 12, Arne Willy Dahl and Camilla Guldahl Cooper give an overview of the Norwegian efforts to implement and disseminate the law of armed conflict, from the ratification of the four 1949 Geneva Conventions to the present. Their particular focus is to describe the extent to which references are made, or not made, to a 'principle of humanity' or to humanitarian considerations in national implementation and dissemination efforts. They demonstrate how the increased participation of Norway in armed conflicts (such as through the contribution of troops to the ISAF operation in Afghanistan) has led to increased attention to international humanitarian law in general, and also to an increased focus on the humanitarian aspects of these rules. It is suggested that the Norwegian perspective on international humanitarian law is influenced by the lack of armed conflicts involving Norwegian territory and interests.

Finally, in Chapter 13, two of the editors, Kjetil Mujezinović Larsen and Camilla Guldahl Cooper, provide their personal views and conclusions to the questions raised in the book.

Notes

1 The provisions in, inter alia, Additional Protocol I to the Geneva Conventions pertaining to distinction, unnecessary suffering and proportionality are often referred to as 'principles'.

2 A useful overview of different meanings of the term 'humanity' is given by R. Coupland, 'Humanity: What is it and how does it influence international law?' (2001) 83 *International Review of the Red Cross* 969.

3 A general overview of the history of IHL is given by, e.g., L.C. Green, *The Contemporary Law of Armed Conflict* (2nd edn, Manchester: Manchester University Press, 2000) 20 ff., C. Greenwood, 'Historical development and legal basis' in D. Fleck (ed.), *The Handbook of International Humanitarian Law* (2nd edn, Oxford University Press, 2008) 1–43 at 15–27, and in the present book by Robert Kolb, Chapter 2.

4 2 Kings 6:22.

5 Cited by Green, *Contemporary LOAC*, 21 and Greenwood, 'Historical development', 16.

6 Green and Greewood *ibid.*

7 See generally Green, *Contemporary LOAC.*, 23–5.

8 Greenwood, 'Historical development', 20.

9 Instructions for the Government of the United States in the Field, 24 April 1863. General academic comments to the Lieber Code include, e.g., G.B. Davis, 'Doctor Francis Lieber's Instruction for the Government of Armies in the Field' (1907) 1 *American Journal of International Law* 13; E. Root, 'Francis Lieber' (1913) 7 *American Journal of International Law* 453; T. Meron, 'Francis Lieber's Code and principles of humanity' (1998) 36 *Columbia Journal of Transnational Law* 269 (also published in *War Crimes Law Comes of Age: Essays* (Oxford: Clarendon Press, 1998) 131–41); or B.M. Carnahan, 'Lincoln, Lieber and the laws of war: the origins and limits of

the principle of military necessity' (1998) 92 *American Journal of International Law* 213.

10 Root,'Francis Lieber', 456.

11 Meron, 'Lieber's Code', 271.

12 *Ibid.* 272–3.

13 *Ibid.* 274.

14 Declaration Renouncing the Use, in Time of War, of Explosive Projectiles under 400 Grammes Weight, made in St Petersburg, 29 November/11 December 1868.

15 See e.g., Y. Dinstein, *The Conduct of Hostilities under the Law of International Armed Conflict* (Cambridge University Press, 2004) 57; Greenwood, 'Historical development', 23; S. Oeter, 'Methods and means of combat' in Fleck, *Handbook*, 119–235 at 128.

16 Academic comments on the Martens Clause include, e.g., V.V. Pustogarov, 'The Martens Clause in international law' (1999) 1 *Journal of the History of International Law* 125; A. Cassese, 'The Martens Clause: half a loaf or simply pie in the sky?' (2000) 11 *European Journal of International Law* 187; or T. Meron, 'The Martens Clause, principles of humanity, and dictates of public conscience' (2000) 94 *American Journal of International Law* 78.

17 Cassese, 'Martens Clause', at 188 (original emphasis).

18 Protocol Additional to the Geneva Conventions of 12 August 1949, and relating to the Protection of Victims of Non-International Armed Conflicts (Protocol II), 8 June 1977, Preamble, para. 4.

19 Convention on Prohibitions or Restrictions on the Use of Certain Conventional Weapons which may be Deemed to be Excessively Injurious or to Have Indiscriminate Effects, 10 October 1980, Preamble, para. 5.

20 Convention on Cluster Munitions, 30 May 2008, Preamble, para. 11.

21 Geneva Conventions of 12 August 1949, see Article 63 of Geneva Convention I, Article 62 of Geneva Convention II, Article 142 of Geneva Convention III, and Article 158 of Geneva Convention IV.

22 Dinstein, *Conduct of Hostilities*, 17.

23 Cassese, 'Martens Clause', 189–92.

24 *Ibid.* 214.

25 *Ibid.* 208.

26 Meron, 'Martens Clause', 87–8.

27 *Kupreskić et al.* (IT-95-16), ICTY, Trial Judgment, 14 January 2000, paras. 525–6. The Appeals Chamber did not discuss the Martens Clause.

28 UK Ministry of Defence, *The Manual of the Law of Armed Conflict* (Oxford University Press, 2004) 23.

29 Interpretive Guidance on the Notion of Direct Participation in Hostilities under International Humanitarian Law, Adopted by the Assembly of the International Committee of the Red Cross on 26 February 2009, published in (2008) 90 *International Review of the Red Cross*, 1041.

30 *Ibid.* 1042.

31 *Ibid.* 1041.

32 For an overview of the controversy, see Summary Report, Fourth Expert Meeting on the Notion of Direct Participation in Hostilities (2006) 75–9. For a critique of the position taken in the *Guidance*, see e.g., Major R.S. Taylor, 'The capture versus kill

debate: is the principle of humanity now part of the targeting analysis when attacking civilians who are directly participating in hostilities?' (2010) 5 *Army Lawyer*, 103.

33 Convention on the Prohibition of the Use, Stockpiling, Production and Transfer of Anti-Personnel Mines and on their Destruction, 18 September 1997.

34 *Supra* note 20.

35 T. Meron, 'The humanization of humanitarian law' (2000) 94 *American Journal of International Law* 239.

36 S. Maslen, *Anti-Personnel Mines under Humanitarian Law: A View from the Vanishing Point* (Antwerp/Oxford/New York: Intersentia-Transnational Publishers, 2001) 202 ff. describes the military *utility* of anti-personnel mines, and concludes that the effectiveness of these mines is low, but that it 'is not possible to argue convincingly that anti-personnel mines have no military utility whatsoever' (at 208).

37 N. van Woudenberg, 'The long and winding road towards an instrument on cluster munitions' (2007) 12 *Journal of Conflict and Security Law* 447 describes (at 450) some standard arguments for and against the use of cluster weapons.

38 In Lao PDR, for example, there is still an average of 300 casualties per year as a result of explosive remnants from the 1970s (www.handicap-international.org).

39 Protocol Additional to the Geneva Conventions of 12 August 1949, and relating to the Protection of Victims of International Armed Conflicts (Protocol I), 8 June 1977.

40 UN doc. ST/SGB/1999/13, para. 6.2.

41 Protocol on Prohibitions or Restrictions on the Use of Incendiary Weapons (Protocol III to the Convention on Certain Conventional Weapons), 10 October 1980, and the ICRC Customary Law Study, rules 84 and 85.

42 See e.g., O. Bøe-Hansen, 'Taliban og ISAFs propagandakrig – Kampen om den mest overbevisende historien' in Oslo Files on Defence and Security (01/2010).

PART I

Theoretical perspectives

2

The main epochs of modern international humanitarian law since 1864 and their related dominant legal constructions

ROBERT KOLB

1. Introduction

The date of birth of modern international humanitarian law (IHL) is normally placed in the post-Solferino creation of the Red Cross Movement, and in particular the creation of the Geneva International Committee of the Red Cross dedicated to promoting the care of wounded or sick military personnel.[1] Since these times, in the 1860s, almost 150 years have elapsed. International society, the concept and the practice of war, the body of international humanitarian law, the practical problems posed for its varying subject matters – all these aspects have undergone significant, if not fundamental, changes.

The history of modern IHL has been expounded on numerous times and there would be no significant advantage to be gained in adding a further contribution to the numerous writings.[2] Nevertheless, very few written works have attempted to set out synoptically the main phases of evolution of this body of law, each characterised by a set of common fundamental understandings, problems and operational principles within the applicable IHL. If such a perspective is adopted, it may be possible to shed some light on the manner in which IHL has been perceived and applied in differing social and legal settings in order to address significantly different practical needs and aspirations. For even if there is an obvious continuity in the history of IHL, there are also fundamental departures and separate developments in certain phases. Thus, for example, the early phase saw states produce, construe and deal with IHL essentially as a matter of municipal military law, codified in the international sphere mainly through model rules, where lacunae and sub-regulations constituted a salient feature (1864–1899); the next phase saw the evolution of a system where the predominance of sovereignty, as influenced by the famous (if not infamous) *Lotus* principle of state freedom,[3] tended to prevail over the Martens Clause and to enhance the centrality of military necessities, i.e., a system where the presumption rested on the belligerent's freedom of action (1899–1946). A further phase developed in which IHL became centred around the concept of humanitarian protection of the victims of war through the introduction of very detailed and non-derogable rules, thereby restricting the freedom of state action, even in non-international armed conflicts (1949–1993). Finally, in the current phase, IHL is becoming progressively 'humanised', i.e., 'homo-centred' instead of 'state-centred', but also increasingly 'supplementary', in the sense that it progressively merges with human rights law considerations while being sanctioned and developed through the growing branch of international criminal law. At the same time, military functions are themselves becoming increasingly diverse and multifunctional, creating a need for further regulation of branches of international law other than IHL (1993 to date).

These four phases, which have here only been briefly presented, quite clearly portray and offer a basis for the operation of different types of IHL. The application of these different ways of interpreting IHL will lead to differing results, among others with regard to belligerent reprisals and reciprocity, the role of treaty law or customary law, the function ascribed to special agreements between the belligerents, the application of military necessity and other principles such as proportionality, the distinction between international and non-international armed conflicts, and the relation to other bodies of international law such as human rights law.

The danger of such categorisations is, of course, to overstate the sharpness of the distinction between the phases and to understate the existence of continuity and the subtle merging of one phase into another. Perhaps such over-emphasis is not only a danger, but is indeed an inescapable drawback of such an approach. The risk of doing so, however, may be justly incurred in light of the many insights which such an original approach may yield. There always remains the possibility of placing these findings in a broader context and to blunt their sharp edges in order to properly address the legitimate concerns of the caveat just presented.

The first of the phases will be explored in somewhat more detail, for two reasons. First, it is the formative period of IHL from which all subsequent epochs take reference. Secondly, as it is today more remote, its essential features are less well known and will gain greater clarity through a more thorough treatment.

I must also warn the reader that because of space constraints imposed by the editors, the often space-consuming explanations of basics or of legal concepts has been avoided in the following chapter; this means that a reasonable understanding of IHL is necessary in order to comfortably follow all the arguments presented. By the same token, I have provided the reader with footnote references quite unevenly; sometimes the notes are more absent than present, in an effort to save space; at other times, I have allowed myself a somewhat freer rein. I quote more extensively from older sources than from newer ones in the belief that these are less well known and accessible. Further, I have not hesitated to quote texts in French or other languages than English – it is today of the greatest usefulness to remind triumphant Anglo-Saxons that, in international relations at least, it is utterly insufficient to know only one language. Let us now plunge *in medias res.*

2. First phase (1864–1899): predominance of domestic law, 'codification' and gaps

This first phase[4] spans from the adoption of the first Geneva Convention of 1864 (for the Amelioration of the Condition of the Wounded in Armies in the Field),[5] to the St Petersburg Declaration of 1868 (on Explosive Projectiles under 400 Grammes Weight, important essentially for its Preamble which contains an outline of sorts on the philosophy and teleology underlying the modern law),[6] to the first series of the three Hague Conventions of 1899 to which three declarations were added.[7] Between these, there has been a series of codification efforts resulting in non-binding sets of rules: one may here mention the Brussels Declaration of 1874[8] and the Oxford Manual of 1880,[9] both attempting to cover the whole ground of the then applicable law of warfare. There has also been a set of remarkable codifications of the law of warfare in various national laws, the most influential of them being the seminal 'Lieber Code' (1863)[10] proclaiming as compulsory legal rules for the federal armed forces during the American Civil War. There is no need to comment upon the precise scope and meaning of all these texts; one may in that regard refer to the existing literature. The focus here will rather be on the system of the law of war at this time. The following aspects may be emphasised here.

2.1 *Predominance of municipal law as* 'droit public externe'

In the nineteenth century, many peoples in the 'civilised' part of the world achieved constitutional and democratic autonomy. This political process resulted in a focus on constitutional law, i.e., on the municipal law of their state, which stood for their hard-acquired independence and legislative power. The United States, France, later Germany and Italy, are particularly conspicuous cases of this evolution. The challenge quickly arose as to how to square this municipal 'constitutional' (or public) law with the external commitments of the state, in a world moving towards constantly higher levels of interdependence. This way of perceiving the problem, however, contained in itself a limitation of the range of possible solutions. The point of departure was the constitutional law, the subjective 'I', and hence the freedom and autonomy of every state. The point of arrival was a way of construing a restriction on this freedom of action in order to reconcile it with some form of international law allowing ordered interrelations among nations, when these (as *prius* in the system) chose to have such ordered interrelations. It is especially in nations that most cherished their recent and hard-won freedom, and which had a pronounced preference for theoretical thinking (Germany and Italy), that the new way of thinking took a bright and distinct form. In this construction, international law is the part of each state's public law which relates to external relations; its binding force is thus derived from the municipal law. It is the state that binds itself to a certain course of conduct in its external relations (*Selbstverpflichtungslehre*).[11] Thus, there is no single or objective international law; the latter is simply the (ever-changing) area where the municipal laws of various states converge. International law is thus not binding in itself; its rules will be binding by virtue of the binding nature of municipal law, thus it will be binding for a particular state only so long as the relevant rule still exists in its municipal law. Nevertheless, only cogent reasons should lead a state to change such laws, lest all properly ordered international intercourse would be jeopardised. The theorists of the time firmly believed in practical reason and harmonious progress; they thus assumed that no state would abuse such a freedom. Consequently, this power of change was not seen as dangerous to international law. The circle was thus completed: a state is absolutely free, i.e., sovereign, and yet bound by international law through its own sovereign will. The famous phrase of the Permanent Court of International Justice (PCIJ) in the *S.S. Wimbledon* case here springs to mind, a phrase so magnificently smooth and optimistic (besides being manifestly true) as to immediately disclose its nineteenth century lineage: 'The Court declines to see in the conclusion of any Treaty by which a state undertakes to perform or to refrain from performing a particular act an abandonment of its sovereignty … [T]he right of entering into international engagements is an attribute of state sovereignty'.[12] The sovereignty is the pivotal point: it signifies both freedom and (relative) constraint. Moreover, public law and international law, the internal and external side of the state and of the law, at once merge into one another.

This type of systematic approach had a much greater influence on the law of war in the second part of the nineteenth century than is commonly perceived today. There are few efforts, up to the Hague Conference of 1899, which pursue a more or less exhaustive codification of the laws of war through a set of comprehensive conventions at the international level. During the second part of the nineteenth century, the path followed was rather that of either producing quite short and generic legal texts which would be spelled out in the municipal law of the various states (Geneva Convention of 1864), or non-binding model rules intended to inspire national military legislation and the drafting of national military manuals. This course of conduct was a result of the fact that, as the fate of the Brussels Declaration of 1874 or the additional Articles to the Geneva Convention adopted in 1868 showed, states were not yet ready to accept any extensive international codification of binding rules on the question of warfare.

The Geneva Convention of 1864 contains only ten Articles, both incomplete and underdeveloped. These Articles are not self-sufficient; they culminate in the duty of national legislators to pass municipal legislation and to take other related action. Thus, for example, the Convention obliges states to prepare sufficient medical services for the eventuality of war. This duty is not stated directly but indirectly, through the obligation placed on each belligerent to collect and care for the wounded and ill combatants of whatever nationality (Article 6). Article 1 states that the ambulances and military hospitals shall be recognised not only as neutral, but also 'protected', which means that states, for example, must enact legislation to repress pillage and looting. The distinctive emblem of the Red Cross must be protected by national legislation against abuses.[13] The sanction for punishing offences against the provisions is left entirely to be enacted in national criminal law; such a sanction is not included in the Convention. Overall, the eight substantive Articles of the Convention are hardly able to cover the entire ground, even on such a narrow subject as the amelioration of the condition of the wounded in armies in the field. The thrust of its concrete application is thus left to internal legislation.

The Oxford Manual (1880) Preamble states the point of its existence very clearly:

> The Institute [of international law], too, does not propose an international treaty, which might perhaps be premature or at least very

> difficult to obtain; but … it believes it is fulfilling a duty in offering to the governments a Manual suitable as the basis for national legislation in each state, and in accord with both the progress of juridical science and the needs of civilised armies.[14]

Indeed, in the United States and in almost all European states, being the essential military powers of the day, an intense process of national legislation and adoption of military manuals took place during these years.[15] It is no coincidence that legal writings extensively refer to the various pieces of national legislation and military manuals on almost every point of the law of war. The relevant law is thus formed through international soft law (Brussels 1874, Oxford 1880, Lieber 1863) and various national laws in a complex array of interrelationships. Some authors rightly point out that the development of the modern *jus in bello* rests heavily upon progressive national legislation, such as that of France, the United States, Germany or Italy.[16] This approach can still be felt to some extent in the landmark legislation of 1899 (The Hague). The 1899 Hague Convention II (on land warfare) opens as follows: 'The High Contracting Parties *shall issue instructions* to their armed land forces, which shall be in conformity with the [annexed Regulations]' (Article 1) (emphasis added). Understandably, the Convention requires some action from the states parties intending to implement it; at the same time it is still an echo of the older approach of inserting an obligation to enact specific instructions to the armed forces, only thereafter to recall that these instructions must of course conform (but not be limited to!) the duties under the Convention.[17]

There are several consequences resulting from this way of developing the law of war through municipal law influenced by international 'model' rules. The most important aspects are that the law becomes not unitary but divided; and that in a particular armed conflict, the applicable law will be defined by the converging or reciprocal rules contained in the municipal legislations of the warring states. In other words, the area of overlap between the national legislations will produce some common rules to be applied. Rather than being based on objective rules of international law, the gist of applicable law was in concrete cases the sum of varying subjective rules based on national law. Some common or objective rules of international law did exist, such as the Geneva Convention of 1864 or the St Petersburg Declaration of 1868; but such rules were exceptional, whereas the national rules were commonplace. It is only the repeated experiences of considerable differences in military usages and practice, provoking numerous complaints about violations of the laws and of bad faith, which finally inspired a process of codification. This process produced a series of more detailed and objective rules on the international level, directed at silencing such complaints.[18] The Franco-Prussian War of 1870–1871 was a landmark experience in that area, but it was not the only one.

2.2. *Principle of 'necessity' as the pivotal rule of the system*

The laws of war of the second half of the nineteenth century were replete with gaps and uncertainties.[19] The older 'usages' of war were not considered to be fully legal: they were a mixture of religious, moral and other practices, falling short of the modern, purportedly strictly scientific, concept of law, originating in the nineteenth century positivistic ideal. Then again, legal codification was only in its earliest stages. Since there was a ready-made, complete set of precise rules to be relied on, it became essential to sum up the whole subject matter within some guiding principles. These principles could immediately inspire the work of both the legislator, when enacting new laws, as well as those applying the law in order to seek a legal answer to a concrete problem.

One way of approaching the issue is the time-honoured principle that the laws of war emerge out of a conciliation of two countervailing principles, those of military necessity and humanity.[20] But this equation is both too complicated and too limited: too complicated since it would perhaps be possible to state a clearer and easier principle, which should then be preferred; and too limited, because the equation presented addresses itself principally to the legislator and is of less avail to the law-applier. So what would be a simpler way of stating this? It would be to make 'military necessity' or 'war necessity' the *pivot* of the whole system, thereby creating a synthesis of the two concepts. This concept of 'necessity' encompasses both a positive, expansive, violence-permitting role, and a negative, restrictive, violence-limiting role. The equation reads as follows: (1) everything which is necessary to overpower the enemy must be permitted, and it would be pointless to attempt to prohibit it, even on account of humanity; (2) but everything which is not necessary remains incompatible with war and must be considered a superfluous, inhuman and prohibited destruction.[21] The first component is thus always lawful while the second is always unlawful. In the absence of concrete prohibitive rules, this principle offers criteria for deciding the lawfulness of means of warfare. The principle of necessity therefore plays an essential residual role in a legal environment where detailed rules are rare and gaps frequent. Evolutions in warfare, new weapons systems, changes in the configuration of the relationships between civilians and combatants, all these and other factors constantly shift the boundaries between what appears 'necessary' or not at any certain time. It is the main task of the legislator to take all these factors into account and to weigh them in the different historical situations.

The principle of humanity and all other restrictions on warfare developed within the second, restrictive component of necessity. The philosophy of this restrictive 'necessity' is admirably summarised in the Preamble to the St Petersburg Declaration (1868).[22] Indeed, many authors of the time concluded that an action is unlawful simply because it involves more use of force than necessary to achieve a particular military objective.[23] Restrictive necessity also inspires entire branches of the law of armed conflict: thus, for example, the principle of 'unnecessary suffering' permeates the entire law of weapons.[24] How could such a restriction on warfare be accepted at all? One of the reasons for such a moderation flows from *jus ad bellum*: it is the old maxim, known since Augustine,[25] that a war involving excessive use of force renders the return to peace (which is the final aim) much harder because of the long-lasting resentment of the victims.[26] The other reasons arise from *jus in bello*: the aim of restricting behaviour is to encourage military discipline and focus on important rather than secondary objectives, as well as reducing injury to the bystanders of war. The aim is also to avoid reprisals and thus excessive losses.[27]

The principle of necessity (expansive and restrictive) has the advantage that it may to a significant extent mask the absence of precise legal rules. It offers a guiding criterion, appearing reasonably precise enough to, *faute de mieux*, decide on what is lawful and what is unlawful in warfare. Moreover, the principle has a distinguished origin. It can be found in works by almost all classical authors, especially in Grotius,[28] Wolff,[29] Vattel,[30] and even in J. J. Rousseau;[31] it furthermore appears more or less subliminally in many other passages of the classic writers.[32] It can be encapsulated in the maxim: *in bello licere quae ad finem sunt necessaria*. What is easier than to cling to tradition?

The principle, however, could only produce increasingly significant clashes in a world where military conceptions and configurations of *raison d'Etat* widely differed: what could be common to a German militaristic conception of war (and thus of necessity), an Anglo-Saxon commercial conception of war (and thus of necessity[33]) or a French, at that time more moderate conception of defensive patriotic war (and thus of necessity)? When there is no common conception of war and its principal aims, a general principle such as necessity allows excessive strain on particular rights and duties. The recurrence of abuse is mainly the reverse of lack of common conceptions. It was thus understood, at the turn of the century, that the 'necessity' criterion was too vague and open to abuses,[34] and had to be complemented (and to some extent superseded) by a codification of particular rules in international conventions. It may also be recalled that in the more militarist visions of the law, *Kriegsräson* preceded *Kriegsmanier*, so that the rules on warfare always remained subject to the restrictions of necessity and to *rebus sic stantibus*.[35] Notwithstanding, we may here note that the principle of 'necessity' admirably fitted the system of the law of war as it stood in the nineteenth century, with its many gaps and uncertainties, its reliance on internal law (and thus also of municipal conceptions of the war), its military rather than humanitarian character, and its still formative impulse. All these aspects have been heavily nourished by the seminal general principle of necessity – chameleonic in its nature, at once expansive and then again restrictive.

2.3 A subjective rather than an objective trigger for the applicability of the law of war

The system of the law of war in the nineteenth century, and up until 1949, was based on a subjective rather than objective trigger for determining the applicability of that body of the law.[36] Traditionally, the application of the law of war depended on the existence of a state of 'war'. Since the concept of war was all but clear, shifting between formal (declared) and material (intensity) war, international and civil war, the necessary legal certainty as to what was going to be applied to whom was achieved through some acts of will by the concerned states. An international war was held to exist essentially when it was declared (this being a unilateral legal act, expressing a will), or at least when there was an ascertainable subjective *animus belligerendi* of at least one state to the violent contest. This explains the extraordinary importance of the declaration of war in the nineteenth century.[37] It was of the essence, especially for the neutral states and their commerce at sea, since their rights and duties towards the warring states would be altered from the declaration of war onwards. A civil war could also bear heavily on the rights of neutral states. Therefore, it was accepted that a 'recognition of belligerency' (again a unilateral legal act embodying an expression of will) would allow the two parties in a civil war to be treated as belligerents placed on an equal footing. Hence, the law of war, especially neutrality, would apply to both.[38] This recognition could emanate from the local government or from third states. A civil war could thus be transformed from a legal point of view into a full-fledged 'war' between the recognising state and the recognised opposing entities, so that the law of war and of neutrality would apply.

These two devices (declaration of war and recognition of belligerency) fitted perfectly into the sovereignist and positivist frame of the nineteenth century:

1. Humanitarian protection was not paramount, thus gaps in protection were not felt as being inadmissible; if a particular violent contest were not formally classified as 'war' (e.g., armed reprisals), the law of war would simply not apply.[39] The formal aspect dominated the material one.
2. The sovereign will of the different states was decisive, each state remaining free in the application of the law according to its perception of a particular violent struggle (if it declares or recognises the war, the law of war applies; if not, the law of war would not apply).
3. This will is expressed through a unilateral act (declaration of war, recognition of belligerency), not through an agreement between the belligerents. We here once again confront a projection of the 'I' which reflects very well the above-mentioned paradigm of the primacy of municipal law;
4. The legal picture ensuing from such a system is fraught with relativity: the war formally exists or does not exist depending on the will of each state. Thus, the question of the existence of war was subjective rather than objective. It must be added that the sharp edges of such a doctrine were sometimes softened in legal writings, e.g., by the development of a category of 'material war' to be treated analogously to a 'formal' or declared war. The essence of the system, however, was subjective in the described sense and therefore material criteria were not easily applied.

This subjective system was abandoned in 1949. With the Geneva Conventions, through their Common Article 2, the trigger for the applicability of the law of armed conflicts now became neatly objective. The law of armed conflicts applies in cases of 'declared wars', 'international armed conflicts', 'occupation of territories without resistance' (hostile occupation even without hostilities), and to non-international armed conflicts (Common Article 3). All these concepts, with the exception of the first, are objectively defined and do not depend on declaration or recognition. Thus, for example, the concept of 'armed conflict' refers to effective hostile contacts between armed forces or to the existence of wounded and sick, prisoners of war, enemy civilians in need of protection (international armed conflicts), or to a military organisation of the armed forces and a certain intensity of the armed contest (non-international armed conflicts). If there is such a situation in the field, which is to be objectively determined through the key concept of modern law, i.e., effectiveness, then the law of armed conflict applies. It is not by coincidence that the term 'law of war' was now progressively abandoned in favour of the larger term 'law of armed conflict' in order precisely to underscore this shift from a subjective to an objective system. The concept of 'war' essentially depended on a subjective will to be at war; 'armed conflict' refers to a fact on the *terrain*.

The main aim of this shift was to ensure the applicability of IHL to all situations of effective hostile contact. This reflects the major shift of the law from military matters (pre-1949) to the humanitarian protection of the victims of war (post-1949). Thus, while lacunae in applicability could easily be accepted before 1949, when the questions focused on military matters to be sorted out between professional armies, after 1949, such lacunae in protection could no longer be accepted, in view of the new paramount humanitarian aim of the law.[40] No victim may be left without protection because of legal subtleties surrounding the concept of war. It may be added that the subjective aspects have not, however, completely disappeared, especially in the context of non-international armed conflicts. Governments fighting internal rebellion are often reluctant to accept that an 'armed conflict' is ongoing; they prefer to claim that they face, at most, internal disturbances. This way, they seek to avoid the application of international obligations under the Geneva Conventions, the *droit de regard* of the international community and of the ICRC which this inevitably triggers (resented as interventions in internal affairs in an extremely sensitive moment), and the granting of an unwelcome political and legal status to the insurgents, who would then have to be treated as 'belligerents'. This margin of appreciation hardly fits modern law, but it is in fact exercised. Moreover, recognition of rebels as belligerents, in order to apply the whole body of the law of armed conflicts instead of only Common Article 3, was still possible after 1949, but in fact such recognition of belligerency fell quickly into disuse. To some extent, the modern law of armed conflict still faces difficulties in its application. These are ordinarily overcome through special agreements between the warring parties. Such ad hoc agreements grant some practical humanitarian guarantees, while at the same time reserving the correct legal qualification of the situation.

We may thus notice that the subjective approach of the nineteenth century augmented the gaps in the law. Not only was the law of warfare incomplete in itself (gaps within the law), it was also easy to escape its application by not declaring war or by not recognising belligerency, thus creating a second type of gap (gaps in the application of the law).

2.4 *Fundamental paradigm of progress and civilisation (with its related beliefs)*

The modern movement for developing the law of war sprung from a deeply rooted sense of progress, philanthropism and civilisation, which was predominant in Europe in the nineteenth century.[41] This sociological 'law of progress' was considered to be scientific law. It was much the same approach as applied by Hegel, Marx and others, who had presented ineluctable laws of evolution. In this context, the dominant belief was that almost everything done in the warfare of past centuries, where war had been cruel and inhuman, had been lawful; that limitations were now being imposed on the destructiveness of war through the progress of humanitarianism, and that the social phenomenon 'war' would become completely eliminated.[42] The maxim could be paraphrased as follows: 'formerly nothing; now something; tomorrow everything'. This evolution from darkness to light was thought to be inevitable; it was implicit in the objective laws governing social evolution (nineteenth century scientism). Martti Koskenniemi[43] has shown with great clarity (but perhaps sometimes excessively through the critical lens of the modern man) how this idea of progress permeated the work of the founding fathers of the Institut de droit international, which incidentally gave much weight to the law of armed conflicts. This gospel of progress was particularly marked in continental thinking, especially in France, whereas the Anglo-Saxon concept of war remained somewhat more traditional.

Moreover, the laws of war were no longer, as they had often been with Grotius, Vattel and other classical writers, questions of natural law (as opposed to the positive law of nations)[44] or of personal morals (the personal conscience before God, as Vattel often put it).[45] They were now laws imposed by the positive law of nations itself, at once binding and incontrovertible.

References to progress and civilisation abound in the old treatises on the law of war.[46] Through that particular lens, the whole subject matter receives an unmistakable teleological, temporal and sometimes almost eschatological colouration, spanning from moral considerations, on the one hand, to the firm belief that growing enlightenment created by arguments[47] and conventions[48] will improve warfare, on the other. Thus:

> La 'civilisation' de la guerre n'est plus aujourd'hui reculée dans le lointain d'un avenir idéal. S'il n'est pas permis encore d'affirmer que l'adoucissement des mœurs et le développement de la raison publique aient complètement et définitivement substitué à la primauté de la force la primauté du droit, il est impossible du moins de méconnaître le mouvement progressif qui, de nos jours, s'accomplit à cet égard dans l'ordre des idées et des faits.[49]
>
> Or: L'humanité, dans sa marche ascendante vers un idéal social, tend à asseoir de plus en plus sa constitution sur le respect du droit. Aucun critère du progrès n'est plus infaillible que l'idée juridique; plus elle s'épure, plus le règne de la force va s'affaiblissant.[50]

This religion of progress had some characteristic corollaries. One of them was unlimited faith in the support of public opinion for the cause of progress.[51] By a sort of fiction, public opinion was held to be automatically enlightened.[52] Another corollary is that the law of war is perceived as a technical humanitarian question, permeated by the scientific laws of social evolution, and not a political question with all its inevitable fluctuations.[53] A third corollary is that the law of war applies only to 'civilised' states; they do not apply in colonial territories or in the 'barbarian' and 'savage' world.[54] The threefold classification of James Lorimer[55] of civilised, barbarian and savage communities was very common at that time.[56] The law of war was perceived as a specific Christian and Occidental practice, developed through centuries. The group benefiting from this practice was a closed one. Finally, another corollary was the concept that progress implied centralisation of all acts of warfare within professional armies, and thus within the organs of the state. Private wars are disordered, intrinsically unlimited and barbaric. Progress means rendering the war more professional; to this effect, it must be concentrated in the public domain. Hence, privateering and other forms of private participation in war were considered remnants of older practices which ought to be abolished.[57]

2.5 *Varia*

There are some other aspects of the law of war of the nineteenth century which are of interest from a systemic perspective. They may be summed up very briefly.

Prevalence of the normative approach

The nineteenth century preserved an unbroken faith in the strength of legal norms and treaty arrangements. Its focus was to produce model rules for insertion in the municipal law of the various sovereign states; it was far from being concerned with ensuring sanctions for the few rules adopted on the international level. Every government was considered to acclaim the principle of *pacta sunt servanda* and its international repute; public opinion was thought to emphasise the respect of law. How optimistic the view of the times could be may be illustrated by the following sentences: 'Le droit hospitalier international [c'est-à-dire le droit humanitaire] porte avec lui sa sanction; car le connaître, c'est le respecter. Aussi bien, pour en assurer la scrupuleuse application, il suffit que chacun soit informé de ses règles et de l'esprit utilitaire qui les inspire';[58] 'La Convention de Genève en particulier est due à son influence [of public opinion], et nous pouvons nous fier à elle du soin de l'exécution des ordres qu'elle a dictés. C'est par un louable sentiment de justice et d'humanité que les souverains ont signé la Convention; les peines morales sont par conséquent celles qu'ils doivent redouter le plus, puisqu'elles sont plus que d'autres en harmonie avec les mobiles qui les ont guidés'.[59]

It was only occasionally that the glaring insufficiencies of this approach were perceived. The troublesome experiences with applying the Geneva Convention of 1864 in the following wars (such as the gaps in the laws governing sea warfare shown by the Battle of Lissa, 1866; or the ignorance of the conventional provisions and the breaches which occurred in the Franco-Prussian War of 1870–1871) culminated in the proposal of Gustave Moynier, of the Geneva Committee (later the ICRC), for an international criminal tribunal.[60] This proposal was criticised in legal literature. The most these critics were ready to allow was the insertion of criminal provisions in the various national criminal codes or in special military legislation.[61] The proposal was even less popular with states. Hence, again the national approach was preferred; every state was free to adopt penal legislation to the extent they wished. It was only through the shock of the First World War, with the massive (though often exaggerated by propaganda) contempt of the rules and the glaring violation of Belgian neutrality, that the problem really came to the forefront and that the 'failure' of international law (or rather, the old approach to it) became widely acknowledged.[62] From then on, efforts to introduce some criminal sanction for violations of the rules on warfare on the international level were made. After the First Word War, this led to the Leipzig trials; after the Second World War to the Nuremberg, Tokyo and other post-war trials; and in the 1990s to the ad hoc criminal tribunals, the mixed criminal tribunals, and the International Criminal Court (ICC).

Importance of the humanitarian initiative of the ICRC

Due to the fact that the law of war of the nineteenth century was replete with so many gaps and uncertainties, its development, strengthening and implementation rested essentially on the devoted action of its principal champion, the Geneva Committee, now called the ICRC. The main means at the disposal of the ICRC to push forward the legal body it championed was (and remains) the so-called 'humanitarian initiative'.[63] The ICRC exercised this initiative on a great number of occasions throughout the nineteenth century. It thus expanded its area of action from the wounded and sick military personnel in land warfare to the wounded, sick and shipwrecked at sea, later to non-injured prisoners of war, and finally to civilians.[64] From these times onwards, there has been an indissoluble connection between 'IHL' and the ICRC. Equally, in modern times the concept of the law of war (or IHL) is much more than the black letter law that was first introduced; it is also a spirit of protection and action. In this larger domain, the ICRC will seek to obtain guarantees and protections for the various victims of war by – if necessary separate – concessions of the belligerents. By this course of conduct, it will thus often attempt to go beyond the formal law, fraught with all its insufficiencies. But the letter killeth ...

Some attempts to uniform maritime and land warfare

In the nineteenth century, maritime warfare still had a paramount importance. The main communication lines for vital resources, and the bulk of commerce, were at that time maritime. To secure military victory, it was essential to disrupt or inflict damage on the enemy's maritime communications. Maritime warfare had thus, since time immemorial, been geared to hampering commerce. This inevitably meant inflicting damage not only on the state and its agents, but also on private individuals, enemies (confiscation, destruction) or neutrals (contraband of war, blockade). The Anglo-Saxon states accepted this as a necessity in maritime war; while many continental authors opposed it as an infringement on the rule that war should take place only between states and not between private persons. These rather progressive authors thus sought to harmonise maritime warfare and land warfare by subjecting them to the same core principles: the protection of private property.[65] This was one of the most important and controversial questions of the law of war of the nineteenth century. It produced a great array of legal arguments of a most interesting nature,[66] on which it is impossible to dwell here. It may just suffice to say that the stern resistance of England and some other important maritime states did not allow the realisation of the proposed reforms towards protecting private property. Systemically speaking, the law of sea warfare remained under the guiding polar star of different principles from land warfare: for the former, a continued tribute to the older conception of war as taking place against the whole enemy community, state and private persons alike (collective responsibility); whilst the latter saw an increasing adherence to the famous Rousseauist theorem that war and its effects must be confined to the state, sparing private individuals from attack (state responsibility). Hence, private property was not protected at sea; but it was, at least to a greater extent, protected on land. The battle for unity within the law of war between its maritime and land branches was lost. The dichotomy has remained untouched until today, with the rider that the law of sea warfare has to a great extent lost its practical importance.

Absence of the 'civilian'

The law of war of the nineteenth century was only marginally concerned with civilian persons and their protection. The law was essentially a part of military law, concentrating on means and methods of warfare (referred to as 'Hague Law', flowing from the codifications of 1899/1907) and on the care of wounded, sick or shipwrecked military persons ('Geneva Law'). The civilian was thought to stand 'outside' the war and hence, being aloof, not to be in need of any specific regulation (except in sea warfare, as already explained). Civilians undoubtedly might suffer in certain situations, such as siege warfare or occupied territories; however, even in these cases, the law considered them at best as persons indirectly affected, having to suffer the inevitable course of hostilities. It was only in the particular situation of occupied territories that the civilian obtained direct legal protection.[67] This relative absence of the civilian had many causes.[68] First was the optimistic belief that land warfare, with its focus on professional armies, would barely impinge on civilians, and in those exceptional cases where it did, this impingement would in any case be inevitable (such as in besieged towns) so that the law would not be able to do much about it, except by special agreement between the belligerents. Second was the somewhat exacting concept of sovereignty, repelling any idea that the dealings of a state with private individuals (even if foreigners) could easily be made subject to international regulation. Third was the tradition of viewing the 'innocents' not as individual persons but rather in terms of categories such as the elderly, women, children, priests, the insane, who tended to remain alive. Finally, was the very fact that the law of war was considered to be 'military' and not properly 'humanitarian' law, i.e., it was a special law for the combating forces rather than a general law protecting persons in general. The result of this eclipse of the 'civilian' was at least twofold. First, the law had to be further developed in order to fill the gap of protection of civilians, faced with ever-increasing suffering caused by ideological and technically improved warfare. This occurred first through some prudent humanitarian initiatives of the ICRC, such as the humanitarian assistance mission in Montenegro to the benefit of 40,000 refugees from Bosnia (1875–1878).[69] Secondly, the concept of prisoners of war was expanded to cover as many persons in the hands of the enemy as possible, on account of the non-existence of any parallel protective status of civilian internees. Thus, in the nineteenth century, the status of prisoners of war was accorded not only to combatants and to certain persons accompanying the armies, but also to a series of enemy persons performing a public function, such as ambassadors, ministers, heads of state, kings, etc.[70] Frequently,[71] authors stressed that 'all persons' not clearly innocent, i.e., persons who could serve in the adverse army or support the adverse war effort, could be taken captive. Since there was no regulation of civilian captivity under the law of war, these persons were by necessity placed under the category of prisoners of war. This functional interpretation of the latter status ensured these persons some degree of protection. Hence, the concept of prisoners of war performed a broader function in the nineteenth century than it does today.

Permanence of conceptual problems

As regards many aspects of the law of war of the time, conceptual uncertainties continued to loom large. One of the branches of the law most obviously affected was the law of belligerent occupation. This concept, now generally construed as a transient and limited control of foreign territory, had only lately emerged from the fogs and clouds of conquest. This process of transformation was unfolding throughout the nineteenth century.[72] If control of foreign territory under occupation was now considered to be only temporary, limited and precarious, and the right of 'ownership' of the original sovereign was preserved, the most acute problem was explaining how two titles to territorial control could coexist and be coordinated one with the other: the title of the original and ousted sovereign, which continued to exist, and the provisional title of the effective occupier, which was superposed on the former. This problem produced a series of theories, which placed the law of belligerent occupation under substantial strain of uncertainties for a considerable time. Some examples of such theories may be mentioned here without venturing into further explanations. For some authors, occupation remained under the shadow of conquest;[73] for others, the occupier was a quasi-sovereign, able to change all institutions and laws of the occupied territory, and limited simply *ratione temporis* to the time of effective occupation.[74] For others again, occupation was nothing more than a mere power of fact (never a power of law), consequential to effective control of foreign territory and rooted in military necessity,[75] while some saw it as legal power (not a simple fact) flowing from effective control.[76] A small number of authors considered it to be based on private law, the occupier 'representing' the sovereign power of the occupied territory and being thus able to exercise all powers granted to the ousted state within its territory by its local municipal law.[77] These different theories tended to result in different approaches to the rights of the occupier.

2.6 *Summary*

The phase spanning from 1864 to the turn of the century, and indeed to the First World War, was essentially dominated by a municipal law approach to the law of war. The predominant idea was that international 'model rules' would serve as the basis for a substantially progressive municipal codification of the law. The applicable law of war would then in most cases be the area of convergence of the various national laws. This approach left significant divergences in the legal regulation and also a considerable number of gaps in the applicable law. The prevailing view of the day was optimistic, derived from ever-growing progress and civilisation. It believed in enlightened practice, not in detailed regulation. Since the evolution towards civilisation was considered to be an inescapable social law, there was no attempt to regulate the rules of warfare extensively or to protect against derogations, attempts at escape or covert subversion through legal subtleties. The law was one thing; the spirit was much more. This impressive but shaky edifice came down with a loud crash in the First World War.

3. Second phase (1899–1946): the law of war between fundamental criticism and configuration as a system of 'limited limitations'

The persisting differences in national regulations combined with experiences with abuse, disputes and accusations of violation provided a strong impetus to an international 'codification' of the law of warfare. This was first attempted in the Hague Conferences of 1899/1907 (the 1907 Conference producing fourteen agreements) and later in the London

Naval Conference of 1909. The First World War, however, witnessed a breakdown of many of the codified rules. Sea warfare became chaotic (long-distance blockade by England, unlimited *U-Bootkrieg* by Germany); and the law of land warfare was put under heavy strain by the progressive unfolding of total war (intense hate and national propaganda, participation of civilians in the war effort, targeting of industrial plants, aerial warfare over vast areas of territory including towns, etc.). It is true that the extent of the breakdown of the law has been exaggerated for propaganda purposes[78] or as a result of war psychosis.[79] Claiming that the enemy has violated the law reinforced the population's determination to resist and it also justified reprisals. Such claims were thus made more often than they should have been, illustrating the wisdom of the saying that the first casualty in war is truth. Nonetheless, the breakdown of the law cannot generally be negated; and its importance should not be minimised. The result of this overwhelming and grim experience was a plunge into cynicism and resignation,[80] at least as remarkable as the older ages' (at least superficial) optimism in its gospel of progress, civilisation and the invisible hand of an enlightened public opinion. These developments generated a phase characterised by two aspects: first, a full-fledged rejection of the law of armed conflict by a non-negligible number of commentators; and secondly, the systematic conception of the law of war as a modest set of rules limiting the general rule of freedom of belligerents. This latter approach was to some extent intended to counterbalance the excessive expectations and demands that had previously been formulated around a triumphant law of warfare, which had turned out in practice to be anything but that.[81]

3.1 *Condemnation of the law of war*

In a series of concordant articles,[82] the most important of which was an anonymous contribution in the *British Yearbook of International Law*, several authors proposed that: (i) it had been a mistake to concentrate on the law of war instead of focusing on the ways of avoiding war in the first place (*jus contra bellum*);[83] and (ii) that on any account, it is impossible to regulate war by so-called rules on warfare since the volcanic violence of war is intrinsically unsuitable for legal restrictions.[84] The focus of legal attention, in the wake of the League of Nations, thus turned to the avoidance of war; the laws of war were neglected, classified as being illusory, bygone *naïvetés*, or 'child's play'. It was held that 'total war'[85] had made legal regulation of wars impossible: the new wars, involving all components of society in the war effort, were unavoidably lawless; thus one could only attempt to prohibit them, not try to regulate them. This short-sighted attitude has been criticised with good arguments;[86] it was, however, dominant during the inter-war period. It hampered further adaptation and progress in the laws of war, especially with regard to weapons, aerial warfare and protection of civilians. The essential conventions adopted in this time period were the Geneva Gas Protocol of 1925[87] and the two Geneva Conventions of 1919 concerning the wounded and sick, and prisoners of war.[88] The first was the result of disarmament efforts by the League of Nations (supervision of international trade in arms) and thus fitted the *jus contra bellum* approach; the second was essentially humanitarian (not forming part of the laws of war in the narrow sense), being a result of the ICRC's efforts.

3.2 The law of war as a system of concrete limitations on the general rule of residual freedom

The authors particularly sensitive to systematic questions had already foreseen[89] what now tended to become a major feature in the *exposé* of the law of war:[90] its character as a set of restricted rules, limiting a residual freedom of belligerent action. As we have seen, military necessity had been the great principle for determining the lawfulness or illegality of a certain conduct. It was held that everything necessary to overpower the enemy had to be considered allowed. In times of extreme necessity such as war, permissive action included a peculiarly vast array of things. These cannot be listed or expressed individually. Residually to this main and vast category of allowed courses of conduct, some limitations could be imposed, because an action is irrelevant and superfluous to the aims of war (necessity in the restrictive sense), or due to dictates of humanity (cruel or excessively devastating means), or finally because of reasons of prudence (fear of reprisals). The presumption was freedom of action; the exception was a concrete limitation contained in the positive law. According to this conception, the law of war could not aim at more; and it was better to achieve less than to fall into illusions and delusions. This state of affairs had two immediate corollaries.

First, the law of war thus to a great extent strengthened the leading legal principle of the time, namely the concept that a state could not be bound by a rule without its express or implied consent. In the first part of the century, legal positivism (and its corollary: sovereignism) was still in its heyday in international law. The whole body of international law thus tended to become a set of rules formed by particular agreements: where there was consent, the states consenting would be bound; where there was no consent, there would be no legal constraint on action. The result of such a conception was that the law was endlessly fragmented and 'archipelised'. There were scarcely any general rules of international law but rather particular rules of international law applicable to certain consenting states. Hence, the general rule was freedom from constraint. This was a sort of default modus in cases where no consent to a rule is expressed. The exception was the existence of a legal rule binding upon states, but only when such corresponding consent existed. When no particular will to bind itself was expressed, a state remained in the ordinary modus of not being bound; when a particular will was expressed, a state would be bound according to the terms of this undertaking. This concept of state freedom as the underlying and ordinary condition of international relations was admirably expressed in the much celebrated (and not less criticised) *Lotus* case (1927), where the PCIJ remarkably illustrated the general atmosphere of the time:

> International law governs relations between independent states. The rules of law binding upon states therefore emanate from their own free will as expressed in conventions or by usages generally accepted as expressing principles of law and established in order to regulate relations between these co-existing independent communities or with a view to the achievement of common aims. Restrictions upon the independence of states cannot therefore be presumed.[91]

Sovereignty, independence and power were the dominant ideals of that system; the law ideally reduced itself to transactions (treaties, diplomacy), responsibility and war.[92] This conception permeated the law of the inter-war period. True, this conception was attacked by progressive legal doctrine, but it remained dominant in practice. It dominated even the most progressive pieces of law, such as the Covenant of the League of Nations. This is demonstrated especially in Article 5(1) of the Covenant, where unanimity is posed as the general voting rule. This voting modality was chosen precisely in order to maintain the equality and unaltered sovereignty of every state through the power of *liberum veto*.

Secondly, it meant that the 'Martens Clause'[93] was not really taken seriously before the post-Second World War trials. The residual rule was not humanity; it was state freedom. Geoffrey Best is thus right, I think, when he expressed the following:

> The Martens Clause was, to begin with, not much more than a swallow announcing a summer still some way off. Much more attention has been paid to it in the second half-century of its life than was paid to it in the first. It attracted no significant attention until the public conscience of the

> victorious civilised peoples, establishing on ground as firm as possible the post-war trials[94] of notoriously uncivilised enemies, found the idea of 'laws of humanity' peculiarly interesting and useful.[95]

A reading of the old literature on the law of armed conflict, especially from the inter-war period, confirms this finding. This evanescence of the Martens Clause is nothing more than the reverse of the coin already discussed: that the dominating principle was state freedom in all cases of absence of a binding, prohibitive rule.

The most sensitive authors[96] went further in their painstaking legal analysis. They insisted on the fact that the law of armed conflict was based not on a residual 'right' to perform specific acts of violence, flowing from the absence of prohibitions, but on a simple '*de facto* freedom' to engage in such courses of action, due to the absence of legal regulation. Indeed, the law of war did not grant a subjective right to undertake and impose a belligerent action on the counterpart. The adverse party was in no way bound to suffer such action, as would be the case if there were a correlative subjective right granted to the belligerent state. The right of the adverse state to resist in order to ward off the coercion which it was being threatened with or subjected to, was rather unquestioned. The freedom to act was thus recognised by the legal order as a *de facto freedom* in the sense that the law abstained from prohibiting certain courses of conduct or regulating certain subject matters, thereby leaving them automatically to be sorted out by power and force. The freedom to act was not recognised by the legal order as a *legal freedom*, sanctioned as such by the law through a granting of rights of action and correlative duties of suffering (*facere et patire*). In the first case, the law referred to a fact; in the second, it referred to a norm. The 'freedom of fact' theory perfectly fits the system of the law of war in the inter-war period, at once decried, jeopardised and shaky.

3.3 *Summary*

This second phase was characterised by a profound crisis of the law of war. For the first time in the history of the law of nations, it was marginalised within the international body. Moreover, this phase was characterised by a legal construction of the law of war as a set of limited, residual and prohibitive rules set against the backdrop of the unlimited number of hostilities which the modern sovereign state, at the heyday of its might, was faced with. The abuses and destructiveness of such permissive premises would necessarily trigger a brutal shift of the law towards new constructions and values, as happened after the Second World War: the law of war now placed at its centre humanitarian concerns. It would thus transform itself into 'international humanitarian law' (IHL).

4. Third phase (1949–1993): the humanitarian age of the Geneva Conventions of 1949

The adoption of the Geneva Conventions in 1949 (to which the two major Additional Protocols of 1977 were later added) marked a radical departure from old concepts and generated a new universe with regard to the law of war. Their importance as a breakthrough of new perspectives, substantive rules and systematic coordinates was epochal.[97] Essentially, the Geneva Conventions (GC) transformed the law of armed conflict into a 'humanitarian law'. The protection of the individual war victims became the pivotal centre of the system; IHL ceases to be merely (or even essentially) the old 'military law'. This new IHL, with its humanitarian outlook, would in due course necessarily come closer to the nascent and growing arm of international human rights law (HRL). To be able to ensure protection of all victims of (modern) war, it became necessary to abandon both the old concept of international model norms in national legislation (phase I) and the approach of minimum codification as in the Hague Conferences (phase II). The law was now clearly influenced by the idea of a thorough international codification of mandatory norms of behaviour imposed on belligerents, norms which do not permit derogation or reprisals. The three main features of this third phase were: (i) humanitarian protection; (ii) a friendly and cooperative relation with human rights; and (iii) detailed international codification. At this juncture, it may be useful to pause for a moment to analyse the meaning and construction of these great Geneva Conventions of 1949.

4.1 What are the Geneva Conventions?

After the end of the Second World War, new drafts on the law of armed conflict, taking into account the experiences gained during the war, were prepared. This war had shown that the traditional law of armed conflict had been insufficient, especially with regard to the protection of persons *hors de combat*. The treatment of prisoners of war (e.g., Russian prisoners in Germany or Allied prisoners in Japan) and the deportation of civilians bore tragic testimony to this. For the wounded and sick military personnel and for prisoners of war, there was already a set of Geneva Conventions which only needed to be updated: the Geneva Conventions of 1929. Nonetheless, there had been a complete absence of conventional protection for civilians, especially if some scattered provisions applying to occupied territories are left out of account (Hague Convention IV, Regulations, Articles 42 ff.). It was therefore thought in 1949 that a new codification effort was necessary on four accounts:

1. The law of armed conflict had since 1919 suffered from regular criticism regarding its much-debated viability: can there truly be a law in armed conflict? Is the law of armed conflict not created in hindsight, and thus a war too late? Is it not unrealistic to think that a law of armed conflict can work? The law had also suffered serious violations during the Second World War. It was thus felt necessary to solemnly reaffirm this branch of international law and to give it a new impetus, starting from a clean slate: the GC codification.
2. The Second World War had shown that there existed a considerable urgency in protecting persons *hors de combat*. Thus, the new law was centred on that humanitarian issue, largely leaving aside the more military part of the law of armed conflicts (conduct of hostilities). For the conduct of hostilities, the old Hague Regulations of 1907 were still applicable.
3. The Second World War had shown the tendency of some belligerents to manipulate and to try to evade the law, as well as to use all the gaps and uncertainties to enable self-serving interpretations (e.g., on hostages). It was consequently considered in 1949 that the new law should be much more detailed than the previous general summary and optimistic law of 1907. This produced a codification with considerably more and longer provisions. Secondly, the drafters prohibited states from opting out of the conventional protection provided in the GCs through bilateral agreements between belligerents, or through unilateral renunciation of the accorded protection by the beneficiaries (see Articles 6–7 GC I–III, and Articles 7–8, 47 GC IV).
4. Experience had shown, through the Spanish Civil War (1936–1939), that some regulation was also needed for non-international armed conflicts (roughly speaking, 'civil wars'). Thus, Common Article 3 of the four GCs was adopted. It provided a sort of 'minimum convention' within the Conventions, granting some elementary protections in the context of non-international armed conflicts.

In the 1970s, it was considered necessary to adapt the Geneva Conventions. This led to the adoption of the two Additional Protocols (AP) to the GCs in 1977. Adaptations of the law were necessary, especially in the following contexts:

1. *Non-international armed conflicts*: Most armed conflicts after 1949 had been civil wars (with or without some form of foreign military intervention). Common Article 3 of the GCs proved to be too sketchy to provide adequate protection for these multifaceted and numerous civil wars. Thus, Additional Protocol II was adopted, devoted only to non-international armed conflicts.
2. *Definition of combatants*: In the many struggles for liberation of colonised people, and also in other warfare situations (e.g., Vietnam), asymmetric guerrilla warfare had frequently occurred. The GCs (Article 4 GC III) did not permit such guerrilla fighters to be considered regular combatants: the conditions were too strict and could only be fulfilled when the rebels in fact controlled a part of the territory. This inequality in status (guerrilla fighters could not be regular combatants, and could not claim prisoner of war status or combatant privilege) led to discrimination and thus to problems of applying the law of armed conflict. Additional Protocol I, in Articles 43–4, somewhat relaxed the criteria for regular combatancy. Nevertheless, it attempted to avoid an excessive relaxing of the relevant criteria since this would have paved the way for terrorist action and placed the principle of distinction between civilians and combatants under too heavy a strain. The question as to whether AP I succeeded in striking a proper balance has remained controversial.
3. *The law relating to conduct of warfare*: The means and methods of warfare had not been reformed since 1907. The Vietnam War in particular had shown that some new efforts to better protect the civilian population were needed, especially in the case of bombardments. This led to the adoption of the most important Article 48 ff. of AP I, protecting civilians during hostilities (principle of distinction, targeting, collateral damages, precautions in attack, etc.).
4. *Human rights law*: Since 1949, human rights law had constantly evolved. In 1977, it was felt necessary to extend some fundamental protections flowing from the growing field of human rights law to the protected persons under the GCs. Thus, Article 75 AP I and Articles 4–6 AP II were adopted. These are quite detailed provisions.

4.2 *Applicability of the Geneva Conventions*

The adoption of the Geneva Conventions in 1949 marks a shift in the scope of application and in the substance of the law of warfare. Prior to 1949, the law of warfare or of armed conflict was applicable essentially to one event: 'the state of war'. This supposed, on the part of a state, a subjective intent to consider itself at war with another state. The required intent was generally notified through a declaration of war. As to the substance of the law, it was largely centred on the conduct of hostilities, as is evidenced by Hague Convention IV. Some Geneva Conventions (1864, 1906, 1929), however, were already concerned with the protection of the wounded and sick, and of prisoners of war. With the adoption of the GCs of 1949, the substantive focus of the law changed: due to the horrific abuses of prisoners and civilians by the Axis powers during the Second World War, the new law of armed conflict developed essentially to protect all persons *hors de combat*, i.e., those who do not take part in hostilities (civilians) and those who have laid down their arms (combatants *hors de combat*). This new focus on the properly humanitarian protection of persons aroused a greater concern with the applicability of the law. It was considered that such elementary protection should be applicable as widely as possible and without any exceptions, at least in international armed conflicts (armed conflicts between states). Moreover, after the experience of the Spanish Civil War (1936–1939), it was considered necessary to introduce some provisions on non-international armed conflicts in order to ensure a minimum standard of humanity in this particular context also. The scope of application of the GCs is thus much more articulated and overall significantly broader than that of the older law, due to its focus on a humanitarian minimum standard. The essential provision for defining the material scope of application of the GCs is Common Article 2.[98]

1. Some provisions of the GCs apply even in peacetime, from the time of ratification and entry into force of the Conventions for the particular state. Thus, for instance, the duty to disseminate the law of the Conventions applies immediately. This dissemination will have to be performed in training courses for armed forces and through information of the population at large, as far as feasible. See Articles 47/48/127/144 GC I–IV. See also, for other examples, Article 14 GC IV or Article 58 AP I.
2. The bulk of the provisions apply in times of armed conflict. The definition of that concept is very wide for international armed conflicts (armed conflicts among states), but somewhat stricter for non-international armed conflicts (civil wars). For international armed conflicts, there is no necessity of a full-fledged war or large-scale hostilities for the GCs to apply (these being obviously included *a fortiori*). A simple small incident between armed forces at the border, even the simple adverse

taking of a prisoner without any exchanges of fire, suffices to trigger the application of the Conventions under the heading of an 'armed conflict'. This purely functional perspective is warranted since there is no reason why humanitarian protection should be granted only for conflicts of a certain intensity. On the contrary, the Convention must apply to the first prisoner when captured, since he is in need of that protection. The only requirement is thus that armed forces of states come into hostile contact and thereby substantively trigger some protection granted by the Conventions. This broad approach is today accepted.

The meaning of armed conflict is different for non-international armed conflicts. Here, only Common Article 3 of the GCs applies, and potentially also AP II if ratified or acceded to. A non-international armed conflict exists only if: (i) the armed forces of the rebels are militarily organised to such a degree that there is discipline and a responsible command; (ii) the conflict has reached a certain intensity, so that it has become protracted and has affected a significant number of victims. As a rule of thumb, there is a non-international armed conflict if the police alone are unable to cope with the situation and military forces must be used. As far as AP II is concerned, according to its Article 1, it applies only to non-international armed conflicts where the rebel forces 'exercise such control over a part of its territory [of a High Contracting Party] as to enable them to carry out sustained and concerted military operations and to implement this Protocol'. These three respective criteria (degree of organisation and intensity of the conflict for the GCs, to which territorial control is added by AP II) should not be interpreted narrowly, bearing in mind the humanitarian nature of the protection accorded. The threshold for reaching an international armed conflict, however, is significantly lower that the one for admitting the existence of a non-international conflict, be it for the purpose of Common Article 3 or AP II.

3. The GCs also apply to cases of declared war. If a declaration of war is followed by hostilities, there will be an armed conflict in the sense just discussed. There may, however, be a time gap between the declaration of war and the effective start of hostilities. To this initial timespan the GCs apply through the trigger of 'declared wars' in Common Article 2. If a declaration of war is eventually not followed by effective hostilities, the GCs equally apply by the same token. There are a series of provisions which may become relevant in such cases of declared war without hostilities, e.g., the treatment of enemy civilians on the territories of the belligerents (see Article 35 ff. GC IV). The fact that

the declaration of war is lawful (e.g., self-defence) or unlawful (e.g., aggression) is irrelevant: the law of armed conflict applies equally to all belligerent parties whatever the cause of their involvement (separation of *jus in bello* from *jus ad bellum* issues). Declarations of war have fallen into disuse since 1945.

4. The GCs apply also to territories occupied without resistance (Common Article 2(2) GCs). There may be cases where a territory is militarily occupied by hostile forces without any resistance from the attacked state. In such cases, there might be neither an armed conflict (no hostilities, no prisoners, no wounded) nor a declaration of war. Thus, a gap could emerge in the protection of the population of occupied territories. The GCs close that gap by the rule contained in Common Article 2(2). It is to be noted that paragraph 2 applies only in cases where a territory is occupied without resistance (residual clause). If a territory is occupied after or in the course of an armed conflict, it is paragraph 1 of Common Article 2 which applies ('armed conflict'). The distinction may have legal importance.[99]
5. AP I adds one specific case to the category of international armed conflicts: namely wars of national liberation (see Article 1(4) AP I). This category belongs to the history of decolonisation.

It can be seen that the main thrust of the Geneva Conventions is to ensure the widest and most complete application of the GCs, as the residual mention of declared wars and of territories occupied without resistance shows. The main reason for this generosity is the humanitarian focus of the GCs.

To sum up, the Geneva Conventions bear testimony to a humanitarian shift of the law: the centre of the new law is the individual, military or civilian, as a victim of the war for whom non-derogable rules of protection must be ensured in all necessary contexts. The law of armed conflict becomes an 'international humanitarian law' (a terminology that was developed in ICRC circles of the 1950s, around Jean Pictet). This new approach allows more weight to be given to the Martens Clause, as state freedom of action is restrained wherever possible, inter alia, through excluding the possibility for derogation, reprisals, etc.

4.3 Synergies with human rights law

International humanitarian law of the Geneva period is rooted in 'humanitarianism'.[100] Hence, progressive interrelations with human rights law were unavoidable. Geneva Convention IV (by its protection of civilians the Convention is structurally nearest to HRL) was the first to undertake interactions with HRL. Nothing is nearer to the 'human being' without qualification in the field of HRL than the newly discovered 'civilian' in the field of IHL. In the territories occupied by Israel after the Six Days War, this new approach of mixing and complementing HRL and IHL for the protection of civilians has been applied for many years, until the present time.[101] All this contributed to the progressive demise of the old ideology of distrust with regard to IHL, prevalent in the United Nations at the beginning of its history. The belief that a focus on IHL could in any way jeopardise the effectiveness of the UN Charter's preventive arrangements against the use of force, which had turned out to be more modest in result than hoped for, had faded. A second essential factor for the two branches of law being drawn closer to each other was the immense growth of the number of civil wars (non-international armed conflicts). IHL was notoriously underdeveloped in the context of non-international armed conflicts. Therefore, it was quite natural to seek additional protection for suffering civilians by applying HRL, as developed since the 1960s. Indeed, HRL could easily be applied to such situations. Civil war takes place within a state. The state driven into civil war continues to be bound by HRL instruments. The only step that must be taken is to define which human rights cannot be derogated from in times of emergency and civil war. Today, the existence of the many HRL monitoring bodies and tribunals also accounts for the improved human rights protection of persons in armed conflicts. Since there are no true monitoring bodies (and even less tribunals) ensuring respect for IHL, it is quite natural to bring abuses of force during armed conflicts within the four corners of HRL violations, and to seek the jurisdiction of an HRL court in order to ensure a sanction.[102] The interrelationship between IHL and HRL has consequently constantly improved and become more interconnected.

4.4 *Summary*

This phase is characterised by a shift from 'military' law to 'humanitarian' law (protection of war victims); this humanitarian law progressively opened itself to human rights law. The Martens Clause now found fertile soil for growth and gained some importance, whereas the rule of the residual freedom of the state was resolutely pushed back. The 'Hague' Law on conduct of hostilities has only been progressively developed in 1977 through the Additional Protocols. But even in this context, the thrust of the legal regulation is the protection of persons. One may quote Article 48 ff. AP I, 'Protection of the Civilian Population against Effects of Hostilities', which is the heart of the Protocol.

5. Fourth phase (1993 to date): a phase of progressive 'humanisation' of IHL but also loss of autonomy

It is always difficult to encapsulate current developments within a clear-cut set of theoretical explanations. Only some reflections on the current systematic construction of IHL can here be offered to the reader, and only in a tentative tone. The starting date of this last phase is also rather fluid: 1993 was chosen as it is the year of the creation of the ICTY, marking a rebirth of international criminal law. This particular branch of international law is of non-negligible importance for the configuration of modern IHL. From the perspective of systematic construction of the law, there are two major developments in this phase.

5.1 Progressive 'humanisation' of IHL

The humanisation of IHL started in 1949 at the latest, through the Geneva Conventions; it continued in the 1960s to the 1990s through the fraternisation of IHL with HRL; but its heyday was in the 1990s, where it was in itself made the object of doctrinal attention.[103] This unclear concept connotes essentially two ideas, one more general, the other more specific:

1. On the general level, 'humanising' IHL means rendering it progressively 'homo-centric' instead of 'state-centred'. Traditionally, it is claimed, the law of war was essentially inter-state law, driven by collective responsibility, reprisals, means and methods of warfare, and reparations *post bellum*. Then, increasingly, homo-centred seeds have flourished: individual criminal responsibility (Nuremberg trials, ad hoc tribunals, ICC); human rights concerns (due process of law, torture, inhuman treatment, arbitrary arrest/detention, non-refoulement, non-discrimination, etc.); an extended applicability of IHL in order to ensure increased protection; special agreements concluded to the same effect; development of minimum humanitarian standards for situations of internal disturbances; strengthening of the principle of proportionality limiting collateral damages during attack (Article 51(5)(b) AP I), etc. This process has clearly been significantly accelerated in

the 1990s. Many actors contributed to its gaining momentum, be it the human rights monitoring organs, the UN Security Council, political bodies of regional organisations, the international criminal tribunals, etc. Moreover, this humanised IHL becomes a part of international public order: *jus cogens*, obligations *erga omnes*, and universal jurisdiction. One may find a symptomatic statement to such a perspective of humanisation in the *Kupreskić* judgment of the ICTY (Trial Chamber, 14 January 2000).[104]

2. On the more specific level, the humanisation of IHL progressively leads to postulations of 'absolute' prohibitions. Being part of public order, the IHL obligations are protected against any attempts of evasion: reservations, reciprocity/reprisals, derogations by special agreements, evasion by applicability issues, all these tend to be eschewed by legal constructions guaranteeing the applicability of the protections stipulated for in any circumstances. It is undoubted that this effort often remains doctrinal; military practice is less inclined to be enthusiastic. But it cannot be doubted that this perspective and the practice to which it gives rise exerts pressure on the actors – humanitarian, political and military. A conspicuous example of the power of such arguments can be found again in the *Kupreskić* case (2000),[105] with regard to a prohibition of reprisals against civilians in customary international law. There are, however, also areas where IHL tends to be put aside under the influence of other norms of public order: one may think of the law of belligerent occupation, yielding at least partially to Security Council resolutions under Chapter VII of the UN Charter. The process of 'hardening' the obligations in IHL is thus a complex one.

5.2 *Progressive loss of autonomy of IHL*

Another notable feature of the current state of IHL is its relative loss of autonomy. Two distinct devices nourish this process.

First, it is hardly possible to fully expose the law relating to specific protection under IHL without taking into account many other areas of international law: HRL, refugee law, international criminal law, international police law (to the extent it exists), etc. Many modern military manuals, rules of engagement, training programmes in IHL, and the like, do contain such references to extra-IHL sources. When I have been asked myself to contribute to concrete solutions in the context of my military service in the 'Law of Armed Conflicts' Section of the Swiss Army (where

I perform my military service), I have often needed to consider issues of human rights law, interlinked with IHL. Moreover, the extent to which the contemporary international criminal tribunals have contributed to the development of IHL can hardly be overstated.[106] The importance of that contribution, especially in the area of non-international armed conflicts, is well known. The ICTY, more than all other criminal tribunals, has applied many rules of IHL for international armed conflicts also in non-international armed conflicts, declaring the former also applicable in the latter on the basis of customary international law.[107]

Secondly, the tasks of modern armies have themselves diversified. They are no longer limited to strictly military or fighting roles, but also include humanitarian tasks (e.g., providing and securing humanitarian aid), policing tasks (e.g., riot control, road checkpoints, fighting piracy on the high seas), and even contributions to nation rebuilding programmes under the aegis of the United Nations or regional arrangements. Furthermore, these different functions tend to merge together. It is not often the case that there are clear-cut periods where the army will do one task, later another and still later something else. On the contrary, it will most often be necessary to perform many of these tasks at the same time, in the same place, with respect to different actors: fighting, police control, humanitarian services. This multidisciplinarity puts a heavy strain on modern armies. Military personnel are often not trained to do all these tasks. Thus, American soldiers in Iraq had not received adequate training for the police functions they were required to exercise (checkpoints, riot control, etc.). The Swiss Army itself is aware of the challenges faced by it through such multiple functions, including potential police functions within the boundaries of Switzerland (e.g., securing sensitive installations). Therefore, training exclusively geared towards the combat function and its IHL counterpart would not be adequate. This multifunctionality accentuates the loss of relative autonomy of IHL. Hence, it is not only the human rights bodies or the criminal tribunals that look at IHL through the lens of their specific competence, which succeed in splitting up its old-fashioned autonomy; the military branch itself, to some extent the guardian of IHL, is today increasingly aware that in the multifunctional modern world, its missions require a mix of different legal supports and abilities.

Both evolutions mentioned consequentially lead to a reshaping of IHL. Like an unsaturated molecule, IHL seeks more and more the complementation of other sources of international and national law.

5.3 *Summary*

From the systematic perspective, the current phase of development is characterised by two conflicting tendencies. On the one hand, there is the strengthening of a 'humanised' IHL. It is considered as expressing a set of norms of public order, which is hailed as an 'absolute' in a world where the human rights logic, since the 1990s, has celebrated a triumphant victory. On the other hand, IHL tends to be enmeshed in an ever more complex network of legal sources, all attempting to give some legal guidance or direction to situations of conflict. The particular flavour of our time is the rise towards the 'absolute', on the one hand, and being caught up in the 'relative', on the other. The two movements are by no means contradictory: both movements strengthen IHL, one in itself, the other by adjoining fresh and supplementary resources to its combat. In the meantime, the situation on the ground remains as dramatic as ever.

6. Conclusion

This contribution has attempted to show that the modern law of armed conflict underwent profound systematic changes to an extent paralleling Ovid's *Metamorphoses*. Even if many essential concrete rules have remained unaltered (e.g., prohibition of poisoned weapons, declaring that no quarter will be given, the protection of prisoners of war, etc.), their systematic surroundings at different times have been as varied as a landscape in different seasons, different weather conditions, and day or night. Few areas of international law have witnessed such profound upheavals. Regulating boundaries of human existence, the law of warfare will certainly continue to respond to important systematic and structural changes in the future. At the same time, some more permanent lines emerge out of the mist of time. A distinguished feature in this body of law is the Geneva Conventions of 1949, which, on the whole, are to be regarded as the most advanced effort made to introduce some humane regulation to wartime situations. It responds to the quest of modern man to secure as far as possible the overriding aim of human dignity. The Conventions of 1949 are in that sense a *Gipfelkomplex*, a sovereign mountain dominating the surrounding landscape, in the long chain of events and texts spanning the changing continent of war.

Notes

1 On this formative stage, see H. Haug, *Humanité pour tous, Le Mouvement international de la Croix-Rouge et du Croissant-Rouge* (Berne/Stuttgart/Vienna, 1993) 19 ff.; F. Bugnion, *Le Comité international de la Croix-Rouge et la protection des victimes de la guerre* (Geneva, 1994) 11 ff. (there exists an English translation of this major book, but French is the original version and it will be quoted in this text). See also J. de Senarclens, *Gustave Moynier, Le bâtisseur* (Geneva, 2000).

2 See P. Boissier, *Histoire du Comité international de la Croix-Rouge, de Solférino à Tsoushima* (Geneva, 1963); A. Durand, *Histoire du Comité international de la Croix-Rouge* (Geneva, 1978); C. Rey-Schyrr, *Histoire du Comité international de la Croix-Rouge, De Yalta à Dien Bien Phu, 1945–1955* (Geneva, 2007); Bugnion, *Le Comité international de la Croix-Rouge*; G. Best, *Humanity in Warfare: The Modern History of the International Law of Armed Conflicts* (London, 1980); H. Coursier, *Etudes sur la formation du droit humanitaire* (Geneva, 1952). See also S.C. Neff, *War and the Law of Nations, A General History* (Cambridge, 2005). For a short introduction, see C. Greenwood, 'Historical development and legal basis' in D. Fleck (ed.), *The Handbook of International Humanitarian Law* (2nd edn., Oxford, 2008) 20 ff. For the period after 1945, see G. Best, *War and Law Since 1945* (Oxford, 1994). In general see also: C. F. Amerasinghe, 'History and sources of the law of war' (2004) 16 *Sri Lanka Journal of International Law* 263; K.H. Ziegler, 'Zur Entwicklung von Kriegsrecht und Kriegsverhütung im Völkerrecht des 19. und frühen 20. Jahrhunderts' (2004) 42 *Archiv des Völkerrechts* 271 ff.

3 On this point, see P. M. Dupuy, 'L'unité de l'ordre juridique international – Cours général de droit international public', *RCADI* 297 (2002), 93, who speaks of a 'Lotus-type' of international society.

4 There are countless writings on the law of war in this period. Almost any international law textbook will contain a substantial section on the law of war, unlike the textbooks of the twentieth century. Since Grotius' *De iure belli ac pacis* (1625), the law of war has been a prominent part of the law of nations, to which all the classic works on international law devoted a great part of their publications. In the nineteenth century, with the renewal of the law of war through the Paris Declaration on Maritime Warfare (1856) and through the Red Cross Movement, there have been further reasons to devote keen attention to this branch of the law. There can be no point in providing a complete list of such publications here; only some of the most important treatises will be mentioned. Some of them are published slightly after the dates of the phase mentioned, but are inspired by the law of the nineteenth century. In the French language: C. Calvo, *Le droit international théorique et pratique* (5th edn., Paris, 1896) vol. IV, 41 ff.; vol. VI, 481 ff.; P. Pradier-Fodéré, *Traité de droit international public européen et américain* vol. VII (Paris, 1897) 1 ff.; vol. VIII (Paris, 1906) 24 ff.; H. Bonfils, *Manuel de droit international public* (3rd edn., Paris, 1901) 571 ff.; F. Despagnet (and C. de Boeck), *Cours de droit international public* (4th edn., Paris, 1910) 802 ff. In the English language: W. O. Manning, *Commentaries on the Law of Nations* (London, 1839) 94 ff.; J. Kent, *Commentary on International Law* (ed. by J.T. Abdy) (Cambridge/London, 1866) 186ff; H. W. Halleck, *Elements of International Law and Laws of War* (Philadelphia, 1874); S. Amos, *Lectures on International Law* (London, 1874) 54 ff.; E. S. Creasy, *First Platform of International Law* (London, 1876) 412 ff.; J. H. Ferguson, *Manual of International Law* (London/The Hague/Hong Kong, 1884) vol. II 262 ff.; T. Twiss, *The Law of Nations*

considered as Independent Political Communities (Oxford, 1884) vol. II; R. Phillimore, *Commentaries upon International Law* (3rd ed., London, 1885) vol. III 115 ff.; H. S. Maine, *International Law* (London, 1888) 57 ff.; T. A. Walker, *A Manual of Public International Law* (Cambridge, 1895) 102 ff.; S. Baker, *First Steps in International Law* (London, 1899) 184 ff.; G. B. Davis, *The Elements of International Law* (New York/London, 1900) 271 ff.; H. Taylor, *A Treatise on International Public Law* (Chicago, 1901) 447 ff. In the Italian language: L. Casanova, *Del diritto internazionale* (2nd edn., Florence, 1870) vol. II 47 ff.; P. Fiore, *Il diritto internazionale codificato* (2nd edn., Turin, 1898) 430 ff. In the German language: E. Lueder, 'Krieg und Kriegsrecht im Allgemeinen' in F. v. Holtzendorff, *Handbuch des Völkerrechts* (Hamburg, 1889) vol. IV 169 ff. and F. H. Geffcken, 'Das Seekriegsrecht', in *ibid.* 545 ff. In the Spanish language: M de Olivart, *Tratado de derecho internacional publico* vol. III (4th edn, Madrid, 1903) 59 ff. and vol. IV, 1 ff. See also the various specialised monographs: G. Moynier, *Etude sur la Convention de Genève pour l'amélioration du sort des militaires blessés dans les armées en campagne (1864 et 1868)* (Paris, 1870); F. Dahn, *Le droit de la guerre* (Antwerp, 1871) (*Das Kriegsrecht*, Würzburg, 1870)); A. Morin, *Les lois relatives à la guerre* (Paris, 1872); J. C. Bluntschli, *Das moderne Kriegsrecht der civilisierten Staaten* (2nd edn, Nördlingen, 1874); F. Lentner, *Das Recht im Kriege* (Vienna, 1880); C. A. Notebaert, *Droit, lois et coutumes de la guerre* (Mons, 1881); J. Guelle, *La guerre continentale et les personnes* (Paris, 1881); J. Guelle, *Précis des lois de la guerre* (Paris, 1884); P. Resch, *Das moderne Kriegsrecht des civilisierten Staatenwelt* (Graz/Leipzig, 1885); E. Linde, *Das Völkerrecht im Kriege* (Berlin, 1888 (extract)); H. Hetzel, *Die Humanisierung des Krieges in den letzten hundert Jahren* (Frankfurt an der Oder, 1891) (compendium of documents showing the progress of the law of war); A. Pillet, *Le droit de la guerre* (Paris, 1892); H. Triepel, *Die neuesten Fortschritte auf dem Gebiete des Kriegsrechtes* (Leipzig, 1894); J. S. Risley, *The Law of War* (London, 1897); A. Pillet, *Les lois actuelles de la guerre* (2nd edn, Paris, 1901).

5 See D. Schindler and J. Toman, *The Laws of Armed Conflicts* (4th edn, Leiden/Boston, 2004) 365 ff. On this Geneva Convention, see e.g., Calvo, *Le droit international*, vol. IV, 207 ff.; Pradier-Fodéré, *Traité*, vol. VII, 318 ff.; Guelle, *Guerre*, 103 ff.; Guelle, *Précis*, vol. I, 144 ff.; Moynier, *Etude*; Lueder, '*Krieg*', 289 ff., 398 ff.; C. Lueder, *Die Genfer Convention* (Erlangen, 1876); Pillet, *Lois*, 165 ff. It is much less frequent that Anglo-Saxon treatises indulge in lengthy treatments of the Geneva Convention of 1864; the treatment of the question is here much shorter, see e.g., Risley, *Law of War*, 132–3. See also G. Münzel, *Untersuchungen über die Genfer Konvention* (Freiburg im Breisgau, 1901); L. E. Visser, *La Convention de Genève du 22 août 1864 et les Sociétés de la Croix-Rouge* (La Haye, 1902); C. Meurer, *Die Genfer Konvention und ihre Reformen* (Munich, 1906); H. Coursier, 'The Geneva Convention of 1864 in International Law' (1954) 7 *Revue Internationale de la Croix-Rouge*, English Supplement 144 ff.; P. Boissier, 'Centième anniversaire de la 1ère Convention de Genève' (1964) 46 *Revue internationale de la Croix-Rouge* 379 ff.; J.H. Dunant, 'La Convention de Genève de 1864' in H. Maza, *Neuf meneurs internationaux* (Paris, 1965) 87 ff.; D. Bujard, 'The Geneva Convention of 1864 and the Brussels Conference of 1874' (1974) 14 *International Review of the Red Cross* 527 at 575 ff.

6 Schindler and Toman, *Laws*, 91. See H. Meyrowitz, 'Reflections on the Centenary of the Declarations of St. Petersburg' (1968) 8 *IRRC* 611; Best, *War and Law Since 1945*, 42–3.

7 Schindler and Toman, *Laws*, 41 ff., 95 ff., 309 ff., 373 ff. On these Conferences, see amongst others A. Mérignhac, *La Conférence internationale de la paix* (Paris, 1900);

J. B. Scott, *The Hague Conferences of 1899 and 1907* (Oxford, 1909); A. Bustamante y Sirven, *La Seconde Conférence de la Paix réunie à La Haye en 1907* (Paris, 1909); O. Nippold, *Die zweite Haager Friedenskonferenz, Teil II: Das Kriegsrecht* (Berlin, 1911); J. H. Choate, *The Two Hague Conferences* (Princeton, 1913); W. I. Hull, *The Two Hague Conferences and their Contributions to International Law* (New York, 1972).

8 Schindler and Toman, *Laws*, 21 ff., and on the substance Lentner, *Das Recht*, 33 ff.

9 Schindler and Toman, *Laws*, 29 ff.

10 *Ibid.* 3 ff. On these instruments, see also R. Kolb, *Ius in bello, Le droit des conflits armés* (2nd edn, Basel/Brussels, 2009) 42 ff.

11 On this doctrine, see A. Truyol y Serra and R. Kolb, *Doctrines sur le fondement du droit des gens* (Paris, 2007) 59 ff; M. Giuliano, *La Comunità internazionale e il suo diritto* (Padua, 1950) 77 ff. Writers such as Hegel, G. Jellinek, Wenzel, Bergbohm, Triepel, the early Anzilotti, the early Verdross, and others could be recalled here, each one with their own nuances. See e.g., G. Hegel, *Grundlinien der Philosophie des Rechts* (Berlin, 1821); G. Jellinek, *Die rechtliche Natur der Staatsverträge* (Vienna, 1880); K. Bergbohm, *Staatsverträge und Gesetze als Quellen des Völkerrechts* (Dorpat, 1887).

12 *Wimbledon* Case, PCIJ, ser. A, no. 1, 25.

13 Cf. Pradier-Fodéré, *Traité*, vol. VII, 411.

14 Schindler and Toman, *Laws*, 30.

15 For the sake of brevity, no list will be provided here. See the information contained in Pradier-Fodéré, *Traité*, vol. VII, 80 ff., 111 ff., 123 ff., 131–2; 172–3, 184, 200–1, 231–5; Bonfils, *Manuel*, 575; Maine, *International Law*, 107. The municipal law approach was commended by many authors, who warned against an extensive codification at the international level: see e.g. Triepel, *Fortschritte*, 55.

16 G. Balladore-Pallieri, *La guerra* (Padua, 1935) 116.

17 This model value of Hague Convention II of 1899 was perceived in the legal writings of the time, see e.g., Despagnet, *Cours*, 806.

18 See Best, *War and Law Since 1945*, 40.

19 This is noted by almost all the commentators; see e.g., Bonfils, *Manuel*, 574–5; Lueder, 'Krieg', 265. This is also noted in various Preambles to international instruments, e.g., to the Brussels Declaration and the Oxford Manual already quoted.

20 See e.g., Bonfils, *Manuel*, 572.

21 See e.g., Lueder, 'Krieg', 186 ff., 254, 265, 276, 388 ff., 389, 391. See also the references in: Calvo, *Le droit international*, vol. IV, 124–6; Pradier-Fodéré, *Traité*, vol. VII, 474; Bonfils, *Manuel*, 571–2, 607, 644; Guelle, *Guerre*, 173; Despagnet, *Cours*, 802–3; Pillet, *Lois*, 6; Halleck, *Elements*, 179; Amos, *Lectures*, 60; Baker, *First Steps*, 204; Risley, *Law of War*, 106. Some authors particularly stressed the restrictive aspect of necessity, in order to better bring to the frontline the exigencies of humanity: see e.g., Moynier, *Etude*, 15 ff. See also P. A. Pillitu, *Lo stato di necessità nel diritto internazionale* (Perugia, 1981) 356–7. One attributes to Napoleon the following phrase: 'My great maxim has always been, in politics and war alike, that every injury done to the enemy even though permitted by the rules, is excusable only so far as it is absolutely necessary; everything beyond that is criminal', quoted in Best, *War and Law Since 1945* 242.

22 Schindler and Toman, *Laws*, 92. The relevant passage reads as follows: 'That the only legitimate object which States should endeavour to accomplish during war is to weaken the military forces of the enemy; That for this purpose it is sufficient to disable the greatest possible number of men; That this object would be exceeded by the employment of arms which uselessly aggravate the sufferings of disabled men, or

render their death inevitable; That the employment of such arms would, therefore, be contrary to the laws of humanity.' Note that the principle of humanity is a consequence of the principle of (restrictive) necessity, not an autonomous rule.

Additionally, some parallel can be drawn to the *jus ad bellum*, where the concept of just war or defensive war turned around the concept of self-preservation, i.e., war waged for vital interests in a situation of 'necessity' (see I. Brownlie, *International Law and the Use of Force by States*, (Oxford, 1963) 19 ff.). This demonstrates the pervasive influence of the principle of necessity in *jus in bello* and *jus ad bellum* alike, as far as the nineteenth century is concerned (the principle of necessity is not defined identically in both branches of the law, *jus in bello* and *jus ad bellum*).

23 See e.g., Calvo, *Le droit international*, vol. IV, 147, 148 (for bombardment of a besieged town). Or even in general terms: Lueder, 'Krieg', 391: all milder means to achieve a certain military result must be preferred to harsher means to achieve the same result (principle of *civiliter uti*). One finds the same principle applied to arms in Balladore-Pallieri, *La guerra*, 193.

24 See E. David, *Principes de droit des conflits armés* (4th edn, Brussels, 2008) 357 ff., with further references.

25 *De civitate Dei*, ch. XIX. See V. Hrabar, 'La doctrine de droit international chez Saint Augustin' (1932) *Archives de philosophie du droit et de sociologie juridique* 437 ff.

26 See e.g., Pradier-Fodéré, *Traité*, vol. VII, 595, 945, 1088.

27 On the reasons for respecting rules on warfare and humanitarian protections, see R. Kolb, *Ius in bello, Le droit international des conflits armés* (Basel/Brussels, 2003) 5–9.

28 In Grotius, only the positive side of the rule is stressed, the negative remains somewhat implicit (and hence there are some controversies about the exact scope of the Grotian *exposé*): *De jure belli ac pacis* (1625) Book III, ch. I, s. 2: 'In war things which are necessary to attain the end are permissible' (which incidentally is not a phrase in the text but in the Index). P. Haggenmacher, 'Grotius et le droit international: Le texte et la légende' in A. Dufour, P. Haggenmacher and J. Toman (eds.), *Grotius et l'ordre juridique international* (Lausanne, 1985) 129 stresses that this sentence implies also the negative (restrictive) principle in the system expounded by Grotius: 'Car la règle en question sous-entend un aspect limitatif [...]: le juste belligérent est certes autorisé à faire ce qui est nécessaire pour atteindre sa fin – c'est là le rétablissement de son droit violé – mais rien de plus!'. Haggenmacher (*ibid.* 131, note 65) refers also to all the *temparamenta belli* contained in chs X to XVI expounding limitations of warfare in natural law (as opposed to the law of nations, or positive law). For a different view, see F. Kalshoven in *ibid.* 89–90. The truth seems to be somewhere in between: Grotius foreshadows the modern 'necessity' criterion but does not develop its potentialities. The negative rule clearly emerges in Wolff and Vattel. See also the further references given by Haggenmacher, in the quoted pages.

29 C. Wolff, *Jus gentium methodo scientifica pertractatum* (1749), ch. VII, s. 781: 'Qui bellum justum gerit, illi in bello licitum est, sino quo jus suum ab adversa parte consequi nequit; quod ad hunc finem consequendum non facit, illicitum est.' To this he adds the following sentence (translated): 'For by the law of nature a right in war exists only to that without which one cannot attain the right, for the sake of which the war is waged.' The restrictive part of the principle is here clearly developed.

30 E. de Vattel, *Le Droit des gens ou principes de la loi naturelle* (1758) Book III, chs. VIII and IX, s. 136: 'Tout cela [what is lawful in war] doit se déduire d'un seul principe, du but de la guerre juste. Car dès qu'une fin est légitime, celui qui a le droit de tendre à cette fin, est en droit par cela même d'employer tous les moyens qui sont nécessaires

pour y arriver.' See also s. 137: 'La fin légitime ne donne un véritable droit qu'aux seuls moyens nécessaires pour obtenir cette fin: tout ce qu'on fait au delà est réprouvé par la loi naturelle.' Since the law of war must be composed of some general rules and not only of circumstantial necessity arguments, varying from situation to situation, however, it is possible that a belligerent has recourse to a means which is held lawful in the law of war in general, but which is not necessary in the particular context. In this case, the recourse to that means constitutes a moral tort (s. 137): 'Ainsi, dès qu'il est certain et bien reconnu que tel moyen, tel acte d'hostilité, est nécessaire dans sa généralité, pour surmonter la résistance de l'ennemi et atteindre le but d'une guerre légitime, ce moyen, pris ainsi en général, passe pour légitime et honnête dans la guerre, suivant le droit des gens, quoique celui qui l'emploie sans nécessité, lorsque des moyens plus doux pouvaient lui suffire, ne soit point innocent devant Dieu et dans sa conscience. Here as elsewhere in that great treatise emerges Vattel's obsession with legal certainty.' It may be added that Vattel in more than one passage condemns any military action having recourse to more destructive means than necessary in the particular context: see Book III, ch. IX, s. 168; Book III, ch. X, s. 178; and he extends that principle even to peacetime: Book III, ch. XIII, s. 201 (peace treaty); Book IV, ch. IV, s. 43 (self-defence). The principle is, in these passages (except the last one), presented as a moral or humanitarian guidance, beyond the strict law.

31 *Du contrat social* (1762), Book I, ch. IV: '[L]a guerre ne donne aucun droit qui ne soit nécessaire à sa fin.'

32 See e.g., J. W. Textor, *Synopsis juris gentium* (1680) ch. XVIII (Carnegie Edition, translation, 1916) 191: 'A great distinction, therefore, must be drawn between such a destruction of property as can materially conduce to victory in war, and the destruction of other things. The former kind of destruction of enemy property is not only lawful in itself, but absolutely free from blame; but one may object, to the latter kind of destruction, that if not improper by Law it is at any rate contrary to the dictates of humanity.' The distinction made here between strict law and moral law is not material for the strength of the necessity argument.

33 Including, thus, private individuals in the legitimate targets of war, as far as commerce and private property is concerned.

34 Up to the violation of Belgian neutrality in 1914. For an early critique of 'necessity', see Pradier-Fodéré, *Traité*, vol. VII, 71, 80, who, however, still relies heavily on it: *ibid*, vol. VI, 474.

35 See Lueder, 'Krieg', 254–6 (but such precedence is only exceptional and must remain so). See generally, on the question: L. Oppenheim, *International Law*, vol. II, *War and Neutrality* s. 69 (e.g., 3rd edn, London, 1921, 90–2). Some authors subjected the entire *jus in bello* to the *rebus sic* stantibus rule, always implied: see e.g., F.W. Jerusalem, *Kriegsrecht und Kodifikation* (Breslau, 1918) 72 ff., following the important thesis of E. Kaufmann, *Das Wesen des Völkerrechts und die Clausula rebus sic stantibus* (Tübingen, 1911). In many writings, we find the implication that a rule of the law of war may always be derogated from by military necessities (implied clause): see e.g., Pillet, *Lois*, 100. On the whole question of necessity in warfare, see Y. Dinstein, 'Military necessity' (1997) *EPIL* III 395; R. Kolb, 'La nécessité dans le droit des conflits armés: Essai de clarification conceptuelle' in SFDI, *Colloque de Grenoble, La nécessité en droit international* (Paris, 2007) 151 ff.; J. Gardam, *Necessity, Proportionality and the Use of Force by States* (Cambridge, 2004) 59 ff.; Y. Dinstein, *The Conduct of Hostilities under the Law of International Armed Conflict*

(Cambridge, 2001) 16 ff.; C. Greenwood, 'Historical development and legal basis', in D. Fleck (ed.), *The Handbook of Humanitarian Law in Armed Conflicts* (Oxford, 1995) 30–33; L. Sbolci, 'Sulla necessità militare nel diritto internazionale applicabile nei conflitti armati' in *Mélanges G. Barile* (Padua, 1995) 653 ff.; H. McCoubrey, 'The nature of the modern doctrine of military necessity', *Revue de droit pénal militaire et de droit de la guerre* 30 (1991) 215; G. Venturini, *Necessità e proporzionalità nell'uso della forza militare in diritto internazionale* (Milan, 1988) 123 ff.; P.A. Pillitu, *Lo stato di necessità nel diritto internazionale* (Pérouse, 1981) 347 ff.; E. Rauch, 'Le concept de nécessité militaire dans le droit de la guerre', *RDPMDG* 19 (1980) 205 ff. Among the older contributions, see N.C.H. Dunbar, 'Military necessity in war crimes trials' (1952) 29 *BYIL* 442; W.G. Downey, 'The law of war and military necessity' (1953) 47 *AJIL* 251; W.V. O'Brien, *The Development of the Concept of Military Necessity and its Interpretation in the Modern Law of War* (Georgetown, 1953); W.V. O'Brien, 'The Meaning of Military Necessity in International Law' (1957) *World Polity* 109; G. Schwarzenberger, 'Military necessity: a misnomer' in *Mélanges S. Séfériadès* (Athens, 1961) 13 ff.; G.I.A.D. Draper, 'Military necessity and humanitarian imperatives', *RDPMDG* 12 (1973) 129. See also M.G. Cowling, 'The relationship between military necessity and the principle of superfluous injury and useless suffering in the law of armed conflict' (2000) 25 *South African Yearbook of International Law* 131; P. A. Ragone, 'The applicability of military necessity in the nuclear age' (1984) 16 *New York University Journal of International Law and Politics* 701; M. Messerschmidt, 'Völkerrecht und Kriegsnotwendigkeit in der deutschen militärischen Tradition seit den Einigungskriegen ', *RDPMDG* 22 (1983) 211; J. De Breucker, 'La réserve des nécessités militaires dans la Convention de La Haye de 1954 sur la protection des biens culturels', *RDPMDG* 14 (1975) 255; C. Eustathiadès, 'La réserve des nécessités militaires et la Convention de La Haye pour la protection des biens culturels en cas de conflit armé' in *Essays J. Basdevant* (Paris, 1960) 183 ff. For a digest of old documents on military necessity see M. Whiteman, *Digest of International Law* (Washington, 1968) vol. 10, 298 ff.

36 On this question, see R.R. Baxter, 'The definition of war' (1960) *Revue égyptienne de droit international* 4 at 13; H.J. Wolff, *Kriegserklärung und Kriegszustand nach klassischem Völkerrecht* (Berlin, 1990) 64 ff. See also R. Kolb, 'Le droit international public et le concept de guerre civile depuis 1945' (2001) 105 *Relations internationales* 9.

37 The Congress of Paris of 1856 (after the Crimean War) recognised that the declaration of war is necessary and thus required, except in the case of invasion and spontaneous self-defence: see Calvo, *Le droit international*, vol. IV, 47.

38 E.C. Stowell, *International Law* (New York, 1931) 401: '[S]ome intercourse with the insurrectionists is often necessary. In the troubled conditions of civil warfare it becomes especially urgent for other States to look out for the protection of their nationals within the zone of operations, and the economic demands of war greatly increase the trade in contraband and a variety of articles. In these circumstances, forced by the necessity of providing for effective protection of their nationals, and urged by the desire to continue and extend an authorized trade with all portions and parties of the state engaged in the conflict, other states accord what is called Recognition of Belligerency'. See also H. Wheaton, *Elements of International Law* (8th edn, Oxford, 1866) 35.

39 L. Kotzsch, *The Concept of War in Contemporary History and International Law* (Geneva, 1956) 50 ff.

40 H.J. Taubenfeld, 'The applicability of the laws of war in civil war' in J.N. Moore (ed.), *Law and Civil War in the Modern World* (Baltimore/London, 1974) 502 ff.

41 On the idea of civilisation in the nineteenth century, see W. G. Grewe, *The Epochs of International Law* (Berlin/New York, 2000) 445 ff., with further references.

42 This conception of the progress of limitations on war moving from an almost complete licence of action to binding legal rules of an ever-growing scope, can be found in many writings of the time, e.g. in Guelle, *Guerre*, 99 (in the context of reprisals); Risley, *Law of War*, 73. It was later still noted in Balladore-Pallieri, *La guerra*, 113 ff.

43 M. Koskenniemi, *The Gentle Civilizer of Nations, The Rise and Fall of International Law 1870–1960* (Cambridge, 2001) 11 ff.

44 This distinction has a prominent place in Grotius' *De jure belli ac pacis* (1625) Book III. See P. Haggenmacher, *Grotius et la doctrine de la guerre juste* (Paris, 1983) 568 ff.

45 See e.g., *Le droit des gens* (1758) Book III, ch. VIII, s. 137.

46 See e.g., Calvo, *Le droit international*, vol. IV, 190, 213, 218, 237, 243, 256, 287, 504; Pradier-Fodéré, *Traité*, vol. VII, 18, 191, 303, 320, 430, 757, 924, 927, 1085, 1133, 1161; vol. VIII, 72 ff., 510, 786–7, 810, 831; Guelle, *Guerre*, 99–100; Guelle, *Précis*, vol. I; Despagnet, *Cours*, 838 ff. (on means and methods of warfare); Halleck, *Elements*, 211; Maine, *International Law*, 75 ff.; Moynier, *Etude*, 1 ff., 22 (the idea of progress in on almost every page); Pillet, *Lois*, 7–11; see also Bluntschli, *Kriegsrecht*; Hetzel, *Humanisierung*; Triepel, *Fortschritte*; the argument here permeates the whole treatise, as their titles aptly suggest.

47 Hence the belief that legal doctrine prepared the progress: Pradier-Fodéré, *Traité*, vol. VII, 956. A contrast was sometimes created between enlightened science and stubborn military personnel clinging on to past prejudices: *ibid.* vol. VIII, 24 ff.

48 The belief that the adoption of a convention solved the problem and insured a definitive breakthrough to progress was also very common: see e.g., Moynier, *Etude*, 24: 'Il suffira dorénavant d'un trait de plume pour bannir du jour au lendemain les pratiques vieilles[…]'. One may then understand the shock produced in civilised circles by the scrap of paper doctrine and the violation of Belgian neutrality in the First World War.

49 P. Pradier-Fodéré, 'Préface', in Guelle, *Précis*, vol. I.

50 Moynier, *Etude*, 1.

51 See e.g., Pillet, *Lois*, 11; Moynier, *Etude*, 12–15.

52 There is here perhaps something of the Kantian idea that republican or democratic states do not go to war against one another (*Zum ewigen Frieden*, 1795), translated from *jus ad bellum* into *jus in bello*: republicans do not go to war; if they happen to go to war, they will more easily accept rules of war (*debitus modus*).

53 On the change of this paradigm in the twentieth century, see Best, *War and Law Since 1945*, 403 ff.

54 See e.g., Guelle, *Précis*, vol. I, 5–6.

55 J. Lorimer, *The Institutes of the Law of Nations* (Edinburgh, 1883) vol. I, 101.

56 It can, e.g., be found in the works of such a thoughtful and prudently progressive author as Bonfils, *Manuel*, 572, and not only in those of that somewhat curious author, J. Lorimer.

57 See e.g., Calvo, *Le droit international*, vol. IV, 50; Pradier-Fodéré, *Traité*, vol. VIII, 44 ff., 151 ff. On the necessity of professional armies, see Moynier, *Etude*, 8.

58 N. Politis and P. Fauchille, *Manuel de la Croix-Rouge* (Paris, 1908) 157.

59 Moynier, *Etude*, 301.

60 G. Moynier, 'Note sur la création d'une institution judiciaire internationale propre à prévenir et à réprimer les infractions à la Convention de Genève', *Bulletin international* (no 11, April 1872) 122 ff.

61 See e.g., Pradier-Fodéré, *Traité*, vol. VII, 441–53; Guelle, *Guerre*, 127–8; Lueder, 'Krieg', 416–17. This was also the original approach of Moynier, *Etude*, 299 ff.

62 See, amongst other critical pieces, the very instructive book by O. Nippold, *Das Völkerrecht nach dem Weltkriege* (Zurich, 1917).

63 Article 5 of the Statutes of the International Movement of the Red Cross and the Red Crescent contains a general statement as to the missions of the ICRC. It also contains the following sentence: 'The International Committee may take any humanitarian initiative which comes within its role as a specifically neutral and independent institution and intermediary, and may consider any question requiring examination by such an institution'. To the extent the ICRC remains within the bounds of humanitarian action (which by reason of its Statutes it cannot overstep) it can propose any practical improvement or solution to a humanitarian problem arising during an armed conflict (or even in peacetime). The ICRC can also be contacted at any time in order to help in a particular situation where war-related humanitarian and practical problems are faced. The ICRC will not refuse to provide help to the extent of its possibilities and the limits of its mandate. This right of initiative is also recognised in Common Article 3 of the GCs of 1949, and in Articles 9/9/9/10 GCs.

64 See the precise account in F. Bugnion, *Le CICR et la protection des victimes de la guerre* (Genève, 1994) 31 ff.

65 In favour of harmonisation, see e.g., Pradier-Fodéré, *Traité*, vol. VIII, 24 ff.; Despagnet, *Cours*, 950–1; Moynier, *Etude*, 27; against such harmonisation, see e.g., Pillet, *Lois*, 118 ff; simply exposing the law as it stands, probably implying that it should remain such, see e.g. Halleck, *Elements*, 215 ff; Manning, *Commentaries*, etc.

66 See the very powerful discussion of these arguments in Bonfils, *Manuel*, 705 ff.

67 See Article 42 ff. of the Hague Regulations (1907).

68 As to some important aspects of this evolutions, see J. F. Quéguiner, *Le principe de distinction dans la conduite des hostilités*, thèse no. 706 (Genève, 2006) 37 ff; on the evolution after 1919 in the context of the modern war, see *ibid.* 115 ff.

69 On the action of the ICRC in the Oriental War of 1875–1878, see F. Bugnion, *Le CICR et la protection des victimes de la guerre* (Genève, 1994) 43 ff.

70 See e.g., Pradier-Fodéré, *Traité*, vol. VII, 133 ff; Lueder, 'Krieg', 430–1 (any person who could contribute to the war effort); Pillet, *Lois*, 151–2 (only the innocent inhabitants cannot be captured as prisoners of war). Balladore-Pallieri, *La guerra*, 136 still in 1935 goes as far as to affirm that even civilians able to serve in the adverse army could be held captive [...] as prisoners of war. That such persons may be interned is conceded today by Geneva Convention IV of 1949, but as civilian internees, not prisoners of war.

71 See *supra* note 70.

72 On the reasons for these transformations and on their development, see R. Kolb and S. Vité, *Le droit de l'occupation militaire* (Brussels, 2009) 7 ff.

73 Halleck, *Elements*, 330 ff.

74 Maine, *International Law*, 108–10. All legislative and executive power passes to the invader. Contrary to Halleck, quoted *supra* note 73, Maine avoids the term 'conquest', *i.e.*, the hallmark of definitiveness.

75 See e.g., Pradier-Fodéré, *Traité*, vol. VII, 686, 696, 703, 715–16, 754. The manifest aim of this theory is not to allow the 'usurper' to enjoy true 'rights' over his spoils; it would be anti-patriotic to grant such rights to the enemy, organising in advance a regime of defeat. See also Bonfils, *Manuel*, 645, 671. This view was cherished most by French and Belgian authors, who feared more than anything an occupation of their territories by Germany. Occupation was thus often compared to mere possession

of fact: Guelle, *Guerre,* 160. The law of occupation derives then essentially from military necessity and is thus circumstantial: Despagnet, *Cours*, 903.

76 Lueder, 'Krieg', 510 ff. Later, very clearly, Balladore-Pallieri, *La guerra*, 329 ff.

77 M. Marinoni, *Della natura giuridica dell'occupazione bellica* (Rome, 1911) 50 ff, 58–9, 155 ff.

78 J.K. Blaschek, *Das bedrohte Völkerrecht* (Perchtoldsdorf, 1915).

79 See J. Kunz, 'Plus de lois de la guerre?', *RGDIP* 41 (1934) 30.

80 See E. Zitelmann, *Haben wir noch ein Völkerrecht?* (Bonn, 1914); P. Eltzbacher, *Totes und lebendes Völkerrecht* (Munich, 1916); H.E. Richards, *Does International Law Still Exist?* (London/New York, 1915).

81 English language treatises of international law containing informed chapters on the law of war written in this period: F.E. Smith, *International Law* (4th edn, J. Wylie (ed.), London, 1911) 110 ff; C.H. Stockton, *Outlines of International Law* (New York/Chicago/Boston, 1914) 293 ff; L. Oppenheim, *International Law: A Treatise*, vol. II, *War and Neutrality* (R.F. Roxburgh (ed.), London, 1921); W.E. Hall, *A Treatise on International Law* (8th edn, Oxford, 1924) 444 ff.; A.S. Hershey, *The Essentials of International Public Law and Organization* (New York, 1927) 557 ff.; Stowell, *International Law* 489 ff.; G.G. Wilson, *Handbook of International Law* (3rd edn, St Paul, 1939) 253 ff.

82 See Anonymous, 'The League of Nations and the laws of war' (1920–1921) 1 *BYIL* 109; J.B. Moore, *International Law and Some Current Illusions* (New York, 1924) 5, 38–39; E. Dickinson, 'The new law of nations' (1925–1926) 32 *West Virginia Law Quarterly* 4; F.W. Jerusalem, *Kriegsrecht und Kodifikation* (Breslau, 1918) 3 ff, 72 ff; O. Nippold, *Das Völkerrecht nach dem Weltkriege* (Zurich, 1917) 8–9. Contrast these writings with the tone still prevailing some years before the war; see e.g., H. Kägi, *Die Kriegsführenden im Landkrieg* (Rostock/Basel, 1909).

83 Thus the argument was: (i) excessive focus on the *jus in bello* has resulted in a loss of time and energy spent on improving the law of peace and devices to protect the peace (peaceful settlement of disputes), the latter being much more useful for international law; (ii) to continue to devote attention to the law of war today is to convey the idea that one doubts the capacity of the League of Nations to protect the peace. See Anonymous, 'League of Nations' 114–15; Dickinson, '*New law*', 25, 29; M. Huber, 'Der Wert des Völkerrechts', in *Neue Zürcher Zeitung*, 20 November 1916. For the argument that devoting attention to the *jus in bello* may weaken the belief in *jus contra bellum*, see Politis (Greece) et Sokal (Poland) in the disarmament commission of the League of Nations (*Documents de la Commission préparatoire de désarmement* [Société des Nations], sér. VIII, 1929, 87 [Sokal], 91 [Politis]). *Contra* Rutgers (Holland), *ibid.* 90. See also K. de Strupp, *Eléments du droit international humanitaire universel, européen et américain* (Paris, 1930) vol. II, 503, note 1. The same approach was taken in the first years of the United Nations: (1949) *Yearbook ILC* 281, s. 18: 'It was considered that if the Commission, at the very beginning of its work, were to undertake this study [on the laws of war], public opinion might interpret its action as showing lack of confidence in the efficiency of the means at the disposal of the United Nations for maintaining peace'. See also C.G. Fenwick, 'The progress of international law during the last forty years', *RCADI* 79 (1951), 60 at 63–4: '[the laws of war are indeed a] law of lawlessness'; 'gone is the naïve belief that it is possible to draft new laws of war'. From the military and political point of view, see B.H. Liddel Hart, *The Revolution in Warfare* (New Haven, 1947). See also,

generally, D. Costantopoulos, 'Les raisons de la crise du droit de la guerre' (1957) 7 *Jahrbuch für internationales Recht* 22.

84 The argument here was as follows: (i) technological advance and progress of total war have made it impossible to limit war by rules and regulations; (ii) the law of war always codifies the experiences of the last war and is thus inevitably out of tune with the necessities of the next war; (iii) the laws of war are the weakest part of international law and have contributed to discrediting that branch of the law; (iv) law is violence (like a tempest), and this cannot be regulated by law; it is chameleonic, ever-changing, and thus inaccessible to legal regulation. See Anonymous, 'League of Nations' 111 ff.; Dickinson, 'Law of Nations' 24 ff.; Jerusalem, *Kriegsrecht* 3 ff., 72 ff.; Nippold, *Völkerrecht*, 8–10. It has also been argued that a functioning law of war is structurally impossible: if its prohibitions are sufficiently firm and absolute in order not to allow evasion, the prohibitions will quickly turn out to be outmoded and ineffective; conversely, flexible prohibitions allowing for exceptions on the basis of military necessity will as such prove more realistic, but will be distorted to advance egoistic interests in case of war, thereby depriving the prohibitions of almost all their practical value: see M.W. Royse, *Aerial Warfare* (New York, 1928) particularly 132 ff.

85 The following passage gives a vivid account of the challenges of the time: 'Under the stress of the war even Great Britain, notwithstanding a strong tradition of individualism, was forced to become totalitarian. When the national effort reached its maximum the whole population, male and female, within very wide limits of age, was mobilised for the prosecution of the war. Exemption from compulsory war service was only granted if the applicant could prove that he or she was privately engaged upon work of national importance. No person within the age limits had any free choice of occupation, and every individual could be told by the government what kind of work he or she had to do. Whatever the particular order given might be, whether the conscript was told to join the army or to work in a factory, in every case the only test was how that individual might be most usefully employed for the purpose of winning the war.

To this it must be added that many millions of men and women, in addition to those enrolled in the regular forces, were mobilised for a form of active service which was known as "civil defence". The main purpose of this organisation was to reduce as far as possible the damage caused by enemy attacks, and it was therefore a form of direct resistance to the enemy's military effort. Millions of men were also enrolled in what was called the "Home Guard". These were combatant troops in the strictest sense when they were on duty and in uniform, but they were only on duty for limited hours and for the rest of their time they were employed on their ordinary work. If so, it follows that every town and every village in the country contained a large number of combatants who could quite lawfully be the objects of direct and deliberate attack at any time. This is quite a different matter from the incidental destruction of civilian life to which I have referred.

What is true of Great Britain is substantially true of all belligerent countries which took a major part in the recent war. To this we must add that the principle of complete mobilisation which was applied to persons was applied equally to industry and to property. The whole system of production, importation, and distribution was organised under a single control with a view to the prosecution of the war effort, and nothing more than the barest minimum was permitted for the satisfaction of normal civilian requirements.

In short, the traditional distinction between combatants and non-combatants rested upon the fact that in practice it was usually quite easy to draw a line between those who were taking an active part in the war and those who were not. The great change has entirely taken place within living memory. In all wars previous to 1914 only a small minority of the population was put into uniform and employed by the government for the purpose of fighting the enemy. The great majority were left free to carry on their ordinary occupations in their own way, and usually there was no difficulty in doing this, except in the immediate neighbourhood of the fighting forces. This distinction was sound in principle, and is still valid today, whenever the facts enable it to be drawn. If it cannot today be observed in practice, the responsibility lies with the governments and peoples who have decided, rightly or wrongly, that the modern war cannot be carried on with anything less than the combined effort of the whole nation. We must accept the consequences of our choice. We cannot boast, as we have done, that every man and woman in the country is now mobilised for war service, and at the same time claim for them immunity of non-combatants'. See H. A. Smith, *The Crisis in the Law of Nations* (London, 1947) 75–7.

86 See in particular A. De La Pradelle, 'Négligera-t-on longtemps encore l'étude des lois de la guerre?', *Revue de droit international (Paris)* 12 (1933) 511; J. Kunz, 'Plus de lois de la guerre?', *RGDIP* 41 (1934) 22, the perplexity of both authors emerging clearly through the use in both cases of question marks. The same criticisms were voiced in the first phase of the existence of the United Nations, where similar arguments against the law of war had prevailed: *Ann. IDI*, vol. 47-I (1957) 323 ff. and the opinion of the Rapporteur, J.-P. A. François, *ibid.* 367 ff. See also J. Kunz, 'The chaotic status of the laws of war and the urgent necessity for their revision' (1951) 45 *AJIL* 37; J. Kunz, 'The laws of war' (1956) 50 *AJIL* 313; H. Lauterpacht, 'The revision of the laws of war' (1952) 29 *BYIL* 360; A.P. Sereni, *Diritto internazionale* (Milan, 1965) vol. IV, 1823–6.

87 See Schindler and Toman, *Laws*, 105 ff.

88 *Ibid.* 405 ff.

89 See e.g., Bonfils, *Manuel*, 607: in war, everything that is not prohibited is permitted. Thus, there is no point in compiling lists of acts permitted; it is sufficient to state the prohibited acts and deeds. See also Risley, *Law of War*, 106: the rules on warfare are essentially negative, being restrictions upon the primitive right of devastation in war.

90 See in particular the most penetrating analysis in Balladore-Pallieri, *La guerra*, 163–4; M. Cruchaga Tocornal, *Nociones de derecho internacional* (3rd edn, Madrid, 1925) vol. II, 51 ff. (all acts 'que tiendan a procurar la victoria' are lawful, subject to certain legal prohibitions); J. de Louter, *Le droit international public positif* (Oxford, 1920) vol. II, 276; L. Oppenheim, *International Law*, vol. II, *War and Neutrality* (3rd edn, R. F. Roxburgh (ed.), London, 1921) 167 (reserving the principle of restrictive necessity). See also P. A. Pillitu, *Lo stato di necessità nel diritto internazionale* (Perugia, 1981) 359; A. P. Sereni, *Diritto internazionale* (Milan, 1965) vol. IV, 1924. Some authors do not really spell out the principle but address the whole subject matter by supposing it, i.e. by focusing on the prohibitions of the law; see e.g., E. Ullmann, *Völkerrecht* (Freiburg im Breisgau, 1898) 323; K. Strupp, *Eléments du droit international public universel, européen et américain* (2nd edn, Paris, 1930) vol. II, 548 ff; F.V. Liszt, *Das Völkerrecht* (11th edn, Berlin, 1918) 296 ff. Some authors maintained the classical principle of necessity: the (only) means prohibited are those not necessary

for securing the legitimate war aim or excessive in that respect; see e.g., S. Gemma, *Appunti di diritto internazionale* (Bologna, 1923) 304; L. Olivi, *Manuale di diritto internazionale pubblico e privato* (Milan, 1911) 509: '[I] mali della guerra vengono limitati al *minimum* occorrente alle operazioni militari perchè queste ottengano il loro fine' (emphasis in the original); P. Fauchille, *Traité de droit international public* (8th edn, Paris, 1921) vol. II, 114–15; and also of humanity or Christianity, see G. Bry, *Précis élémentaire de droit international public* (Paris, 1910) 534. In these conceptions too, the underlying rule is for residual freedom: if the law essentially contains the limitation of necessity (in the restrictive sense), all necessary means of warfare are lawful since they are not prohibited. Instead of being limited only by specific rules, the limitation can also follow from a general principle; but the inherent logic of the system remains the same. Some authors further refine the system: see e.g., W.E. Hall, *A Treatise on International Law* (8th edn, Oxford, 1924) 635, who admits that *prima facie* all acts of violence are unlawful, and then proceeds to limit them by specific rules and by the principle of necessity, but adds a further limitation – wanton acts and disproportionate acts: 'In a general sense a belligerent has a right to use all kinds of violence against the person and property of his enemy which may be necessary to bring the latter to terms. *Prima facie* therefore all forms of violence are permissible. But the qualification that the violence used shall be necessary violence has received a specific meaning; so that acts not only cease to be permitted as soon as it is shown that they are wanton, but when they are grossly disproportioned to the object to be attained; and the sense that certain classes of acts are of this character has led to the establishment of certain prohibitory usages … Some questions not falling under either of these heads [specific prohibitions listed] have to be determined by reference to the general limitation forbidding wanton or disproportionate violence'. One may easily see that the more general principles of this kind are admitted, the more the law moves from the principle of 'what is not prohibited is permitted' (a negative rule) to an intermediary status of the kind 'what is not prohibited is permitted only if compatible with the rule of necessity, the rule on wantonness, the rule on proportionality (or disproportionality), the dictates of humanity'. At a certain juncture, the residual principles of limitation become so dense as to erase the negative approach thereby transforming it into a positive one; then, quantity has become quality. Finally, some authors do not take a position on our problem and simply address lawful and unlawful acts, side by side: see e.g., J. Hatschek, *Völkerrecht* (Leipzig/Erlangen, 1923) 305 ff. Overall, it may be said that the practice of states in the inter-war period was clearly inspired by the idea that the military licence was full and unbridled as long as the law imposed no clear limitations. On the whole question of lawful and unlawful means of warfare, see also, in the literature of the first fifteen years of the twentieth century: L. Fatoux, *La guerre continentale: limitation des moyens de nuire* (Paris, 1903); A. Zorn, *Kriegsmittel und Kriegsfuhrung im Landkrieg nach den Bestimmungen der Haager Konferenz* (Königsberg, 1902); R. D. de Trobriand, *Les moyens de guerre nouveaux et des principales objections qu'ils soulèvent au point de vue du droit international* (Paris, 1909); A. Tettenborn, *Prinzip und Richtungen der Kriegsmittelverbote des Landkriegsrechtes* (Würzburg/Bonn, 1909); R. Jacomet, *Les lois de la guerre continentale* (3rd edn, Paris, 1913). See also A. Rolin, *Le droit moderne de la guerre, Les principes, les conventions, les usages et les abus* (Brussels, 1920–1921).

91 PCIJ, ser. A, no. 9, 18. See also P.M. Dupuy, 'L'unité de l'ordre juridique international: Cours général de droit international public', *RCADI* 297 (2002) 93.

92 See B. Simma, 'From bilateralism to community interest in international law', *RCADI* 250 (1994) 229.

93 In the Preambles to Hague Convention II (1899) and Hague Convention IV (1907) one finds a peculiarly styled clause, known as the Martens Clause (after the name of the Russian delegate at the Hague Conference of 1899, who proposed it) which has gained some celebrity in international law: 'Until a more complete code of the laws of war has been issued, the High Contracting Parties deem it expedient to declare that, in cases not included in the Regulations adopted by them, the inhabitants and the belligerents remain under the protection and the rule of the principles of the law of nations, as they result from the usages established among civilized peoples, from the laws of humanity, and the dictates of public conscience.' This clause has been repeated in Articles 63/64/142/158 Geneva Conventions I–IV. It has also been recalled in Article 1(2), of Additional Protocol I of 1977 with the following, somewhat modernised wording: 'In cases not covered by this Protocol or by other international agreements, civilians and combatants remain under the protection and authority of the principles of international law derived from established custom, from the principles of humanity and from the dictates of public conscience.' Considering that there thus remained important gaps in the emerging law of armed conflict, the delegates unanimously agreed to include the so-called Martens Clause, requiring the belligerents to behave in a civilised and humane way even if in a particular instance no specific rule could be found in the corpus of codified law of armed conflict. The Martens Clause requires any belligerent always to consider if a proposed conduct, even if not explicitly prohibited, is compatible with the principle of humanity and compassion. The rule should not simply be: what is not prohibited is therefore allowed. On the Martens Clause, see H. Strebel, 'Martens Clause' (1997) III *EPIL* (Amsterdam e.a.) 326–7; F. Münch, 'Die Martens'sche Klausel und die Grundlagen des Völkerrechts', *ZaöRV* 36 (1976) 347; S. Miyazaki, 'The Martens Clause and international humanitarian law' in *Essays in Honour of J. Pictet* (Geneva, 1984) 433 ff.; T. Meron, 'On custom and the antecedents of the Martens Clause in medieval and renaissance ordinances of war' in *Essays in Honour of R. Bernhardt* (Berlin e.a., 1995) 173 ff.; V.V. Pustogarov, 'The Martens Clause in international law' (1999) *Journal of the History of International Law*; A. Cassese, 'The Martens Clause: half a loaf or simply pie in the sky?' (2000) 11 *EJIL* 187; R. Ticehurst, 'The Martens Clause and the laws of armed conflict' in N. Sanajaoba (ed.), *A Manual of International Humanitarian Laws* (New Dehli, 2004) 312 (see already in (1997) 37 *IRRC* 125); M.N. Hayashi, 'The Martens Clause and military necessity' in H.M. Hensel (ed.), *The Legitimate Use of Military Force, The Just War Tradition and the Customary Law of Armed Conflict* (Alderhot e.a., 2008) 135 ff.

94 See in particular the *Krupp* case (1948), (1948) 15 *Annual Digest of Public International Law Cases (ILR)* 622.

95 Best, *War and Law Since 1945*, 250.

96 Balladore-Pallieri, *La guerra*, 163–4.

97 On the Geneva Conventions of 1949, see J. A. C. Gutteridge, 'The Geneva Conventions of 1949', (1949) 26 *BYIL* 294; L. Orcasitas Llorente, 'La Conferencia de Ginebra de 1949 para mejorar la suerte de la victimas de la guerra' (1949) 2 *Revista española de derecho internacional* 605; F. Siordet, 'La Conférence diplomatique de Genève' *RICR* 31 (1949) 475 at 554; J. Pictet, 'La Croix-Rouge et les Conventions de Genève', *RCADI* 76 (1950–I) 1; M. Bourquin, 'Les Conventions de Genève du 12 août 1949', *RICR* 32 (1950) 90; E. Djafari, *Les Conventions de Genève du 12 août 1949 sur la protection*

des victimes de la guerre (Paris, 1950); S. Tschirkovitch, 'Les nouvelles Conventions internationales de Genève relatives à la protection des victimes de la guerre du 12 août 1949', *RGDIP* 54 (1950) 97 at 525; P. De La Pradelle, *La Conférence diplomatique et les nouvelles Conventions de Genève du 12 août 1949* (Paris, 1951); R.D. Paine, *The 1949 Geneva Conventions Concerning War Victims* (thesis, Nothwestern University, Evanston, Ill., 1951); A. Schickelé, 'L'avenir des Conventions de Genève', *RICR* 33 (1951) 496; R.T. Yingling and R.W. Ginane, 'The Geneva Conventions of 1949' (1952) 46 *AJIL* 393; J. Kunz, 'The Geneva Conventions of August 12, 1949' in G.A. Lipsky (ed.), *Law and Politics in the World Community* (Berkeley/Los Angeles, 1953) Part III, 279 ff.; E. Lodemann, 'Die Genfer Rotkreuzabkommen vom 12. August 1949' (1953) 4 *Archiv des Völkerrechts* 72; G.I.A.D. Draper, *The Red Cross Conventions* (London, 1958); H. Coursier, *Cours de cinq leçons sur les Conventions de Genève* (Geneva, 1963); G.I.A.D. Draper, 'The Geneva Conventions of 1949', *RCADI* 114 (1965–I) 59; A. Maresca, *La protezione internazionale dei combattenti e dei civili: Le Convenzioni di Ginevra del 12 agosto 1949* (Milan, 1965); D. Schindler, 'Die Anwendung der Genfer Rotkreuzabkommen seit 1949' (1965) *ASDI* 22 75; C. Pilloud, 'Les Conventions de Genève – 1949 – 1969 – Bilan et perspectives', *RICR* 51 (1969) 465; C. Pilloud, 'Les Conventions de Genève, 1949–1969', *RICR* 51 (1984) 465; T. Meron, 'The Geneva Conventions as customary law' (1987) 81 *AJIL* 348; F. Bugnion, *Le Comité international de la Croix-Rouge et la protection des victimes de la guerre* (Geneva, 1994) 354; Best, *War and Law Since 1945*, 80; Y. Sandoz, 'Le demi-siècle des Conventions de Genève', *RICR* 81 (1999) 241; C. Rey-Schyrr, 'Les Conventions de Genève de 1949: une percée décisive', *RICR* 81, no. 834 (1999) 209; 81, no. 835 (1999) 499; F. Bugnion, 'Les Conventions de Genève du 12 août 1949', *RSDIE* 9 (1999) 371; D. Schindler, 'Significance of the Geneva Conventions for the contemporary world' in N. Sanajaoba (ed.), *A Manual of International Humanitarian Laws* (New Dehli, 2004) 42 ff.; D. Forsythe, '1949 and 1999: making the Geneva Conventions relevant after the Cold War' in *ibid.* 56 ff.; C. Rey-Schyrr, *De Yalta à Dien Bien Phu, Histoire du Comité international de la Croix-Rouge, 1945–1955* (Geneva, 2007) 239 ff. One may further consult the commentaries to the four Geneva Conventions edited by the CICR under the direction of J. Pictet in the 1950s: J. Pictet (ed.), *Commentary I, Geneva Convention for the Amelioration of the Condition of the Wounded and Sick in Armed Forces in the Field* (Geneva, ICRC, 1952); J. Pictet (ed.), *Commentary II, Geneva Convention for the Amelioration of the Condition of Wounded, Sick and Shipwrecked Members of Armed Forces at Sea* (Geneva, ICRC, 1960); J. Pictet (ed.), *Commentary III, Geneva Convention relative to the Treatment of Prisoners of War* (Geneva, ICRC, 1960); J. Pictet (ed.), *Commentary IV, Geneva Convention relative to the Protection of Civilian Persons in Time of War* (Geneva, ICRC, 1958). For the Additional Protocols of 1977, see essentially Y. Sandoz, C. Swinarski and B. Zimmermann (eds.), *Commentary on the Additional Protocols of 8 June 1977 to the Geneva Conventions of 12 August 1949* (Geneva, 1987); M. Bothe, K.J. Partsch and W. Solf (eds.), *New Rules for Victims of Armed Conflicts* (The Hague/ Boston/ London, 1982).

98 This provision is today held to express customary international law. Its content applies to all conventions on armed conflicts, including the older ones, such as the Hague Convention of 1907, which according to the text, applies only to war.

99 See e.g., ICJ, *Legal Consequences of the Construction of a Wall in the Occupied Palestinian Territory*, Advisory Opinion [2004] ICJ Reports 136 (the *Israeli Wall* case), para. 95.

100 On these evolutions, see R. Kolb, 'Aspects historiques de la relation entre le droit international humanitaire et les droits de l'homme' (1999) 37 *Canadian Yearbook of International Law* 57; R. Kolb, 'Human rights and humanitarian law' in *Max Planck Encyclopaedia of Public International Law* (2008) www.mpepil.com. See also Centre pour les droits de l'homme (ed.), *Bulletin des droits de l'homme* (United Nations, Geneva, 1992); L. Doswald-Beck and S. Vité, 'International humanitarian law and human rights law' (1993) 293 *IRRC* 94; R. Provost, *International Human Rights and Humanitarian Law* (Cambridge, 2002); H.P. Gasser, 'International humanitarian law and human rights law in non-international armed conflict: joint venture or mutual exclusion?' (2002) 45 *German Yearbook of International Law* 149; T. Meron, 'International law in the age of human rights', *RCADI* 310 (2003) 68; H.J. Heintze, 'On the relationship between human rights law protection and international humanitarian law' (2004) 856 *IRRC* 789; F.F. Martin, S.J. Schnably, R. Wilson, J. Simon and M. Tushnet, *International Human Rights and Humanitarian Law: Treaties, Cases and Analysis* (Cambridge, 2006); R. Arnold and N. Quénivet (eds.), *International Humanitarian Law and Human Rights Law: Towards a New Merger in International Law* (Boston, 2008).

101 See e.g., the *Israeli Wall* Advisory Opinion of the ICJ (2004), *supra* note 99.

102 As to the contribution of the ECHR, see e.g., G. Gaggioli and R. Kolb, 'A Right to Life in Armed Conflicts? The Contribution of the European Court of Human Rights, (2007) 37 *Israel Yearbook on Human Rights* 115. See generally the case law of these tribunals, in particular: (1) UN Human Rights Committee: *Pedro Pablo Camargo* v. *Colombia*, 31 March 1982: Communication No. 45/1979, UN doc. CCPR/C/15/D/45/1979; *Baboeram et al.* v. *Suriname*, 4 April 1985: Communications Nos. 146/1983 and 148 to 154/1983, UN doc. CCPR/C/24/D/146/1983; *Concluding Observations, Israel*, 21 August 2003: UN doc. CCPR/CO/78/ISR; *Concluding Observations, USA*, 15 September 2006: UN doc. CCPR/C/USA/CO/3. (2) European Commission of Human Rights: *Cyprus* v. *Turkey*, 10 July 1976: Appl. No. 6780/74 and 6950/75. (3) European Court of Human Rights: *Kaya* v. *Turkey*, 19 February 1998; *Ergi* v. *Turkey*, 28 July 1998; *Ahmet Özkan and others* v. *Turkey*, 6 April 2004: *Isayeva, Yusupova and Bazayeva* v. *Russia*, 24 February 2005; *Isayeva* v. *Russia*, 24 February 2005; *Khatsiyeva* v. *Russia*, 17 January 2008; *Akkum and others* v. *Turkey*, 24 March 2005. (4) Inter-American Commission of Human Rights: *Arturo Ribon Avila* v. *Colombia*, 30 September 1997; *Juan Carlos Abella* v.. *Argentina*, 18 November 1997(the *La Tablada* case); *Guerrero et al.* v. *Colombia*, 13 April 1999; *Coard et al.* v. *USA*, 29 September 1999; *Report on Terrorism and Human Rights*, 22 October 2002; (5) Inter-American Court of Human Rights: *Bámaca-Velásquez* v. *Guatemala*, 25 November 2000; *Mapiripán Massacre* case, 15 September 2005; *Pueblo Bello Massacre* case, 31 January 2006; *Ituango Massacres* case, 01 July 2006; *De la Rochela Massacre* case, 11 May 2007; *Myrna Mack Chang* v. *Guatemala*, 25 November 2003; *Plan de Sánchez Massacre* case, 29 April 2004; *Moiwana Community* v. *Suriname*, 15 June 2005; (6) African Commission of Human and People's Rights: *Commission Nationale des Droits de l'Homme et des Libertes* v. *Tchad*: Comm. No. 74/92 (1995); *Free Legal Assistance Group and others* v. *Zaïre*, Comm. Nos. 25/89, 47/90, 56/91, 100/93 (1995); *Organisation Mondiale Contre La Torture* v. *Rwanda, African*, Comm. Nos. 27/89, 46/91, 49/91, 99/93 (1996); *Civil Liberties Organisation, Legal Defence Centre, Legal Defence and Assistance Project* v. *Nigeria*, Comm. No. 218/98 (1998); *Amnesty International and others* v. *Sudan*, Comm. No. 48/90, 50/91, 52/91,

89/93 (1999); *Social and Economic Rights Action Center and Center for Economic and Social Rights* v. *Nigeria*, Comm. No. 155/96 (2001).

103 See in particular Meron, 'Age of human rights' 24 ff.; T. Meron, 'The Humanization of Humanitarian Law' (2000) 94 *AJIL* 239.

104 Paragraphs 518–520. We may here just quote para. 518: 'The absolute nature of most obligations imposed by rules of international humanitarian law reflects the progressive trend towards the so-called "humanisation" of international legal obligations, which refers to the general erosion of the role of reciprocity in the application of humanitarian law over the last century. After the First World War, the application of the laws of war moved away from a reliance on reciprocity between belligerents, with the consequence that, in general, rules came to be increasingly applied by each belligerent despite their possible disregard by the enemy. The underpinning of this shift was that it became clear to States that norms of international humanitarian law were not intended to protect State interests; they were primarily designed to benefit individuals *qua* human beings. Unlike other international norms, such as those of commercial treaties which can legitimately be based on the protection of reciprocal interests of States, compliance with humanitarian rules could not be made dependent on a reciprocal or corresponding performance of these obligations by other States. This trend marks the translation into legal norms of the "categorical imperative" formulated by Kant in the field of morals: one ought to fulfil an obligation regardless of whether others comply with it or disregard it.'

105 *Ibid.*, para. 527 ff.

106 On the customary status of the rules of the Additional Protocols (including a reference to the case law of the criminal tribunals), see J.M. Henckaerts and L. Doswald-Beck, *Customary International Humanitarian Law* (Cambridge, 2005) vol. I–III. On the development of IHL though the criminal tribunals, see C. Greenwood, 'The development of international humanitarian law by the International Criminal Tribunal for the Former Yugoslavia' (1998) 2 *Max Planck Yearbook of United Nations Law* 97; G. Abi-Saab, 'International Criminal Tribunals and the development of international humanitarian and human rights law' in E. Yakpo and T. Boumedra (eds.), *Liber Amicorum Judge Mohammed Bedjaoui* (The Hague, 1999) 649 ff.; J.-F. Quéguiner, 'Dix ans après la création du Tribunal pénal international pour l'ex-Yougoslavie: évaluation de l'apport de sa jurisprudence au droit international humanitaire' (2003) 85 *IRRC* 271; M. Sassòli, 'Humanitarian law and international criminal law' in A. Cassese (ed.), *The Oxford Companion to International Criminal Justice* (Oxford, 2009) 111 ff. See also R. Kolb, 'The jurisprudence of the Yugoslav and Rwandan Criminal Tribunals on their jurisdiction and on international crimes' (2000) 71 *British Yearbook of International Law* 259 ff and R. Kolb, 'The jurisprudence of the Yugoslav and Rwandan Criminal Tribunals on their jurisdiction and on international crimes (2000–2004)' (2004) *BYIL* 269; R. Kolb, 'International humanitarian law and its implementation by the international criminal court' in J. Doria, H.-P. Gasser and M.C. Bassiouni (eds.), *The Legal Regime of the International Criminal Court: Essays in Honour of Professor Igor Blishchenko* (The Hague, 2008).

107 See e.g., Meron, 'Age of human rights', 49 ff.

3

The principle of proportionality

YORAM DINSTEIN

1. The so-called 'principle of humanity'

The present book is supposedly dedicated to the 'principle of humanity' in international humanitarian law (IHL). This raises a preliminary question: is there really such a 'principle'? In theory, the answer is patently affirmative, inasmuch as the 'principle of humanity' can be traced back to the Martens Clause (named after F. de Martens, a leading international lawyer who served as a Russian delegate to both Hague Peace Conferences of 1899/1907). A 'modern version of that clause' – in the words of the International Court of Justice[1] – is to be found in Article 1(2) of 1977 Additional Protocol I to the Geneva Conventions, which sets forth:

> In cases not covered by this Protocol or by other international agreements, civilians and combatants remain under the protection and authority of the principles of international law derived from established custom, from the principles of humanity and from the dictates of public conscience.[2]

I do not contest the Martens Clause. The Court said about the Clause that its 'continuing existence and applicability is not to be doubted'.[3] Indeed, the Clause is reiterated in the Preamble to the 1980 Convention on Prohibitions or Restrictions on the Use of Certain Conventional Weapons which may be deemed to be Excessively Injurious or to Have Indiscriminate Effects.[4] The Clause has also been relied upon (on more than one occasion) by the International Criminal Tribunal for the Former Yugoslavia (ICTY).[5] In part, the Martens Clause simply restates the obvious default rule: in the absence of a treaty norm (as well as in its place, where a treaty is denounced or is no longer in force), customary international law will apply. But the Martens Clause goes beyond this self-evident truth by adding a reference to the 'principles of humanity'. It is by no means clear what value is added to the default formula by an allusion to such principles. As a matter of record, there is no empirical evidence in the practice of states that 'principles of humanity' have ever been relied upon independently of the ordinary application of customary international law.[6]

In my opinion, the reference to a principle (in the singular) or principles (in the plural) of humanity is rather loose and partly misleading. It is important not to equate principles of humanity with other principles that will be adduced in this chapter, namely the principles of distinction (see this section below), unnecessary suffering (see section 5 below) and proportionality (see section 2 below). The three latter principles are integrated in positive IHL and they are legally binding as such, even if (due to their somewhat abstract nature) they usually require more concrete rules to resolve specific cases. By contrast, the principles of humanity should be viewed not as legal norms but as extra-legal considerations. I therefore much prefer the language used by the International Court of Justice in the *Corfu Channel* case of 1949: 'elementary considerations of humanity'.[7] The expression 'requirements of humanity', appearing in the 1868 St Petersburg Declaration (see this page below) will also do.

The difference between principles and considerations (or requirements) transcends semantics and goes into substance. Humanity is not an obligation (or a set of obligations) incorporated per se in positive IHL. There is no overarching, binding, norm of humanity that tells us what we must do (or not do) in wartime. What we actually encounter are humanitarian considerations, which pave the road to the creation of legal norms and thus explain the evolution of IHL. While impacting on the law, these considerations do not by themselves amount to law: they are meta-juridical in nature.

Considerations of humanity are inspiring and instrumental, yet they are no more than considerations. And they do not monopolize the field. If benevolent humanitarianism were the only factor to be weighed in hostilities, war would have entailed no bloodshed, no human suffering and no destruction of property; in short, war would not be war. IHL must be predicated on a subtle balance – and compromise – between conflicting considerations of humanity, on the one hand, and the demands of military necessity, on the other. Differently phrased, IHL generally takes a middle road between military necessity and considerations of humanity, reconciling them in one form or another. The idea is well expressed in the Preamble to the 1868 St Petersburg Declaration, which speaks of the desire to fix 'the technical limits at which the necessities of war ought to yield to the requirements of humanity'.[8]

The most outstanding illustration of the balance between humanitarian considerations and military necessity is the cardinal principle of distinction between combatants/civilians and military objectives/civilian objects, which is encapsulated in Article 52 of Additional Protocol I[9] and is referred to by the Court in the *Nuclear Weapons* Advisory Opinion as 'intransgressible'.[10] The purpose of the principle of distinction is to grant civilians/civilian objects maximal protection from attack while exposing combatants/military objectives to the havocs of war.

Distinction, albeit a binding norm, is an abstract principle. More concrete rules spell out the details as regards civilian protection from direct attacks or even indiscriminate attacks.[11] The more one descends from lofty levels of abstraction, the more one realizes that it is a mistake to believe that IHL can provide civilians and civilian objects with airtight safeguards. IHL cannot yield only to the requirements of humanity: it must also yield to the countervailing demands of military necessity. For that reason, incidentally, I personally usually prefer the designation of the law of armed conflict (LOAC) over that of IHL, which tends to create the frequently false impression that humanitarianism is always dominant in IHL. To give just one prime example, let me quote T. Meron: 'Unlike human rights law, the law of war allows, or at least tolerates, the killing and wounding of innocent human beings not directly participating in hostilities, such as civilian victims of lawful collateral damage'.[12] More on lawful collateral damage to civilians in section 3 below.

2. The principle of proportionality

It is sometimes maintained (for instance, by the Supreme Court of Israel, in the *Beit Sourik* case of 2004) that '[p]roportionality is recognized today as a general principle of international law'.[13] This is a completely untenable proposition. Indeed, proportionality is not even a general principle of IHL: it is patently excluded insofar as combat operations are concerned (see section 5 below).

The main thrust of the principle of proportionality in IHL is strictly limited to the theme of 'collateral damage'. This is a relatively novel idea in IHL: as late as the Second World War, it was not fully acknowledged. Yet, there is no shred of doubt that proportionality in collateral damage is part and parcel of contemporary customary international law. Proportionality is an add-on to distinction (see section 1 above). The starting point is the concept of distinction whereby only lawful targets (combatants/military objectives) can be attacked, but proportionality brings into the equation a new element. What it denotes is that the unambiguous identification of an object as a lawful target for attack does not suffice. A crucial supplementary consideration in gauging the legality of a prospective attack against a lawful target is whether the expected collateral (or ancillary) damage to civilians comes within the bounds of proportionality. Collateral damage means (a) incidental losses or injury to civilians; (b) destruction of or damage to civilian objects; or (c) a combination of both.

The essence of the principle of proportionality in attack is that, as phrased by Judge R. Higgins, in her Dissenting Opinion in the *Nuclear Weapons* Advisory Opinion: 'even a legitimate target may not be attacked if the collateral civilian casualties would be disproportionate to the specific military gain from the attack'[14] (and the same applies to damage to civilian property). The attack of a military objective will be illegal if the incidental injury to civilians or damage to civilian objects is expected to be 'excessive' (see section 3 below). The principle of proportionality provides 'a further restriction' by disallowing attacks against impeccably lawful targets owing to the envisaged disproportionate injury/damage to civilians or civilian objects.[15]

The principle of proportionality is the key to the effective protection of civilians and civilian objects from the consequences of attacks in warfare. The trouble is that, while everybody pays lip-service to the principle in the abstract, its specific dimensions are not always understood. Obviously, proportionality is a relative term: it presupposes a comparison between *A* and *B*. What are these *A* and *B* in the context of IHL? It is frequently believed by laymen that the proper comparison to be drawn is between the number of human losses sustained (and the amount of property destroyed) by both sides. Nothing is further from the legal truth. The proportionality that really counts for the purposes of weighing collateral damage is between (*A*) the expectation of excessive incidental loss of civilian life, injury to civilians, damage to civilian objects, or a combination thereof, compared to (*B*) the anticipation of the concrete and direct military advantage to be gained (see Article 51(5)(b) of Additional Protocol I).[16]

An obvious breach of the principle of proportionality would be the destruction of a whole village, with hundreds of civilian casualties, in order to eliminate a single enemy sniper.[17] By contrast, if, instead of a single enemy sniper, an artillery battery would operate from within the village, such destruction may be warranted.[18] This is all a matter of evaluation and assessment. A representative case relating to sea warfare would be that of an enemy passenger liner. Such a vessel is a civilian object, provided that it is engaged only in carrying civilian passengers.[19] If it were to carry also a run-of-the-mill military cargo (the way the *Lusitania* did in its fatal voyage during the First World War), although becoming a military objective, its sinking with all passengers on board would be unlawful, for the act would be expected to generate 'excessive' civilian losses compared to the military advantage anticipated.[20] The position may be different only if the military cargo is of prodigious value (consisting, say, of a nuclear device).

Proportionality is by no means determined by purely crunching numbers of casualties and destruction on both sides. The quintessence of proportionality is that the expectation of collateral damage to civilians and civilian objects must not be 'excessive'. The International Committee of the Red Cross (ICRC) Commentary on Additional Protocol I seems to mix up the term 'excessive' with 'extensive'.[21] This is a misreading of the text.[22] Even extensive civilian casualties may be acceptable, if they are not 'excessive' in light of the concrete and direct military advantage anticipated (see section 3 below).

From the text of Article 51(5)(b) of Additional Protocol I, one can clearly deduce that the appraisal of proportionality is not about results: it is about the initial expectation (of injury to civilians or damage to civilian objects) and anticipation (of the military advantage factored in). In other words, what counts is foresight (before the event) rather than hindsight.

The concrete and direct military advantage must be perceived in a contextual fashion. According to Article 8(2)(b)(iv) of the 1998 Rome Statute of the International Criminal Court, what counts is the 'overall' military advantage anticipated.[23] By introducing the term 'overall', the Statute clearly permits looking at the larger operational picture, as distinct from focusing on the particular point under attack. The attacker may argue, e.g., that an air raid of no perceptible military advantage in itself is justified by misleading the enemy to shift its strategic gaze to the wrong sector of the front (the extensive air raids in the Pas-de-Calais on the eve of the Allied landings in Normandy on D-Day in the Second World War are an emblematic illustration).[24] Nonetheless, 'an attack as a whole' is a finite event. The Eritrea-Ethiopia Claims Commission said that 'a definite military advantage must be considered in the context of its relation to the armed conflict as a whole at the time of the attack' – or to 'the military operations between the Parties taken as a whole' – and 'not simply in the context of a specific attack'.[25] This is a gross exaggeration: the admissible *mise-en-scène* is only 'an attack as a whole' and not 'the armed conflict as a whole'.[26]

3. Lawful collateral damage to civilians

The danger of incidental civilian losses is omnipresent in war. The Eritrea-Ethiopia Claims Commission unequivocally pronounced that civilian losses may be 'regrettable and tragic consequences of the war, but they do not in themselves establish liability' under international law, if they are not expected to be 'excessive' in relation to the military advantage anticipated.[27] In every specific military operation, the risk of injury to civilians (or damage to civilian objects) may very well be foreseen. The fact that it is foreseen does not mean that it has to be forestalled. Albeit foreseen, collateral damage to civilians (or civilian objects), resulting from attacks against lawful targets and unintended as such, need not be avoided if it is not expected to be 'excessive' compared to the anticipated military advantage.

The most obvious dangers, affecting large numbers of civilians (frequently women), are incurred by the employees of industrial plants that constitute military objectives, such as factories manufacturing armaments and munitions. It is clear that the presence of large numbers of civilian employees does not immunise these targets. The importance of a munitions factory is often so critical that, notwithstanding the principle of proportionality, casualties among the labourers may reach very high levels without coming under the rubric of 'excessive'. Thus, the bombardment of a vital industrial plant producing military aircraft or missiles, where there are hundreds or even thousands of civilian employees, need not be aborted merely because of the palpable hazards to those civilians.[28]

This is not to say that presence in a perilous working place leads to loss of civilian status. Admittedly, the notion has been advanced that civilians working in munitions factories assume the status of so-called 'quasi-combatants' and, inasmuch as they may be lawfully bombed when on site in the factories, they may as well be bombed before having reached the factories and after having left them.[29] However, the concept of a 'quasi-combatant' workforce is completely spurious.[30] When civilian labourers are killed or wounded in air raids against munitions factories, the human losses are sustained not because the victims are 'quasi-combatants', but (notwithstanding their civilian status) because they are present within military objectives. That presence does not permanently contaminate the labourers, turning them *ipso facto* into 'quasi-combatants'. Upon leaving the factories, civilian labourers shed the risk of being subject to attack. The attacker is forbidden to follow the workforce home and hit civilians there.[31]

Given the significant military advantage that can generally be gained from the destruction of a strategically located bridge, relatively high civilian casualties would ordinarily be deemed a reasonable collateral damage.[32] 'Whether a bridge is worth five or fifty lives will be dependent upon the attendant values placed on the destruction of that particular bridge in those particular circumstances.'[33] But, surely, it is disallowed to level an entire urban area (as distinct from a few houses) merely in order to hit a bridge.[34]

4. Proportionality in a special context: belligerent reprisals

Although the main application of the principle of proportionality in IHL is in the context of collateral damage to civilians (and civilian objects), proportionality plays a role also in the more peripheral domain of belligerent reprisals. 'A belligerent reprisal consists of action which would normally be contrary to the laws governing the conduct of armed conflict (the *ius in bello*) but which is justified because it is taken by one party to an armed conflict against another party in response to the latter's violation of the *ius in bello*'.[35] Many forms of belligerent reprisals are prohibited by treaties (some reflecting customary international law and others applicable only among contracting parties).[36] The ICTY Trial Chamber, in the *Martić* case of 2007, took it for granted that some belligerent reprisals are permitted, provided that they meet strict conditions prescribed by customary international law.[37] In 2008, the ICTY Appeals Chamber confirmed this line of approach.[38]

Proportionality is the most important condition of the lawfulness of belligerent reprisals.[39] Yet, the proportionality which is the key to the legality of belligerent reprisals ought not to be confused with the proportionality underlying the expectation of 'excessive' collateral damage to civilians and civilian objects (see section 2 above). In the context of collateral damage, the comparison for purposes of proportionality is made between the military advantage anticipated from an attack and the incidental civilian losses (or damage to civilian property) expected. In the setting of belligerent reprisals, the comparison is drawn between the losses (or damage) caused by the enemy's original breach of IHL and the losses (or damage) wreaked in retaliation.

Proportionality in belligerent reprisals does not mean equivalence. Belligerent reprisals need not, and sometimes cannot, be identical to the original breach of IHL by the enemy. If state A bombs certain civilian objects in state B, state B is not bound to respond by paying back with exactly the same coin, i.e., bombing similar civilian objects in state A.

Sometimes there are no direct counterparts in state A for the objects struck in state B. It is also possible that state B lacks the technical (air or missile) capability of meting out to state A, measure for measure, the same devastation inflicted in the original attack. IHL therefore allows state B to respond with belligerent reprisals of a different nature, provided that proportionality is observed. Typically, when belligerent reprisals are not in kind, the degree of proportionality to the original breach may be harder to gauge accurately.[40] In any event, experience demonstrates that belligerent reprisals tend to be somewhat harsher than the original breach of IHL by the enemy.[41]

5. Proportionality out of context: unnecessary suffering

Side by side with the cardinal principle of distinction, the International Court of Justice (in the Advisory Opinion on *Nuclear Weapons*) underscored another cardinal – and 'intransgressible' – principle, namely that of prohibiting unnecessary suffering to combatants.[42] This twin cardinal principle – going back to the St Petersburg Declaration of 1868[43] and reiterated in Article 35(2) of Additional Protocol I[44] – is equally indisputable. It resonates in particular in the field of weaponry. In the words of the International Court of Justice, it is prohibited to employ weapons 'uselessly aggravating' the suffering of combatants, the test being 'a harm greater than that unavoidable to achieve legitimate military objectives'.[45]

A weapon is not banned on the ground of unnecessary suffering merely because it causes 'great' or even 'horrendous' suffering or injury.[46] The effects of the use of certain weapons may be appalling, but this is not, 'in and of itself, enough to render these weapons illegal'.[47] A weapon is proscribed only if it causes injury or suffering that can be avoided, given the military constraints of the situation. Some commentators speak about proportionality between the injury or suffering and the military advantage anticipated.[48] However, the reference to proportionality in this context is inappropriate.[49] Proportionality has nothing to do with injury or suffering sustained by combatants.

In essence, the injunction against unnecessary suffering hangs on a determination whether injury/suffering is avoidable or unavoidable. This requires a comparison between the weapon in question and other options.[50] The two main yardsticks are: (a) is there an alternative weapon available in the military menu, causing less injury or suffering?; and, shifting the focus, (b) are the effects produced by the alternative weapon sufficiently effective in neutralizing enemy personnel?[51]

Inescapably, the double test is 'valid only for weapons designed exclusively for antipersonnel purposes', inasmuch as (for instance) artillery explosives designed to pulverize military fortifications 'may be expected to cause injuries to personnel in the vicinity of the target which would be more severe than necessary to render these combatants *hors de combat*'.[52]

6. Proportionality excluded: combatants

Unlike the principle of unnecessary suffering which applies to combatants, the principle of proportionality – in providing protection against 'excessive' civilian losses (see section 2 above) – ignores combatant losses. Nothing brings into relief the restricted confines of the principle of proportionality in IHL more than the fact that no proportionality is required between combatant losses on the two warring sides. Thus, outside the special context of belligerent reprisals (see section 4 above), the losses sustained by the combatants of one belligerent party may be vastly greater than the counterpart casualties and destruction suffered by the other. There is no legal fault in such one-sided military success of a belligerent party over its enemy. Indeed, IHL does not preclude a belligerent party benefiting from supremacy of means and methods of warfare from pursuing a 'zero casualties policy', leaving its own combatants intact, while inflicting horrific losses on the enemy's armed forces.

7. Proportionality relaxed: 'human shields'

Article 51(7) of Additional Protocol I lays down:

> The presence or movements of the civilian population or individual civilians shall not be used to render certain points or areas immune from military operations, in particular in attempts to shield military objectives from attacks or to shield, favour or impede military operations.[53]

This is the issue of 'human shields', which has become the hallmark of recent battlefields.

There are two types of 'human shields': voluntary and involuntary. The question whether 'human shields' are voluntary or involuntary depends on whether they are deliberately trying to screen lawful targets. When the factual background is shrouded in doubt, 'human shields' must be presumed to be involuntary.

Voluntary 'human shields' ought to be 'excluded in the estimation of incidental injury when assessing proportionality'.[54] This proposition is contested by the ICRC,[55] but it is impossible to hold the attacking force liable for the fact that civilians have deliberately decided to screen military objectives and combatants. Whether or not voluntary 'human shields' are regarded as civilians who are directly participating in hostilities, they cannot possibly be considered as victims of a situation which they have brought upon themselves. If voluntary 'human shields' are excluded from the calculation of proportionality, it means that they are unable to achieve what they set out to do, namely, effectively bar an attack against lawful targets.

As for involuntary 'human shields' (and this is a far more important category of persons), it is evident that, acting as they do under duress and absent complicity, they remain innocent civilians. The crucial question is whether recourse by the enemy to such tactics, in flagrant breach of IHL, would tie the hands of a belligerent party planning to attack a lawful target, effectively obliging it to call off an attack in view of the prohibition of 'excessive' collateral damage (see section 2 above).

Article 51(8) of Additional Protocol I insists that a violation of the prohibition of shielding military objectives with civilians does not release a belligerent party from its legal obligations *vis-à-vis* the civilians.[56] This is a curious 'provision that seems to punish the complying party for an adversary's bad faith'.[57] In essence, what it signifies is that the principle of proportionality remains applicable in every respect. In my opinion that cannot be the case. It is submitted that, even if the principle as such endures, the test of what amounts to 'excessive' injury to civilians (see section 2 above) must be relaxed in the exceptional circumstances of 'human shields'. To paraphrase, the appraisal whether civilian casualties are expected to be 'excessive' in relation to the military advantage anticipated must make allowances for the fact that, by reason of the presence (albeit involuntary) of civilians at the site of the military objective, the number of civilian casualties can be foreseen to be higher than usual. Thus, for instance, in the words of L. Doswald-Beck, '[t]he Israeli bombardment of Beirut in June and July of 1982 resulted in high civilian casualties, but not necessarily excessively so given the fact that the military targets were placed amongst the civilian population'.[58] The basic approach is confirmed by the UK *Manual on the Law of Armed Conflict*:

> Any violation by the enemy of this rule [the prohibition of 'human shields'] would not relieve the attacker of his responsibility to take precautions to protect the civilians affected, but the enemy's unlawful activity may be taken into account in considering whether the incidental loss or damage was proportionate to the military advantage expected.[59]

Customary international law is certainly more rigorous than Additional Protocol I on this point. It has traditionally been perceived that, should civilian casualties ensue from an illegal attempt to shield combatants or a military objective, the ultimate responsibility lies with the belligerent party placing civilians at risk.[60] A belligerent party is not vested by IHL with the power to block an otherwise lawful attack against combatants or military objectives by deliberately placing civilians in harm's way.[61]

8. Conclusions

It is plain to see that, despite the non-existence of a normative 'principle of humanity', humanitarian considerations are playing a major role in the forging and fostering of IHL. The normative principles of distinction, unnecessary suffering and proportionality are all testimony to that. The principle of proportionality is particularly noteworthy in that it provides civilians protection from collateral damage even when they are not the direct target of attack.

Humanitarian considerations are nevertheless not alone in the process of creation of IHL. The demands of military necessity frequently offset humanitarian considerations and even prevail over them. The fact that proportionality does not impose any limitations on combatant losses is a good illustration of humanitarianism being sidelined by reason of military requirements. To be fully effective, IHL must occasionally render unto Mars what is due to Mars.

Notes

1 Advisory Opinion on the *Legality of the Threat or Use of Nuclear Weapons* [1996] ICJ Rep. 226, 257.

2 Protocol Additional to the Geneva Conventions of 12 August 1949, and relating to Protection of Victims of International Armed Conflicts (Protocol I), 1977, D. Schindler and J. Toman (eds.) *The Laws of Armed Conflicts: A Collection of Conventions, Resolutions and Other Documents* 4th edn., Leiden: Martinus Nijhoff, 2004) 711, 715.

3 Advisory Opinion on *Nuclear Weapons, supra* note 1, 260.

4 Geneva Convention on Prohibitions or Restrictions on the Use of Certain Conventional Weapons which may be deemed to be Excessively Injurious or to Have Indiscriminate Effects (CCW), 1980, Schindler and Toman, *The Laws of Armed Conflicts, supra* note 2, 181, 184.

5 See e.g., *Prosecutor* v. *Furundzija*, ICTY, Trial Chamber, 1998, 121 *International Law Reports* 213, 255; *Prosecutor v. Kupreškić et al.*, ICTY, Trial Chamber, 2000, paras. 525–6; *Prosecutor* v. *Martić*, ICTY, Trial Chamber, 2007, paras. 466–7.

6 See T. Meron, 'The Martens Clause, principles of humanity, and dictates of public conscience', (2000) 94 *American Journal of International Law* 78 at 87.

7 *Corfu Channel* case (Merits) [1949] ICJ Rep. 4, 22.
8 St Petersburg Declaration Renouncing the Use, in Time of War, of Explosive Projectiles under 400 Grammes Weight, 1868, Schindler and Toman, *The Laws of Armed Conflicts, supra* note 2, 91, 92.
9 Additional Protocol I, *supra* note 2, 737.
10 Advisory Opinion on *Nuclear Weapons, supra* note 1, 257.
11 For details, see Y. Dinstein, *The Conduct of Hostilities under the Law of International Armed Conflict* (2nd edn, Cambridge University Press, 2010) 124–8.
12 T. Meron, 'The humanization of humanitarian law' (2000) 94 *American Journal of International Law* 239, 240.
13 *Beit Sourik Village Council* v. *Government of Israel*, Supreme Court of Israel, 2004, (2004) 43 *International Legal Materials* 1099, 1113.
14 Advisory Opinion on *Nuclear Weapons, supra* note 1, 587.
15 E. Rauch, 'Conduct of combat and risks run by the civilian population'(1982) 21 *Revue de Droit Militaire et de Droit de la Guerre* 66 at 67.
16 Additional Protocol I, *supra* note 2, 736.
17 See W.H. Parks, 'Air war and the law of war' (1999) 32 *Air Force Law Review* 1 at 168.
18 See W.M. Reisman, 'The lessons of Qana' (1997) 22 *Yale Journal of International Law* 381 at 395–6.
19 See *San Remo Manual on International Law Applicable to Armed Conflicts at Sea* (L. Doswald-Beck (ed.), (Cambridge University Press, 1995), 132.
20 See L. Doswald-Beck, 'Vessels, aircraft and persons entitled to protection during armed conflicts at sea' (1994) 65 *British Yearbook of International Law* 21 at 249.
21 See C. Pilloud and J. Pictet, 'Article 51' in ICRC, *Commentary on the Additional Protocols of 8 June 1977 to the Geneva Conventions of 12 August 1949* (Y. Sandoz *et al.* (eds.), 1987) 613,626.
22 See C. Greenwood, 'Current issues in the law of armed conflict: weapons, targets and international criminal liability'(1997) 1 *Singapore Journal of International and Comparative Law* 441, 461–2.
23 Rome Statute of the International Criminal Court, 1998, Schindler and Toman, *The Laws of Armed Conflicts, supra* note 2, 1309, 1318.
24 See W.A. Solf, 'Article 52' in M. Bothe, K. J. Partsch and W. A. Solf (eds.), *New Rules for Victims of Armed Conflicts: Commentary on the Two 1977 Protocols Additional to the Geneva Conventions of 1949* (The Hague: Martinus Nijhoff, 1982) 318, 325.
25 Eritrea-Ethiopia Claims Commission, Partial Award, Western Front, Aerial Bombardment and Related Claims, Eritrea's Claims 1, 3, 5, 9–13, 14, 21, 25, 26, 2005, (2006) 45 *ILM* 396, 417, 418.
26 See G. Venturini, 'International law and the conduct of military operations' in A. de Guttry, H.H.G. Post and G. Venturini (eds.), *The 1998–2000 War between Eritrea and Ethiopia: An International Legal Perspective* (The Hague: TMC Asse Press, 2009) 279, 301.
27 Eritrea-Ethiopia Claims Commission, *supra* note 25, 415.
28 See H. Parks, 'The protection of civilians from air warfare' (1997) 27 *Israel Yearbook on Human Rights* 65 at 110.
29 See J. Stone, *Legal Controls of International Conflict: A Treatise on the Dynamics of Dispute – and War – Law* 629 (2nd edn., Sydney: Maitland, 1959).
30 See M. Sassòli and A.A. Bouvier, *How Does Law Protect in War? Cases, Documents, and Teaching Materials on Contemporary Practice in International Humanitarian Law* (ICRC, 2nd edn., 2006) 204

31 See D. Bindschedler-Robert, 'Problems of the law of armed conflict', in C.M. Bassiouni and V.P. Nanda (eds.) *A Treatise on International Criminal Law* (Springfield: Thomas, 1973) vol. I, 295, 318.

32 'If, for example, the destruction of a bridge has a crucial importance for the success of a particular campaign, higher [civilian] casualties will be tolerable to achieve this than, for example, the destruction of a munitions factory of secondary importance'. L. Doswald-Beck, 'The value of the 1977 Geneva Protocols for the Protection of Civilians' in M. A. Meyer (ed.), *Armed Conflict and the New Law: Aspects of the 1977 Geneva Protocols and the 1981 Weapons Convention* (London: BIICL, 1989) 137, 156.

33 See D. Stephens and M.W. Lewis, 'The law of armed conflict: a contemporary critique' (2005) 6 *Melbourne Journal of International Law* 55, 76.

34 See Pilloud and Pictet, 'Article 57', *supra* note 21, 677, 684.

35 C. Greenwood, *Essays on War in International Law* (London: Cameron May, 2006) 297.

36 For details, see Dinstein, *The Conduct of Hostilities*, *supra* note 11, 257–8.

37 *Prosecutor* v. *Martić*, *supra* note 5, para. 465.

38 *Prosecutor* v. *Martić*, ICTY, Appeals Chamber, 2008, paras. 263–7.

39 See *Prosecutor* v. *Martić*, *supra* note 5, para. 465.

40 See G. Schwarzenberger, 2 *International Law as Applied by International Courts and Tribunals: The Law of Armed Conflict* (London: Stevens, 1968), 453.

41 See US Naval War College, *Annotated Supplement to the Commander's Handbook on the Law of Naval Operations*, 73 ILS 339–40 n. 43 (A.R. Thomas and J.C. Duncan (eds.), 1999).

42 Advisory Opinion on *Nuclear Weapons*, *supra* note 1, 257.

43 St Petersburg Declaration, *supra* note 8, 92.

44 Additional Protocol I, *supra* note 2, 730.

45 Advisory Opinion on *Nuclear Weapons*, *supra* note 1, 257.

46 See the Dissenting Opinion of Judge Higgins, *ibid*, 585–7.

47 R. Cryer, 'The fine art of friendship: *jus in bello* in Afghanistan', (2002) 7 *JCSL* 37, 60.

48 See Solf, 'Article 35', *supra* note 24, 192, 196.

49 See H. Meyrowitz, 'The principle of superfluous injury or unnecessary suffering from the Declaration of St. Petersburg of 1868 to Additional Protocol I of 1977',(1994) 34 *IRRC* 98 at 109–10.

50 See Greenwood, *Essays on War*, *supra* note 35, 240.

51 See Solf, 'Article 52', *supra* note 24, 196.

52 *Ibid*, 196–7.

53 Additional Protocol I, *supra* note 2, 736.

54 M.N. Schmitt, 'War, technology and the law of armed conflict' in A. M. Hel, (ed.), *The Law of War in the 21st Century: Weaponry and the Use of Force*, 82 International Law Studies (2006) 137, 177.

55 See ICRC, *Interpretive Guidance on the Notion of Direct Participation in Hostilities under International Humanitarian Law* (N. Melzer (ed.), 2009) 57.

56 Additional Protocol I, *supra* note 2, 736–7.

57 N.A. Canestaro, 'Legal and policy constraints on the conduct of aerial precision warfare' (2004), 37 *Vanderbilt Journal of Transnational Law* 431 at 461.

58 See L. Doswald-Beck, 'The civilian in the crossfire' (1987), 24 *Journal of Peace Research* 251 at 257.

59 *UK Manual of the Law of Armed Conflict* (UK Ministry of Defence, 2004) 68.
60 See Parks, 'Air war', *supra* note 17, 162–3.
61 See A.D. McClintock, 'The law of war: coalition attacks on Iraqi chemical and biological weapon storage and production facilities' (1993) 7 *Emory International Law Review* 633 at 663–664.

4

The Geneva Conventions and the dichotomy between international and non-international armed conflict: curse or blessing for the 'principle of humanity'?

CECILIE HELLESTVEIT

In recent years, the dichotomy introduced in the Geneva Conventions between international armed conflicts (IAC) and non-international armed conflicts (NIAC) has come under increased strain due to its perceived impediment to the principle of humanity. As famously expressed in the *Tadić* case: what is inhumane in international conflicts cannot but be inhumane in civil strife. Nevertheless, efforts to remove or downscale the importance of the dichotomy in the name of the principle of humanity are not without problems. This chapter briefly depicts the historical background of the dichotomy, and presents the rationale and efforts in recent years to move towards a unified body of humanitarian law. It then lists seven arguments that support upholding the binary structure of IAC and NIAC, making the case that despite *prima facie* inadequacies of the rules regulating NIAC, the dichotomy enables and sustains important protective features. It concludes that sixty years on, the dichotomy between international and non-international armed conflicts should be seen as a blessing to be upheld rather than a curse to be dismantled, if the aim is maximising protection and furthering the principle of humanity for persons caught up in armed conflict.

The Geneva Conventions of 1949 introduced several novelties which had profound effects on the nature of international regulation of armed conflict. In their Common Article 3, the Geneva Conventions extended certain elementary principles of protection – a miniature Bill of Rights for victims in situations of internal armed violence that had previously been beyond the reach of international treaty law.[1] This truly represented a major blessing for humanitarian protection. By doing so, however, the Geneva Conventions also introduced a dubious dichotomy, differentiating between rules applicable to international armed conflict (IAC), including belligerent occupation on the one hand, and rules applicable to non-international armed conflict (NIAC) on the other;[2] the former bestowing upon its victims the protection of the entire body of humanitarian law, the latter offering only very rudimentary protection. This arrangement eventually led to the crystallisation of two separate and distinct regimes of humanitarian law. The extensiveness and level of detail in the regulation of international armed conflict is one with which few other disciplines of international law can compete – largely due to the Geneva Conventions. In stark contrast to this stands the regulation of non-international armed conflict – less impressive in terms of *quantity* (fewer rules), *quality* (less protective) and *clarity* (less detailed). Over the years, the perception has increasingly been that this dichotomy represents a true curse for humanitarian protection.

The dichotomy between international armed conflict and non-international armed conflict does not sit well with the most basic of moral instincts. How can victims of war be entitled to different levels of protection depending on formalistic legal technicalities that may be arbitrary and over which the victims have no influence at all? The steady increase in the number of NIACs over the decades since 1949 has made the dichotomy a barrier excluding victims of *most* armed conflicts from the full protection of the Geneva Conventions, a discriminatory effect that has been subject to much criticism. The paucity of rules, the practical need for rules that cover the majority of armed conflicts in our times and the strong moral repulsiveness of such a dichotomy, have driven tribunals, supervisory bodies and scholars to vindicate the humanitarian dichotomy between IAC and NIAC introduced by the Geneva Conventions in 1949. It goes against the 'fundamental humanitarian principle',[3] and as succinctly expressed by the ICTY Appeals Chamber in the *Tadić* case: 'What is inhumane, and consequently proscribed, in international wars, cannot but be inhumane and inadmissible in civil strife'.[4]

Is the dichotomy between international and non-international armed conflicts a curse to the principle of humanity, depriving victims in armed conflict of protections that they would be entitled to absent this distinction? It is argued here that this approach is too simplistic, as it ignores the structural incompatibilities between IAC and NIAC. Certain incompatibilities between the regulation of IAC and NIAC that were present at the time of negotiation of the Geneva Conventions very much persist today, and seem to impede the rise of a unified regime of IHL applicable to all armed conflicts. The dichotomy sixty years on deserves to be seen as a blessing in disguise, a structural feature with the potential to maximise humanitarian protection for victims of armed conflicts. With the strengthening of adjacent regimes of law applicable to armed conflict such as human rights, the dichotomy seems to offer a stratification by which legal protection can in fact be increased rather than weakened. The dichotomy may also provide a certain protective feature. The case is made here that with the advances made in IHL over the past decades, the dichotomy should be regarded as a blessing rather than a curse of the Geneva Conventions, as it is a mechanism that may serve to maximise humanitarian protection in both stereotypes of conflict.

1. Background of the dichotomy: Geneva Conventions Common Article 3

Article 3 common to the Geneva Conventions (GC Article 3) marked the introduction in *lex scripta* of certain basic rules applicable to situations of internal armed conflict that had previously been left almost entirely to the discretion of sovereigns. This novelty was not included with the aim of furthering reciprocal interests of states in a strict sense. Made against the background of the ferocity with which numerous civil wars preceding the negotiations had been fought, the regulation of NIAC was inspired by the common interests of *humanity*.[5] The idea that elementary humanitarian standards would henceforth apply to internal conflict on the territory of a High Contracting Party was an expression of mutual interests in the broadest possible sense.

The Conference in 1949 rejected the idea of full application to civil wars amid fierce controversy, and GC Article 3 eventually had a wide scope of applicability, offering only scarce humanitarian protection. If seen in contrast to the fully-fledged protections of IAC, the protections of GC Article 3 were not impressive. Its substantive protection may be summed up in two main rules: the obligation to treat humanely persons who do not (or not any longer) take an active part in the hostilities, and the obligation to collect and care for the sick and wounded. But compared to the alternative of no protections at all, GC Article 3 assumed the function of 'minimum standard rules',[6] subsequently described by the International Court of Justice (ICJ) as a 'minimum yardstick', reflecting 'elementary considerations of humanity'.[7] It was in this sense that GC Article 3 was 'revolutionary'.[8]

GC Article 3 has promoted humanitarian protection for victims of internal armed conflict both in direct and indirect ways. It went against the historical bias of humanitarian law to regulate only inter-state war, dramatically expanding the material scope of application of IHL. In so doing, GC Article 3 established, beyond doubt, the legitimacy of the concern by international law with internal armed conflict. And although the protection offered by GC Article 3 is rudimentary, it is commonly held that no Article in the Geneva Conventions has applied so widely and with comparable effects.[9] As the Geneva Conventions have attained universal ratification, it is beyond question that international law and GC Article 3 apply in any NIAC *anywhere*.[10] It is also commonly held that were it not for the existence of GC Article 3, efforts in pursuit of a more effective legal regulation of non-international armed conflicts would have been more difficult.[11] GC Article 3 offers protection to victims of war, *and* enables further regulation to protect such victims.

A less gratifying effect of GC Article 3 was the introduction of a differentiation between conflicts subject to fully fledged regulation by the Geneva Conventions in Common Article 2, on the one hand, and conflict regulation 'lite' provided for in GC Article 3, on the other.[12] Added to that, the precise line between the two categories is unsettled. IAC and NIAC are not clearly delimited terms, and their closer content is controversial. There is no authoritative legal definition of 'armed conflict' in IHL, and the implications of 'international' remains highly unclear.[13] IAC is not limited to inter-state war, nor is NIAC synonymous with civil war, although these situations describe the essence of each category.[14]

In order to circumvent the very controversial definition of war which had marred the laws of war for the preceding decades,[15] the Geneva Conventions introduced the concept of 'armed conflict', thereby setting an 'objective criteria' for the applicability of IHL.[16] The Conventions applied, according to GC Article 2, once there was an 'armed conflict' between states, commonly held to mean any intervention between the armed forces of two states.[17] The replacement of 'war' with the more flexible term 'armed conflict' allowed for inclusion of situations within states that had never qualified as 'war' as such. The definition of internal armed conflict was circumvented by a negative definition that rendered GC Article 3 applicable in 'armed conflicts *not* of an international character', seemingly covering all types of conflicts not falling into the category of GC Article 2. While an IAC is easily identifiable by objective terms, however, the closer criteria for defining a NIAC remained unsettled,[18] evolving around evasive notions of *intensity* of hostilities and the nature of *organisation*.

Hence, although the evasiveness of the term 'war' was largely removed in the Geneva Conventions with respect to IAC, a related problem reappeared in the category of NIAC. The criteria of applicability for NIAC inherited much of the vagueness previously associated with 'war' – unsettled criteria and reluctance on the part of the (state) party involved to acknowledge application. The quagmire of NIAC was henceforth established, and GC Article 3 was seldom applied during the first twenty-five years.[19] A relatively uniform understanding of the term IAC, and identifiable objective criteria alongside it, made the protection of war victims of IAC increasingly common. The situation for NIACs was profoundly different.

The dichotomy and difference in application between IAC and NIAC resulted in an unsatisfactory situation that is often referred to as a gap (lacuna) in humanitarian protection.[20] Victims of internal armed conflicts were left with rudimentary protection only – a situation heavily criticised.[21] Additionally, GC Article 3 was devoid of clear criteria for applicability, largely leaving it to the discretion of hostile parties to 'acknowledge' that a situation amounted to a non-international armed conflict. As could be expected, most states were reluctant to make such concessions to insurgents.[22] Questions were increasingly raised concerning the dichotomy, barring victims of internal conflict from the full protection of the Geneva Conventions,[23] and alternative structures were proposed.[24] An increasing unease about the inadequate regulation of NIAC melded with more general efforts to improve and expand the standards of the Geneva Conventions.

2. Attempts to fill the normative gap from within the framework of the Geneva Conventions

At the request of the General Assembly, the ICRC prepared for the Diplomatic Conference that took place from 1974–1977 in Geneva ('the CDDH'), leading to the adoption of Additional Protocol (AP) I and AP II. AP I filled a normative gap that had been present for years, in particular with regard to conduct of hostilities.[25] The context in which these efforts crystallised was one where armed conflicts formally falling into the category of NIAC were abundant.[26] During the CDDH, the question of which model to rely on for NIAC resurfaced.[27] Draft AP II proposed a similar set of elaborate rules for NIAC, and a broad scope of applicability; however, during the CDDH, specificity in the law was bought at the price of a materially reduced scope of application,[28] a specificity that was reduced even further at the final session.[29]

The Additional Protocols resulted in a system of four classifications of armed conflict:[30] (1) GC Article 3, providing very rudimentary protection for victims in a wide range of conflicts;[31] (2) AP II Article 1(1), offering somewhat better protection for victims, but with a very narrow scope of applicability;[32] (3) situations within AP I Articles 1(4) and 93(3), offering the fully fledged protection of civilians and combatants in IHL, but with a scope of applicability that is so narrow or controversial that it has never been applied;[33] and (4) situations within GC Article 2, proper IACs. Only the latter refers to inter-state war, while the former three refer to situations in which at least one party is a non-state party, formally falling in the category of NIAC. Other treaty frameworks have subsequently perpetuated this fourfold system of the Geneva Conventions.[34]

This result left an impression of IACs being scrutinised and regulated on a very detailed level, while NIACs were left 'in the void', largely to the discretion of parties (in particular governments) involved in internal conflicts. Critics commonly imply that the wide ratification of AP II is due precisely to its narrow scope.[35] The result was a difference in *lex scripta* between IAC and NIAC that probably appears larger in treaty law than it actually was in customary law.

The Protocols did not remove the dichotomy between IAC and NIAC. On the contrary, the dichotomy was now even more firmly inscribed in conventional law. Application was complicated by the inclusion of two new categories of armed conflict and the politicising of the question of classification by adding a layer of 'just war' to certain NIACs that were then elevated to IACs. Nor did the Protocols remove the humanitarian gap between IAC and NIAC. Rather, they exacerbated the impression of adverse treatment in IHL of victims of NIAC, given the thorough regulation of AP I.

In the following years, the dichotomy was subject to increasingly heavy criticism.[36] This academic debate largely focused not on the character of the adversaries involved in violence, but on the *humanitarian* effects. It increasingly questioned the dichotomy between IAC and NIAC and its role in 'barring' victims of NIAC from the full protections of IHL.

The prevailing opinion was that the avenue of the Geneva Conventions had been exhausted. AP II left numerous unresolved issues with regard to NIAC that needed to be addressed. Alarmed by the experience of the CDDH, where states had expressed strong fears that a comprehensive treaty about IHL in NIAC might affect state sovereignty, prevent governments from effectively maintaining law and order within their borders and be invoked to justify outside intervention, focus then turned to mechanisms *outside* the framework of the Geneva Conventions in order to repair the humanitarian gap of the Conventions.

3. Filling the normative gap outside the framework of the Geneva Conventions

Following the failure of AP II to provide a comprehensive and sufficiently protective framework for NIAC, academic and institutional efforts to improve protection for victims of NIAC increasingly evolved around two approaches: to strengthen the rules applicable to NIAC *outside* the GC framework (treaties or custom) in order to lessen the humanitarian gap; or to extend application of humanitarian principles to all instances of armed conflict irrespective of the dichotomy and gradations other than that of the existence of an armed conflict (disregarding the structural dichotomy upon which the Geneva Conventions rely).

This latter tendency has increasingly been expressed as endeavours towards a unified body of IHL, an approach that *prima facie* has the added value of simplifying questions of application of IHL. The idea of one set of rules applicable to all received impetus from the human rights discourse, increasingly expanding into the realm of armed conflict, and blind to many of the structural premises of humanitarian law. In 1966, the United Nations had successfully adopted the two UN Covenants on human rights, and a breakthrough for IHL came two years later with the International Conference on Human Rights in Tehran, convened by the United Nations.[37] The Conference adopted a resolution on human rights in armed conflicts,[38] making no distinction between *types* of armed conflicts. Increasingly, human rights and humanitarian law were referred to together, with no details about their respective spheres.

Another major impetus to these endeavours came from international jurisprudence. In 1986, the ICJ pronounced in the *Nicaragua* case that the United States was bound by GC Article 3 in view of its customary nature, that GC Article 3 reflects 'elementary considerations of humanity' applicable under customary international law to *any* armed conflict, and thus that 'the minimum rules applicable to international and to non-international conflicts are identical'.[39] The Court thereby lent authority to the idea that certain core rules of IAC and NIAC are the same, applicable to all armed conflicts, thus in some respects making the dichotomy irrelevant.[40] The next leap in development came with the UN ad hoc tribunals for the former Yugoslavia and Rwanda, both of which needed to relate to rules regulating NIAC.[41] Most important in this regard was the *Tadić* decision of 1995.[42] Seminal because of its definition of armed conflict[43] and its conclusion that breaches of GC Article 3 may constitute crimes under international law,[44] the *Tadić* decision also has had more direct influence on reducing the humanitarian gap. It questioned the dichotomy between IAC and NIAC, and it made important findings with regard to what customary rules apply to NIAC.

With respect to the dichotomy, the Appeals Court in *Tadić* held that 'in the area of armed conflict the distinction between interstate wars and civil wars is losing its value as far as human beings are concerned … [the] dichotomy should gradually lose its weight'.[45] The statement was not decisive of the final decision on the character of the conflict in the former Yugoslavia, and is generally considered to be *obiter dicta*. In the subsequent year, the then President of the ICTY, Antonio Cassese, opined in 1996 that 'there has been a *convergence* of the two bodies on international law with the result that internal strife is now *governed* to a large extent by the rules and principles which had traditionally only applied to international conflicts' (emphasis added),[46] implying that the dichotomy as such was not questioned. The same conclusion has been reached in literature somewhat critical about this *dicta*, because it represented a breach with the otherwise and subsequently determined endeavours by the ICTY to abide by the structure of the Geneva Conventions.[47]

The ICTY's arguments concerning the *extension* of IHL norms into the realms of NIAC beyond that of the treaty law in the Geneva Conventions have been more convincing. Basing itself on the fundamental humanitarian principle that what is inhumane in IAC must also be inhumane in NIAC,[48] the Court listed a number of basic rules of protection applicable to NIAC,[49] an approach later upheld and further extended by the subsequent jurisprudence of the ICTY. In the *Martić* case in 1996, the Court concluded that '[t]here exists, at present, a corpus of customary international law applicable to all armed conflicts irrespective of their characterisation as international or non-international armed conflicts. This corpus includes general rules designed to protect the civilian population as well as rules governing means and methods of warfare'.[50]

With regard to the establishment of a set of customary rules going *beyond* that of GC Article 3 and AP II applicable by the tribunal to NIAC, the *Tadić* decision has had a major effect on the development of the lacuna in NIAC. Ad hoc tribunals have built on fundamental humanitarian principles to find that the prohibitions that derive from instruments addressed only in IACs may apply in NIACs, with the result that a common core of IHL applies irrespective of the nature of armed conflict. The resulting effect on IHL has been that the minimum rules deemed applicable in all conflicts by the ICJ in 1986, expanded to a wider array of rules in the *Tadić* case in 1995, including some of the rules of AP II. The *Tadić* case made a huge contribution to bridging the normative gap, although the dichotomy of IAC/NIAC was ultimately left intact by the tribunal.

In the subsequent negotiations for the Rome Statute in 1998, the approach taken by *Tadić* was largely confirmed. The dichotomy between IAC and NIAC was upheld, with acts within GC Article 3 and certain acts within AP II criminalised, in addition to other breaches relating to the laws and customs of war in NIAC. There was unanimous agreement during the Conference that the crimes adopted constituted customary international law. The ICC upheld a threefold system of armed conflict: IACs, and NIACs divided into GC Article 3-type conflicts[51] and conflicts similar to those regulated by AP II.[52] The dichotomy was thus upheld, but a certain part of the bridging of the normative gap suggested in the *Tadić* decision was confirmed by states as declaratory of customary international law in internal armed conflicts.

The most extraordinary development in recent years has nevertheless been the expansion of treaty law other than the Geneva Conventions into the realm of NIAC since the early 1990s.[53] To view this as indicative of a disintegration of the dichotomy between IAC and NIAC does have some merit.[54] Nonetheless, it needs to be accompanied by substantial reservation.

IHL consists of a core of treaty and customary rules regulating the means and methods of warfare, dating back as far as 1868. Once states are willing to outlaw a means or method of war, there is generally no reason why they should reserve their use in certain types of conflicts.[55] This attitude has been noticeable since the negotiations of the Geneva Conventions in 1949, where the United States put forward a proposal to the effect of extending the protections of the 1925 Gas Protocol to civil wars, a proposal that was rejected.[56] The rules of IHL relating to weapons were cut out of the CDDH due to their highly controversial nature. Given the exacerbated controversies surrounding weapons (nuclear weapons in particular) at the height of the Cold War, the issue of weapons threatened to derail the entire CDDH. Consequently, weapons were cut loose from AP I and AP II.[57] The issue was relegated to a later conference, eventually leading to the much-criticised CCW Convention in 1980.[58] During the negotiations on the CCW, which at the outset only applied to IACs, the issue of internal armed conflict was largely off the table.[59]

The Convention on Biological Weapons, concluded in 1972, outlawed such weapons in *all* conflicts.[60] In the early 1990s, in a post-Cold War mood, heavily influenced by the use of chemical weapons during the Iran–Iraq war, including their use by the Iraqi Ba'ath regime against Iraqi

Kurds in what was a parallel internal conflict in Iraq, the Convention on Chemical Weapons was concluded in 1992, entering into force in 1997. States parties now undertook 'never under any circumstances' to use chemical weapons.[61] Riot control agents (RCA) were exempted, but states undertook not to use RCA as 'a method of warfare'.[62] Neither the Biological nor the Chemical Weapons Convention thus relate to the classical dichotomy between IAC and NIAC, signalling that the same rules apply for such weapons irrespective of the type of conflict. The nature of the relevant disarmament agreements may account for some of this, but it nonetheless marked a clear shift in treaty law. The following year, the ICJ delivered its Advisory Opinion on the use of nuclear weapons, in which it labelled the prohibition on causing unnecessary suffering to combatants a cardinal principle of IHL, according to which states do not have unlimited freedom of choice of means in the weapons they use.[63] Here, no reference was made to the character of armed conflict. For what concerns ABC (atomic, biological, chemical) weapons, it can be concluded that at least by the mid-1990s, the dichotomy between IAC and NIAC had become irrelevant – also in *lex scripta*.

With regard to conventional weapons, 1996 also saw the amended Protocol II to the CCW, expanding the scope of application to GC Article 3 conflicts amid fierce debates.[64] At the second review conference in 2001, a US proposal to extend the entire CCW with existing Protocol to NIAC met with no substantial debates concerning the extension into NIAC (in force from 2004). As for weapons conventions negotiated outside the framework of the CCW, the Anti-Personnel Mine Convention of 1997 and the Cluster Munitions Convention of 2008 equally make no distinction between IAC and NIAC. For what concerns prohibition and restrictions on the use of conventional weapons, it may be concluded that the dichotomy between IAC and NIAC has effectively been removed over the past decades.[65]

This recent development in treaty law of weapons is commonly used as an indication of a more a general tendency towards the disintegration of the dichotomy between IAC and NIAC. Nevertheless, it bears repeating that regulation of the use of weapons has always been in a somewhat particular situation in IHL. Although the first multilateral treaties of IHL regulated precisely the use of weapons,[66] their regulation has generally posed serious problems given their intimate link with what is perceived to be in the military interests of states.[67]

Once persuasive arguments convince states to outlaw a weapon, few reasons exist as to why such prohibition should be limited to IAC.

In fact, if a weapon were outlawed, few countries would keep it in their armoury.[68] This disarmament dimension of the regulation of weapons is one reason why the rules of weapons should be kept separate from other rules of IHL. With regard to NIAC, the regulation of weapons is perhaps the area in which a separation between IAC and NIAC is most difficult to defend, and where the moral absurdities are most evident, while it is the area where the structural impediments in a unified body of IHL are least imposing. The main issue is not the legal character of the parties to the conflict, but rather whether use of a given weapon happens inside or outside an armed conflict.[69]

Beyond treaties of international criminal law and weapons, the conventional law of IHL has not been expanding into the realms of NIAC in a parallel way, with a few notable exceptions.[70] The avenue left for filling the normative gap of NIAC therefore seems to be that of customary law.[71]

Over the past decades, practice in the UN Security Council, General Assembly and the Human Rights Council indicates that a distinction between different types of armed conflicts is not made at the United Nations. Similarly, on the domestic level, operational guidelines often make no distinction between IAC and NIAC with respect to which rules apply. Although this may point to a development where the significance of the dichotomy is less marked, other factors may equally explain this trend.[72] In 1995, the ICRC embarked on a study of customary international humanitarian law, a major purpose of which was to determine if customary international law regulated NIACs in more detail than treaty law.[73] The Study, published in 2005, identified 161 rules of customary law, clearly indicating (or perhaps grossly overstating) that there is a large body of IHL rules applicable, irrespective of type of armed conflict.[74] Curiously, the ICRC chose not to examine the definition of armed conflict, nor the dichotomy between IAC and NIAC, although it relied heavily on the latter. The Study ultimately upheld the dichotomy, and by perpetuating it, even reinforced the impression of two distinct sets of rules of IHL. It did confirm, however, that the humanitarian protection offered by either regime is not very different for what concerns customary international law. This approach was also taken in a recent opinion paper by the ICRC on 'armed conflict' in 2008,[75] and in the institutional approach of the ICRC expressed in its Guidance on direct participation in hostilities (DPH) of 2009.[76] The dichotomy between IAC and NIAC is not questioned; emphasis is rather put on the evolution of norms of IHL in NIAC slowly mending the normative gap. Other soft-law instruments, such as the *San Remo Manual on Non-International Armed Conflicts* (2006), also rely on the dichotomy, and similarly attempt to identify what analogous rules apply in NIAC.[77] The *Manual on Air and Missile Warfare* (2009)[78] also relies on the dichotomy, but is structured exclusively on IAC, with indications about parallel rules in NIAC only in the Commentary to the Manual,[79] clearly indicating that IAC and NIAC are still separate regimes of IHL with partly different structures and content.[80]

It is beyond question that the normative gap between IAC and NIAC has diminished considerably over the past decades. The expansion of treaty law into the realm of NIAC in certain areas, the establishment and consolidation of a common enforcement regime for IAC and NIAC through international criminal law, and the trend in practice to assimilate rules of IAC and NIAC unless expressly exempted, all point to an increased level of protection by IHL in NIACs, a development slowly reducing the normative gap of NIAC. While most legal sources indicate that the dichotomy remains largely intact,[81] endeavours to reduce the distinction further have continued.

In the wake of the *Tadić* decision, a substantial number of scholars embraced the ICTY's statements on the reduced importance of the dichotomy between IAC and NIAC. The tendency to refer to a common set of rules applicable to armed conflict irrespective of classification has led many to argue for a gradual demise of the distinction. As the normative regimes applicable to situations of massive violence formally classified under NIAC or IAC are increasingly converging with respect to the level of humanitarian protection, it would be natural to think that calls for a removal of the dichotomy were less outspoken. This seems not to be the case.

There is now extensive literature suggesting that customary international law has developed to a point where the gap between the two regimes is less marked.[82] Some go further. Stewart claims that national legislation, international legal instruments and judicial decisions all show that the disparity between the laws applicable to international and non-international armed conflicts is becoming outmoded and is eroding.[83] Certain practice of judicial bodies implies assimilation of the rules,[84] and numerous international reports relying on IHL seem to presuppose a high degree of assimilation.[85] In recent years, the case for elimination of the dichotomy has regained its intensity.[86] Some argue that minimum standards should be reintroduced.[87] The lack of a more comprehensive legal regulation in *lex scripta* and the continuing normative gap between IAC and NIAC are still fuelling calls for a unified rule of IHL, a disintegration of the dichotomy between IAC and NIAC.

4. Arguments in favour of a uniform body of IHL

Arguments used to advocate for the removal of the distinction between IAC and NIAC may be divided into two main categories. First, there are arguments relating to the *inoperability* of the dichotomy, a problem that may relate to law, to facts, or both. Secondly, there are arguments concerned with the *discriminatory effects* of the dichotomy, given that IHL still provides more extensive and elaborate protection for victims of IAC than for victims of NIAC.

Among the elements of inoperability, some refer to the problem of applicability. There exists the difficulty of laying down *objective criteria* to distinguish NIAC from IAC,[88] the problems of parallel application,[89] described by Meron as 'a crazy quilt of norms that would be applicable in the same conflict'.[90] A slightly different argument relates to the arbitrariness and uncertainty of classification,[91] while another approach emphasises changes in the nature of armed conflict and problems with making the real world 'fit'.[92] There seems to be a prevailing notion that a uniform law would solve many of the challenges involved with the application of IHL.[93]

Foremost in the category of arguments relating to the discrimination in humanitarian protection is the argument that IHL has the same *function* in IAC and NIAC – to humanise and regularise the conduct of hostilities between the parties.[94] If emphasis is put exclusively on the humanitarian function, there is no persuasive reason why different rules should govern the two, and the dichotomy should be removed. Such views were expressed by proponents of a unified rule for IAC and NIAC, discussed during the negotiations of the Geneva Conventions in 1949[95] and during the CDDH.[96] Over the years, policy-makers, military operators and legal experts have argued in line with this, that humanitarian protection should be the same irrespective of the type of armed conflict: gradation of legal protection and regulation based on the type of conflict is portrayed as a false distinction, undesirable,[97] or (increasingly) irrelevant.[98] Inequality before the law is often put forward as the main argument why the distinction between IAC and NIAC should be erased.[99] Underlying reasons for the dichotomy are also being scrutinised,[100] and there seems to be a certain notion that a removal of the distinction between IAC and NIAC would neutralise other functions that the dichotomy may have.[101]

The conclusions drawn from these arguments diverge. Some argue in favour of a unified body, a removal of the distinction in order to have a unified law of IHL applicable to all armed conflicts. There are those who seem to take a more extreme approach, arguing for a unified rule in order to 'do away' with IHL.[102] Most proponents represent more moderate views, however, emphasising a unified application, with overall the same rules applicable to IAC and NIAC.[103] Summed up, critics share the view that the reasons behind the dichotomy between IAC and NIAC cannot justify the arbitrary differences in humanitarian protection resulting from the dichotomy.[104] This call for a uniform body of the laws protecting persons in armed conflicts is unequivocally based on a belief that such a development can only be beneficial to the protective regime.[105] Does this assumption stand up to closer scrutiny?

5. Seven arguments in defence of the dichotomy between international and non-international armed conflict

It may be virtually impossible in many cases to distinguish an IAC from a NIAC by observing the conduct of hostilities, the animosity between the belligerent parties, or by contemplating how an armed conflict is unfolding. Nevertheless, armed conflicts between legal entities with the complete set of rights and duties of states are inherently different in a legal sense from those between one state and one or more non-state parties, or between non-state parties. A basic mantra of contemporary IHL is that all parties to an armed conflict are subject to rights and duties under international humanitarian law, irrespective of their legal status.[106] Notwithstanding, this fact does not affect the legal nature of the non-state parties.[107] It does not bestow obligations from adjacent legal regimes such as human rights law, refugee law or international law more broadly upon the non-state parties to the armed conflict. Nor does it make non-state actors commensurate with states with respect to rights and duties under IHL. Non-state parties remain non-state parties for all purposes within IHL and outside, unless of course the non-state party transforms into a state party by way of force, assuming the role of its state party opponent. A large part of the differences that persist between IAC and NIAC may be traced back to this fact, elementary but of paramount importance. These are differences that a unified body of IHL will not be able to mend. In fact, this fundamental structural difference between the parties involved in IAC and NIAC leads to several arguments in favour of a continued dichotomy between the two types of armed conflicts. The first four relate to applicability, the latter three to discriminatory issues.

1. *The separation between ius ad bellum and ius in bello.* The introduction of the term 'armed conflict' in the Geneva Conventions was part of a process that separated international rules relating to the rights and duties during armed conflict (*ius in bello*) from the question of the overall legitimacy or legality of the resort to the threat or use of armed force (*ius ad bellum*), regulated by the UN Charter.[108] IAC was restricted in international law, while NIAC was not prohibited as such.[109] Subsequent developments may have modified this picture somewhat.[110] Notwithstanding, among the binary structures of IHL that have come under strain over the past decades, the pair *ad bellum–in bello* is the one that seems to have been affected the least, because to insulate questions of lawfulness and legitimacy of the resort to use of armed force from the right and duties of the belligerents is seen as fundamental for the neutral application of humanitarian law.[111] Over the years, numerous IHL scholars have warned against the 'just war' thinking which is inherent in linking issues of *ad bellum* to that of *in bello*, and the inevitable undermining of IHL that will follow.[112] *Ad bellum* issues differ for IAC and NIAC – the former regulated in international law, the latter in domestic law – a difference with several implications for how the rules of *in bello* function.[113] A unified rule of *ius in bello* would have to mitigate this structural incompatibility.[114] Undermining of the distinction in order to accommodate NIACs would clearly not be conducive to the furthering of protections of IHL.

2. *The lower threshold of violence.* The threshold of violence required for applicability of IHL is different for IAC and NIAC. In IACs, the mere intervention by states of armed force against each other is enough to satisfy the criteria of applicability of IHL.[115] This criteria, however, is closely linked to armed conflicts where states are parties on both sides.[116] The criteria for applicability in NIAC are different.[117] In addition to a certain level of organisation for establishing identifiable parties to a conflict, applicability is dependent on a non-state party, and the intensity and protraction of hostilities. Any other solution does not sit well with humanitarian protection. States must have certain room for the use of force on their own territory. If mere 'intervention of the armed forces'[118] were sufficient to trigger application of IHL, a vast array of domestic deployments would become subject to the body of IHL, opening up the possibility of a displacement of domestic law and a curbing of certain international obligations. IHL therefore excludes internal disturbances and tensions, as well as isolated and sporadic acts of violence from the ambit of IHL in NIAC.[119]

A similarly high threshold for IAC would leave victims of foreign states with much reduced protection, if the rules of IHL did not protect them unless a certain intensity had been reached in the clashes between armed forces.

What is more, the idea that states may resort to 'a certain degree of hostilities' not amounting to armed conflict would not only undermine IHL protection, but could potentially recreate the very unsatisfactory situation of the 1930s, where the laws of war were paralysed over arguments about the threshold criteria of 'war'.

Proponents of a unified law acknowledge the need to 'ensure that states continue to enjoy an ability to deal with internal disturbances under domestic law but that international conflicts of low intensity remain subject to international humanitarian protection'.[120] The idea that the threshold for armed conflict happening between the armed forces of two states should be subject to the same kind of threshold as that of the resort to the use of force by a state on its own territory does not seem to promote either humanitarian protection of armed conflict, by raising the threshold for IAC, nor the best humanitarian protection of peace, by allowing states to apply IHL at an earlier stage, to the detriment of the full application of domestic law and human rights law.

3. *The issue of occupation.* Despite its structural resemblance with that of a NIAC, occupation has always been seen as an impediment to a unified law of IHL,[121] a problem also noted by certain proponents of a unified rule.[122] This is also linked to the inherent difference in rights and duties of a state involved in an armed conflict on its own territory, and the limitations imposed by IHL on a belligerent power that has effective control over foreign territory, assuming the role of occupying power. Such an entity may not be equated with that of the rights of the sovereign. Given that numerous challenges faced by a state with an incipient insurgency and that of a belligerent occupying power are in fact very similar, a unified body of IHL would probably see the end to this distinction, a development clearly not beneficial for the humanitarian protection bestowed by the Geneva Conventions upon persons living under military occupation.

4. *The interplay and function of international human rights law.* It is common to refer to the influence of human rights to explain current trends in IHL – and to advocate for development in one direction or another. The ICTY in the *Tadić* case observed that 'recent trends in state practice and the whole doctrine of human rights ... tend to blur in many respects the traditional dichotomy between international wars and civil strife'.[123]

In international armed conflict, however, human rights law primarily regulates the relationship between a state and persons subject to its control, and not as such the relationship with enemy combatants or enemy civilian populations. Although certain treaties may remain in force between the belligerents, the rules applicable if IHL did not apply (the default regime) are highly rudimentary. In NIAC happening on the territory of a state, the situation is the reverse. The default regime, even under laws of emergency, is generally more specific, more precise and more advantageous to persons caught up in the unrest, obliging the state actor to comply in respect of all its subjects, within the confines of its ability. In such a setting, however, the entire function of IHL transforms, since the default regime is better (not, as in IAC, worse), even to the point where one may question the humanitarian function of IHL in NIAC. Given that its function differs in this way, a unified body of IHL may not be able to appropriately adjust to these two different settings, potentially to the detriment of the humanitarian protection offered. In NIAC, a certain paucity of rules might ideally open the way for a more expansive influence of the human rights regime, an avenue that is not equally evident in IAC.

5. *The principle of distinction*. This is one of the most fundamental tenets of IHL, and at the core there is not much difference between the obligations of warring parties *vis-à-vis* civilians in IAC and NIAC.[124] Nevertheless, efficient protection of the principle of distinction depends on a certain degree of clarity concerning the categories between which to distinguish. IHL has always been stretched to cover three categories of persons: those who are allowed to take part in hostilities and may be directly targeted (combatants),[125] those who do not take part in hostilities and are immune against direct attacks (civilians),[126] and those who are not allowed to, but take part in hostilities nonetheless (irregulars).[127] The latter group is constantly posing a threat to an otherwise orderly principle of distinction.[128] In IAC, there will be combatants and civilians on both sides, and even in the messier conflicts of our days, the vast majority of persons will belong to the groups either of combatants or the derived notion of civilians.[129] With regard to the principle of distinction, combatants may be directly targeted at all times, unless they are rendered *hors de combat*. In NIAC, the situation is less clear. No legal category of combatant exists, and consequently nor does the derived notion of civilian. State armed forces and the fighters of non-state parties may be targeted during hostilities, but the criteria determining the loss and regaining of target immunity for state and non-state parties is controversial. Proponents of a unified body

of IHL for IAC and NIAC accept that this issue must be 'resolved'.[130] The ICRCs institutional position has been made clear through the Guide on DPH in 2009, adopting a similar structure for NIAC.[131] In IAC, the principle of distinction and the categories upon which it rests are fairly clear. In NIAC, the situation is much more unsettled. Extending IHL or IAC into NIAC will not resolve this uncertainty. It is far from evident that a solution where citizens of a state in a NIAC are designated targetable based on a model resembling that of IAC, or a progressive assimilation into one prototype of rules for both situations, will provide increased protection for victims in either type of conflict.

6. *Prisoners of war.* The concept of prisoner of war (POW), regulated for IAC in GC III, does not exist in NIAC. In IAC, the corollary of target immunity for civilians is prosecutorial immunity for combatants for lawful acts of war if detained by the enemy belligerent. The entire POW concept relies on the premise that members of the armed forces are functional instruments of the state will, and that neutralising them from battle is sufficient to gain a certain military advantage. Since the purpose of their detention is not punitive, they are also given certain privileged treatment. POW status is given primarily to persons who have the right to participate in hostilities.[132] This 'right' in IHL is translated into a duty of the belligerent capturer not to prosecute the POW in domestic law for lawful acts of war.[133] POWs may instead be kept in quarters until the end of the armed conflict.

No parallel structure exists in NIAC, for rather obvious reasons. States will not, and arguably may not, bestow on non-state actors en bloc immunity for lawful acts of war against the state on its own territory. Such a 'concession' would implicitly question the ability and willingness of state authorities to uphold the monopoly of use of force. The human rights obligations of most states would probably preclude such treaty provisions. The compromised solution that has been negotiated for NIAC is a discretionary option to give amnesty, in reality an immunity for lawful acts of war given *ex post facto*. It is generally believed that one of the main reasons why states are reluctant even to operate openly under the laws of NIAC is the fear of giving some sort of implicit status to non-state belligerents. This dimension of the 'combatant' issue – in terms of fully fledged immunity in domestic (or international) law for lawful acts of war – is perhaps what is posing the most serious problems for the prospect of a unified body of IHL. Even the most staunch adherents of eliminating the distinction between IAC–NIAC acknowledge that this issue 'must be resolved'.[134]

7. *Relationship to third parties: neutrality.* Historically, the law of neutrality was the background for the doctrine of belligerency,[135] a practice that is generally perceived to have fallen into desuetude.[136] Despite certain indications to the contrary,[137] the law of neutrality has a role to play. The pillars of the law of neutrality are non-discrimination as well as non-participation.[138] While the second may be less problematic, the former does not sit well with the structure of NIAC, and it is unclear how this issue could be resolved if the dichotomy of IAC and NIAC disintegrated.

These inherent differences between IAC and NIAC will not disappear merely by suppressing the formal dichotomy between the two types of armed conflict.

The intricate binary categories of IHL in IAC, upon which much of the protection of the human person is in fact contingent, disintegrate, disappear or at least are less clear in NIAC. It therefore seems compelling to argue that since IAC provide more extensive, more clear-cut and more detailed provisions of IHL, it would serve the interests of humanity if they were expanded to situations of NIAC. This presumption from a moral perspective, however, does not stand up to closer scrutiny. There are evident structural incompatibilities between IAC and NIAC that seemingly impede a unified law of armed conflict. Trying to force the two into one basket, IAC with its clear-cut binary structures, and NIAC comprising a whole range of different situations, with a messy and fluid legal nature, does not seem prudent. Rather than bringing the clarity of IAC into NIAC, the risk is high that the quagmire of NIAC will contaminate the regime of IAC.[139]

Arguments in favour of a unified body of IHL because of the differences in humanitarian protection have lost some of their urgency as the normative protection of NIAC is slowly improving. Arguments in favour of a unified body due to the inoperability of the criteria of classification are more persuasive, but unfortunately this is unlikely to be solved by disregarding the dichotomy between NIAC and IAC altogether. Given the legal incommensurability, there must be some differentiation between situations where a state is at war with another state, and that of a state at war with its own citizens. If the distinction between IAC and NIAC is suppressed, the incommensurability will in all likelihood move deeper into the fabric of IHL, causing problems for operability simply on a different level, fragmenting the body of IHL – most likely at the expense of humanitarian protection.

IHL is built upon a set of binary relations: war–peace, *ad bellum–in bello*, IAC–NIAC, combatant–civilian. Traditionally, the most rigid distinction was that between 'a state of peace and a state of war'.[140] As this most profound distinction has become less evident, other binary pairs that constitute the fabric of IHL have also come under pressure, perceived as impediments to increased protection. It bears repeating, however, that the binary structures of IHL do have protective functions, modelled on the reality of armed conflict. The distinction between IAC and NIAC, for a long time barring victims of NIAC from humanitarian protection, is now increasingly protecting the clear-cut structures of IAC from the much messier category (in legal and factual terms) of NIAC.

IHL is intended to cover a whole range of increasingly divergent situations of armed conflicts. To distinguish in law between the two types of conflicts which, from a legal perspective, pose different kinds of problems, is not irrational, nor ultimately is it detrimental to humanitarian protection.

6. Concluding remarks

The normative gap between international and non-international armed conflicts has decreased over the past decades. Suppressing the dichotomy between IAC and NIAC further, however, will most likely *not* serve to advance the humanitarian purposes of the Geneva Conventions – on the contrary.

As the most appalling consequences of the differences between the two sets of rules are being mended, more constructive and even protective functions of the 'insulation' of NIAC are coming to light.

First, the dichotomy shields IAC from the quagmires of NIAC; the issue of lower threshold is absent, the question of lawfulness of the use of force has no bearing on the rules relating to conduct of hostilities and treatment of persons, and the system of privileges (rules relating to target immunity and prosecutorial immunity for lawful acts of war), are fairly clear and coherent for international armed conflict. This clarity reinforces compliance in providing solid ground for a common understanding of humanity in this particular type of conflict that may not be very common in the present era, but (and it bears repeating) which nevertheless represent the most potent danger in terms of massive destruction and havoc. Adjustment of these rules to fit a more asymmetric reality in present-day conflict risks introducing elements that will substantially reduce the protective force and level of compliance associated with the Geneva Conventions in situations of inter-state armed conflicts.

Secondly, the more unsettled and flexible set of rules applicable to NIAC offers a different type of potential in terms of humanitarian protection. Although this flexibility certainly poses problems, in NIAC it also opens the door for an increased role for other regimes of international law in such conflicts, notably human rights law. Different models of interaction adjusted to specific types of asymmetric conflicts can be envisaged, offering optimised balances between humanitarian considerations and military necessities, very much to the benefit of victims of such conflicts.

Several serious challenges nevertheless remain, including differences in the level of protection offered by the rules. These differences, however, are mostly traceable to structural incompatibilities between inter-state conflicts, on the one hand, and conflicts where at least one party to the conflict is a non-state actor, on the other. A disintegration of the dichotomy between the rules of international and non-international armed conflict will *not* solve the intangible issues at the core of this distinction: the legal regulation of the relationship between a state at war with its own subjects, or with the subjects of other states, or that of war among its own subjects. The rules of IAC remain incommensurate with armed conflict where one or more actors are non-state actors. Certain key rules will not – and in some cases cannot – be extended to apply to non-state actors: hence the entire systemic construct of rules of IAC disintegrate.

In order to respond appropriately to humanitarian considerations, the body of IHL must offer a scope of application so wide that it protects those affected by hostilities when other legal rules can no longer protect them, but so narrow that it does not come at the expense of other areas of international law that may offer better protection. IHL rules must be framed in ways that leave no doubt about the outer limits, but that may be flexible for improved protection based on the wider context of the armed conflict. It is submitted/concluded that in both these respects, the optimal solutions for maximised humanitarian protection are different for IAC and NIAC.

Removing the dichotomy will therefore not lift the level of humanitarian protection of non-international armed conflict to that provided in international conflicts. A more likely scenario in case of a meltdown of the distinction is that the intangible problems associated with asymmetric conflict will contaminate the entire fabric of IHL, disintegrating the binary structures from within, undermining the delicate balance between military necessity and humanitarian protection increasingly adjusted to IAC and NIAC based on their similarities *and* differences. At the end of the day, such a disintegration may jeopardise the most important gains made by the Geneva Conventions for protection of civilians and combatants in IAC. It bears remembering that the rules of international armed conflict in the Geneva Conventions represent some of the most precious legal heritage of the twentieth century. They should not be easily discarded.

Developments in the normative regulation of NIAC over the past few decades seem to create a system where protection can be optimised within each of the two binary systems, on their own terms. Seeking to resolve the inadequacies of each system by a reference to the other is not conducive to strengthening humanitarian protections for persons caught up in armed conflict. Rather than trying to disintegrate the distinction, efforts should aim at improving humanitarian protection within each category of armed conflict, based on the legal particularities of each type. The much-cursed dichotomy of the IHL under Geneva Conventions into IAC and NIAC may then finally be turned into a blessing for humanitarian protection.

Notes

1 R. Baxter, 'Ius in cello interno: the present and future law' in J.N. Moore (ed.), *Law and Civil War in the Modern World* (Johns Hopkins University Press, 1974) 518–39 at 520.

2 The terms 'IAC' and 'NIAC' derive from the titles of Additional Protocol I (AP I) and Additional Protocol II (AP II) to the Geneva Conventions respectively. Full titles are 1977 Protocol (I) Additional to the Geneva Conventions of 12 August 1949, and relating to the Protection of Victims of International Armed Conflicts, 1125 UNTS 3, and 1977 Protocol (II) Additional to the Geneva Conventions of 12 August 1949, and relating to the Protection of Victims of Non-International Armed Conflicts, 1125 UNTS 609. The acronyms have gained increased use after their extensive use in the 2005 ICRC Customary Study. See J.-M. Henckaerts and L. Doswald-Beck (eds.), *Customary International Humanitarian Law* (Cambridge University Press, 2005), vol. I: Rules. See also San Remo International Institute of Humanitarian Law, M.N. Schmitt, C.H.B. Garraway and Y. Dinstein, 'The Manual on the Law of Non-International Armed Conflict' (2006) 36 *Israel Yearbook on Human Rights, Special Supplement*, and Program on Humanitarian Policy and Conflict Research at Harward University, *Commentary on the HPCR Manual on International Law Applicable to Air and Missile Warfare* (Harvard University, 2009), both using 'non-international armed conflict' as a generic term.

3 D. Fleck, *The Handbook of International Humanitarian Law*, 2nd edn, (Oxford University Press, 2008) para. 1201 (5.c).

4 *Prosecutor* v. *Tadić* (Case No IT-94-I-AR72), ICTY, Decision on the Defence Motion for Interlocutory Appeal on Jurisdiction, 2 October 1995, para. 119.

5 The Russian Civil War (1917–1923) and the Spanish Civil War (1936–1939) had been shockingly brutal, with almost complete disregard for the laws of war, see F. Bugnion,

'Jus ad bellum, jus in bello and non-international armed conflicts' (2003) 4 *Yearbook of International Humanitarian Law* 167 at 185. Neither the Chinese Civil War (1945–1949) nor the Greek Civil War (1946–1949), ongoing during the preparations for the Geneva Conventions, led to recognition of belligerency and thereby application of the laws of war.

6 *Final Record of the Diplomatic Conference of Geneva of 1949*, vol. II–B (Federal Political Department, Berne, 1949), 35 and 326. This name was first used by the delegation of the USSR.

7 *Case Concerning Military and Paramilitary Activities in and against Nicaragua (Nicaragua* v. *United States)* (Merits) [1986] ICJ Reports 14, 76 ILR, para. 218.

8 D.P. Forsythe, 'Legal management of internal war: the 1977 Protocol on Non-international Armed Conflicts' (1978) 72 *American Journal of International Law* 272 at 274. See also International Law Association (ILA) Committee on Use of Force, *Initial Report on the Meaning of Armed Conflict in International Law* (Rio de Janeiro, 2008), 8 available at www.ila-hq.org/en/committees/index.cfm/cid/1022 referring to GC Article 3 as 'revolutionary'.

9 For an early overview, see Forsythe, 'Legal management of internal war'. See also L. Moir, *The Law of Internal Armed Conflict* (Cambridge University Press, 2002).

10 For a recent confirmation to this effect, see the US Supreme Court in *Salim Ahmed Hamdan* v. *Donald H. Rumsfeld, Secretary of Defense*, 548 US 1, 68 (2006).

11 See Forsythe, 'Legal management of internal war', 274.

12 '[D] eclared war or … armed conflict which may arise between … High Contracting Parties, even if the state of war is not recognized by one of them', GC Common Article 2(1); 'armed conflict not of an international character', GC Article 3(1).

13 The definition of armed conflict is frequently referred to as the 'lower threshold', while the distinction between non-international and international conflict is referred to as the 'upper threshold', primarily because AP II is circumscribed by AP I ('shall apply to all armed conflicts which are not covered by … Protocol I'). Under certain circumstances, a NIAC may be regarded as an IAC on account of the involvement of a state on the side of the non-state party to the conflict. The term 'upper threshold' may be misleading, however, implying that a NIAC may turn into an IAC simply on account of its severity. On a general note, the actual fighting required for IHL to apply is lower for IACs than for NIACs.

14 For an overview of current trends in interpreting the closer content of 'armed conflict', see ILA Committee on Use of Force Initial Report 2008.

15 The laws of war were habitually circumvented because states denied the existence of war. During the 1930s, this practice led to evasion of international obligations in virtually all armed conflicts.

16 '[T]he applicability of international humanitarian law was henceforth to be unrelated to the will of governments. It was no longer based solely on the subjectivity inherent in the recognition of the state of war, but was to depend on verifiable facts in accordance with objective criteria … The relevant rules apply when certain specific factual conditions are met.' J.S. Pictet *et al.* (eds.), *Geneva Convention I for the Amelioration of the Condition of the Wounded and Sick in Armed Forces in the Field: Commentary* (Geneva: ICRC, 1952) 32. The preceding Geneva Conventions of 1864, 1906 and 1929 either spoke of 'war' or were silent, implicitly referring to the war in which the 'belligerents' or 'belligerent Powers' were involved. According to J.S. Pictet *et al.* (eds.), *Geneva Convention III relative to the Treatment of Prisoners of*

War: Commentary (Geneva: ICRC, 1952) 23, the wish to avoid linking applicability of IHL to 'war' in the technical legal sense was the reason why the notion of armed conflict was introduced. For the legal position of 'war' after the Geneva Conventions, see E. Lauterpacht, 'The legal irrelevance of the "state of war"' (1968) 62 *Proceedings of the American Society of International Law* 58; R. Baxter, 'The legal consequences of the unlawful use of force under the Charter' (1968) 62 *Proceedings of the American Society of International Law* 68; M.E. O'Connell, 'The legal case against the global war on terror' (2004) 36 *Case Western International Law Journal* 349 at 353, and C. Greenwood, 'War, terrorism and international law' (2004) 56 *Current Legal Problems* 505 at 529; see also ILA Committee on Use of Force Initial Report 2008.

17 See Pictet, *Commentary on GC I*, 32: 'any difference arising between two States and leading to the intervention of armed forces is an armed conflict within the meaning of Article 2'.

18 This deceptively simple notion has been the object of much controversy and criticisms: '[o]ne of the most assured things that might be said about the words "not of an international character" is that no one can say with assurance precisely what they were intended to convey'. T. Farer, 'The humanitarian laws of war in civil strife: towards a definition of "international Armed Conflict" (1971) 7 *Revue Belge de Droit International* 20 at 26.

19 Forsythe, 'Legal management of internal war'.

20 Commonly described as the 'normative gap', see L. Zegfeld, *Accountability of Armed Opposition Groups in International Law* (Cambridge University Press, 2002), or the 'normative loophole', see M. Bothe, 'Customary international humanitarian law: some reflections on the ICRC Study' (2008) 8 *Yearbook of International Humanitarian Law* 143.

21 R. Baxter, 'Some existing problems of humanitarian law' (1975) XIV *Revue de Droit Militaire et droit de la Guerre* 297, observing that 'the law on different types of conflicts has pursued different courses to the prejudice of a common core of humanitarian principles', at 301. Critical voices have called GC Article 3 a 'statement of affectionate generalities' rather than precise guidelines, see Forsythe, 'Legal management of internal war', 273, and they are commonly referred to as skeletal, see C. Greenwood, 'International humanitarian law and the United Nations military operations' (1998) 1 *Yearbook of International Humanitarian Law* 3 at 9. Rules of NIAC are 'skeletal' compared to those of IAC, or embryonic, see J.S. Pictet, *Development and Principles of International Humanitarian Law* (Dordrecht/Geneva: Martinus Nijhoff and Henry Dunant Institute, 1985) 47.

22 Certain regimes nevertheless resorted to the vocabulary of IHL to justify their use of force against their own subjects. In Chile, following the military *coup d'etat* in 1973, authorities insisted that the country found itself in an armed conflict, to which 'appropriate response' was necessary. The Supreme Court reached the conclusion that there *was* an internal armed conflict, then reached the decision that it was not, reversed it again, and finally reversed it in 2009, currently with the conclusion that there was no internal armed conflict in 1974.

23 It was referred to as a legally radical separation, see G. Abi-Saab, 'Non-international armed conflicts' in UNESCO, *International Dimensions of Humanitarian Law* (Dordrecht, 1988); and an arbitrary division, see R.-J. Dupuy and A. Leonetti, 'La notion de conflict armé à caractère non international' in A. Cassese (ed.), *The New Humanitarian Law of Armed Conflict* (Naples: Editoriale scientifica, 1971) 258: 'Elle

produitune dichotomie arbitraire entre les conflits, puisque la distinction, purement formelle, ne se fonde pas surune observation objective de la réalité.'

24 See, among others, M. Veuthey, *Guerillas et droit humanitaire* (Geneva: ICRC 1976) proposing a legal framework that would not consist in binary oppositions between war and not-war, priviledged and unpriviledged combatants, IAC and NIAC, but a series of flexible posisions, absence of rigidity in their application and a range of protective rules, based on continuums rather than dichotomies (at 356–7).

25 Fundamental principles of the Hague Conventions of 1899 and 1907 on the conduct of hostilities were reaffirmed and elaborated. This was particularly important in view of the considerable age of these Conventions and the many states that had no part in their drafting.

26 The Biafran and the Vietnam war, in addition to wars of national liberation in countries like Algeria, Indonesia, Tunisia, Morocco and Angola, all defied the formal categories of the Geneva Conventions. A particular need was felt to accommodate such mixed conflicts, formally falling into the category of NIAC. In the Biafran conflict in 1967, state authorities applied GC III and parts of GC IV in its dealings with the rebel forces and the civilian population, indicating that such extended application of (parts of) the Geneva Conventions to NIAC was not improbable. See ICRC Annual Reports 1967 to 1970.

27 For AP II, the ICRC originally proposed an extensive Protocol, a mini-convention, broad material scope of application, and broad obligations on parties and third parties. See *Draft Additional Protocols to the Geneva Conventions of August 12, 1949, Commentaries* (Geneva: ICRC, October 1973).

28 Forsythe, 'Legal management of internal war,' 284.

29 The extensive draft Protocol, elaborated over the preceeding seven years, was radically changed during the last two weeks. The inclusion of Article 1(4) into AP I led certain states to argue that there was no longer a need for a Protocol on internal armed conflict, prompting a debate about 'selective humanitarianism', brought to an end by a Pakistani proposal which significantly reduced the substantive content, from forty-seven to twenty-eight Articles, eliminating most provisions concerning the conduct of hostilities. See CDDH/I/SR.24 at 10. Pakistan was a state which had recently recovered from an internal conflict with East Pakistan to which IHL had not been applied, see Baxter, 'Ius in bello interno', 528. Pictet has referred to this process as a 'summary and ill-considered mutilation' of AP II, Pictet, *Development and Principles of International Humanitarian Law,* 48. Commonly, this stripping of AP II is explained by reference to the fear that the Protocol might affect state sovereignty, prevent governments from effectively maintaining law and order within their borders and that it might be invoked to justify outside intervention.

30 See e.g., W.A. Solf, 'Problems with the application of norms governing interstate armed conflict to non-international armed conflict' (1983) 13 *Georgia Journal of International and Comparative Law* 291, identifying four situations other than interstate armed conflicts.

31 '[A]rmed conflicts not of an international character occuring in the territory of one of the High Contracting Parties', GC Article. 3.

32 '[A]ll armed conflicts that are not covered by [Protocol I] and which take place in the territoriy of a High Contracting Party between its armed forces and dissident armed forces or other organized groups which, under responsible command, exercise such control over a part of the territory as to enable them to carry out sustained and concerted military operations and to implement this Protocol', AP II Article 1(1).

33 '[A]rmed conflicts in which people are fighting against colonial domination and alien occupation and against racist régimes in the exercise of their right of self-determination', AP I Article 1(4)

34 See e.g., UN International Convention against the Taking of Hostages (1979) Article 12, and the 2001 Amendment of Article 1 of the 1980 UN Convention on Prohibitions or Restrictions on the Use of Certain Conventional Weapons which may be deemed to be Excessively Injurious or to Have Indiscriminate Effects (CCW), 1342 UNTS 137.

35 During the first fifteen years, AP II was formally applied only to a limited number of NIACs: El Salvador (1980–1993), the Philippines (1991) and Bosnia-Herzegovina (1992–1994). The number of states parties to AP II currently stands at 165, with the latest accession by Afghanistan in 2009. Key states with ongoing or incipient internal conflicts have largely refrained from ratifying AP II.

36 It was held that the injustice of having less protective regimes for victims of certain types of war was inevitable as long as IHL distinguished between IAC and NIAC, see D. Schindler, 'The different types of armed conflicts according to the Geneva Coventions and Protocols' (1972) 163 *Receuil des Cours* 125 at 138. The dichotomy was perceived as no longer factually tenable or compatible with the thrust of humanitarian law, see M. Reisman and J. Silk, 'Which law applies to the Afghan conflict' (1988) 82 *American Journal of International Law* 465. It was also described as an exclusion device, an unacceptable 'policy error' in need of rectification, M. Reisman, 'Application of humanitarian law in non-international armed conflicts, remarks by W. Michael Reisman' (1991) 85 *American Society of International Law Proceedings* 83 at 90.

37 Schindler is of the opinion that this involvement by the United Nations was what in fact brought IHL forward, and that both the impact of and the interest for the Geneva Conventions of 1949 was almost absent during their first twenty years, see D. Schindler, 'International humanitarian law: its remarkable development and persistent violation' (2003) 5 *Journal of the History of International Law* 173.

38 Requesting the General Assembly to invite the Secretary-General to study '(a) steps to secure better application of existing humanitarian international conventions and rules in *all* armed conflicts, and (b) the need for additional humanitarian international conventions to ensure better protection of civilians, prisoners and combatants ... and the prohibition of the use of certain methods and means of warfare'. This was later followed up by the UN General Assembly in Resolution 2444 relating to (a) restrictions of means, (b) no targeting of the civilian population as such and (c) principle of distinction (GA Res. 2444, UN doc. A/7218 (1968)). This resolution is generally believed to constitute custom, e.g., subsequent US confirmation of its position that GA Res. 2444 was declaratory of existing customary law, see 'Letter from J. Fred Buzhardt, General Counsil of the Department of Defense, to Senator Edward Kennedy, Chaiman of the Subcommittee on Refugees of the Committee on the Judiciary' (1973) 67 *AJIL* 124, and subsequent Resolutions; no reference was made to classification in a subsequent resolution in 1970 (GA Res. 2675, UN doc A/8028 (1979)), while calls were made for equal treatment of persons irrespective of the classification of the armed conflict in yet another (GA Res. 2676, UN doc. A/80 (1979)).

39 Nicaragua case, ICJ paras. 218–19.

40 The idea of minimum standards was carried further, e.g., in the 'Declaration of Minimum Standards of Humanity, intended to apply in all circumstances [Turku

Declaration]' (1991) 85 *American Journal of International Law* 375. Inspired primarily by human rights law, the Turku Declaration was intended to mend the gap created by derogation of human rights obligations in times of emergency. The minimum standards were to apply to all situations, irrespective of the existence of an armed conflict.

41 On the influence of the ad hoc tribunals on international humanitarian law in NIAC, see T. Meron, 'War crimes in Yugoslavia and the development of international law' (1994) 88 *American Journal of International Law* 78; C. Greenwood, 'The development of international humanitarian law by the International Criminal Tribunal for the Former Yugoslavia' (1998) 2 *Max Planck Yearbook of United Nations Law* 97; W. Fenrick, 'The development of the law of armed conflict through the jurisprudence of the International Criminal Tribunal for the Former Yugoslavia' (1998) 3 *Journal of Armed Conflict Law* 197; L.J. van den Herik, *The International Criminal Tribunal for Rwanda and the Development of International Law* (Leiden: Koninklijke Brill, 2005); E. La Haye, *War Crimes in Internal Armed Conflicts* (Cambridge University Press, 2008).

42 *Tadić* case, ICTY, paras. 75–7. The issue at hand was jurisdiction. The draft Statute and the ensuing debate led the ICJ to conclude that the conflicts in ex-Yugoslavia had been recognised to have both internal and international aspects, and that the Security Council had intended 'to empower [the Tribunal] to adjudicate violations of humanitarian law that occurred in either context'.

43 *Tadić* case, ICTY, para. 70: 'an armed conflict exists whenever there is a resort to armed force between States or protracted armed violence between governmental authorities and organized armed groups or between such groups within a State. International humanitarian law applies from the initiation of such armed conflicts and extends beyond the cessation of hostilities until a general conclusion of peace is reached; or, in the case of internal conflicts, a peaceful settlement is achieved.' This is widely relied on as an authoritative definition of armed conflict. See e.g., Moir, *The Law of Internal Armed Conflict*, 42–5; N. Balendra, 'Defining armed conflict' (2008) 29 *Cardozo L Rev.* 2461 at 2475, and ILA Committee on Use of Force Initial Report 2008 at 13 where it was stated that 'The ICTY *Tadić* decision is nowadays widely relied on as authoritative for the meaning of armed conflict in both international and non-international armed conflicts.'

44 In affirming that breaches of GC Article 3 could incur individual criminal responsibility under international law, the ICJ initiated a process of closing the gap of enforcement mechanisms between IAC and NIAC by extending the concept of war crimes also to NIACs. The ICTY chose a different approach in attempting to close the gap with respect to another enforcement mechanism of IHL, belligerent reprisals, arguably applicable only in IAC, see J.S. Pictet *et al.* (eds.), *Geneva Convention IV relative to the Protection of Civilian Persons in Time of War: Commentary* (Geneva: ICRC, 1952) 39, implying that they are becoming outlawed altogether, see *Prosecutor* v. *Josipović et al. (Kupreskić)* (Case No. IT-95-16-A), ICTY, Appeals Chamber, Judgment, 14 January 2000, para. 530. This interpretation by the ICTY has been heavily criticised. It must be seen as *obiter*, and its weight beyond the ICTY is dubious.

45 *Tadić* case, ICTY, para. 97.

46 Memorandum of 22 March 1996 to the Preparatory Committee for the Establishment of the International Criminal Court, cited in Moir, *The Law of Internal Armed Conflict*, 51.

47 See e.g., C. Greenwood, 'International humanitarian law and the *Tadić* case', (1996) 7 *European J Int'l L* 265 at 269–75, pointing to 'the general tenor of that ruling, where insistence was placed on the importance of the dichotomization of armed conflicts and of the importance of the implementation of that dichotomization in practice'. For a general analysis of the notion of international and internal armed conflict in the ICTY, see C. Gray, 'Bosnia and Herzegovia: civil war or inter-state conflict' (1996) 67 *BYBIL* 155; C. Byron, 'Armed conflicts: international or non-international?' (2001) 6 *Journal of Conflict and Security Law* 63, 80–3; J. Stewart, 'Towards a single definition of armed conflict in international humanitarian law: a critique of internationalized armed conflict' (2003) 85 *IRRC* no. 850 313, and La Haye, *War Crimes in Internal Armed Conflicts*.

48 *Tadić* case, ICTY, para. 119. Insofar as Tadić was not accused of any offences involving unlawful use of weapons, the statement on the prohibition of certain weapons in NIAC were unquestionably *obiter*, see D. Turns, 'At the "vanishing point" of international humanitarian law: methods and means of warfare in non-international armed conflicts' (2003) 45 *German Yearbook of International Law* 115 at 128, and R. Cryer, 'Of custom, treaties, scholars and the gavel, the influence of the International Criminal Tribunals on the ICRC Customary Law Study' (2006) 11 *Journal of Conflict and Security Law* 239 at 254.

49 *Tadić* case, ICTY, paras. 120–5.

50 *Prosecutor* v. *Martić*, (Decision No. IT-95–11-R61), ICTY, 8 March 1996, para. 11.

51 '[A]rmed conflicts not of an international character,' a threshold taken verbatim from AP II Article 1(2), excluding 'internal disturbances and tensions', see Article. 8(2) (c) and (d) of the 1998 Rome Statute of the International Criminal Court, 2187 UNTS 90.

52 '[A]rmed conflicts not of an international character .... that take place in the territory of a State when there is protracted armed conflict between governmental authorities and organized armed groups or between such groups', 1998 Rome Statute Article 8(2)(f).

53 For a comprehensive overview of these developments, see L. Perna, *The Formation of the Treaty Law of Non-International Armed Conflicts* (Leiden: Martinus Nijhoff, 2006).

54 Schindler points out that practically all humanitarian law treaties adopted since 1995 have been made applicable to both IAC and NIAC, something that he interprets as demonstrative of a growing acceptance of a 'progressive assimilation' of the dual laws of armed conflicts into one body of law. Schindler, 'International humanitarian law', 177.

55 An entirely different issue is the use of certain weapons *outside* of armed conflict. Various means that international treaties explicitly outlaw in combat situations are not unlawful in law-enforcement settings, e.g., dum-dum bullets or riot control agents (RCA), primarily due to the inherent differences between IHL and the law applicable to law-enforcement situations. In law-enforcement situations, a highly discriminate projectile such as a dum-dum bullet may decrease the risk to innocent bystanders at the expense of the criminal posing such an imminent threat that the use of lethal force against him may be lawful. In IHL, 'guilt' or 'innocence' are irrelevant notions in this respect civilians are no more 'innocent' than combatants are 'guilty'. The humanitarian considerations of one collective group ('civilians') and their protection against indiscriminate weapons may not come at the

complete expense of the humanitarian considerations of that of another collective group ('combatants' or persons directly participating in hostilites) and their protection against weapons that cause unnecessary suffering or superfluous injury. Dum-dum bullets are therefore prohibited in warfare. The issue of riot control agents poses slightly different problems. Whilst having an appeasement function in law-enforcement settings, where the level of force must not exceed that which is strictly necessary for its purpose, RCA are prohibited in warfare, see Convention on the Prohibition of the Development, Production, Stockpiling and Use of Chemical Weapons and on their Destruction (CWC), 13 January 1993, 32 ILM 800, Article 1(5). IHL does not have a corresponding requirement of proportionate use of force obliging a belligerent to use only the amount of force strictly necessary in order to obtain a specific military advantage. Proportionality in *ius in bello* is relevant in relation to damage to civilians and civilian objects, not to the use of force as such. RCA are therefore prohibited based on the logic of IHL: civilians may not be targeted in IHL, civilians must be protected against indiscriminate weapons, while combatants must be protected against weapons that cause unnecessary or superfluous injury. The end result of this balancing may therefore sometimes be at odds with rules of human rights law.

56 *Final Record of the Diplomatic Conference of Geneva of 1949*, vol. II-B, 90.

57 Except for the rather vague general statements of AP I Article 35, and the national review mechanisms in Article. 36. The first draft proposal to the AP II during the CDDH contained a parallel proposal to prohibit the use of means and methods of a nature to cause unecessary suffering or superfluous injury, but this was also removed as part of the last compromise. See CDDH Official Records vol. VII, CDDH /SR.51, 3 June 1977, 114.

58 Conventions on Certain Conventional Weapons (CCW), *supra* note 34.

59 See CCW Article 1, referring to GC Common Article 2 and AP I Article 1(4) conflicts. Likewise, the three Protocols to CCW in 1980 on Non-Detectable Fragments (Protocol 1), on Prohibitions or Restrictions on the Use of Mines, Booby-Traps and Other Devices (Protocol 2), and Protocol on Prohibitions or Restrictions on the Use of Incendiary Weapons (Protocol 3).

60 See Convention on the Prohibition of the Development, Production and Stockpiling of Bacteriological (Biological) and Toxin Weapons and on their Destruction, 10 April 1972, 1015 UNTS 164, according to which states parties undertake '*never in any circumstances* to develop, produce or stockpile … weapons … designed to use such agents or toxins for hostile purposes or *in armed conflict*' (emphasis added). Article 1(2). The Convention was heavily inspired by a disarmament idea, see the Preamble to the Convention.

61 CWC Article 1(b).

62 See CWC Article 1(5).

63 *Legality of the Threat or Use of Nuclear Weapons* (1994–1996) ICJ Advisory Opinion of 8 July 1996, para. 78.

64 CCW Protocol on Prohibitions or Restriction on the Use of Mines, Booby-Traps and Other Devices as amended on 3 May 1996 (Am. Prot. II), entered into force 1998, 35 ILM 1209, Article 1(2). The amended Protocol also contains in Article 3 a rather wide set of rules relating to conduct of hostilities when using such weapons. These rules are applicable to 'each party to the conflict', irrespective of the type of armed conflict, see Article 1(3).

65 One notable exception is the 1976 UN Convention on the Prohibition of Military or Any Other Hostile Use of Environmental Modification Techniques, 1108 UNTS 151. The distinction still poses a significant challenge to the applicability and enforcement of IHL for environmental protection, see UN Environment Programme Report of 2009: Protecting the Environment During Armed Conlict, DEP/1191/GE, para. 2.1.

66 Notably the Declaration Renouncing the Use, in Time of War, of Explosive Projectiles under 400 Grammes Weight, St Petersburg, 29 November/11 December 1868 (St Petersburg Declaration of 1868), and Hague Convention III of 1899.

67 As pertinently observed by Kennedy: 'Military leaders outlaw weapons that they no longer need, against which defence would be too expensive or difficult, or that they feel will be potent tools only for their adversaries', D. Kennedy, *Of War and Law* (Princeton University Press, 2006) 86. For a general history of the legal regulation of weapons, see H. Parks, 'Conventional weapons and weapons review' (2005) 8 *Yearbook of International Humanitarian Law* 55.

68 For the view that most protocols to the CCW should be considered arms control agreements, see Parks, 'Conventional weapons and weapons review'.

69 See e.g., the mutual accusations in 2009 between the Taliban and US forces in Afghanistan concerning who was responsbile for the use of white phosphorous in Farah, an issue of entirely different nature than questions about the legal rights and duties of Taleban fighters on and off the battlefield, and in detention.

70 See the Second Protocol to the Hague Convention of 1954 for the Protection of Cultural Property in the Event of Armed Conflict, The Hague (1999), Article 22. The Hague Convention of 1954, however, already applied to NIAC, see Article 19(1), albeit with far fewer provisions. See also the Optional Protocol to the Convention on the Rights of the Child on the Involvement of Children in Armed Conflict (2000), with no specific qualification of the type of armed conflict. (Seemingly, the Protocol only contains one article applicable to non-state actors, i.e., armed groups that are distinct from the armed forces of a state, prohibiting them from recruiting or using persons under the age of eighteen in hostilites, see Article 4).

71 As expressed by Judge C.G. Weeramantry, retired judge with the ICJ, speaking of the irredeemably difficult situation of making states subject to treaties of a certain kind, that states may still be bound 'if you can get them caught within the network of customary international law'. See L.M.B. Chakka (ed.), *Custom as a Source of International Humanitarian Law*, Proceedings of the Conference to Mark the Publication of the ICRC Study 'Customary International Humanitarian Law' held in New Delhi, 8–9 December 2005 (New Delhi: ICRC, 2006) 49

72 The United Nations has traditionally avoided classifying armed conflicts for the purpose of IHL. In most resolutions regarding situations of violence in internal armed conflicts, UN bodies call on the parties to respect humanitarian law and human rights law, with no further qualifications. There is no need for the UN Security Council to make such classifications. And it risks becoming quite politicised. With regard to operational guidelines, the military has different needs. It may also reflect policy considerations.

73 J.-M. Henckaerts, 'Assessing the laws and customs of war: the publication of customary international humanitarian law' (2006) 13 *Human Rights Brief* 8.

74 159 rules apply to IAC, two were only applicable to NIAC. Of these 159, however, 146 were applicable irrespective of type of armed conflict. Essentially, insofar as

the conduct of hostilities is concerned, the rules are the same. The somewhat bold conclusions of the Study with regard to NIAC has earned it substantial criticism, primarily due to the perceived lack of sufficiently convincing indications in sources for extending rules of IAC into the realms of NIAC: See e.g., Parks, 'Conventional weapons and weapons review', 121 and D. Turns, 'Weapons in the ICRC Study on Customary International Humanitarian Law' (2006) 11 *Journal of Conflict and Security Law* 201 at 209–11.

75 *How is the Term 'Armed Conflict' Defined in International Humanitarian Law?*, International Committee of the Red Cross Opinion Paper (Geneva : ICRC, March 2008).

76 *Interpretive Guidance on the Notion of Direct Participation in Hostilities under International Humanitarian Law*, ICRC Interpretive Guidance (Geneva: ICRC, 2009).

77 See San Remo Manual on the Law of Non-International Armed Conflict.

78 See Program on Humanitarian Policy and Conflict Research at Harward University, *HPCR Manual on International Law Applicable to Air and Missile Warfare* (Harvard University, 2009).

79 See *Commentary on the HPCR Manual on Air and Missile Warfare*.

80 See *HPCR Manual on Air and Missile Warfare*, section 2(1), and the explanation as to why such a solution was chosen in the Commentary.

81 See also L. Zegveld, *Accountability of Armed Opposition Groups in International Law* (Cambridge University Press, 2007), 35, identifying a clear trend in diminishing the distinction in international practice, but still asserting that the distinction between these conflicts has not been abolished.

82 Byron, 'Armed conflicts: international or non-international?'; J.-M. Henckaerts, 'The conduct of hostilities: target selection, proportionality and precautionary measures under international humanitarian law' in *Protecting Civilians in 21st-Century Warfare: Target Selection, Proportionality and Precautionary Measures in Law and Practice* (The Netherlands Red Cross, 8 December 2000) 11.

83 Stewart, 'Towards a single definition'.

84 With regard to conduct of hostilities, Dieter Fleck interprets the *Targeted Killings* case of the Israeli Supreme Court sitting as the High Court of Justice as convincingly underlining that a differentiation between IAC and NIAC is not really relevant for the conduct of hostilities, see Fleck, *The Handbook of International Humanitarian Law*, para. 1201(3.c).

85 Recent fact-finding reports have taken fairly progressive approaches, see e.g., the 2009 Report of the United Nations Fact Finding Mission on the Gaza Conflict to the UNHRC, UN doc. A/HRC/12/48, the so-called 'Goldstone report', declaring that 'the substantive rules applicable to either international or non-international armed conflicts are converging'. The Fact Finding Mission nonetheless recognises that certain differences exist in relation to the regime of enforcement established by treaty law, in particular the regime of grave breaches contained in the Geneva Conventions, at 86–7. See also the Human Rights Watch report *So Much to Fear: War Crimes and Devastation of Somalia*, 8 December 2008, 27, stating that it is fairly common to assume that the international law relating to the conduct of hostilities is now recognised as largely the same whether it is applied to an international or a non-international armed conflict. See also the 2004 Report of the International Commission of Inquiry on Darfur to the UN Secretary-General (*Cassese Report*),

paras. 164–5, enumerating twenty-four rules of customary international law that the report deems to be applicable to NIAC.

86 See Stewart, 'Towards a single definition' and E. Crawford, *Unequal before the Law: the Case for the Elimination of the Distinction between International and Non-international Armed Conflicts* (Leiden, 2007).

87 D. Kretzmer, 'Symposium on Complementing IHL, exploring the need for additional norms to govern contemporary conflict situations', (2009) 42 *Israeli Law Review* 8 at 23. Others argue that the distinction should be removed for the purpose of particular aspects, see D. Willmott, 'Removing the distinction between international and non-international armed conflict in the Rome Statute of the International Criminal Court' (2004) 5 *Melbourne Journal of International Law* 196.

88 I. Detter, *The Law of War* (London: Cambridge University Press, 2002), 49.

89 The ICJ in the *Nicaragua* case found a parallel applicabiliy of rules pertaining to IAC and NIAC: 'The conflict between the contras' forces and those of the Government of Nicaragua is an armed conflict which is "not of an international character". The acts of the contras towards the Nicaraguan Government are therefore governed by the law applicable to conflicts of that character; whereas the actions of the US in and around Nicaragua fall under the rules relating to international conflict.' [1986] ICJ Reports 3 at 114, 76 ILR 1 at 448. Such a system of parallel applicability has the advantage of identifying conflict-dyads (pairs of legal parties to a conflict) and applying the correct set of rules to each pair, depending on the legal status of the parties in each pair, in certain types of messy conflicts, with various parties with varying degree of state involvement with unclear links between them, or in larger conflicts with a set of different parties; however, the complexity of such diverging conflict-dyads creates a system not conducive to the clarity and simplicity required in IHL.

90 T. Meron, 'Classification of armed conflict in the former Yugoslavia: Nicaragua's fall-out' (1998) 92 *American Journal of International Law* 238.

91 Stewart argues for the abandonment of the distinction between IAC and NIAC primarily with reference to the problems of classification and the intricate issues of internationalised armed conflict. Stewart, 'Towards a single definition,' 328; see also Byron, 'Armed conflicts: international or non-international?' and H.-P. Gasser, 'Internationalized non-international armed conflicts: case studies of Afghanistan, Kampuchea, and Lebanon' (1983) 33 *Auckland University Law Review* 145.

92 G.H. Aldrich, 'The laws of war on land' (2000) 94 *American Journal of International Law* 42, 62: 'armed conflicts in the real world do not always fit neatly into the two categories';. A. McDonald, 'The year in review' (1998) 1 *Yearbook of International Humanitarian Law* 121: '[w]ith the increase in the number of internal and internationalized armed conflicts is coming greater recognition that a strict division of conflicts into internal and international is scarcely possible, if it ever was'.

93 Crawford suggests that '[i]t is reasonable to surmise that if a uniform law had been in place, there would be no need to ascertain whether the duty arose in treaty or custom, whether the war was international, non-international or some hybrid, or whether the participants were privileged combatants or unlawful combatants. The *prima facie* approach would always be one of "does an armed conflict exist" and "have the laws of armed conflict been breached" rather than having to debate the origins, status and character of the conflict and the participants.' Crawford, *Unequal before the Law*, 464.

94 A view that can be traced back to the time of the negotiations of the Geneva Conventions. See H. Lauterpacht, *Recognition in International Law* (Cambridge, 1947) 246: 'International law ought to step in in order to fulfil the same function which it performs in wars between sovereign states, namely to humanize and regularize the conduct of hostilties as between the parties.'

95 A proposal to apply all rules of the GC to internal conflicts was raised during the negotiations of the GC IV. In the orginal Draft Convention for the Protection of War Victims Article 2(4), a 'maximalist approach' was taken that would have resulted in application of the entire GC to NIAC. See Abi-Saab, 'Non-international armed conflicts', 220. See also Y. Sandoz *et al.*, *Commentary on the Two 1977 Protocols Additional to the Geneva Conventions of 1949* (Geneva : ICRC, 1982) 1322.

96 See e.g., the delegates of Finland at CDDH/SR.18, para. 15, Sweden at CDDH/SR.14, para. 7 and Norway at CDDH/SR.10, para. 3, advocating for a removal of the distinction between IAC and NIAC. Nordic countries seemingly have had a prominent role in efforts to disregard the dichotomy. Alas being representatives, as pertinently observed by Solf, from 'stable western state[s] not bothered by incipient separatist movements'. Solf, 'Problems', 291.

97 Detter, *The Law of War*, 49.

98 See B. Simma and A. Paulus, 'The responsibility of individuals for human rights abuses in internal conflicts: a postivist view' (1999), *Symposium AJIL* 302 at 316, 303.

99 E.g. Crawford, *Unequal before the Law*.

100 A. Duxbury, 'Drawing lines in the sand: characterising conflicts for the purpose of teaching international humanitarian law' (2007) 8 *Melborne Journal of International Law* 1 at 8: 'Very few, if any, commentators would argue that there is a purely humanitarian reason for distinguishing between international and internal armed conflict for the purposes of applying rules that aim to protect the victims of armed conflict or that regulate the means and methods of warfare.'

101 Stewart, 'Towards a single definition', 344: 'A single definition of armed conflict within the confines of a uniform body of humanitarian law would … prevent political agendas from so negatively affecting humanitarian principles applicable in those contexts.'

102 F.F. Martin, 'Using international human rights law for establishing a unified use of force rule in the law of armed conflict' (2001) 64 *Saskatchewan Law Review* 347. R. Arnold and N. Quénivet (eds.), *International Humanitarian Law and Human Rights Law: Towards a New Merger in International Law* (Martinus Nijhoff Publishers, 2008).

103 See Moir, *The Law of Internal Armed Conflict*, 51: 'What will matter as regards legal regulation will not be whether an armed conflict is international or internal, but simply whether an armed conflict exists per se.'

104 Traditionally, those concerns have been based on a fear of premature recognition of belligerence, the potential for promoting internal uprisings, a real reluctance to be prevented from dealing with individuals participating in such groups under domestic law and, in some instances, an uneasiness about applying the full body of international humanitarian law to internal conflicts.

105 Crawford, *Unequal before the Law*, 463.

106 If and how non-state actors may be bound by treaty law has been debated for decades. It is beyond doubt that non-state parties to an armed conflict *are* bound by IHL, see Zegfeld, *Accountability of Armed Opposition Groups in International Law*,

and Moir, *The Law of Internal Armed Conflict*. For recent expressions to this effect, see e.g., Preamble to the 2000 Optional Protocol to the Convention on the Rights of the Child on the involvement of children in armed conflict, para. 12: 'recalling the obligation of each party to an armed conflict to abide by the provisions of international humanitarian law'.

107 A point made explicitly clear by all treaties implying applicability of IHL to non-state actors. The more extensive the duties and rights implied, the more thorough the reservations that the application of the article or treaty 'shall not influence the legal status of the parties to the conflict', see GC Article. 3(4), AP I Article 4. See also Hague Convention for the Protection of Cultural Property in the Event of Armed Conflict (1954), Article 19(4); Second Protocol to the Hague Convention for the Protection of Cultural Property in the Event of Armed Conflict (1999), Article 22(6); Optional Protocol to the Convention on the Right of the Child (2000), Article 4(3). For treaties with extended reservation clauses, see CCW Amended Protocol II (1996), Article 1(6), CCW (2001) Amended Article 1(6): 'shall not change their legal status or the legal status of a disputed territory, either explicitly or implicitly'. AP II does not have such a clause, since it contains no reference to 'parties to the conflict'. See Sandoz *et al.*, *Commentary on the Two 1977 Protocol*, para. 4439.

108 See the Preamble to AP I. For the origin of the twin terms of *ad bellum/in bello*, see R. Kolb, 'Sur l'origine du couple terminologique ius ad bellum/ius in bello' (1997) 827 *IRRC* 593. See also C. Greenwood, 'The relationship of ius ad bellum and ius in bello', (1983) 9 *Review of International Studies* 133. Bugnion ascribes the confirmation of the autonomy of *in bello* over *ad bellum* to the Nuremberg trials, see Bugnion, 'jus ad bellum, Jus in bello and non-international armed conflicts', 172. See also M. Sassòli, 'Ius ad bellum and ius in bello: the separation between the legality of the use of force and humanitarian rules to be respected in warfare: crucial or outdated?' in M. Schmitt and J. Pejić (eds.), *International Law and Armed Conflict: Exploring the Faultlines – Essays in Honour of Yoram Dinstein* (Martinus Nijhoff, 2007) 243.

109 See J. Siotis, *Le Droit de la Guerre et les conflits armes d'un caractere non international* (Paris: Libr. générale de droit et de jurisprudence, 1958) 24 for the period of the League of Nations, and E. Castren, *Civil War* (Helsinki: Suomalainen Tiedeakatemia, Helsinki, 1966) 19 for the period of the United Nations. See also Sandoz *et al.*, *Commentary on the Two 1977 Protocols*, para. 4354. Intimately linked with the very nature of NIAC. International law presumes that states have a monopoly on the use of force on their own territory. Resort to the use of force by non-state actors within the borders of a state is not regulated by international law, but is normally prohibited in domestic law.

110 In fact, several subsequent developments have brought this issue into question. The strengthening of the human rights regime, circumvention of the principle of non-intervention through practice in the UN Security Council since 1990 relating to NIACs constituting a 'threat to international peace and security', questions about humanitarian intervention more generally, and the conclusion following 2001 that an armed attack by a non-state actor constituted an (unlawful) armed attack in international law that triggered the right to self-defence, are all indications that a corollary *ius ad bellum* proper to (specific kinds of transborder) NIACs may be crystallising in international law. *Ius ad bellum strictu sensu*, however, is

still perceived as a set of rules that exclusively regulate the relationship between states, and to the extent that a NIAC may come under *ius ad bellum*, it is because it affects international relations (i.e., international borders) in such a way that it may give rise to the right to self-defence under UN Charter Article 51. See e.g., Y. Dinstein, *War, Aggression and Self-Defence* (4th edn., Cambridge University Press, 2005) 206.

111 See e.g., Greenwood, 'The relationship of *ius ad bellum* and *ius in bello*'; E. Benvenisti, 'Rethinking the divide between *jus ad bellum* and *jus in bello* in warfare against non-state actors' (2009) 34 *Yale Journal of Intl, L* (2009) 541 at 542; R.D. Sloane, 'Cost of conflation: preserving the dualism of *jus ad bellum* and *jus in bello* in the contemporary law of war' (2009) 24 *Yale Journal of Intl, L* 47; T. Franck, 'On proportionality of countermeasures in international law', (2008) 102 *AJIL* 715 at 723–4.

112 Pictet, *Development and Principles of International Humanitarian Law,* 14–15; Bugnion, '*jus ad bellum, jus in bello* and non-international armed conflicts', 172.

113 The prohition in domestic law of the resort to use of force by non-state actors does not only have consequences for the question of status of rebels, it also destroys the basic structure of protected persons (civilians of enemy nationality) see GC IV Article 4. In NIAC, civilians normally do not have different nationality. Nor may they be identified through allegiance with the enemy ('enemy civilians'), because if such allegiance is to a non-state party, it will in itself constitute a crime under domestic law.

114 For attempts to propose a common set of elements for IAC and NIAC, see Bugnion, '*jus ad bellum, jus in bello* and non-international armed conflicts'. This may explain why certain advocates of a unified law commonly point to the irrelevance of the distinction between *ad bellum* and *in bello*. See e.g., Martin, 'Using international human rights law' or Benvenisti, 'Rethinking the divide between *jus ad bellum* and *jus in bello*'.

115 See Pictet, *Commentary on GC I,* 32: 'It makes no difference how long the conflict lasts, or how much slaughter takes place'. See Richard Baxter, 'The duties of combatants and the conduct of hostilities (law of the Hague)' in *International Dimensions of Humanitarian Law (*Paris/Geneva/Dordrecht/Boston/London, Henry Dunant Institute, UNESCO, Martinus Nijhoff, 1988) 93–135 at 98: 'The proper view would seem to be that "any other armed conflict which may arise between two or more of the High Contracting Parties" should be taken as referring to any outbreak of violence between the armed forces of two states, regardless of the geographical extent and intensity of the force employed'. This has also been reafirmed in the jurisprudence of the ICTY, see *Prosecutor* v. *Mucic et al.*, (Case No. IT-96–21-T), ICTY, Judgment, 16 November 1998, paras. 184, 208. See also the Commentary to the 1998 Rome Statute, where Fenrick argues that 'the firing of weapons by soldiers of opposing sides across a contested border on the uninvited intervention of the armed forces of one State, even in small numbers, in the territory of another State may trigger the application of the Geneva Conventions in totality'. M. Cottier, W.J. Fenrick, P. Viseur Sellers and A. Zimmermann, 'Article 8, War Crimes' in O. Triffterer (ed.), *Commentary on the Rome Statute of the International Criminal Court, Observers Notes, Article by Article* (Baden-Baden: Nomos, 1999) 182. See also *Commentary on the HPCR Manual on Air and Missile Warfare*, section 2(r): '"international armed conflict" is wider, and includes not only "wars" (whether or

not declared), but also situations "short of war". What counts is that two or more States are engaged in hostilities with each other'. For certain contrary state-practice see ILA Committee on Use of Force Initial Report 2008 and references to the 'Red Crusader Incident' (Great Britain and Denmark, International Commission of Inquiry, 1961) and the Cod Wars (Great Britain and Iceland, 1970s), see also A.M. Weisburd, *Use of Force: The Practice of States Since World War II* (University Park, PA: Pennsylvania State University Press, 1997) referring to numerous incidents of 'limited use of force' between states that were not treated as armed conflicts.

116 There is an increasing tendency to refer to all armed conflicts between states as IAC, and all other armed conflicts as NIAC, see e.g., *HPCR Manual on Air and Missile Warfare*, sections 1(r) and 2(1).

117 ILA Committee on Use of Force Initial Report 2008 at 11–12 takes the view that '[a]s the IHL rules on international and non-international armed conflict converge, the argument for a distinction between the intensity level required for international versus non-international armed conflict will presumably lose its purpose. Indeed, as the cases show, making a meaningful distinction between the two types of conflicts is increasingly difficult. The distinction that appears to remain important is between armed conflict – of whatever type – and peace'.

118 See Pictet, *Commentary on GC III*, 23.

119 AP II Article 1(2) and 1998 Rome Statute Article 8(2)d).The question of a NIAC taking place outside of the territory of the state party to the conflict may come in a different position with respect to threshold.

120 Stewart, 'Towards a single definition', 345.

121 Baxter, observing that 'much of the Geneva Conventions simply cannot be applied in civil conflicts because their operation turns on notions of belligerent occupation of territory and enemy nationality, concepts that are alien to civil conflicts'. R. Baxter, 'Comments' in P. Trooboff (ed.), *Law and Responsibility in Warfare: The Vietnam Experience* (Chapel Hill:, University of North Carolina, under the auspices of ASIL, 1975). See also Bugnion, '*Jus ad bellum, jus in bello* and non-international armed conflicts', 182.

122 Schindler noting that occupied territory does not have a correlate in NIAC: Schindler, 'International humanitarian law', 173. Although Crawford also concedes that there are several other barriers to a unified law of armed conflict: in addition to status and the issue of occupied territory, she also mentions the question of belligerent reprisals.

123 *Tadić* case, ICTY. See also Benvenisti, 'Rethinking the divide between *jus ad bellum* and *jus in bello*', 542, IAC–NIAC as 'muted' by the recognition that both IHL and human rights law are relevant to both types.

124 R. Mullerson, 'International humanitarian law in internal conflicts' (1997) 2 *Journal of Armed Conflict* 109, at 122.

125 See AP I Article 43.

126 See e.g., AP I Article 51(2).

127 AP I Article 51(3): persons lose their target immunity 'for such time as' they take a direct part in hostilities.

128 For an early identification of the three categories, see Institut du Droit International, in its commentary to the Brussels Declaration: Session de La Haye (1875), IDI Examen de la Déclaration de Bruxelles de 1874 (Rapporteur: M. Gustave Rolin-Jaequemyns) (reproduced at www.idi-iil.org/idiF/resolutionsF/1875_haye_02_fr.pdf). During

the Diplomatic Conference leading to the Geneva Conventions the issue of partisans were discussed. The issue of guerrilla fighters was much debated during the CDDH, while terrorists have been the centre of attention over the past two decades. From an IHL perspective, all fall into the category of irregulars, if and when IHL is applicable. They lose immunity against direct attack when directly participating in hostilites (AP I Article 51(3)), and are not bestowed with the priviledge of prosecutorial immunity for lawful acts of war upon capture by the enemy, given to 'combatants'.

129 'Members of the armed forces of a Party to the conflict … are combatants', AP I Article 43(2). The definition of (civilian) is distinguishned from combatant, see AP I Article 50(1).

130 See Crawford, *Unequal before the Law,* in particular 459 ff.

131 N. Melzer, *Interpretive Guidance on the Notion of Direct Participation in Hostilites under International Humanitarian Law* (Geneva: ICRC, May 2009). The ICRC take the approach that there is a structure in NIAC parallel to that in IAC. State armed forces and the 'organized armed groups of a party to the conflict' – persons with continuous combat function – constitute the corollary of combatants in NIAC, who may be targeted for as long as they retain their combat function, see at 27–36. Everyone else, the corollary civilians, retain target immunity, which they may lose only 'for as long as' they participate in hostilities, see at 70–3.

132 See GC III Article 4(2) and AP I Article 44(1).

133 Accordingly, a belligerent state capturing an enemy combatant who has caused the death of some of its own citizens (combatants or civilians), is prevented from honouring its obligations according to human rights treaties and domestic law to guarantee the right to life of its dead citizens through investigation and prosecution of the perpetrator, provided that the combatant was acting in accordance with IHL.

134 See Crawford, *Unequal before the Law,* in particular 459 ff. Schindler discusses the impracticality of a uniform code without consideration of the POW situation, Schindler, 'International Humanitarian Law' 173.

135 Recognition of belligerency by the government of a state in which a NIAC is taking place, with the effect of making the laws and customs of war applicable between the government and its adversaries, on the one hand, must not be conflated with the recognition of belligerency by the government of *another state*, with the effect of making the law of neutrality applicable between that state and the parties involved in the civil war. Recognition by a state of belligerency would make the rules of IAC apply to the civil war, while third party recognition of belligerency entailed application of the laws of neutrality.

136 It was last formally recognised during the Boer War of 1902. H.-P. Gasser, 'International humanitarian law' in H. Haug (ed.), *Humanity for All: The International Red Cross and Red Crescent Movement* (Henry Dunant Institute and Paul Haupt Publishers, 1993) 559.

137 The rules of neutrality have been put under strain by the increased tendency that one party to armed conflicts operate under UN Security Council mandates, in which case the role of the law of neutrality becomes highly dubious. Another issue is the development of the *erga omnes* obligation to ensure compliance with IHL, obliging neutral states to be vigilant and to take actions. See Benvenisti, 'Rethinking the divide between *jus ad bellum and jus in bello*', 542.

138 See 'Draft Convention on Rights and Duties of Neutral States in Naval and Aerial War' (P.C. Jessup, reporter) (1939) 33 *AJIL Sp Supp* 167, at 176, Article 4.5. See also W. Heintschel von Heinegg, '"Benevolent" third states in international armed conflicts: the myth of the irrelevance of the law of neutrality' in M. Schmitt and J. Pejić (eds.), *International Law and Armed Conflict: Exploring the Faultlines* (Martin Nijhoff Publishers, 2007) 543–69.

139 One example may be strain under which the rules of NIAC has come following 9/11 and the 'war on terrorism', or 'contingency operations'. There is also reason to be vigilant about the impact it may have on IAC, such as the decision by the United States to label a part of the Iranian special forces, Pasdaran, as a terrorist organisation in 2007. Despite ideological and political functions, the Pasdaran constitute a part of the Iranian armed forces. This labelling happened in a period when there were heightened risks for encounters between Iranian soldiers (Pasdaran) and US soldiers on Iraqi soil.

140 C. Greenwood, 'Scope of application of humanitarian law' in D. Fleck, *The Handbook of Humanitarian Law in Armed Conflicts* (1st ed, Oxford University Press, 1995) 39.

5

A 'principle of humanity' or a 'principle of human-rightism'?

KJETIL MUJEZINOVIĆ LARSEN

1. Introduction

The present chapter makes an inquiry into the relationship between international humanitarian law (IHL) and international human rights law (HRL) with a view (i) to examine the current impact of the latter regime on the conduct of hostilities, and (ii) to discuss the relevance of that impact for the existence and/or status of a 'principle of humanity' in IHL. This inquiry can best be introduced by describing two important premises for the discussion.

First, in Chapter 3, Yoram Dinstein has argued forcefully that there exists no 'principle of humanity' in international humanitarian law, if one, by this term, refers to a *legal norm* of humanity. There 'is no overarching, binding, norm of humanity that tells us what we must do (or not do) in wartime', as he puts it.[1] He speaks instead, both in this volume and in other works,[2] of *humanitarian considerations*, which can have legal effects only through their impact on the creation of binding, positive norms. In this norm-creation process, humanitarian considerations must be weighed against the demands of military necessity. Every single norm of IHL represents a compromise between these considerations.[3] This is the first premise for the discussion.

Secondly, a wide consensus has emerged in recent years, both in practice and in legal doctrine, that HRL in principle remains applicable during (international and non-international) armed conflicts, and hence matters may arise that are governed both by HRL and by IHL. This is the second premise for the discussion.

These two premises lead to the following inquiry, which in an abbreviated form describes the key issue in the present chapter: To what extent does HRL impact on the conduct of hostilities to such an extent that one can say that IHL must now nevertheless be interpreted in light of a set of purely humanitarian norms, i.e., norms that do *not* represent a compromise between humanitarian considerations and demands of military necessity? If a 'principle of humanity' were to exist as an independent, legally binding norm in IHL, its primary impact would presumably have been to entail a general obligation for combatants to act in a humane manner, so that a conduct which complies with a positive norm under IHL could still be considered unlawful on grounds of being 'inhumane'. The present chapter inquires whether HRL now has a comparable legal impact on the conduct of hostilities. If this question is answered in the affirmative, one may inquire whether in practice it is largely irrelevant whether a 'principle of humanity' exists or not in IHL, since a similar effect in any case follows from the application of HRL. Or one may, alternatively, inquire instead as to whether the impact of HRL on the conduct of hostilities suggests that a 'principle of humanity' is *emerging* as a legal norm in IHL, perhaps in the form of a 'principle of human-rightism',[4] if one prefers.

This chapter addresses these issues primarily through an analysis of the case law from the European Court of Human Rights[5] in cases concerning alleged human rights violations during armed conflicts. The single perhaps most important issue in the Court's case law in this regard concerns incidental civilian casualties,[6] and this is therefore the focus of the study. Other issues will be discussed to the extent that the scope of the study so permits.

The inquiry will be conducted in two steps. First, the study examines the impact of IHL on the Court's considerations (section 2 below): To what extent *can* or *does* the Court take IHL into consideration? Although the section considers the impact of IHL in general, a particular inquiry is whether there can be found traces of a 'principle of humanity' in the Court's case law. The study thereafter considers (in section 3 below) what impact, if any, the Court's considerations in return have on IHL, on the conduct of hostilities, and on the development of a 'principle of humanity'. Section 4 provides necessary conclusions.

2. Impact of IHL on human rights law: the case law of the European Court of Human Rights

2.1 Jurisdiction of the ECtHR to take IHL into consideration

It is common knowledge that international human rights bodies, including the ECtHR, with increasing frequency are called upon to consider allegations of human rights violations during situations of armed conflict. In such cases, the bodies must – voluntarily or not, explicitly or not, consciously or not – consider how the applicability of IHL influences the interpretation of the human rights treaty in general, and on specific human rights norms in particular. This challenge is not new,[7] but it remains controversial as to how tribunals should respond to this challenge. These issues are discussed at some length in the following, and the reason for this is that one may argue that the impact of HRL on the conduct of hostilities may be influenced partly by the legitimacy of the Court to make proclamations about IHL.

The first issue is to what extent the ECtHR (and other human rights bodies) has *jurisdiction* – or even an *obligation* – to apply IHL or to take this legal regime into consideration. IHL represents external rules in relation to human rights treaties. The clear starting point is that the Court is vested with the jurisdiction to supervise the Contracting States' compliance with the European Convention on Human Rights,[8] and not their compliance with other rules under international law.[9] Nevertheless, in exercising its jurisdiction, the Court must of course interpret the ECHR, and the relevant question at present is to what extent a tribunal can (or must) interpret the provisions of a human rights treaty in light of other rules of international law, including IHL.[10] When faced with the same challenge, the Inter-American Court of Human Rights has described its competence in a manner which is illustrative also for the competence of other human rights bodies such as the ECtHR. In the *Las Palmeras* case, the Court described how it is competent 'to determine whether any norm of domestic or international law applied by a state, in times of peace or armed conflict, is compatible or not with the American Convention', and that:

> [i]n order to carry out this examination, the Court interprets the norm in question and analyzes it in the light of the provisions of the Convention. The result of this operation will always be an opinion in which the Court will say whether or not that norm or that fact is compatible with the American Convention. The latter has only given the Court competence to determine whether the acts or the norms of the states are compatible with the Convention itself, and not with the 1949 Geneva Conventions.[11]

Along the same lines, the ECtHR cannot 'apply' IHL if this term is intended to refer to the competence of the Court to consider a state's compliance with norms under IHL. Nevertheless, there exist several mechanisms that allow the Court to take external rules, including IHL, into consideration. First, Article 15(2) ECHR states that no derogation is permitted from Article 2 on the right to life except 'in respect of deaths resulting from lawful acts of war', and this is commonly understood as an *explicit* reference to IHL; whether this requirement is met can only be decided by interpreting IHL.[12] Secondly, the general derogation clause in Article 15(1) contains an *implicit* reference to IHL, as it requires that a derogation measure must not be inconsistent with the state's other obligations under international law, such as IHL.[13] The ECtHR can therefore apply IHL in order to consider the validity of a derogation measure. Thirdly, an implicit reference to IHL is also found in Article 7 concerning the principle of legality in criminal law, which prohibits the criminalisation of acts or omissions which at the time of commission or omission did not constitute a criminal offence 'under national or international law'. This allows the Court to consider whether a particular conduct violates IHL.[14] Fourthly, Article 53 ECHR[15] contains a so-called 'consistency clause' (or 'highest standard of protection' clause, if one prefers), whereby Contracting States are prevented from restricting human rights that are guaranteed by international agreements to which the state is a party on the pretext that the state is not required by the ECHR to protect these rights or that the rights in question are ensured to a lesser extent.[16] Consequently, if IHL offers a higher degree of protection to an individual than human rights, the Contracting State cannot limit that protection to the lower standard required by the ECHR, and the Court may therefore be required to interpret IHL to determine the relevant levels of protection. And *finally*, the Court can apply external rules even in the absence of any explicit or implicit references thereto in the Convention; Article 31(3)(c) of the Vienna Convention on the Law of Treaties provides that 'any relevant rules of international law applicable in the relations between the parties' can be taken into consideration when interpreting a treaty.[17] In the *Demir and Baykara* case, which concerned the right to form trade unions and enter into collective agreements, the Court discussed at length its practice of interpreting Convention provisions in light of other international texts and instruments, and some (if not all) of the statements there are relevant also for the specific issue of how to apply IHL. The Court reiterated the general principle that the Convention must be interpreted and applied in a manner which renders its rights practical and effective, not theoretical and illusory, since 'the Convention is first and foremost a system for the protection of human rights', as the Court put it.[18] The Court went on to hold, inter alia, that it 'has never considered the provisions of the Convention as the sole framework of reference for the interpretation of the rights and freedoms enshrined therein. On the contrary, it must also take into account any relevant rules and principles of international law applicable in relations between the Contracting Parties.'[19] More specifically, the Court considered that the 'precise obligations that the substantive provisions of the Convention impose on Contracting States may be interpreted, firstly, in the light of relevant international treaties that are applicable in the particular sphere',[20] or in light of 'general principles of law recognized by civilized nations'.[21] Further, of particular importance for IHL, the Court described how it has taken 'into consideration the principles laid down by *texts of universal scope* in developing its case-law'.[22] But the Court does not confine itself to taking into consideration those rules that are binding for the respondent state in a particular case. When the Court 'considers the object and purpose of the Convention provisions, it also takes into account the international law background to the legal question before it', since 'the common international or domestic law standards of European States reflect a reality that the Court cannot disregard'.[23] Further, when 'searching for common ground among the norms of international law [the Court] has never distinguished between sources of law *according to whether or not they have been signed or ratified* by the respondent state'.[24] The Court's concluding remark was that:

> in defining the meaning of terms and notions in the text of the Convention, [the Court] can and must take into account elements of international law other than the Convention, the interpretation of such elements by competent organs, and the practice of European States reflecting their common values. The consensus emerging from specialised international instruments and from the practice of Contracting States may constitute a relevant consideration for the Court when it interprets the provisions of the Convention in specific cases.
>
> In this context, it is not necessary for the respondent state to have ratified the entire collection of instruments that are applicable in respect of the precise subject matter of the case concerned. It will be sufficient for the Court that the relevant international instruments denote a continuous evolution in the norms and principles applied in international law or in the domestic law of the majority of member states of the Council of Europe and show, in a precise area, that there is common ground in modern societies.[25]

When applied to the specific situation of IHL, these principles have some noteworthy implications. One implication is that the Court may consider itself competent to take into consideration the Additional Protocols to the Geneva Conventions, even if the respondent state has not ratified these. As we will see, however, when the Court applies IHL, it ordinarily does so in quite a subtle manner, by adopting terminology and standards from IHL when interpreting provisions in the human rights conventions, without necessarily making it explicit that this is being done. The Court has never given a similarly detailed explanation about the application of external rules for the specific situation of IHL, but in the *Varnava* case, the Court held along the same lines that 'Article 2 must be interpreted in so far as possible in light of the general principles of international law, *including the rules of international humanitarian law* which play an indispensable and universally-accepted role in mitigating the savagery and inhumanity of armed conflict'.[26]

2.2 *Relevance for the ECtHR of the general theories on the relationship between IHL and HRL*

The second issue is how the Court *should* interpret the ECHR in a case relating to an armed conflict, i.e., where IHL is applicable. Which position is taken on this issue may depend, inter alia, on how concerned one is about the so-called fragmentation of international law.[27] Those who are concerned about this development will presumably consider that the Court should apply IHL in a manner which is consistent with norms and principles under general international law concerning the relationship between IHL and HRL, while those who are less concerned about the 'fragmentation' are presumably more ready to accept that the Court develops its own *sui generis* approach to the relationship between these two regimes. Without pursuing this matter further, the former of these two positions touches upon a more important concern, namely the fact that there exists no universally accepted theory about the relationship between IHL and HRL, and that the Court in any case would be unable to apply an 'objectively correct' theory. At least four different theories can be identified.[28] First, it is well known that the International Court of Justice in the *Wall* case held that if a matter is covered by both IHL and HRL, 'the Court will have to take into consideration both these branches of international law, namely human rights law and, as *lex specialis*, international humanitarian law'.[29] This does not mean that IHL is *lex specialis* in the sense that HRL is rendered inapplicable altogether, but rather that a particular norm of IHL may be considered *lex specialis* to a particular norm of HRL.[30] Secondly, an alternative approach is offered by the *complementarity* theory, which holds that the two regimes do not contradict each other, but rather that they are based on the same principles and values, and therefore complement and mutually reinforce each other.[31] There are two aspects in particular where this theory of complementarity is advocated: one, with regard to the possibility for HRL to fill gaps in IHL; and two, the potential for HRL to provide mechanisms for the implementation of specific IHL norms.[32] Thirdly, a variety of the complementarity theory is what can be described as 'the most favourable protection of victims' theory. This theory is teleological in its nature, as it accentuates one particular value as the key consideration: when there is a conflict between norms under IHL and HRL, the norm which provides better protection of individuals shall prevail.[33] The theory has been criticised for not taking the reality of a conflict environment sufficiently into consideration,[34] and for making it necessary to establish which regime actually provides the better outcome, something which can be difficult to determine.[35] And fourthly, some commentators advocate a pure *human rights-based* theory. While there exist different varieties of this theory, a common core is that HRL should be applied in full during armed conflicts and that combat operations accordingly must comply in full with HRL. While advocates of this theory often appear to acknowledge that the theory is *lex ferenda* only,[36] it is worth noting in the present context that Abresch has argued that 'unified rules for the use of lethal force' (meaning that the use of force against combatants and against non-combatants is assessed by the same standards) are emerging as the approach of the ECtHR in non-international armed conflicts, and thus represent the *lex lata* in that context.[37]

2.3 Application of IHL when the respondent state does not recognise its applicability

One final point to be made is that it is often difficult for the Court to determine the applicability of IHL. This is partly because it is difficult in itself to determine whether an armed conflict exists, and subsequently to qualify the conflict as international or non-international, and partly because the respondent state often will not acknowledge the existence of an armed conflict. To what extent should the Court take IHL into consideration if the respondent state does not recognise the applicability of the legal regime? This question is particularly accentuated in situations where HRL provides a higher level of protection for the individuals concerned than IHL does. As Hampson has pointed out, IHL 'is, or is not, applicable as a matter of law, and not because a state recognizes its applicability',[38] and the lack of recognition by the respondent state of the applicability of IHL is therefore arguably irrelevant. Nevertheless, the Court stated in the so-called *Isayeva II* case that in the absence of a derogation or of a declaration of a state of emergency, the 'operation in question … has to be judged against a normal legal background',[39] which implies that in the view of the Court, IHL is relevant for the Court's assessment only if the respondent state recognises its applicability through making a derogation. This position does not correspond well to the general rule in IHL that it is the factual circumstances that define the existence and the qualification of an armed conflict.

2.4 *Norms concerning incidental civilian casualties in IHL*

In order to discuss the impact of IHL on HRL, or *vice versa*, one must have a clear understanding of what the IHL rules in fact are. It is therefore necessary at this stage to provide a short summary of the norms concerning incidental civilian casualties, also referred to as 'collateral damage', since this will form the basis for the subsequent analysis. Since any IHL textbook will describe these norms more extensively, however, an in-depth presentation is unnecessary here.[40]

First, the attack in question must be directed at a legitimate military objective and satisfy the principle of distinction. Direct and deliberate attacks against civilians are prohibited, as are indiscriminate attacks.[41] Military operations which fail to comply with these fundamental rules fall outside the scope of this study, as they do not create *incidental* civilian casualties.

Secondly, even if the attack satisfies these requirements, the principle of proportionality must be respected. An attack is prohibited as indiscriminate if it may be expected to cause incidental loss of civilian life or other civilian damage which 'would be excessive in relation to the concrete and military advantage anticipated'.[42] Two terms should be highlighted here, namely (i) that only 'excessive' civilian casualties are unacceptable,[43] and (ii) that the relevant factors in the comparison are the *expected* civilian damage and the *anticipated* military advantage.[44]

And thirdly, to ensure that civilians and civilian objects are spared, certain precautionary measures must be taken with respect to the attack. Particularly important at present is the obligation to 'take all feasible precautions in the choice of means and methods of attack with a view to avoiding, and in any event to minimizing, incidental loss of civilian life, injury to civilians and damage to civilian objects'.[45]

2.5 *ECtHR case law on incidental civilian casualties*

The ECtHR has considered a number of cases concerning events that took place during situations which objectively could be characterised as armed conflicts, and several of these cases concern military operations which have resulted in incidental civilian casualties.[46] A common feature in these cases is that the Court never expressly applies IHL in order to replace or qualify the provisions in the ECHR, but IHL is occasionally used – implicitly rather than explicitly – as an interpretative factor when considering the obligations of the respondent state.

Nonetheless, for the purposes of the present book, a necessary starting point is this: the Court has never expressly referred to a 'principle of humanity' in any form. The Martens Clause, which often is considered to reflect such a principle,[47] appears to be referred to only once, in a dissenting opinion in the Chamber judgment in the *Kononov* case.[48] In this writer's opinion, it is also impossible to identify situations where such a principle can realistically be said to have had any implicit, independent legal impact on the Court's considerations. On the contrary, at least one case implies that a 'principle of humanity' does not exist within the framework of the ECHR: the case of *Akpınar and Altun* v. *Turkey* concerned the killing of two individuals in a military operation in 1999, where both victims had their ears cut off after their death. The mutilation of dead bodies is prohibited under IHL, in both international and non-international armed conflicts,[49] and this prohibition is clearly based solely on humanitarian considerations. The Court, however, considered (in para. 82) that the events were not covered by Article 3 ECHR (which prohibits torture and inhuman or degrading punishment or treatment) with regard to the victims:[50]

> Nevertheless, the Court has never applied Article 3 of the Convention in the context of disrespect for a dead body. The present Chamber concurs with this approach, finding that the human quality is extinguished on death and, therefore, the prohibition on ill-treatment is no longer applicable to corpses ... despite the cruelty of the acts concerned.

The Court's formal argument that the human rights protection of an individual ceases at the time of death, suggests that the provisions in the Convention are not supplemented by any independent notions of 'humanity' beyond the framework of the Convention itself.

The present section will therefore not focus on the use of a 'principle of humanity' in the Court's case law, but instead address more generally the impact of IHL on the Court's considerations.

The first case before the Court where the issue of incidental civilian casualties was addressed, *Ergi* v. *Turkey*,[51] concerned an ambush operation by military forces directed against PKK members in the village of Kesentaş, where a civilian woman was killed while standing on her own veranda.

Beyond this, the facts of the case were disputed. The applicant submitted that the security forces had opened fire that 'lasted for about one hour and consisted of indiscriminate bombardment of civilian houses',[52] while the government submitted that the security forces had not been in the area from which the fatal shot must have been fired (thus implying that the shot was fired by the PKK), and that 'only a few houses were slightly damaged, which does not support the allegations of prolonged, indiscriminate firing'.[53] The Court held that there was 'an insufficient factual and evidentiary basis on which to conclude that the applicant's sister was, beyond reasonable doubt, intentionally killed by the security forces',[54] and could therefore not consider whether an intentional deprivation of life in violation of Article 2 ECHR had occurred. Instead, the Court considered the case from the perspective of the state's obligation to 'secure' the right to life of individuals, i.e., the so-called *positive* obligation under Article 2. This allowed the Court to review the planning and conduct of the operation despite the factual uncertainties, and the Court held that:

> the responsibility of the state is not confined to circumstances where there is significant evidence that misdirected fire from agents of the state has killed a civilian. It may also be engaged where they fail to take all feasible precautions in the choice of means and methods of a security operation mounted against an opposing group with a view to avoiding and, in any event, to minimising, incidental loss of civilian life.[55]

More specifically, the Court inquired 'whether the security forces' operation had been planned and conducted in such a way as to avoid or minimise, to the greatest extent possible, any risk to the lives of the villagers, including from the fire-power of the PKK members caught in the ambush'.[56] In assessing this issue, the Court held that the operation had been conducted in a manner which placed the villagers at considerable risk of being caught in cross-fire, and that even 'if it might be assumed that the security forces would have responded with due care for the civilian population in returning fire against terrorists caught in the approaches to the village, it could not be assumed that the terrorists would have responded with such restraint'.[57] The Court continued to conclude that 'insufficient precautions had been taken to protect the lives of the civilian population'.[58]

It has been argued that the Court in this case 'resorted directly to international humanitarian law',[59] but other commentators disagree.[60] It is clear, however, that the Court formulated a standard of precaution which is almost identical to that found in Article 57(2)(a)(ii) of Additional Protocol I to the Geneva Conventions, which places an obligation on those who plan or decide upon an attack to 'take all feasible precautions in the choice of means and methods of attack with a view to avoiding, and in any event to minimizing, incidental loss of civilian life, injury to civilians and damage to civilian objects'.[61] While this provision in itself clearly was inapplicable *de jure* in the case, since Additional Protocol I applies to international armed conflicts only,[62] an identical standard is considered applicable in non-international armed conflicts as customary international law.[63] It is also worth noting that the *Ergi* case represents the first time for the Court to apply this standard, and thus the standard was clearly not based on previous case law. There is therefore no reason to doubt that the Court incorporated the IHL standard, but it did so by adapting it to the human rights paradigm. The Court makes no direct reference to IHL, and it is clear that the Court both in principle and in reality considered the case under Article 2 ECHR. In this writer's opinion, it is most appropriate to say that the Court took IHL into consideration when interpreting and applying Article 2 ECHR in the specific legal and factual context, rather than to say that the Court 'resorted directly' to IHL. This may, however, be a question of semantics rather than of content.

The next relevant case is the *Özkan* case, which concerned events in 1993 in the Şırnak province in south-east Turkey.[64] Among the events complained of was an attack by security forces which led to the death of two children and the detention of many male villagers, along with the burning of several houses in the village. The government claimed that the forces had come under fire from the village while being out on a search mission. The Court reiterated the general principles from the *Ergi* case, including the standard of precaution, and continued to accept as fact that shots had been fired at the forces who had then returned fire.[65] This led the Court to conclude that this 'tactical reaction to the initial shots fired at them' was compatible with Article 2 ECHR, since it could not be regarded as 'entailing a disproportionate degree of force' and that it was 'absolutely necessary' for the purpose of protecting life.[66]

The Court nevertheless found a violation of Article 2 to have occurred. The Court considered that once the security forces had taken control of the village and had assembled its entire population, they had failed to make any attempt to verify whether there were any civilian casualties, which was a realistic possibility under the circumstances. Thus, the Court held 'that the callous disregard displayed by the security forces as to the possible presence of civilian casualties amounted to a breach of the Turkish authorities' obligation to protect life under Article 2 of the Convention'.[67] The result of this judgment is that even if incidental civilian casualties could be justified under Article 2, the state has an obligation to search for possible casualties and to provide necessary medical assistance to injured civilians after the cessation of the attack. IHL also sets forth an obligation to search for killed and wounded civilians,[68] but this obligation appears not to have had any independent influence on the Court's considerations.

Two famous cases from Chechnya, the so-called *Isayeva I* and *Isayeva II* cases,[69] also concern incidental civilian casualties during military operations, namely during the hostilities that took place in the autumn of 1999 between federal military forces and Chechen fighters. The factual background to the *Isayeva I* case was the bombing of a civilian convoy near Grozny, where sixteen civilians were killed and eleven injured. The convoy consisted of civilians who were leaving Grozny, but Russian authorities claimed that the convoy also included trucks with Chechen rebel fighters and that these had been the target of the attack. The *Isayeva II* case concerned the bombardment of the village Katyr-Yurt, where the applicant's son and three nieces were killed. The government alleged that the village had been taken over by rebel Chechen fighters. Both cases concerned the application of Article 2 ECHR, and it is useful at this point to take a closer look at the Court's description of the general principles concerning the interpretation of this provision.

According to the Court, it is clear that Article 2 'covers not only intentional killing but also the situations where it is permitted to "use force" which may result, as an unintended outcome, in the deprivation of life'.[70] This obviously includes incidental civilian casualties during military operations. A starting point, even during such operations, is that the use of force must be 'absolutely necessary' for the achievement of one or more of the purposes set out in Article 2(2)(a)–(c), which means that 'the force used must be strictly proportionate to the achievement of the permitted aims'.[71] Article 2 is also considered to be of such an importance that the Court must 'subject deprivations of life to the most careful scrutiny, taking into consideration not only the actions of state agents but also all the surrounding circumstances'.[72] Two different standards in this regard are recalled by the Court.

The first is, 'whether the operation was planned and controlled by the authorities so as to minimise, to the greatest extent possible, recourse to lethal force. The authorities must take appropriate care to ensure that any risk to life is minimised. The Court must also examine whether the authorities were not negligent in their choice of action.'[73]

And second is, that 'the state's responsibility is not confined to circumstances where there is significant evidence that misdirected fire from agents of the state has killed a civilian. It may also be engaged where they fail to take all feasible precautions in the choice of means and methods of a security operation mounted against an opposing group with a view to avoiding and, in any event, minimising, incidental loss of civilian life.'[74]

Both standards are applicable to military operations, and both have obvious counterparts in IHL.[75] Nevertheless, the relationship between them is not entirely clear. They are clearly similar, but inquisitive minds may certainly ask whether standards of 'appropriate care' and 'not negligent' in fact are entirely identical to a standard of 'all feasible precautions'. If the standards are considered identical, a question arises as to why the Court distinguishes between them in *Isayeva II*. If taken literally, the first standard pertains to situations where it is established that it was the acts of state agents that caused the civilian damage, while the second standard pertains to situations where it is unclear if the damage was caused by state agents.

But in these specific cases, *Isayeva I* and *Isayeva II*, the Court once again avoided any direct reference to the rules and principles under IHL concerning civilian casualties.[76] Instead, the Court considered the operations in light of the law enforcement paradigm[77] and assessed the operations in relation to Article 2(2)(a) ECHR, which legitimises use of force that is absolutely necessary 'in defence of any person from unlawful violence'.[78] In doing so, the Court did *not* refer to the standard of precaution from the *Ergi* case, but instead to the first standard cited above, namely 'whether the operation was planned and conducted in such a way as to minimise, to the greatest extent possible, harm to civilians, *as is required by Article 2 of the Convention*'.[79] This reference to Article 2 clarifies, at least from a formal point of view, that the Court applies ordinary human rights standards and not IHL. It is nevertheless worth noting that the Court elsewhere refers to 'the conflict in Chechnya'[80] which 'called for exceptional measures on behalf of the state in order to regain control over the Republic and to suppress the illegal armed insurgency. These measures could presumably include employment of military aviation equipped with heavy combat weapons.'[81] The Court also refers to the 'military operation' in both cases,[82] and criticises the Russian failure to provide information concerning measures taken to assess and prevent 'possible harm to the civilians who might have been present on the road or elsewhere in the vicinity of what the military could have perceived as legitimate targets'.[83] This vocabulary is a clear indication of the Court's recognition of the armed conflict and of the military character of the operations in question, despite its assertion that the operation must be considered under a law enforcement paradigm. Again, it is most appropriate to say that the Court applied Article 2 ECHR, but that the Court took IHL into consideration in the process.

The conclusion in both cases was that Article 2 was violated, since the operations were not 'planned and executed with the requisite care for the lives of the civilian population'.[84]

For the present study, the general points to be drawn from the Court's case law are the following: first of all, the Court does only to a small extent make express references to IHL in its judgments. But this does not mean that IHL has no influence on the Court's interpretation of the ECHR. Even though the influence is only implicitly acknowledged (or even implicitly *denied*), IHL has in some cases had a *significant* impact on the Court's considerations, which is evident through the word-for-word incorporation of IHL standards in the decisions. The Court nevertheless adapts these standards to the human rights paradigm, which means that the standards under HRL may not necessarily correspond to the standards under IHL even though the wording is similar. To suggest a new term, one might say that the IHL standards are being adapted to the human rights paradigm, thereby becoming 'human-rightified'. And this is the key point to bear in mind for further analysis. In practice, human rights courts and tribunals have, or assume, competence to examine the conduct of military forces during armed conflicts, and through this mechanism, HRL becomes the applicable standard by which the legality of military operations are assessed.

3. Impact of human rights law on IHL: a 'principle of human-rightism'?

This section makes the opposite inquiry from that above. Rather than inquiring what impact IHL has in the case law of the ECtHR, the present section discusses whether this case law has had a general impact on the application of norms and principles under IHL by other actors. With regard to the specific example of incidental civilian casualties, one inquiry is whether the case law from the ECtHR contributes to a lower threshold for considering such casualties to be disproportionate in relation to the military objective that is sought, thereby creating a shift in the assessment of whether a military operation is considered proportionate and lawful.

Notwithstanding, it is useful at first to consider more generally in what manner, and to what extent, the jurisprudence of international human rights tribunals in principle *may* or *should* influence the interpretation and application of substantive norms and general principles under IHL. For the purposes of this study, one might suggest three alternative responses, all of which carry some merit.

First, any proclamation concerning IHL by a human rights tribunal is, and should be, relevant only for the interpretation of the human rights treaty in question. The tribunal is competent to apply the relevant human rights treaty, and it lacks the formal competence to resolve issues under IHL. The tribunal's conclusions on questions under IHL therefore do not bind actors outside the framework of the treaty. Specifically, the ECtHR may decide authoritatively what impact norms and principles of IHL should have on the interpretation of the provisions in the ECHR and how specific norms shall be interpreted for that purpose, but it cannot decide with binding effect for other (domestic or international) courts or for other actors, how specific norms of IHL shall be interpreted in other contexts.

Secondly, there is supposedly a presumption that the contracting states to a human rights treaty wish to act in compliance with that treaty, in the manner that the treaty is interpreted by the competent supervisory body. If so, proclamations by the supervisory body concerning IHL will inevitably influence the contracting states' conduct during military operations, at least *de facto* if not *de jure*. If a specific conduct is lawful under IHL while HRL prohibits this conduct, then the state may seek to adjust its conduct during military operations to comply with the latter.[85] Such a situation does not concern the application of a norm under IHL, however, but rather the application of a norm under HRL. The state's *conduct* can be affected, but not the state's interpretation of IHL.

And thirdly, proclamations made by human rights tribunals concerning IHL will have an impact not only on the practice, but also on the *law*. This impact can even apply for states who are not parties to the particular human rights treaty. The reason is that the proclamations may be a relevant factor in the development of customary IHL or in the development of general principles of that law. If one accepts the methodology in the ICRC Customary Law Study (and as far as the present issue is concerned, it is difficult to see any compelling reason not to do so), then decisions by international judicial bodies are in fact recognised as being relevant in this regard.[86] A long list of cases from the ECtHR and the European Commission of Human Rights has been included in the Study, and the practice is clearly relevant for the formation of customary law.[87] This concerns also the issue of incidental civilian casualties. The *Ergi* case[88] is cited in support of rule 17 as 'further evidence of the customary nature of this rule in both international and non-international armed conflicts'.[89]

But in order to consider the impact of HRL on IHL with greater precision, it is necessary to divide the issue. A necessary, initial question is whether HRL in fact provides a different standard than IHL. If HRL adopts an identical standard to IHL, it makes little sense to inquire whether HRL in turn has an impact on the standard in IHL. Only to the extent that a difference is identified is it necessary to discuss the impact of HRL on IHL or on the conduct of hostilities. While the first of these issues may be properly addressed here, the second issue requires empirical studies that fall beyond the scope of the present study, which must therefore be limited to providing some theoretical (or even anecdotal) reflections on the matter.

It is necessary for the following discussion to distinguish between different norms governing incidental civilian casualties. First, it should be recalled from section 2.2 above that incidental civilian casualties are unlawful only if the *expected* civilian casualties are *excessive* in relation to the *anticipated* military advantage. This standard is not incorporated in the case law cited above, where the Court instead refers to the human rights standard that any use of force must be strictly proportionate to the achievement of a permissible aim. The Court applies the proportionality standard which belongs to HRL rather than the principle of proportionality under IHL. At least in *general* terms, the HRL standard permits less in terms of civilian casualties than the IHL standard does, even though they may lead to the same result in concrete situations.

Secondly, section 2.2 above also describes that in order to ensure that civilians and civilian objects are spared, there is an obligation under IHL to take all feasible precautions in the choice of means and methods of attack with a view to avoiding, and in any event to minimising, incidental loss of civilian life, injury to civilians and damage to civilian objects. We have seen above that this standard is adopted by the Court, and the existing case law does not suggest that the HRL standard is less permissible than the IHL standard in this regard.

Thirdly, the Court requires that the operation must be executed in pursuit of one of the objectives in Article 2(2) ECHR, rather than to inquire more generally about legitimate military objectives. Any use of force must, in the Court's view, be absolutely necessary for the achievement of one or more of the purposes set forth in Article 2(2) ECHR, typically that it is necessary 'in defence of any person from unlawful violence' (litra a) or 'for the purpose of quelling a riot or insurrection' (litra b). That an attack is directed at a legitimate military target does not in itself satisfy this requirement, even though the Court was prepared to accept (or to assume) that a legitimate purpose was pursued in the *Isayeva* cases.[90]

And finally, the Court applies a clear human rights standard with regard to the obligation to search for victims of military operations and to investigate civilian casualties. Again, the same results may follow from the application of IHL norms, but not necessarily.

The case law leaves no doubt that HRL places extensive obligations on the states during armed conflicts, both in terms of clear positive obligations to secure the right to life of civilians, in terms of a rigorous scrutiny of the planning and execution of an operation, and in terms of an independent obligation to search for casualties and to provide medical assistance after the operation. But whether these obligations in reality differ from the corresponding obligations under IHL is a question that is not yet exhaustively resolved. For example, *Sassòli and Olson* have argued with regard to the case law above that 'even on such a typical humanitarian law subject as precautionary measures, which have to be taken for the benefit of the civilian population when attacking military objectives, human rights can lead to the same result as humanitarian law'.[91] But that the legal regimes *can* 'lead to the same result' in particular cases does not necessarily mean that they *are* 'the same'. If, in a later case, the facts are different, the Chechen and Turkish cases offer in themselves no guarantee that the Court will reach the same result as would an application of IHL.

Thus, even though the present writer agrees with those commentators who argue that the differences between IHL and HRL should not be exaggerated and that the two regimes will often lead to the same results, there are undeniable differences which inevitably mean that HRL places independent requirements on the conduct of hostilities in addition to what is required by IHL. This is an impact which takes place not only in the norm-creation process (where human rights concerns have an impact on the creation of legally binding norms under IHL[92]), but which concerns the execution of concrete operations as well. An operation that satisfies the requirements under IHL may very well be found to be unlawful under HRL. But this triggers two questions, as already suggested in the introduction.

First, one may inquire as to whether the impact of HRL on the conduct of hostilities means that a 'principle of humanity' is, at least, *emerging* as an independent norm in IHL. This appears, however, to be a futile inquiry. HRL has an undeniable impact on the conduct of hostilities and on the norm-creation process in IHL, but that is quite a different thing from saying that even a more general notion of 'humanity' has become legally binding as a norm under IHL. Perhaps the most easily conceivable argument in support of this proposal would be that HRL norms and standards now acquire a significance in situations where the codified human rights law is *de jure* inapplicable, for example, through their inclusion in military manuals, Rules of Engagement, etc. This is particularly relevant in conflicts during which the state in question does not exercise any 'jurisdiction' (which is the threshold requirement for the application of human rights treaties, see e.g., Article 1 ECHR). Let us, hypothetically speaking, suppose that an ECHR norm were incorporated into the Rules of Engagement for the armed forces in an international armed conflict, where the forces are operating outside of the territory of their home state. That state would then, ordinarily, lack 'jurisdiction' in the sense that this term is used in the Convention, and it could not be held responsible if the norm were violated by its armed forces. The individual soldiers could, however, under the circumstances be held responsible for having violated a binding order. But this still does not suggest that 'humanity' enters into the equation as an independent norm, as it is only yet another example of the impact of humanitarian considerations (here in the form of HRL norms) on the norm-creation process in IHL (here, norms in the Rules of Engagement).

Secondly, the apparent non-existence of a 'principle of humanity' as an independent legal norm, combined with the undeniable legal impact of HRL, leads to the inquiry of whether it is even *relevant* to search for a 'principle of humanity' in IHL. Wouldn't the application of HRL in any case achieve the same results? For example, let us recall that it is sometimes said that a possible impact of the Martens Clause (which reflects a 'principle of humanity') is to provide an argument against a finding of *non liquet* during the conduct of hostilities.[93] But the increasing impact of HRL on the conduct of hostilities renders this possible legal impact largely redundant, particularly in non-international armed conflicts, since HRL will fill the relevant 'gaps' in the legal regulation provided by IHL more effectively than the Martens Clause could do. Nevertheless, the obvious response to this is that since HRL is not legally applicable in all situations, an independent 'principle of humanity' in IHL would make an impact in those other situations where HRL is inapplicable.

But as a final point, let us approach this issue of *relevance* from another perspective. Let us recall that the application of HRL to the conduct of hostilities remains a controversial issue. Supporters may consider that HRL provides the best legal framework for the alleviation of human suffering during armed conflicts, and that IHL is insufficient in this regard. Such supporters may even consider that the indifference of IHL (*jus in bello*) to the origin of a conflict (*jus ad bellum*) in itself is detrimental to the protection of individuals during armed conflicts,[94] and they may be concerned that humanitarian considerations continue to have too little impact on the conduct of hostilities. On the other hand, opponents may consider this position to be unrealistic and inappropriate, and that it may disturb the fine balance between humanitarian considerations and considerations of military necessity which is inherent in IHL. Another concern is that HRL does not necessarily provide the better protection,[95] and that the eagerness to apply HRL occasionally may be based on a lack of understanding of IHL. It is important to bear in mind that an opposition to the application of HRL in armed conflicts is not necessarily 'pro-war' or 'anti-humanitarian', since the opposition may be founded on a fear that placing (arguably) unrealistic and unachievable human rights obligations on the parties to an armed conflict would result in weakened respect for legal obligations altogether, even for IHL. More formal arguments may also be put forward, for example that HRL creates *de jure* obligations for a state party only and not for a non-state party, thereby creating asymmetric legal obligations and unreasonably curtailing the state's ability to conduct hostilities (which again, in turn, may reduce the state's respect for its obligations under international law). And finally, some may fear that a strict compliance with HRL may hamper the ability to effectively conduct hostilities to the extent that a solution to a conflict may be postponed and the hostilities prolonged, with self-evident negative consequences for the affected population.

But in this light, the question arises as to whether the development of a stronger, clearer and more general 'principle of humanity' would actually represent a constructive middle road between these opposing sides. Such a principle could reduce the more expansionist tendencies in HRL, i.e., the tendency to advocate the applicability of HRL in situations that are more appropriately assessed in light of IHL. It could further contribute to a more coherent relationship between IHL and HRL, since a 'principle of humanity' could function as a 'humanitarian exception' *entirely within the framework of IHL* and thereby reduce the need to turn to external rules, such as HRL, which may or may not fit in the particular context, and thereby reduce the need for courts, military actors, lawmakers and others to discuss the relationship between the two regimes. The existence of a general 'humanitarian exception' to positive norms under IHL could, potentially, alleviate some of the concerns of both the supporters and the opponents of a stronger impact of HRL on the conduct of hostilities. It is, however, certainly not difficult to develop forceful counter-arguments, for example, that this would reduce the clarity and foreseeability of IHL. It must in any case be stressed that this is not a part of the *lex lata* at present, and the present study does not allow for further elaboration into the possible viability or content of such a 'humanitarian exception'.

4. Conclusions

The introductory Chapter 1 raised a number of key questions to be addressed in the volume, and one of these questions concerned the legal impact of a 'principle of humanity' in contemporary IHL. Other chapters in this book suggest that such an impact can be found only in the norm-creation process, and the present chapter does not argue against this view. Even when the conduct of hostilities is assessed from a human rights perspective, no independent 'principle of humanity' can be identified. This chapter, however, suggests that a 'principle of *humanity*' in any case may be less relevant than a 'principle of *human-rightism*'. There is an increasing trend in human rights tribunals, exemplified above by the European Court of Human Rights, to consider the conduct of state actors in armed conflicts in light of HRL, and the practical consequence is that IHL is supplemented by a much more detailed and forceful set of norms than what a 'principle of humanity' in any case could offer. Norms which provide protection of the individual under HRL, such as the right to life, are detailed and clear, whereas a 'principle of humanity' would be vague and uncertain; HRL is undoubtedly legally binding, on certain conditions, whereas a 'principle of humanity' has little (if any) legal effect; HRL is also perceived as legally binding by the states, whereas a 'principle of humanity' can, at best, be perceived as a moral obligation. And perhaps most importantly: HRL must be considered to be more extensive than a 'principle of humanity' would have been, both in terms of its substantive content and in terms of its scope of application. The relevant place for a 'principle of humanity' would be in situations where HRL is not legally applicable, but this chapter does not suggest that such a principle exists as an independent legal norm. The purpose of this chapter has been far more modest, as it has merely attempted to introduce the hitherto unexplored alternative view that the possible future emergence of such a principle could in fact be considered advantageous both by supporters and opponents of a more humanitarian IHL, as it could create a more coherent relationship between IHL and HRL.

Notes

1 Yoram Dinstein, Chapter 3.
2 Y. Dinstein, *The Conduct of Hostilities under the Law of International Armed Conflict* (Cambridge University Press, 2004) 16 ff.
3 *Ibid.* 17.
4 'Human-rightism' is not a legal term, and is used by different writers to denote different things; for example, Pellet uses it to describe (and criticise) the notion that human rights is somehow 'special' in international law (A. Pellet, '"Droits-de-l'hommisme" et droit international', Conférence commémorative Gilberto Amado, 18 July 2000), while Pronto uses it to describe the direct and indirect influence of human rights on general international law (A. Pronto, '"Human-rightism" and the development of general international law' (2007), 20 *Leiden Journal of International Law* 753). In this study, the term is used in the latter meaning.
5 Hereinafter 'ECtHR' or 'the Court'.
6 The term refers to the unintended killing of civilians in attacks against a lawful military target. This is an issue where the relationship between IHL and HRL is much discussed, since the IHL norms (which are described in section 2.4 below) to a certain extent permit such casualties while HRL prohibits intentional or arbitrary killing unless a valid derogation has been made with regard to lawful acts of war (see e.g., Articles 2 and 15 ECHR).
7 For instance, the European Commission on Human Rights addressed already in the 1970s complaints in relation to the Turkish invasion of Northern Cyprus in 1974, but this was at that time the only international armed conflict which had led to applications under the ECHR. See A. Reidy, 'The approach of the European Commission and Court of Human Rights to international humanitarian law' (1998) 38 *International Review of the Red Cross* 513, note 11.
8 Hereinafter called 'ECHR' or 'the Convention'. See Article 32(1): 'The jurisdiction of the Court shall extend to all matters concerning the interpretation and application of the Convention and the protocols thereto.'
9 For an overview of arguments against allowing the Court to apply other branches of international law, see G. Pinzauti, 'The European Court of Human Rights' incidental application of international criminal law and humanitarian law' (2008) 6 *Journal of International Criminal Justice* 1043 at 1044.
10 For a doctrinal analysis of the impact of external rules on treaty interpretation, see D. French, 'Treaty interpretation and the incorporation of extraneous legal rules' (2006) 55 *International and Comparative Law Quarterly* 281.
11 *Las Palmeras* v. *Colombia* Series C no. 67, (2000), IACtHR, paras. 32–33. See also A. Orakhelashvili, 'The interaction between human rights and humanitarian law: fragmentation, conflict, parallelism, or convergence?' (2008) 19 *European Journal of International Law* 161 at 168.
12 Orakhelashvili, *ibid*, 165, argues that the Court 'is duty-bound to test whether the conduct and measures of the derogating state are in accordance with international humanitarian law'.
13 See (with regard to the corresponding provision in Article 5 in the International Covenant on Civil and Political Rights) the UN Human Rights Committee's General Comment No. 29 on states of emergency (Article. 4), UN doc. CCPR/C/21/Rev.1/add.11 (31 August 2001) para. 9, or M. Nowak, *U.N. Covenant on Civil and Political Rights: CCPR Commentary* (2nd edn., Kehl: N.P. Engel, 2005) 99.

14 Examples are *Kononov* v. *Latvia*, appl. no. 36376/04, ECtHR, Judgment, 24 July 2008, or *Korbely* v. *Hungary*, appl. no. 9174/02, ECtHR, Judgment 19 September 2008.

15 Formerly Article 60 (amended by Protocol No. 11 which entered into force on 1 November 1998).

16 See F. Bruscoli, 'The rights of individuals in times of armed conflict' (2002) 6 *International Journal of Human Rights* 45 at 51, or (with regard to the similar clause in Article 5 ICCPR), Nowak, *CCPR Commentary*, 118.

17 For an analysis of this provision, see e.g., U. Linderfalk, 'Who are "the Parties"? Article 31, paragraph 3(C) of the 1969 Vienna Convention and the "principle of systemic integration" revisited' (2008) 55 *Netherlands International Law Review* 343.

18 *Demir and Baykara* v. *Turkey*, appl. no. 34503/97, ECtHR, Judgment 12 November 2008, para. 66. For an analysis of the decision, see R. Nordeide's case note in (2009) 103 *American Journal of International Law* 567.

19 *Demir and Baykara* v. *Turkey*, para. 67.

20 *Ibid.* para. 69.

21 *Ibid.* para. 71, see Article 38(1)(c) of the Statute of the International Court of Justice.

22 *Demir and Baykara* v. *Turkey*, para. 72 (emphasis added).

23 *Ibid.* para. 76.

24 *Ibid.* para. 78 (emphasis added).

25 *Ibid.* paras. 85–6.

26 *Varnava and others* v. *Turkey*, appl. nos. 16064/90 and others, ECtHR, Judgment, 18 September 2009, para. 185 (emphasis added).

27 See, generally, the International Law Commission's (ILC) report *Fragmentation of International Law: Difficulties Arising from the Diversification and Expansion of International Law*, UN doc. A/CN.4/L.682 (13 April 2006).

28 Despite occasional assertions that there are only two theories, see e.g., W. Schabas, '*Lex specialis*? Belt and suspenders? The parallel operation of human rights law and the law of armed conflict, and the conundrum of *jus ad bellum*' (2007) 40 *Israel Law Review* 592 at 593.

29 *Legal Consequences of the Construction of a Wall in the Occupied Palestinian Territory*, Advisory Opinion, [2004] ICJ Reports 136 (at 178), para. 106.

30 Beyond this, the present study does not allow for an elaboration of the content of the *lex specialis* doctrine, which in itself is controversial. A thorough analysis of this doctrine in international law is provided by the ILC's Study Group on the Fragmentation of International Law (*supra* note 27) in its report UN doc. A/CN.4/L.682 (13 April 2006) 34–65 paras. 56–122.

31 C. Droege, 'Elective affinities? Human rights and humanitarian law' in 90 (2008) *International Review of the Red Cross* 501 at 521.

32 N. Quénivet, 'The history of the relationship between international humanitarian law and human rights law' in R. Arnold and N. Quénivet, *International Humanitarian Law and Human Rights Law: Towards a New Merger in International Law* (Leiden/Boston: Martinus Nijhoff, 2008) 1–12 at 9.

33 Schabas, 'Parallel operation', 593; H. Krieger, 'A conflict of norms: the relationship between humanitarian law and human rights law in the ICRC Customary Law Study' (2006) 11 *Journal of Conflict and Security Law* 265 at 274; N. Prud'homme, '*Lex specialis*: oversimplifying a more complex and multifaceted relationship?' (2007) 40 *Israel Law Review* 356 at 358. See, more generally, Orakhelashvili, 'Interaction',

who addresses different areas where the level of protection in one field can be lower than in the other.

34 Prud'homme, '*Lex specialis*' 358.

35 Schabas, 'Parallel operation', 593.

36 See e.g., the attempts to develop a 'human-rights based law of war' by F. Martin, 'Using international human rights law for establishing a unified use of force rule in the law of armed conflict' (2001) 64 *Saskatchewan Law Review* 347, who proposed a 'unified use of force rule' where the use of lethal force in armed conflict, even against combatants, would be lawful only in the three situations mentioned in Article 2(2) ECHR; or by D. Koller, 'The moral imperative: toward a human rights-based law of war' (2005) 46 *Harvard International Law Journal* 231, who set out to 'develop a new law of war that is based on human rights and is entirely consistent with the requirements of human rights law'.

37 W. Abresch, 'A human rights law of internal armed conflict: the European Court of Human Rights in Chechnya' (2005) 16 *European Journal of International Law* 741 at 752.

38 F. Hampson, 'The relationship between international humanitarian law and human rights law from the perspective of a human rights treaty body' (2008) 90 *International Review of the Red Cross* 549 at 556.

39 *Isayeva* v. *Russia*, appl. no. 57950/00, ECtHR, Judgment, 24 February 2005 ('*Isayeva II*'), para. 191. This case is discussed further below.

40 These norms are also discussed by Yoram Dinstein, Chapter 3.

41 Articles 48, 51(2) and 52(2) of Additional Protocol I to the Geneva Conventions ('GC AP I'), and Rule 1 in the ICRC Customary Law Study (J.-M. Henckaerts and L. Doswald-Beck, *Customary International Humanitarian Law*, vol. I, *Rules* (Cambridge University Press, 2005)). See e.g., Dinstein, *Conduct of Hostilities*, 82 ff. and 113 ff.

42 Articles 51(5)(b) and 57(2)(a)(iii) GC AP I and Rule 14 in the ICRC Customary Law Study, *supra* note 41. See e.g., Dinstein, *Conduct of Hostilities*, 119 ff.

43 Dinstein, *ibid.*, describes (at 120–1) how 'excessive' should not be misread as 'extensive'.

44 See e.g., Dinstein, *ibid.*

45 Article 57(2)(a)(ii) GC AP I and Rules 15 and 17 in the ICRC Customary Law Study, *supra* note 41. See e.g., Dinstein, *Conduct of Hostilities*, 125 ff.

46 These cases are, by now, fairly well rehearsed in academic writings, and their facts and the Court's assessments may therefore be given a somewhat simplified description. See e.g., H.-J. Heintze, 'On the relationship between human rights law protection and international humanitarian law' (2004) *International Review of the Red Cross* no. 856 789; Abresch, 'Chechnya'; L. Doswald-Beck, 'The right to life in armed conflict: does international humanitarian law provide all the answers?' in (2006) 88 *International Review of the Red Cross* no. 864 881; or C. Byron, 'A blurring of the boundaries: the application of international humanitarian law by human rights bodies' (2007) 47 *Virginia Journal of International Law* 839 (especially at 851–6).

47 See the introduction by the editors in Chapter 1.

48 *Kononov*, appl. no. 36376/04, ECtHR, Joint Dissenting Opinion of Judges Fura-Sandström, Björgvinsson and Ziemele, para. 10.

49 See Article 15(1) in the Geneva Convention I and rule 113 in the ICRC Customary Law Study, *supra* note 41.

50 Appl. no. 56760/00, ECtHR, Judgment, 2 February 2007, para. 82. See also *Akkum and others* v. *Turkey*, appl. no. 21894/93, ECtHR, Judgment, 24 March 2005.

51 *Ergi* v. *Turkey*, appl. no. 23818/94, ECtHR, Judgment, 28 July 1998.
52 *Ibid.*, para. 10.
53 *Ibid.*, paras. 16–17.
54 *Ibid.*, para. 78. Since the Court went on to conclude that there was in any case a violation of Article 2 (see below), it was strictly speaking unnecessary for the Court to draw a more concrete conclusion about the facts.
55 *Ibid.*, para. 79.
56 *Ibid.*
57 *Ibid.*, para. 80.
58 *Ibid.*, para. 81.
59 See Heintze, 'Relationship', 810, see also K. Altiparmak, 'Banković: an obstacle to the application of the European Convention on Human Rights in Iraq?' (2004) 9 *Journal of Conflict and Security Law* 213 at 220.
60 Abresch, 'Chechnya,' argues (at 746) that such a conclusion cannot be drawn from the use of the terminology and that the terminology 'belongs as much to human rights law as to humanitarian law'.
61 The differences, namely that 'attack' is replaced with 'security operation', and that 'injury to civilians and damage to civilian objects' is omitted, are insignificant for present purposes.
62 The conflict in south-eastern Turkey is clearly non-international, and Additional Protocol I does not apply. Turkey is in any case not a party to the Protocol.
63 ICRC Customary Law Study, *supra* note 41, rules 15 and 17.
64 *Özkan and others* v. *Turkey*, appl. no. 21689/93, ECtHR, Judgment, 6 April 2004. In this case, the Court directly acknowledged the existence of an armed conflict in the area, see para. 305.
65 *Ibid*, para. 298.
66 *Ibid*, paras. 305–6.
67 *Ibid*, para. 308.
68 Article 16(2) of Geneva Convention II, Article 8 of Additional Protocol II, rules 109 and 112 in the ICRC Customary Law Study, *supra* note 41.
69 The '*Isayeva I*' case is *Isayeva, Yusupova and Bazayeva* v. *Russia*, appl. nos. 57947/00, 57948/00, 57949/00, ECtHR, Judgment 24 February 2005. The '*Isayeva II*' case is cited *supra* note 39.
70 *Isayeva I*, para. 169, *Isayeva II*, para. 173.
71 *Ibid.*
72 *Isayeva I*, para. 170, *Isayeva II*, para. 174.
73 *Isayeva I*, para. 171, *Isayeva II*, para. 175.
74 *Isayeva II*, para. 176, with reference to the *Ergi* case. This paragraph is omitted in *Isayeva I*.
75 See *supra* note 45.
76 See Krieger, 'Conflict of norms', 267–8, who simply asserts that the ECtHR based its findings 'exclusively on human rights law'.
77 This is stated explicitly in *Isayeva II*, para. 191, where the Court stated that the use of heavy weapons 'in a populated area, outside wartime and without prior evacuation of the civilians, is impossible to reconcile with the degree of caution expected from a law-enforcement body in a democratic society', and that the absence of any declaration of martial law, a state of emergency, or derogation, means that the 'operation in question therefore has to be judged against a normal legal background' (see also *supra* note 39).

78 *Isayeva I*, para. 182, *Isayeva II*, para. 181.
79 *Isayeva II*, para. 183 (emphasis added). See also *Isayeva I*, para. 177, where the direct reference to Article 2 is omitted.
80 *Isayeva I*, para. 181.
81 *Isayeva I*, para. 178, *Isayeva II*, para. 180.
82 *Isayeva I*, para. 181, *Isayeva II*, para. 188.
83 *Isayeva I*, para. 175 and, similarly, *Isayeva II*, para. 182.
84 *Isayeva I*, para. 199, *Isayeva II*, para. 200.
85 Let us disregard, for the moment, the many issues concerning the relevant *actors* under IHL and HRL.
86 See, generally, the ICRC Customary Law Study, *supra* note 41, vol. II: *Practice*, and 4308 ff.
87 *Ibid.* 4310–17.
88 See *supra* note 51.
89 ICRC Customary Law Study, *supra* note 41, volume I, 58 and vol. II, 383.
90 *Isayeva I*, paras. 181–2, *Isayeva II*, para. 180.
91 M. Sassòli and L. Olson, 'The relationship between international humanitarian and human rights law where it matters: admissible killing and internment of fighters in non-international armed conflict' (2008) 90 *International Review of the Red Cross* 599 at 601.
92 See e.g., Robert Kolb, Chapter 2 and Katarina Månsson, Chapter 6.
93 *Non liquet* refers to the situation that existing legal rules offer no clear legal answer to a particular legal problem. See T. Meron, 'The Martens Clause, principles of humanity, and dictates of public conscience' (2000) 94 *American Journal of International Law* 78 at 88.
94 See e.g., Schabas, '*Lex specialis*'.
95 See e.g., A.M. Gross, 'Human proportions: are human rights the Emperor's New Clothes of the international law of occupation?' (2007) 18 *European Journal of International Law* 1, who argues (at 4–5) 'that the merging of IHRL into IHL, rather than expanding human protection may serve to undermine it as well as to legitimize violations of people living under occupation'.

6

The principle of humanity in the development of 'special protection' for children in armed conflict: 60 years beyond the Geneva Conventions and 20 years beyond the Convention on the Rights of the Child

KATARINA MÅNSSON

1. Introduction

Mankind owes to the child the best it has to give.[1]

This phrase, formulated as early as 1924 in the Preamble to the Declaration of the Rights of the Child, stipulates in simplicity that children stand in the frontline of mankind's exercise of 'humanity'. In its original English usage, humanity implied 'kindness, graciousness', to later evolve into its modern meaning of 'one who advocates or practices human action', 'the condition of being human' and 'compassion or benevolence'.[2] In the same Declaration from 1924, men and women of all nations declared and accepted as their duty that 'the child must be the first to receive relief in times of distress'. Long before the modern codification of international humanitarian law (IHL) and human rights law (HRL), the child hence held a position of priority in the advocacy and practice of human action, of humanity.

This exposé explores how this duty of humanity towards one of the most vulnerable groups in society has developed into a legal duty of states and other actors under international law and how that legal duty has, or has not, ensured their 'special protection' in times of armed conflict. The intertwinement of the 1949 Geneva Conventions and relevant human rights instruments, the 1989 Convention on the Rights of the Child in particular, is at the heart of the discussion. Particular attention will be given to the plight of children involved in armed conflict, by exploring the legal provisions seeking to protect children from the recruitment and use in armed forces and armed groups. It aspires to demonstrate, as suggested by Popovski, how the codification of the protection of children is particularly illustrative of the convergence between international humanitarian law and human rights law.[3]

In this sense, the issue of protection of children in armed conflict highlights how the principle of humanity as expressed in international humanitarian law cannot be examined in isolation from the philosophy and development of human rights law. On the contrary, by contending that human rights law preceded and influenced the elaboration of child-oriented protection standards in international humanitarian law and by providing for a complementary prevention and protection scheme, this chapter suggests that the principle of 'humanity' has operated as an underlying philosophical tenet, advancing past and present standard-setting concerning child protection in situations of conflict. This normative evolution saw a landmark development with the adoption in 2000 of the Optional Protocol to the Convention on the Rights of the Child on the Involvement of Children in Armed Conflict, described as 'a best example of a potential merger of HRL and IHL with regard to children'.[4] In terms of protection of children in armed conflict, the twentieth anniversary of the Convention on the Rights of the Child in 2009 is thus as important as the sixtieth anniversary of the Geneva Conventions. These accumulated eighty years of international law-making for the protection of children in times of peace as well as in war commenced with the adoption of the United Nations Charter in 1945.

2 Legal frameworks of protection for children in IHL and HRL

2.1 UN Charter and UDHR: enabling a new legal era

It is no coincidence that the law of armed conflict, as noted by Kolb in his contribution to this book, saw a 'radical departure' from earlier tenets and conceptions of this branch of international law and re-emerged under the name of 'international humanitarian law' in the immediate post-Second World War era.[5] The 'humanization' of the old military law through the adoption of the 1949 Geneva Conventions had at its very core the protection of the individual victim of war, especially those *hors de combat*,[6] and found clear expression in the Fourth Geneva Convention relative to the Protection of Civilian Persons in Time of War. Experience from the Spanish civil war had also brought to the forefront the inadequacies of regulations governing civil war, giving birth to Article 3, common to the four Geneva Conventions, providing for humane treatment for all persons taking no active part in hostilities in non-international armed conflicts, including children.

One year prior to the adoption of the Geneva Conventions, on 10 December 1948, the Universal Declaration of Human Rights (UDHR) was adopted by the UN General Assembly. Prompted by outrage at the flagrant disrespect for civilian lives, not only of the enemy state but also of states' own citizens during the Second World War, and the repercussions such violations had on international peace and security, the UDHR gave universal expression to one of the main purposes of the United Nations as spelled out in Article 1(3) of the UN Charter: to promote and encourage respect for human rights and fundamental rights for all. Just as the UN Charter makes no distinction regarding the application of its human rights provisions between times of peace or times of war, the UDHR similarly does not specify its scope of application, but rather sets forth that 'everyone' and 'all' are entitled to the rights and freedoms stipulated in the Declaration.[7] The UN Secretary-General in his 1969 report on *Respect for Human Rights in Armed Conflict* elaborated on the issue in the following way:

> These texts [the Charter and the UDHR] seem to cover all persons living in countries which are at peace as well as inhabitants of countries engaged in, or affected by, armed conflicts. The phraseology of the Charter would apply in its generality to civilian as well as military personnel; it would encompass persons living under the jurisdiction of their own national authorities and persons living in territories under belligerent occupation.[8]

In this way, the UN Charter and the UDHR set the foundation of the principle that human rights applies in all times, also in times of armed conflict. By default, human rights standards and norms inevitably came to infuse the 'post-1945 development' of international humanitarian law.[9] The basis for this fusion is the recognition, and philosophical conviction, of the inherent dignity and worth of the human person and the corresponding inalienable rights accorded to each individual.[10] The similarities of the Preambles to the UN Charter and the UDHR, as well as the proposed text for a Preamble to Geneva Convention IV, are in this regard indicative of the common vision and aspirations shared by the drafters of these treaties:

1. The UN Charter set forth as one of the objectives of the United Nations to 'reaffirm faith in fundamental human rights, in the dignity and worth of the human person, in the equal rights of men and women and of nations large and small'.

2. The UDHR was inspired by the recognition that, 'the inherent dignity and inalienable rights of all members of the human family is the foundation of freedom, justice and peace in the world'.
3. Geneva Convention IV on the Protection of Civilians was designed to 'ensure the respect of human personality and dignity by putting beyond reach of attack those rights and liberties which are the essence of its existence'.[11]

These are all age-neutral provisions, reflective of the fact that 'humanity' as a concept is necessarily holistic and all-embracing, inclusive of all members of the human family in order for it to have any validity, let alone meaning. The general protection in and by law that the UN Charter and the UDHR seek to ensure is manifest in their universality *ratione temporis* (they apply always), *ratione personae* (they apply to everyone), and in terms of *jurisdiction* (they apply everywhere). Drzewicki claims that the 'definition and catalogue of human rights in the Declaration may safely be regarded as a "quasi-authentic" interpretation of the human rights provisions in the Charter. The universal message reflected in the Declaration is further strengthened by the fact that some of its provisions constitute general principles of law or represent elementary considerations of humanity.'[12]

2.2 *General protection of children in armed conflict*

Geneva Conventions: a year after the UDHR

Against this background, the first child-specific provisions of IHL appear in the Geneva Conventions of 1949, primarily in Geneva Convention IV on the protection of civilians.[13] In terms of 'general protection', they concern, inter alia, (i) the establishment of hospitals and safety zones with a view to protect children under fifteen, (ii) the conclusion of local arrangements for the removal of children from besieged or encircled areas, (iii) the free passage of foodstuffs, clothing and tonics intended for children under fifteen, and (iv) the obligation on the parties to the conflict to ensure that children under fifteen who are orphaned or separated from their families as a result of the war are not left to their own resources. Children were also attended to in provisions relating to the obligations of an occupying power: notably in the fields of education, protection against forced labour, prohibition of the application of the death penalty and special treatment of detainees who are minors.

These provisions have been called 'pretty limited and insufficient';[14] not only in terms of their scope of material application, limited to international armed conflict, but moreover by applying only to 'protected persons' or civilian population in occupied territories. Some of the general protection provisions are also limited to special categories of children, namely those who are 'orphaned or separated from their families as a result of war'.[15] An all-encompassing protection shield for all children is lacking, hence also failing to address children as particularly vulnerable individuals in times of conflict. Also, the principle on which rules relating to children is based is not stated explicitly anywhere in the Conventions and a definition of the child is lacking.[16] This is reflected in, and partly explains, the inconsistent approach concerning the age of children in the Geneva Conventions. Geneva Convention III relative to the Treatment of Prisoners of War simply refers to 'age' as a reason for preferential treatment.[17] Geneva Convention IV alternates between 'children' or 'minors' (without an age qualification), 'children under 15', and in one case 'children under 12' in its provisions.[18] The drafters seem to have deviated from this age categorisation of the child as a person under the age of fifteen in the context of forced labour and the application of the death penalty where the age is set at eighteen years.[19] This distinction between 'younger children' (below the age of fifteen) and 'older children' (ages fifteen to eighteen) is retained to a large extent in subsequent humanitarian and human rights law instruments, especially as they relate to the recruitment and use of children in armed conflict.

The lack of a general child-specific protection clause in the Geneva Conventions, the restricted scope of protection with regard to non-international armed conflicts of Common Article 3, and the exclusion of children more *directly* involved in and affected by conflict stand out as major deficiencies of the 1949 international humanitarian law. Nevertheless, the Geneva Conventions marked an important embryonic step towards the elaboration of stronger child-related protection provisions in IHL. In this respect, it should be noted that the UDHR had already specifically set forth in Article 25(2) that 'childhood is entitled to special care and assistance'.[20] It can hence be suggested that emerging human rights law as represented by the UDHR set a precedent and influenced the new protection and victim-oriented focus of the Geneva Conventions, including in relation to children. Mindful of the fact that all the provisions of the UDHR were made universally applicable to 'all' and 'everyone' and that 'no one' should be subjected to its prohibited acts, makes its protection net larger than that of the Geneva Conventions in terms of *duty-bearers* (not restricted to High Contracting Parties), *scope of application* (not restricted to a particular type of conflict), and *rights-holders* (no specified age).

2.3 *Special protection of children affected by and involved in armed conflict*

Additional Protocols of 1977: embodying the interdependency between HRL and IHL

It took another thirty years to remedy some of the protection gaps of the 1949 Geneva Conventions with the adoption in 1977 of the Additional Protocols (AP). They introduced two main novelties in international humanitarian law as a child-oriented protective legal framework. First, they introduced the concept of 'special protection' of children in international humanitarian law. Article 77 of Additional Protocol I, applicable in international armed conflict, states the obligation of High Contracting Parties to show 'special respect' with regard to children. This notion is paralleled in Additional Protocol II, applicable in non-international armed conflict,[21] with the concept of provision of 'care and aid'.[22] Secondly, they were the first international instruments that specifically addressed the issue of the recruitment and use of children in hostilities.[23]

These two novelties reflect the close interrelatedness of international humanitarian law and international human rights law in the evolution of child protection in international law. By 1977, the first core international human rights treaty, the International Convention on the Elimination of All Forms of Racial Discrimination (ICERD), and the two international covenants – the International Covenant on Economic, Social and Cultural Rights (ICESCR) and the International Covenant on Civil and Political Rights (ICCPR) – had been adopted. These developments proved critical to the elaboration of the Additional Protocols where the express concept of 'the principles of humanity' appears for the first time in international humanitarian law:

1. Additional Protocol I (Article 1(1)): In cases not covered by this Protocol or by other international agreements, civilians and combatants remain under the protection and authority of the principles of international law derived from established custom, from the principles of humanity and from the dictates of public conscience.
2. Additional Protocol II (Preamble): Recalling furthermore that international instruments relating to human rights offer a basic protection to the human person;

   Recalling that, in cases not covered by the law in force, the human person remains under the protection of the principles of humanity and the dictates of the public conscience.

Special protection of the child

The concept of 'special protection' starkly illustrates the influence of human rights law on the development of international humanitarian law. Article 77(1) of Additional Protocol I states:

> Children shall be the object of special respect and shall be protected against any form of indecent assault. The Parties to the conflict shall provide them with the care and aid they require, whether because of their age or for any other reason.

This and related principles for the protection of children had already been advanced in a number of binding as well as non-binding international human rights instruments. Principally, the Declaration of the Rights of the Child from 1959, inspired by the protection clauses set forth in the 1924 Geneva Declaration and the UDHR (Article. 24), encompassed the principle of special protection alongside two other principles of fundamental importance to the furthering of international human rights and humanitarian law as they relate to children:

Principle 2: The child shall enjoy special protection.
Principle 8: The child shall in all circumstances be among the first to receive protection and relief.
Principle 9: The child shall be protected against all forms of neglect, cruelty and exploitation and shall in no case be caused or permitted to engage in any occupation or employment which would prejudice his health or education, or interfere with his physical, mental or moral development.

Principle 9 has been proposed as 'an early expression of the United Nations' concern with the use of children in armed forces'.[24] Not only was the 1959 Declaration a forerunner to the 1989 Convention on the Rights of the Child, but the principles set forth in the 1959 Declaration can also be retraced in the two International Covenants on human rights of 1966. Notably, Article 24 of the International Covenant on Civil and Political Rights (ICCPR) sets forth that:

> Every child shall have, without discrimination as to race, colour, sex, language, national or social origin, property or birth, *the right to such measures of protection* as are required by his status as a minor, on the part of his family, society and the state. (emphasis added)

This protection clause should be read as an additional and reinforcing provision to all the other substantive safeguards of the Covenant, such as the right to life, the right to personal liberty and security, freedom from torture and other forms of ill-treatment and freedom from slavery or servitude, which applies to 'everyone' or 'all persons', including children.[25] The Human Rights Committee has interpreted this provision to entail that 'the implementation of this provision entails the adoption of special measures to protect children, in addition to the measures that states are required to take under Article 2 to ensure that everyone enjoys the rights provided for in the Covenant … The right to special measures of protection belongs to every child because of his status as a minor.'[26]

It is interesting to note in this context that the earlier drafts of what is today Article 4 of the Covenant on derogations proposed that derogations from the obligations of states parties would be admissible '*in time of war* or other public emergency' (emphasis added).[27] While the drafters of the UN Commission on Human Rights recognized that the outbreak of war was one of the most important public emergencies, it was felt that the Covenant 'should not envisage, not even contemplate, the possibility of war'.[28] For this reason the express reference to war was omitted from the text of the draft Covenant in 1950. This does not imply in any way that the Covenant does not apply in times of war. On the contrary, the UN Secretary-General underscored shortly after the adoption of the Covenant that 'the provisions set forth in the [ICCPR] apply in times of public emergency, *which term includes the state of an armed conflict*' (emphasis added).[29] The continuing applicability of human rights in times of armed conflict was even upheld by the Security Council in 1967 when it stated that 'essential and inalienable human rights should be respected even in the vicissitudes of war'.[30] The Human Rights Committee, the UN treaty body monitoring and assisting states parties to the ICCPR with respect to domestic implementation of the Covenant, reiterated in 2004 that 'the Covenant applies also in situations of armed conflict to which the rules of international humanitarian law are applicable', noting that 'both spheres of law are complementary, not mutually exclusive'.[31]

The same principle applies to provisions of the International Covenant on Economic, Social and Cultural Rights (ICESCR) from 1966, Article 10 of which obliges states parties to take:

> *Special measures of protection and assistance* … on behalf of all children and young persons without any discrimination for reasons of parentage or other conditions. Children and young persons should be protected from economic and social exploitation. Their employment in work harmful to their morals or health or dangerous to life or likely to hamper their normal development should be punishable by law.

Whereas the plight of children affected by or engaged in hostilities was not explicitly referred to in Article 10, its influence on the provisions concerned with special protection and use and recruitment of children in Additional Protocol I and II is implicit. Around the time of the adoption of the international covenants, there was a strong recognition of the inadequate *de facto* and *de lege* protection of civilians, including children, in situations of armed conflict. This was paralleled with a corresponding realisation that the basic principle for effective civilian protection in armed conflict was fundamental human rights[32] and that a strengthening of existing humanitarian instruments in this respect needed to be made against the basis of the UN Charter and existing human rights law.[33]

It is in this spirit of debate that the Declaration on the Protection of Women and Children in Emergency and Armed Conflict was adopted in 1974. The Declaration can be seen as a soft law bridge between the child-oriented clauses of the international human rights instruments, existing international humanitarian law provisions and the Additional Protocols to come. By identifying children, and women, as 'defenceless' and 'the most vulnerable members of the population', it declares that women and children belonging to the civilian population and finding themselves in circumstances of emergency and armed conflict 'shall not be deprived of shelter, food, medical aid or other inalienable rights, in accordance with the provisions of the [UDHR], [ICCPR], [ICESCR], the Declaration of the Rights of the Child or other instruments of international law'.[34]

In view of the above, the principle of 'special protection' of children embodied in the two Additional Protocols can be seen as a reaffirmation of the duty of states to respect the above-mentioned child-specific provisions set forth in non-binding and binding international human rights instruments since they also apply in times of conflict.

Recruitment or use of children in hostilities

The second novelty of the Additional Protocols concerned the fact that they constituted the first international instruments ever to acknowledge and address the problem of children actively engaged and involved in armed conflict. Article 77(2) of Additional Protocol I, applicable in international armed conflicts, sets out that:

> The Parties to the conflict shall take all feasible measures in order that children who have not attained the age of fifteen years do not take a direct part in hostilities and, in particular, they shall refrain from recruiting them into their armed forces. In recruiting among those persons who have attained the age of fifteen years but who have not yet attained the

> age of eighteen years, the Parties of the conflict shall endeavour to give priority to those who are the oldest.

The corresponding Article in Additional Protocol II, applicable in non-international armed conflicts, is similar but provides for stronger protection in two ways: first, by providing *larger* scope of protection in that it applies not only to government forces but also to rebel groups and dissident groups; secondly, by providing *stronger* scope of protection in that it prohibits altogether the recruitment of children under the age of fifteen in armed forces or groups as well as their active part in hostilities. Article 4(3)(c) hence entails a blanket ban on recruitment and use in hostilities of children under the age of fifteen. It reads:

> Children who have not attained the age of fifteen years shall neither be recruited in the armed forces or groups nor allowed to take part in hostilities.[35]

The human rights instruments and documents adopted prior to the drafting of the Additional Protocols did not, as described above, expressly address the specific protection needs of children taking active part in war. It may be noted, however, that the Human Rights Committee in its General Comment No. 17 (1989) on the rights of the child pointed to the need for states parties to the ICCPR to include in their reports on the Covenant information on 'measures adopted to ensure that children do not take a direct part in armed conflicts'.[36] As was also alluded to, the reference in the 1959 Declaration on the Rights of the Child to 'employment which would prejudice his health or education, or interfere with his physical, mental or moral development', and as replicated in Article 10 of the ICESCR, could be read as normative precedents for the above-mentioned provisions of the Additional Protocols.

In terms of international law, however, the above-mentioned provisions of the Additional Protocols would engender a converse force of influence of international humanitarian law on the development of international human rights law. Specifically, Article 77(2) of Additional Protocol I was transposed twelve years later, almost verbatim, into the 1989 Convention on the Rights of the Child.

2.4 Convention on the Rights of the Child and its Optional Protocol on the Involvement of Children in Armed Conflict

With a twelve-year span between the adoption of the Additional Protocols (1977) and the Convention on the Rights of the Child (CRC) (1989), a much stronger legal protection framework in the Convention, rather than a mere repetition of existing international humanitarian law, was probably expected. Indeed, it is acknowledged that 'one of the most notorious instances where the NGO Group [on the Drafting of the Convention on the Rights of the Child] failed to convince government delegates was in relation to Article 38, which permits the participation of children aged fifteen to seventeen years in armed conflicts, despite massive pressure from NGOs and others for it to be outlawed'.[37] Among all forty-one substantive provisions of the Convention on the Rights of the Child, Article 38 (together with Article 39 on physical and psychological recovery and social reintegration) is the only one specifically dedicated to the protection of children in armed conflict. States parties to the CRC, enjoying close to universal ratification, are under an obligation to:

1. Undertake to respect and ensure respect for rules of international humanitarian law applicable to them in armed conflicts which are relevant to the child.
2. Take all feasible measures to ensure that persons who have not attained the age of fifteen years do not take a direct part in hostilities.
3. Refrain from recruiting any person who has not attained the age of fifteen into their armed forces. In recruiting among those persons who have attained the age of fifteen years but who have not attained the age of eighteen years, states parties shall endeavour to give priority to those who are oldest.
4. In accordance with their obligations under international humanitarian law to protect civilian population in armed conflicts, [and] take all feasible measures to ensure protection and care of children who are affected by an armed conflict.[38]

Article 38 is interesting in that it represents the first time that an international human rights instrument explicitly obliges states parties to respect international humanitarian law. In this regard, Popovski suggests that the CRC 'can be regarded as an instrument of both IHL and HRL'.[39] Indeed, the UN Committee on the Rights of the Child, the treaty body monitoring domestic application of the Convention, has stated that the relevant international humanitarian law rules referred to in paragraphs 1 and 4 include the Geneva Conventions, the Additional Protocols, the Declaration on the Protection of Women and Children in Emergency and Armed Conflict, the Declaration of the Rights of the Child and also the ICCPR.[40]

Such reflection further compounds the disappointment in that the CRC, in regard to its efforts to protect children from armed conflict, offers 'no better protection than those of Additional Protocol I'.[41] Despite the Convention's definition of the child as 'every human being below the age of 18 years', Article 38 adheres to the age limit of fifteen years set forth in international humanitarian law. Furthermore, Additional Protocol II even provides stronger protection than the Convention by *firmly prohibiting* – not merely calling on states to 'refrain from' or 'take all necessary measures' in relation to the phenomenon – states parties from recruiting or allowing children under fifteen years of age to directly engage in hostilities. Why the wording from Additional Protocol I is more or less retained verbatim may be due to similar political considerations and concerns as those that considerably weakened the original language proposed by the International Committee of the Red Cross (ICRC) during the drafting of the Additional Protocols. Vague terms and phraseology such as 'all feasible measures' or 'direct part in hostilities' allow each state to determine the meaning, and hence scope of obligations, of treaty provisions. There had also been resistance from states that supported national liberation movements and that recognized that a large numbers of fighting children and youths involved in these movements were critical to their success.[42] When international law is seen to infringe upon or excessively interfere with core elements of state sovereignty, including issues relative to the armed forces and national security, principles such as that of 'humanity' are more easily sidelined.

In acknowledging these shortcomings, the Committee on the Rights of the Child decided at its first session in 1991 to hold its very first so-called Day of General Discussion specifically on Children and Armed Conflict. This decision was also based, among other things, on the need to 'underline the complexity of the question of children in armed conflicts, which should not simply be reduced to the consideration of one single provision of the Convention, namely article 38'.[43] In reviewing contributions to this Day of General Discussion, the Committee envisaged various measures it could take to address the problem, including the 'preliminary drafting of a future Optional Protocol to the Convention on the Rights of the Child raising the age of recruitment of children into the armed forces to 18 years of age'.[44] A preliminary draft optional protocol on the involvement of children in armed conflict was included in the Committee's outcome document on the Day of Discussion.[45]

The Optional Protocol to the Convention on the Involvement of Children in Armed Conflict (CRC-OPAC) was adopted in 2000. Further development in the field of human rights law, notably the adoption of the African Charter on the Rights and Welfare of the Child (1990),[46] the

Rome Statute on the International Criminal Court (1998),[47] and the ILO Convention No. 182 on the Prohibition and Immediate Action for the Elimination of the Worst Forms of Child Labour[48] were instrumental in raising the minimum age of recruitment into armed forces from fifteen to eighteen in the Optional Protocol. Nonetheless, the Optional Protocol falls short of an absolute prohibition of the recruitment and use of children under the age of eighteen years in the armed forces of states parties: States parties shall take 'all feasible measures' to ensure that members of their armed forces who have not yet turned eighteen do not take a 'direct part in hostilities' (Article 1) and 'shall ensure' that persons under the age of eighteen are not 'compulsorily recruited' into their armed forces (Article 2). Article 3 addresses only to a certain degree the inadequacies of Article 38(3) of the Convention on the Rights of the Child by obliging states parties to raise the minimum age for voluntary recruitment, 'recognizing that under the Convention persons under 18 are entitled to special protection'. An *express* obligation imposed on states parties to actually establish eighteen years as the minimum age for voluntary recruitment is not codified.

While the Protocol's distinction between compulsory and voluntary recruitment has attracted considerable critique,[49] among its main positive innovations is Article 4 which prohibits the recruitment or use in hostilities of persons under eighteen years by 'armed groups' and obliges states parties to prevent such recruitment and use, including legal measures to prohibit and criminalize such practices. In view of realities on the ground today and the proliferation of non-state actors engaging in the recruitment of child soldiers and other child abuses, this is a significant improvement compared to the protection provided by international humanitarian law. In this sense, the Optional Protocol has been described as 'a best example of a potential merger of HRL and IHL with regard to children'.[50] It remains a matter of fact, however, that this merger is setting its highest protection standards *vis-à-vis* non-state actors while permitting states to continue recruitment of children under the age of eighteen.[51] Nevertheless, it should be underlined that the Committee on the Rights of the Child has consistently recommended states parties to the Optional Protocol to raise the minimum age for recruitment to eighteen years with a view to strengthening the protection of children,[52] noting further that a great majority of states parties to the Protocol do not permit voluntary recruitment of children.[53] The jurisprudence of the Committee also establishes that there should be no exceptions to such minimum age.[54]

3. Humanity: child protection from law to practice

The Optional Protocol to the Convention on the Rights of the Child on the Involvement of Children in Armed Conflict has been considered a 'pioneer example of adopting a treaty text in [human rights law] that entirely addresses an issue relevant exclusively to [international humanitarian law]'.[55] Consequently, the Optional Protocol can be seen as setting a precedent for future normative developments in international human rights law on the basis of international humanitarian law. The fact that children are the subjects of this pioneering legal development should not come as a surprise: when, if not towards the youngest and weakest members of the human family, would not states and other actors be willing to demonstrate grace, kindness, and compassion, to refer to the original etymology of the word humanity? In the words of the Committee on the Rights of the Child: 'The distinct nature of children, their initial dependent and developmental state, their unique human potential as well as their vulnerability, all demand for more, rather than less, legal and other protection from all forms of violence.'[56] Does not this prove that the principle of humanity is a living norm of guidance that shapes and reinforces the evolution of standard setting and implementation of both international humanitarian and human rights law?

This reasoning also seems to challenge the contention that the issue of the recruitment and use of children in armed conflict was an issue 'relevant exclusively to international humanitarian law'.[57] In view of the brief exposé above of some key areas of convergence and influence of human rights law and international humanitarian law, special protection for children originally developed from principles and standards set forth in human rights law. In this perspective, the principle of humanity can be interpreted as the philosophical driving force behind the cross-fertilization of child protection provisions in both bodies of law. This backs the argument put forth here that it is probably not a coincidence that the 'principle of humanity' enters the vocabulary of international humanitarian law (AP I and II) only subsequent to the codification of international human rights law instruments. When the UN High Commissioner for Human Rights today calls for respect of the imperative or the principle of 'civilian inviolability' in situations of armed conflict, it is a call for respect of 'humanity' in situations of armed conflict.[58] Different eras, different generations, and different disciplines employ different language, concepts and terminologies intended for the same purpose: upholding and respecting the dignity and worth of each and every individual, which remains a fundamental guiding principle of international human rights law.

Even if the Optional Protocol were to inspire further development of legal standards in either body of law, the question is whether children exposed to the 'scourge of war' really need more standards or more law-making at the international level? First, effective implementation and compliance with existing standards should be assessed. This raises the question: sixty years after the adoption of the Geneva Conventions and twenty years after the Convention on the Rights of the Child, to what extent has 'special protection' of children been ensured? Recalling that there are today 193 states parties to the Convention on the Rights of the Child, 141 states parties to the Optional Protocol to the Convention, and that a majority of UN member states have ratified the Geneva Conventions and their Additional Protocols, the answer is pitiful. Two excerpts from reports of UNICEF and the UN Special Representative of the Secretary-General on Children and Armed Conflict respectively, suffice to illustrate that, with respect to child protection, the principle of 'humanity' remains a legal principle more than a principle of practice:

> More than 2 million children have died as a direct result of armed conflict, and more than three times that number have been permanently disabled or seriously injured. An estimated 20 million children have been forced to flee from their homes and more than 1 million have been orphaned or separated from their families. Some 300,000 child soldiers boys and girls under the age of 18 are involved in more than 30 countries worldwide.[59]
>
> In the past decade, a number of United Nations reports … have noted with concern the fact that the character and tactics of war are changing. These changes have created new and unprecedented threats to children. In many of the new wars, especially in Asia and Africa, conflict remains internal and takes place in peripheral areas where access is difficult. In particular, children and other vulnerable segments of the civilian population are increasingly becoming the direct targets of violence. In addition to thousands of children being killed and wounded as a direct result of fighting, many more children in conflict contexts die from malnutrition and disease. Other fundamental rights, such as education and recreation, are also being denied children in situations of armed conflict.[60]

With the images that these excerpts evoke, it is indeed a paradox that despite the 'pioneering' merger of international humanitarian law and human rights law in the field of children's rights, children and women continue, in virtually all contemporary conflicts, to suffer disproportionally.[61]

4. Enforcing the principle of humanity for children in armed conflict

As emphasized by the UN Special Representative of the Secretary-General for Children and Armed Conflict, priority today should shift collective emphasis from the development of norms and standards of protection, which are comprehensive and robust due to concerted efforts made by the international community, to their practical application and implementation on the ground.[62] Likewise, the head of the ICRC legal division on the occasion of the sixtieth anniversary of the Geneva Conventions stressed that the major challenge is not the rules as such but 'that the law is not being respected nearly enough. Too few people know what the Geneva Conventions are, while too many warring parties ignore or flout them.'[63] In view of the strong interrelation and mutually reinforcing convergence of international humanitarian law and human rights law regarding the protection of children involved in armed conflict, the potential for action to translate standards into practice is arguably greater than with respect to other areas of international humanitarian law.

In particular, this interrelationship facilitates interdisciplinary and concerted efforts by a multitude of actors simultaneously. In view of the complexity and myriad of political, economic and socio-cultural factors that perpetuate armed conflict and the participation of children therein, such multi-track strategies are indispensable. The basis for such complementarity is the state's responsibility under international human rights law to work towards a long-term political, social and institutional environment where the provisions of the CRC and CRC-OPAC can be implemented, through *preventive* (e.g., rigorous recruitment procedures and age verification mechanisms) as well as through *reactive* measures (e.g., application of legislation criminalizing recruitment). The realization of other rights protected under the Convention on the Rights of the Child, not the least the right to an identity, the right to life, survival and development and the right to an education, are equally important preventive mechanisms. Indeed, the Committee on the Rights of the Child, in its General Discussion on children in armed conflict, recalled that the overall realization of the rights of the child should be ensured and that 'this framework was very often also reflected in provisions of humanitarian law'.[64] Concerning international humanitarian law, the basis is the respect for existing rules and regulations by parties to the Geneva Conventions and the Additional Protocols, including through well-trained and disciplined armed forces and armed groups operating under a functioning chain of command where accountability for any breach is ensured.

At the international level, among the key actors to facilitate the translation of the legal complementarity of IHL and HRL into practical complementarity of protection are the Committee on the Rights of the Child, the ICRC, the Office of the Special Representative of the Secretary-General for Children and Armed Conflict, the International Criminal Court, the General Assembly and the Security Council (and its Working Group on Children), and non-governmental organizations. Below follow examples of suggested courses of action by these actors that could foster greater practical application of the above-mentioned and other relevant child-specific IHL and HRL norms.

4.1 *Effective use of relevant UN human rights monitoring mechanisms, in particular the Committee on the Rights of the Child*

Dialogue with states through the reporting procedure under the CRC and the CRC-OPAC

The Committee on the Rights of the Child, monitoring not only the implementation of the Convention on the Rights of the Child but also implementation of the Optional Protocol by states parties to these treaties, plays a key role in promoting realization of the child-related standards in both human rights law and international humanitarian law. The recommendations and concluding observations, as well as General Comments, of the Committee provide useful guidance to states in adopting the appropriate legislative, administrative, educational and other measures necessary to ensure the effective implementation of the relevant provisions of the CRC, the CRC-OPAC, as well as the Geneva Conventions and the Additional Protocols.

The Committee commenced examination of states parties' reports on the CRC-OPAC in January 2005 and has to date examined and issued recommendations with respect to reports submitted by sixty-three states parties.[65] The reporting process (from the preparation and drafting of the report, to the state's dialogue with the Committee on the occasion of the examination of its report, and implementation by the state of the Committee's recommendation) represents a constructive, non-confrontational and voluntary opportunity for each state party to assess progress and identify remaining obstacles in the realization of these standards. For instance, the revised reporting guidelines of the Committee on the Optional Protocol ask states parties to provide information to the Committee on the number of children under the age of eighteen voluntarily recruited into the national armed forces and, when applicable, available data on the number of children recruited and used in hostilities by armed groups in the state party, details of measures taken to prevent recruitment of children by armed forces distinct from the state and whether it cooperates with the ICRC in such efforts, and with the Office of the Special Representative of the Secretary-General on Children and Armed Conflict (SRSG-CAAC) and measures taken to prevent attacks on civilian objects protected under international humanitarian law and other international instruments.[66] The Committee's recommendations to states parties (known as 'concluding observations') likewise seek to strengthen efforts by states parties to ensure respect for international humanitarian law, including by reforming domestic military law;[67] disseminating information related to international humanitarian law in local languages; training members of the armed forces, especially recruitment officers, in international humanitarian law;[68] and extending extra-territorial jurisdiction over war crimes, including the conscription and enlistment of children under fifteen.[69]

Committee on the Rights of the Child and CRC Article 45

Article 45 of the Convention on the Rights of the Child sets out a number of activities that the Committee on the Rights of the Child may undertake with a view to 'foster effective implementation of the Convention and to encourage international cooperation in the field covered by the Convention'. Under this provision, the Committee can: (i) invite UN specialized agencies, UNICEF, and other competent bodies (such as NGOs) to provide expert advice on the implementation of the Convention in areas falling within the scope of their respective mandates (Article 45(a)); (ii) transmit to any of these bodies reports by states parties containing a request or indicating a need for technical assistance or advice (Article 45(b)); and (iii) recommend to the General Assembly that it requests the Secretary-General to undertake on its behalf studies on specific issues relating to children's rights (Article 45(c)). An excellent example of the impact of such initiatives in the context of children and armed conflict is the adoption of General Assembly Resolution 48/157 in 1993, following a recommendation by the Committee, which recommended that the Secretary-General appoint an independent expert to study the impact of armed conflict on children. The outcome document, the Graça Machel report of 1996 on *Impact of Armed Conflict on Children*, further recommended the establishment of a Special Representative on the impact of armed conflict on children (today the Special Representative of the Secretary-General on Children and Armed Conflict).[70]

Support for the establishment of a communications procedure under the Convention on the Rights of the Child

An important step[71] to further strengthen the protection of children's rights was taken in June 2009 when the UN Human Rights Council adopted a resolution providing for the establishment of an Open-ended Working Group with the mandate to 'explore the possibility of elaborating an optional protocol to the Convention on the Rights of the Child to provide a communication procedure'.[72] The Convention is currently the only core UN human rights treaty without a communications procedure attached to it. The possibility of seeking remedy for an alleged violation of the Convention, including violations of Article 38, and of the provisions set forth in the CRC-OPAC, through a communications procedure complementary to the above reporting procedure would, in the words of the Chairperson of the Committee on the Rights of the Child, 'significantly contribute to the overall protection of children's rights'.[73]

In accordance with the above-mentioned resolution, the first session of the Working Group was held from 14–18 December 2009. Little more than a year later, in February 2011, the Working Group adopted a final text of the Optional Protocol, which is expected to be adopted by the General Assembly at its sixty-sixth session in 2011.[74] Under the Optional Protocol, which provides for individual complaints, inter-state communications and an inquiry procedure, complaints on alleged violations of the CRC and its Optional Protocols on the involvement of children in armed conflict and on the sale of children, child prostitution (CRC-OPSC) and child pornography, can be submitted to the Committee on the Rights of the Child for examination.[75] The omission from the final text of the possibility for the Committee to also consider *collective* communications[76] on violations under the Convention and its two substantive Protocols has been regretted among supporters of a strong communications procedure.[77] Such a procedure, which would have allowed non-governmental organizations and national human rights institutions to submit complaints on recurring violations affecting many children, could certainly have played a particularly important role in bringing critical situations concerning violations of children's rights in situations of armed conflict to the Committee's attention.

Nevertheless, the possibility to submit complaints to the Committee under the Optional Protocol for individuals or groups of individuals claiming to be victims of a violation of the rights stipulated in theCRC, CRC-OPAC and CRC-OPSC[78] will, needless to say, constitute an important additional protection mechanism for children affected by armed conflict, and a critical accountability mechanism for states parties, and should, as such, gain solid support from states and other actors.

4.2 Strengthening monitoring and reporting mechanisms on child rights and armed conflict in the field by the United Nations and other actors

There are currently several monitoring and reporting mechanisms in respect of children affected by armed conflicts operating at a field level under the auspices of the United Nations, which are complementary to, should build upon and can reinforce the recommendations issued by the Committee on the Rights of the Child and, as applicable, other UN human rights treaty bodies.

One is the so-called *monitoring and reporting mechanism* (MRM) set up at country-level to report on violations of grave child rights violations, including the recruitment and use of children in armed forces or groups,[79] in line with Security Council resolution 1612 (2005). The reports produced by country task forces set up in accordance with this Security Council resolution are considered by a specific Working Group of the Security Council on Children and Armed Conflict, which can make recommendations to the Security Council such as appropriate mandates for peace-keeping missions, or to other UN bodies,[80] to promote the protection of children affected by armed conflict. An equally important task is the ability of field-based task forces to engage in dialogue with concerned national actors on the practical measures to prevent child rights violations, including time-bound action plans to end and prevent the recruitment and use of children in armed forces.[81] Ultimately, the actions undertaken in the framework of the MRM are designed to support and supplement, as appropriate, the protection and rehabilitation roles of national governments.[82] The MRM has primarily been established in situations of parties to conflict (armed forces of states or armed groups) that recruit and use children in armed conflict, a list of which have been included in reports of the Secretary-General on children and armed conflict since 2002.[83] Subsequent to Security Council resolution 1882 of August 2009, that list also includes 'parties to armed conflict that engage in patterns of killing and maiming of children and/or rape and other sexual violence against children, in situations of armed conflict'.[84]

Another key field-based activity of the United Nations that can address urgent child rights protection concerns, as well as assist states in building more long-term institutional structures, are *UN peace operations*. In particular, child protection, human rights, and rule of law components of peace operations play important roles in supporting and building local and national capacity and preventive measures. The mandate of the UN Mission in the Democratic Republic of the Congo (MONUC) included, for instance, that of providing training in international humanitarian and human rights law, child protection and the prevention of gender-based violence to members of the armed forces of the Democratic Republic of the Congo (DRC), as well as to assist the authorities in human rights promotion and protection, in particular concerning women, children and other vulnerable groups, and cooperate in efforts to bring to justice perpetrators of grave violations of human rights and international humanitarian law.[85]

Thirdly, field presences of the *Office of the High Commissioner for Human Rights* (OHCHR) can play a critical role in promoting respect for human rights and humanitarian law, including by facilitating legislative reform relating to the criminalization of the recruitment and use of under-aged persons in armed and non-armed forces and in accountability measures and monitoring and reporting on cases of violations of children's rights.[86] For instance, the mandate of the OHCHR country office in Colombia includes that of 'observing and reporting on human rights and international humanitarian law, giving advice, providing technical cooperation, promoting and disseminating human rights and international humanitarian law, and strengthening national authorities and civil society'.[87]

4.3 *Role of the Special Representative of the Secretary-General for Children and Armed Conflict and impartial and neutral humanitarian organizations*

Besides the role of supporting and engaging the national task forces on MRM on Security Council resolution 1612 and presenting their findings to the Working Group of the Security Council on Children and Armed Conflict, the Special Representative for Children and Armed Conflict plays an important advocacy role directly *vis-à-vis* states. An important element of such advocacy strategy is the undertaking of field visits, which aim, inter alia, at gaining a first-hand assessment of the situation of children so as to enhance global advocacy for protection and prevention programmes on their behalf and to engage in dialogue with national authorities at the highest levels to gain concrete commitments to prevent and address violations.[88] In her annual report to the General Assembly in

2009, the Special Representative identified 'child protection dialogue with non-state actors' as one of the current critical themes, recognizing that 'the cessation of violations against children in situations of armed conflict and the provision of programmes for victims depends to large extent on the establishment of such dialogue'.[89]

In this respect, examining the ways in which governments can be encouraged to facilitate dialogue between non-state armed groups and the United Nations, especially with regard to awareness and application of the relevant child-specific rules and standards in international humanitarian and human rights law, is critical. In situations of concern where governments have been reluctant to allow for further dialogue with certain armed groups, this has impeded progress on securing the release and rehabilitation of children associated with these groups.[90] Besides the Special Representative, one may contemplate ways in which the Security Council Working Group on Children and Armed Conflict could reach out to local and regional actors, for instance by carrying out on-site visits, and encouraging action where progress has been stalled.

In similar situations, neutral and impartial humanitarian organisations such as Geneva Call and the Coalition to Stop the Use of Child Soldiers can have an important role to play. Geneva Call, dedicated to 'engaging armed non-state actors towards compliance with the norms of international humanitarian law and human rights law',[91] initiated its Children and Armed Non-State Actor (CANSA) programme in 2008. As non-state actors do not have the legal capacity to become party to international treaties, Geneva Call has created a parallel mechanism known as the Deed of Commitment. At a 2009 conference in Geneva, representatives of twenty-eight non-state actors from around the globe endorsed the plans of Geneva Call to follow up the initial Deed of Commitment on the anti-personnel landmine ban with one on children and armed conflict.[92] Such a Deed of Commitment for the Protection of Children from the Effects of Armed Conflict was launched in November 2010. It aims at providing 'armed non-state actors (NSAs), which lack the legal capacity to become party to relevant international treaties, with an opportunity to demonstrate their commitment to international norms protecting children from armed conflict'.[93] Signatories to the Deed of Commitment commit themselves, inter alia:

> (1) to adhere to a total ban on the use of children in hostilities; (2) to ensure that children are not recruited into our armed forces, whether voluntarily or non-voluntarily ...; (3) to never compel children to associate with, or remain associated with, our armed forces.

> Importantly, by signing the Deed, non-state armed groups further agree to allow and cooperate in the monitoring and verification of our present commitment by Geneva Call and other independent international and national organizations associated for this purpose with Geneva Call. Such monitoring and verification include visits and inspections in all areas where we operate, and the provision of the necessary information and reports, as may be required for such purposes in the spirit of transparency and accountability.[94]

As such, the Deed of Commitment represents a groundbreaking novel avenue for independent expert bodies to access and engage in dialogue with non-state armed groups with a view to strengthening the latter's awareness of and compliance with international law as it relates to the protection of children. Noting Article 7 whereby signatories commit to provide children in areas where they exercise authority with aid and care, this includes equivalent 'positive obligations' of non-state armed groups to protect children.[95]

The Coalition to Stop the Use of Child Soldiers is another non-governmental organization now with years of experience in engaging with both armed forces of states and non-state armed groups on prevention of recruitment and use of child soldiers. Local chapters of the organization have been created over the years, for example the DRC Coalition Chapter. Created in 2000, the DRC Coalition Chapter, through an initiative to encourage families of children recruited by armed forces to engage other local networks such as community and religious leaders, teachers and social workers to advocate for child protection, has over time succeeded to engender a 'change in attitude and a noticeable reduction of forced recruitment and military training of under-18s' among armed groups in eastern DRC.[96]

4.4 *Enhance concerted efforts by ICRC, UN system and regional organizations*

As the organisation whose mandate derives in part from the Geneva Conventions and whose exclusively humanitarian mission is 'to protect the lives and dignity of victims of armed conflict and other situations of violence and to provide them with assistance', the ICRC upholds a critical position in advancing effective protection for children caught in or forced into the lines of fire. With its privileged position and contacts with parties to conflicts, both state and non-state actors, the ICRC can, perhaps more readily than other international actors, identify protection needs and shortcomings and advocate for IHL compliance. An interesting area of study in this respect would be to examine the role and possibilities of the ICRC in reminding parties to the Additional Protocol I of the implications of section II of the Protocol on repression of breaches of the Geneva Conventions and the Protocol. If staff members of the ICRC were to observe violations of Article 77(1), it appears to be vital to remind and follow up with national authorities regarding the duty of commanders to initiate disciplinary or penal action against violators who are going to commit or have committed any breach of the GCs or AP I.[97] This is particularly so when keeping in mind the call by the Special Representative for Children and Armed Conflict to the Human Rights Council in September 2009 that in order to halt grave violations against children, 'addressing impunity and holding perpetrators accountable must remain a priority of the international community'.[98]

4.5 Role of the International Criminal Court

The Rome Statute of the International Criminal Court (ICC) introduced a new category of war crimes by making the recruitment of children an international crime. A precedent in the criminalization of the recruitment and use of children in international law had been seen in the case *Prosecutor* v. *Norman* of the Special Court of Sierra Leone in 2004, stating that the enlisting of child soldiers had been prohibited in customary international law and subject to individual criminal responsibility, even before the adoption of the ICC Statute.[99] In January 2009, the ICC made 'legal history' as the Court put on trial its first suspect taken into custody, Mr Thomas Lubanga Dyilo, a Congolese warlord accused of recruiting child soldiers.[100] Mr Lubanga was accused of a series of war crimes, including conscripting and enlisting child soldiers into the military wing of his group and then using them to participate in hostilities in the DRC between September 2002 and August 2003. His case represents not only the debut proceedings of the ICC but also the 'first trial in the history of international law to see the active participation of victims in the proceedings, among which will number child combatants'.[101]

5. Conclusion

By examining the evolution of the legal protection of the child in situations of conflict from a historical perspective, this exposé has attempted to demonstrate the significant influence of human rights law in the development of international humanitarian law, but also to highlight the reverse impact. In particular, it has argued that an underlying tenet and guiding norm behind this beneficial cross-fertilization of international law-making is indeed that of 'the principle of humanity'. The principle is founded on the same philosophical cornerstone as human rights law: the imperative to protect the weakest in society against the abuse of the strong. In the same spirit, the principle of humanity is the principle that guides the ICRC in its purpose 'to protect life and health and to ensure respect for the human being'.[102]

The legal standing of the principle of humanity may be more diffuse, but is still implicit in the principle's status as the normative foundation of both international humanitarian law and human rights law, whose interdependency and interrelatedness in situations of conflict are also seen in the development of customary IHL standards.[103] When the Committee on the Rights of the Child discussed the topic of children and armed conflict in 1992, the need to consider a 'set of minimum humanitarian standards' to be 'applicable in all situations to all children, without discrimination, in a period of armed conflict' was crystallized.[104] With the convergence of international human rights and humanitarian law as outlined in this chapter, such sets of standards have gradually been formed. In practice, these should be translated into concrete preventive and protective action by all actors with obligations established under the two sets of laws and other applicable legal instruments. As phrased by the Special Representative of the Secretary-General on Children and Armed Conflict, '[c]ollectively, we should be guided by a principle of "exceptional consideration for children" as the most vulnerable segment of the population that deserves unconditional protection'.[105] That exceptional consideration comes with better understanding of and unconditional application of the relevant instruments of international humanitarian and human rights law, prompted and supported by collective interaction and cooperation.

Just as the Human Rights Committee noted that international humanitarian law and international human rights law are 'complementary, not mutually exclusive', so are the preventive and protective roles of actors responsible for their effective implementation and of corresponding monitoring bodies complementary and mutually reinforcing. The Security Council acknowledged this interdependency, irrespective of the type of conflict, in its recent resolution 1882 (2009) on Children and Armed Conflict, by:

> calling on all parties to conflicts to comply strictly with the obligations applicable to them under international law for the protection of children

> in armed conflict, including those contained in the Convention on the Rights of the Child and its Optional Protocol on the involvement of Children in Armed Conflict, as well as the Geneva Conventions of 12th August 1949 and their Additional Protocols of 1977.[106]

To effectively prevent and protect children from the violence and abuse of armed conflict, all relevant actors must play their part to cast a complete net of protection. The assessment made by Graça Machel in her landmark 1996 report on the *Impact of Armed Conflict on Children* has not, regrettably, changed dramatically over the past decade. Ms Machel then wrote:

> [The] statistics are shocking enough, but more chilling is the conclusion to be drawn from them: more and more of the world is being sucked into a desolate moral vacuum. This is a space devoid of the most basic human values; a space in which children are slaughtered, raped, and maimed; a space in which children are exploited as soldiers; a space in which children are starved and exposed to extreme brutality. Such unregulated terror and violence speak of deliberate victimization. There are few further depths to which humanity can sink.[107]

Mankind still owes to the child the best it can give.

Notes

1 Geneva Declaration of the Rights of the Child, adopted on 26 September 1924, League of Nations.

2 *Online Etymology Dictionary* and *Oxford Online Dictionary*.

3 V. Popovski, 'Protection of children in international humanitarian law and human rights law', in R. Arnold and N. Quénivet (eds.), *International Humanitarian Law and Human Rights Law: Towards a New Merger in International Law* (Brill, 2008) 384.

4 The Optional Protocol to the Convention on the Rights of the Child on the Involvement of Children in Armed Conflict entered into force on 12 February 2002. To access the text of the Optional Protocol and the Convention on the Rights of the Child, see the webpage of the UN Committee on the Rights of the Child on the website of the Office of the High Commissioner for Human Rights (www2.ohchr.org/english/bodies/crc/index.htm).

5 See Robert Kolb, Chapter 2.

6 The wounded and sick, prisoners of war and the civilian populations as per the Geneva Conventions I–IV.

7 See *Respect for Human Rights in Armed Conflict, Report of the Secretary-General*, UN doc. A/7720 (20 November 1969) paras. 15–24.

8 *Ibid.* para. 23.

9 The third phase in the development of international humanitarian law as per Kolb's categorization, see Robert Kolb, Chapter 2.

10 K. Drewicki, 'The UN Charter and the Universal Declaration of Human Rights' in R. Hanski and M. Suksi (eds.), *An Introduction to the International Protection of Human Rights* (Turku, 1999) 71.

11 International Committee of the Red Cross, *The Geneva Conventions of August 12 1949*, 19.
12 Drewicki, 'UN Charter', 75.
13 For a full list, see the Summary Table of Provisions of international humanitarian law and other provisions of international law specifically applicable to children in war of the International Committee of the Red Cross, available at www.icrc.org.
14 Carolyn Hamilton, 'Armed conflict: the protection of children under international law', available at www.essex.ac.uk/armedcon/international/comment/Text/paper 001.htm.
15 Geneva Convention IV relative to the Protection of Civilians in Time of War Article 24.
16 Denise Plattner, 'Protection of children in international humanitarian law' (1984) 240 *International Review of the Red Cross* 140.
17 Geneva Convention III relative to the Treatment of Prisoners of War, Articles 16 and 49.
18 Geneva Convention IV, Article 12 on measures relating to child welfare.
19 Geneva Convention IV, Article 51: the occupying power may not compel protected persons to work unless they are over eighteen years of age, and then only under specific conditions. Geneva Convention IV, Article 68(4): in any case, the death penalty may not be pronounced against a protected person who was under eighteen years of age at the time of the offence.
20 UDHR, Article 25(2).
21 The purpose of AP II is to develop and supplement Common Article 3 of the 1949 Geneva Conventions and it applies to 'all armed conflicts which are not covered' by Article 1 of AP I and which 'takes place in the territory of a High Contracting Party between its armed groups and dissident armed forces of other organized armed groups which, under responsible command, exercise such control over a part of its territory as to enable them to carry out sustained and concerted military operations'. AP II, Article 1(1).
22 AP II, Article 4(3).
23 AP I, Article 77(2) and AP II, Article 4(3)(c)–(d).
24 Popovski, 'Protection', 394.
25 See also Human Rights Committee, General Comment No. 17 on the Rights of the Child, 1989, UN doc. HRI/GEN/1/Rev.8, para. 1.
26 *Ibid*, paras. 1 and 4.
27 *Respect for Human Rights in Armed Conflict, Report of the Secretary-General*, UN doc. A/7720 (20 November 1969), para. 26.
28 *Ibid.*
29 *Ibid.*, para. 29.
30 Security Council Resolution 237 (1967), welcomed by the General Assembly in its Resolution 2252 (ES-V) (1967).
31 Human Rights Committee, General Comment No. 31 on Nature of the General Legal Obligation Imposed on States Parties to the Covenant, UN doc. CCPR/C/21/Rev.1/Add.13 (26 May 2004) para. 11. See also Human Rights Committee General Comment No. 29 on State of Emergency (Article 4) which states that derogations under Article 4 in situations of armed conflict are allowed 'only if and to the extent that the situation constitutes a threat to the life of the nation', and must not be inconsistent with the state's other international obligations, 'particularly the rules

of international humanitarian law'. UN doc. CCPR/C/21/Rev.1/Add.11 (31 August 2001) paras. 3 and 9.

32 See, inter alia, GA Res 2444 (XXIIII) (9 December). 1966.

33 See GA Res. 2676 (XXV) (1970). See also K. Månsson, 'Implementing the concept of protection of civilians in the light of international humanitarian law and human rights law: the case of MONUC', in Arnold and Quénivet (eds.), *Towards a New Merger*, 572–3.

34 Declaration on the Protection of Women and Children in Emergency and Armed Conflict, GA Res. 3318 (XXIX), (14 December 1974) para. 6.

35 Additional Protocol II, Article 3(c).

36 Human Rights Committee, General Comment No. 17 on the Rights of the Child, 1989, para. 3.

37 C. Breen, 'The role of NGOs in the formulation of and compliance with the Optional Protocol to the Convention on the Rights of the Child on Involvement of Children in Armed Conflict' (2003) 25 *Human Rights Quarterly* 460.

38 See also CRC Articles 6(1)(2) 20(1) and 32(1) which are also relevant in the context of protection of children in situations of armed conflict.

39 Popovski, 'Protection', 384.

40 Committee on the Rights of the Child, Report on its second session, September/October 1992, UN doc. CRC/C/10, para. 65. See also UNICEF, *Implementation Handbook for the Convention on the Rights of the Child* (3rd edn., September) 2007 573–586.

41 S.K. Karanja, 'Child soldiers in peace agreements: the peace and justice dilemma!' (2008) 8 *Global Jurist* 19.

42 D.M. Rosen, 'Child soldiers, international humanitarian law, and the globalization of childhood' (2007) *American Anthropologist* 302.

43 See the document on Children in Armed Conflict, available at www2.ohchr.org/english/bodies/crc/discussion2008.htm or in UN doc. CRC/C/10 (5 October 1992).

44 UN doc. CRC/C/10, 1992, para. 75. The Commission on Human Rights established a working group to elaborate such a draft Optional Protocol to the Convention by means of Resolution 1994/91 in 1994. For an overview of the elaboration of the Optional Protocol, see Breen, 'The role of NGOs', 453–81.

45 See www2.ohchr.org/english/bodies/crc/discussion2008.htm.

46 African Charter on the Rights and Welfare of the Child, 1990, Article 22, reads: 'States Parties to the present Charter shall take all necessary measures to ensure that no child shall take a direct part in hostilities and refrain in particular, from recruiting any child.' Article 2 of the African Charter clearly stipulates that a child means every human being below the age of eighteen.

47 The ICC Statute is applicable to both international and non-international armed conflicts, and defines as a war crime the conscription or enlistment of children under the age of fifteen into armed groups or groups or using them to participate actively in hostilities. See ICC Statute, Article 8(2)(e)(viii).

48 Article 3(a) of ILO Convention No. 182 includes among the 'worst forms of child labour' the forced or compulsory recruitment of children for use in armed conflict.

49 See, e.g., Popovski, 'Protection', 400.

50 *Ibid.* 399.

51 See also Rosen, 'Child soldiers', 302.

52 See, e.g., the Committee's concluding observations on Israel: *Consideration of Reports Submitted by States Parties under Article 8 of the Optional Protocol to the Convention on the Rights of the Child on the Involvement of Children in Armed Conflict*, UN doc. CRC/C/OPAC/ISR/CO/1 (2010) para. 21.

53 Under Article 3 (2), of the Optional Protocol, a states party shall deposit a binding declaration upon ratification of or accession to the Protocol setting forth the minimum age at which it will permit voluntary recruitment into its national armed forces. These declarations are available on the webpage of the United Nations Treaties Collection, see http://treaties.un.org/pages/ViewDetails.aspx?src=TREATY&mtdsg_no=IV-11-b&chapter=4&lang=en.

54 See, e.g., the Committee's concluding observations on Mexico, *Consideration of Reports Submitted by States Parties under Article 8 of the Optional Protocol to the Convention on the Rights of the Child on the Involvement of Children in Armed Conflict*, UN doc. CRC/C/OPAC/MEX/CO/1 (2011) para. 21.

55 Popovski, 'Protection', 399.

56 Committee on the Rights of the Child, General Comment No. 8: the right of the child to protection from corporal punishment and other cruel or degrading forms of punishment (paras. 19, 28, and 37), UN doc. CRC/C/GC/8 (2 March 2007), para. 21.

57 Popovski, 'Protection', 399.

58 The High Commissioner for Human Rights, Ms. Navanethem Pillay, in her opening speech to the 12th session of the Human Rights Council on 14 September 2009 stressed that 'in situations of armed conflict combatants must ensure that effective measures are put in place to guarantee respect for international human rights law and international humanitarian law, including the principle of civilian inviolability'. Opening statement, at 5, available at www.unhchr.ch/huricane/huricane.nsf/view01/2DD5A4BD46C13CEFC1257631002D5B6B?opendocument.

59 *UNICEF Humanitarian Action Report 2005*, quoted in Popovski, 'Protection', 386.

60 *Report of the Special Representative to the Secretary-General for Children and Armed Conflict*, UN doc. A/64/254, (6 August. 2009), para. 5.

61 Speech of the High Commissioner for Human Rights, *supra* note 58, 5.

62 *Ibid.* para. 27.

63 Interview with Mr Knut Dörmann, Head of the ICRC legal division on 8 August 2009, available at www.icrc.org/web/eng/siteeng0.nsf/htmlall/geneva-convention-interview-120809.,

64 See *Children in Armed Conflict*, para 37, available at www2.ohchr.org/english/bodies/crc/discussion2008.htm. The Committee referred to the importance of protecting the family environment; ensuring the provision of essential care and assistance; ensuring access to health, food and education; prohibiting torture, abuse or neglect; prohibiting the death penalty; and the need to preserve the children's cultural environment, as well as the need of protection in situations of deprivation of liberty. *Ibid.*

65 As of May 2011.

66 See *Revised Guidelines regarding Initial Reports to be Submitted by States Parties under Article 8, para. 1, of the Optional Protocol to the Convention on the Rights of the Child on Involvement of Children in Armed Conflict*, UN doc. CRC/C/OPAC/2 (19 October 2007) paras. 8(a), 14(e), 16 and 35.

67 For instance, in regard to Chile, the Committee recommended 'the speedy adoption of the reform of the Code of Military Justice, in conformity with international

standards of international humanitarian law and human rights law'. See UN doc. CRC/C/OPAC/CHL/CO/1 (13 February 2008), para. 20.

68 For instance, in regard to Bangladesh, the Committee recommended the state party to 'further expand and mainstream courses on international humanitarian law to all persons working with children and to military personnel, especially the recruiting officers'. See UN doc. CRC/C/OPAC/BGD/CO/1 (17 March 2006), para. 26.

69 See the recommendation with regard to Monaco: in line with the minimum standards prescribed by the Convention on the Rights of the Child (Article 38), and relevant instruments of international humanitarian law, consider establishing extra-territorial jurisdiction over war crimes which involve conscripting or enlisting children under the age of fifteen into the armed forces. UN doc. CRC/C/OPAC/MCO/CO/1 (18 June 2007) para. 9(a).

70 *Impact of Armed Conflict on Children, Report of the Expert of the Secretary-General, Ms. Graça Machel, submitted pursuant to General Assembly Resolution 48/157*, UN doc. A/51/306 (26 August 1996).

71 Another, and perhaps more familiar, terminology for communications procedure is 'the individual complaints procedure'. The procedure entails the possibility for anyone under the jurisdiction of a state party to a UN human rights treaty to bring a complaint alleging a violation of the rights set forth in that treaty to the UN treaty body set up (under that specific treaty) for quasi-judicial adjudication. For more information on the communications/complaints procedure, see OHCHR Fact Sheet No. 7 on Complaint Procedures (Rev.1), available at: http://www.ohchr.org/EN/PublicationsResources/Pages/FactSheets.aspx.

72 Human Rights Council Resolution 11/1, 17 June 2009, UN doc. A/HRC/11/L.3.

73 Statement by Ms Yanghee Lee, Chairperson of the Committee on the Rights of the Child, 64th session of the General Assembly, Third Committee, Item 65, 14 October 2009, New York.

74 See Draft Report of the Open-ended Working Group on an Optional Protocol to the Convention on the Rights of the Child to Provide a Communications Procedure, UN doc. A/HRC/17/37 (17 February 2011) Annex.

75 Article 5 of the Optional Protocol.

76 See UN doc. A/HRC/17/36, 12, note 7.

77 See CRIN (Child Rights Information Network), 'Summary of the third and final working group meeting to draft the communications procedure under UNCRC', available at www.crin.org/resources/infodetail.asp?id=24180.

78 It could be mentioned that the Committee on the Rights of the Child recommends states parties to CRC-OPAC to ratify the CRC-OPSC 'given the potential connection between the sale of children and their recruitment into armed groups'. See the concluding observations of the Committee with respect to Ireland, UN doc. CRC/C/OPAC/IRL/CO/1, para. 25.

79 The six grave child rights violations are as follows: (i) killing or maiming of children; (ii) recruiting or using child soldiers; (iii) attacks against schools or hospitals; (iv) rape or other grave sexual violence against children; (v) abduction of children; (vi) denial of humanitarian access for children. The six grave child rights violations were first identified in Security Council Resolution 1539 (2004) and in the fifth report of the Secretary-General on Children and Armed Conflict, UN doc. A/59/695 S/2005/72 (2005).

80 Security Council Res. 1612 (2005) para. 8(a), (b).

81 For more information on the six grave violations and the work of the MRMs, please consult the website of the Office of the Special Representative of the Secretary-General on Children and Armed Conflict, www.un.org/children/conflict/english/themostgraveviolations.html.
82 Security Council Res. 1882 (4 August 2009), Preamble.
83 See, e.g., *Report of the Secretary-General: Children and Armed Conflict*, UN Doc. A/63/785-S/2009/158 (26 March 2008).
84 Security Council Res. 1882 (4 August 2009), para. 3.
85 Security Council Res. 1856 (22 December 2008), paras. 3(k) and 4(c).
86 At the end of 2008, the OHCHR ran fifty-two field presences in the form of one of the following four categories: country offices, regional offices, human rights advisers in UN Country Teams, and human rights components in UN peace missions. OHCHR, *2008 Report: Activities and Results*, 68, available at www.ohchr.org/Documents/Press/OHCHR_Report_2008.pdf.
87 See OHCHR Colombia, available at www.ohchr.org/EN/Countries/LACRegion/Pages/COSummary0809.aspx
88 See www.un.org/children/conflict/english/countryvisits.html.
89 See *Report of the Special Representative to the Secretary-General for Children and Armed Conflict*, UN doc. A/64/254 (6 August 2009) para. 19.
90 See *Report of the Secretary-General on Children and Armed Conflict*, UN doc. A/63/785–S/2009/158 (29 March 2009), para. 147.
91 See mission statement of Geneva Call, available at www.genevacall.org.
92 See genevacall.org/news/press-releases/f-press-releases/2001–2010/2009–26jun-gc.htm.
93 See communiqué, Geneva Call, available at www.genevacall.org/.../deed-of-commitment/...deed-of-commitment/DoC_CANSA_%5BEN%5D.pdf.
94 Deed of Commitment, Article. 9.
95 Specifically, Article 7 of the Deed refers to access to adequate food and health care; protection against sexual and other forms of violence; provision of impartial humanitarian assistance to children in need; family reunion; avoiding using for military purposes schools or premises primarily used by children.
96 See L. Withers, 'Child-soldiers: how to engage in dialogue with non-state armed groups' in C. Bellamy and J. Zermatten (eds,), *The Swiss Human Rights Book: Realizing the Rights of the Child* (Zurich, 2007) 232–3.
97 Additional Protocol I, Article 87 on duty of commanders.
98 Human Rights Council, 'A terrible year for children in armed conflict', Press Release, 15 September 2009.
99 Popovski, 'Protection', 401.
100 UN News, 'First-ever trial at International Criminal Court, on use of child soldiers, opens', 26 January 2009, available at www.un.org/apps/news/story.asp?NewsID=29674&Cr=icc. Mr Lubanga was found guilty on 14 March 2012, case no. ICC-09/04–09/06
101 *Ibid.*
102 See www.icrc.org/Web/Eng/siteeng0.nsf/html/ethical-principles-220502.
103 J.-M. Henckaerts and L. Doswald-Beck, *Customary International Humanitarian Law*, Vol. 1, *Rules* (Cambridge University Press and ICRC, 2005).
104 See Committee on the Rights of the Child, *Day of General Discussion, Children and Armed Conflict* (1992), para. 66, available at www2.ohchr.org/english/bodies/crc/

discussion2008.htm.

105 *Report of the Special Representative to the Secretary-General for Children and Armed Conflict*, UN doc. A/64/254 (6 August. 2009) para. 19.

106 Security Council Res. 1882 (4 August 2009) Preamble.

107 *Impact of Armed Conflict on Children, Report of the Expert of the Secretary-General, Ms Graça Machel, submitted pursuant to General Assembly Resolution 48/157*, UN doc. A/51/306 (26 August 1996) para. 3.

PART II

Nordic experiences

7

Military occupation of Eastern Karelia by Finland in 1941–1944: was international law pushed aside?

LAURI HANNIKAINEN

In the course of previous centuries, Nordic states have occupied many foreign territories. Sweden, for instance, was one of the great powers of Europe, and in that capacity occupied several foreign territories. For centuries, Denmark was the sovereign of both Norway and Iceland. In addition, some Nordic occupations were of non-populated or very scarcely populated territories such as Spitzbergen and Greenland.

The latest Nordic occupation of a foreign territory took place in 1941, when Finland occupied Eastern Karelia by military force, until 1944. This territory was located in the border areas of Finland and Russia (from Finland towards the isthmuses between the White Sea and the lakes Onega and Ladoga) and its original inhabitants, the Karelians, belong to the Finno-Ugric ethnic group. The occupation was a part of Finland's Continuation War against the Soviet Union, Finland being an ally of Nazi Germany.

1. Background to Finland's occupation of Eastern Karelia in 1941

1.1 Background to the Occupation: From 1917 to the early 1920s

Finland was under the sovereignty of the Russian Empire as an autonomous territory from 1809 until 1917, when the revolutionary Bolshevik regime was prepared to grant Finland independence in the name of the peoples' right to self-determination. The Finnish declaration of independence was made in December 1917 and was recognized by Russia the same month.

The years before and after Finland's declaration of independence were chaotic, not only in Russia, but in Finland as well. In January 1918, a civil war broke out in Finland when the Reds, representing the lower classes, rebelled against the bourgeois White government. The civil war ended in May, the Whites victorious, with the help of military intervention by Germany.[1]

Eastern Karelia had belonged to Russia since the Peace Treaty of Stolbov in 1617. The newly independent Finland, however, was not satisfied with the eastern border of the autonomous territory of Finland as its border with Russia, and therefore demanded sovereignty over Eastern Karelia. Finland organized three military interventions into Eastern Karelia, which were, however, all unsuccessful.[2]

The disagreements between Finland and Bolshevik Russia were settled by the Peace Treaty of Tartu (Dorpat) in 1920.[3] Finland had some freedom of choice as to whether it would like to gain sovereignty over a part of Eastern Karelia or the Petschenga region in the north. Finland opted for Petschenga as this secured Finnish access to the Arctic Ocean. Eastern Karelia remained a part of Russia.[4] At the time of the signing of the Peace Treaty, however, Russia gave a unilateral declaration assuring that it would grant autonomy to Eastern Karelia.[5] This declaration was not a part of the Peace Treaty.

The preference given by Finland to Petschenga over Eastern Karelia may sound surprising. During the Finnish national awakening since the mid-nineteenth century, Eastern Karelia had gained a status of great significance in Finnish minds as the sacred origin of the Finnish nation.[6] It was in the northern part of Eastern Karelia, Viena, where the singing fields of Kalevala, the Finnish national saga, were located.

In 1921, anti-Bolshevik forces in Eastern Karelia revolted against Bolshevik power. Finland's armed forces played a substantial role in the resulting armed conflict, and the Commander of the rebelling forces was the Finnish Major Paavo Talvela. The revolt was initially successful, but was ultimately defeated by the Bolshevik-led forces.[7]

Finland became a member at the League of Nations in 1921, whereas Russia remained outside. Finland attempted to bring the case of Eastern Karelia to the leading organs of the League and was to some degree successful: the Council decided to request an Advisory Opinion from the Permanent Court of International Justice on the status of the disputed area. Finland argued that Russia's declaration in 1920 to grant autonomy to Eastern Karelia was binding on Russia and that Russia was violating this pledge. To the disappointment of Finland, however, the Court decided that since Russia was not a member of the League and had not recognized the jurisdiction of the Court, the Court lacked jurisdiction in the matter.[8] Ultimately, Finland's effort to get the League involved in the matter failed.

During the 1920s and 1930s, the Finnish government protested against the Soviet policy in Eastern Karelia but made no territorial claims. Nevertheless, support for the pro-Karelian cause was quite high in Finland.[9]

1.2. *Finland's armed conflicts in 1939–1941, including military occupation of Eastern Karelia*

In 1939, alarmed by the aggressive invasions of Nazi Germany, the Soviet Union proposed changes to the Finnish territory in order to protect Leningrad and to enable Russia to keep in touch with events in the Baltic Sea. As compensation, Finland would acquire a territory from the western part of Eastern Karelia twice the size of the area lost. Finland refused, suspecting that Russia had further aggressive plans. As a result, the Soviet Union launched an armed attack against Finland. After fierce fighting, the Soviet Union compelled Finland into signing a peace treaty in March 1940.[10] Finland had been the victim of an aggressive war, losing nearly 12 per cent of its territory, including eastern parts of Finnish Karelia.

During the following period of peace, the Soviet Union maintained a very hostile attitude towards Finland, including strong demands and threats. Finland had ample reasons to suspect that the Soviet Union might attack again and invade the whole of Finland. After complicated secret consultations, Finland became an ally of Nazi Germany. Tens of thousands of German soldiers settled in northern Finland in the first half of 1941. Finland was ready to support Germany's war of aggression against the Soviet Union and participate in the attack.[11]

When Nazi Germany attacked the Soviet Union on 22 June 1941, Finland had already mobilized its armed forces to attack. Finland did not want to be labelled as Germany's aggressive ally, however, and therefore held back its attack for a few weeks. Aware of what the Finnish were planning, the Soviet Union chose to bomb several sites in Finland, in particular airports which were being used or could be used by Nazi bombers. This provided Finland with a basis for declaring that it had been the victim of aggression and was thus entitled to military self-defence. The Finnish forces crossed the Finnish-Soviet border on 10 July 1941, advanced quite rapidly to the 1939 border, and without delay continued eastwards. In early October 1941, the Finnish forces occupied the capital of Eastern Karelia, Petrozavodsk (Äänislinna), and by December, Finland had occupied all of Eastern Karelia with the exception of certain territories in the north. During 1942, the Finnish forces did not attempt to occupy any further areas.

The Finnish occupiers established a provisional military administration in Eastern Karelia with its own commander. This commander was directly subordinated to the Supreme Commander of the Finnish Army, Marshal C.G. Mannerheim, who had his headquarters in the Finnish town Mikkeli, hundreds of kilometres from Eastern Karelia.[12] Even though Mannerheim visited Eastern Karelia several times, he may not have been fully aware of events and developments there, but he was the responsible decision-maker on important questions. Peculiarly, even the leading part of the provisional Military Administration for Eastern Karelia was stationed outside Eastern Karelia in the Finnish town of Joensuu until mid-1943, when it finally moved to Petrozavodsk.

Several officials of the Military Administration in Eastern Karelia were members of the Academic Karelia Society, which since the 1920s had openly advocated ethnic hatred against Russia and Finland's right to Eastern Karelia and Ingria (Ingermanland).[13] The Society had many members and supporters in the Finnish Army as well as university teachers and students.[14] Many active members of the Society had considerable knowledge of Eastern Karelia and personal contacts with Karelians, and Finland's alliance with Nazi Germany offered a golden opportunity to realize their dream of creating a 'Greater Finland'. Their hostility towards Russians was an influential factor as to why the occupying power's treatment of Russians in Eastern Karelia became so problematic.

2. Finland's goals concerning Eastern Karelia

When Finland occupied Eastern Karelia,[15] there was a strong belief in Finland that Nazi Germany would decisively defeat and destroy the Soviet Union. Adolf Hitler was sympathetic to the idea that Finland could annex Eastern Karelia and even some other Russian territories. The Finns did not rush the annexation of Eastern Karelia, but wanted to ensure that the expected destruction of the Soviet-Russian enemy actually took place. After all, Finland was a small country with 3.7 million inhabitants, whereas the Soviet Union had 180 million inhabitants. Nonetheless, the Finnification of the territory began in 1941, upon the initiative of members of the Academic Karelia Society. A prime example was the Finnification of local geographical names – of towns, municipalities, villages and streets – even though Mannerheim expressed doubts and only grudgingly assented to this policy.[16]

Finland wanted to give the international community the impression that it was not acting as an ally of Nazi Germany but rather acting in its own interests. As its leading public justification to take Eastern Karelia, Finland emphasized its need to establish a secure border towards Russia, a border consisting of three isthmuses connected to the White Sea and great lakes Ladoga and Onega. This border would be militarily easier to defend against Russia, Finland's arch-enemy for centuries. Those governments (such as the Swedish and British) that were closely observing Finnish policies, however, well knew that Finland also had further intentions in its occupation of Eastern Karelia – the annexation of this area to Finland.

Finland planned to create an ethnically 'clean' Eastern Karelia, consisting only of a Finno-Ugric population (Finns, Karelians and Ingrians). It was to become a new province under the sovereignty of Finland. How was this going to be done, when over 70 per cent of the population of Eastern Karelia were Russians or other non-Finno-Ugric inhabitants (in 1939, overwhelmingly Slavic)?[17] What were the Finns prepared to do with the thousands of Russian inhabitants? Were the Finns perhaps planning to follow the example of their powerful ally, Nazi Germany, and engage in a policy of extermination?

No, Finland would not resort to extermination. The Finnish plan was to gather the ethnically alien population, i.e., those who ethnically were not Karelians, Finnish or other Finno-Ugric, in concentration camps and transfer them away from Eastern Karelia, supposedly to German-occupied territories in Russia. It was the Finnish wish that the transfer would take place quite rapidly so that Finland could concentrate on the creation and development of a Finno-Ugric Karelia. Thus, after some initial difficulties, the occupation of Eastern Karelia would be a positive thing. The fate of the Russians and other 'aliens' deported to the German-occupied territories would not be the concern of Finland.[18]

However, it did not turn out that way. First, Finland was not able to transfer the 'alien' population out of the area. Secondly, communication with the Karelian population in Eastern Karelia was problematic as the main language of many Karelians was Russian and they had no common language with the Finnish occupying force; neither did they have any strong feelings of kinship towards the Finns.[19] This is not surprising: Eastern Karelia had been a part of Russia since 1617 and its development had been very different from that of Finland. Finally, even by early 1943, the Finnish leadership must have suspected that Nazi Germany would lose the war and that Finland would face harder times. The occupation of Eastern Karelia could fail.

3. International law of belligerent occupation during the Second World War

The prohibition on wars of aggression became a universal rule during the inter-war period. The Nuremberg Tribunal in 1946 declared that a war of aggression was not only an international crime but it was the supreme international crime.[20] Occupation of a foreign territory by armed force was considered a weighty proof of this crime.

The principal instrument regulating the maintenance of belligerent occupation of a foreign territory was at the time the Regulations concerning the Laws and Customs of War on Land annexed to the 1907 Hague Convention (IV) Respecting the Laws and Customs of War on Land ('Hague Regulations').[21] The Regulations contain a specific section on military occupation: 'Military Authority over the Territory of the Hostile State' (Articles 42–56).

From the perspective of the occupation of Eastern Karelia, some Articles of the Hague Regulations are of particular interest. Article 43 calls upon the occupier to ensure, as far as possible, public order and safety. Article 46 stipulates that family honour and rights, the lives of persons, and private property, as well as religious convictions must be respected. Private property cannot be confiscated. Article 50 prohibits collective penalties.

A number of Articles on occupation deal with property. The occupier is entitled to use the property of the state (Article 53). The property of municipalities, however, as well as the property of institutions dedicated to religion, charity and education, the arts and sciences, even when state property, are to be treated as private property (Article 56). Furthermore, requisitions in kind and services may be demanded from municipalities and inhabitants to meet the needs of the occupying army, but they must be in proportion to the occupied country's resources (Article 52). Oppenheim mentions as examples of such services the burying of the dead, repairing roads, bridges and buildings, and acting as drivers or farriers.[22]

Some provisions in other sections of the Hague Regulations should also be noted – analogy in mind. Among the articles on prisoners of war, Article 4 obligates the occupier to treat prisoners of war humanely and Article 7 requires that prisoners are given board, lodging and clothing of the same standard as the troops of the government who captured them.

Finland had ratified Hague Convention IV, as had imperial Russia. When the Bolsheviks came to power, they declared that revolutionary Russia was not a successor state of the Russian Empire and was thus not bound by the Empire's international obligations. In connection with the reorganization of the Russian Red Cross, however, the new government declared to the International Committee of the Red Cross (ICRC) that it would maintain the Conventions relating to the Red Cross to which Russia was an adherent until October 1917. The declaration did not specifically mention Hague Convention IV, but according to the ICRC, it included this Convention, though it was not a formal declaration of accession to Hague Convention IV. In the view of Finland, the Soviet Union was not a party to Hague Convention IV. Finland pointed out that, as Article 2 of the Convention clearly states, the Convention only applies between the contracting states, and only if all the belligerents in a given war are parties to the Convention, the result was that the Convention did not apply to the war of 1941–1944.[23]

Nevertheless, in August 1941, Finland and the Soviet Union specifically agreed on respecting the provisions of Hague Convention IV. Finland emphasized that the agreement required effective reciprocity. Later, the Finnish military authorities claimed that the Convention was not binding upon Finland, because the Soviet Union had not respected the Convention's provisions.[24] In the case of the occupation of Eastern Karelia, it should be kept in mind that it was the occupier, Finland, whose obligations were under consideration, not the defending Soviet Union whose forces had been driven away from the territory by the occupying power.

There is one especially important provision in Hague Convention IV, the famous Martens Clause in the Preamble:

> Until a more complete code of the laws of war has been issued … the inhabitants and belligerents remain under the protection and the rule of the principles of the law of nations, as they result from the usages established among civilized peoples, from the laws of humanity, and the dictates of the public conscience.

Finland certainly wanted to be regarded as a civilized, democratic state and thus had to take the Martens Clause seriously. The Clause emphasized the importance of the laws of humanity and thus strengthened the prevailing view in the international legal community that at least the basic principles and rules of the Hague Conventions were binding on all states as international customary law. I concur with the opinion of Hanski that the basic principles of Hague Convention IV (including those of the Hague Regulations) in any case were binding on Finland and the Soviet Union as customary law.[25]

It is regrettable that the Regulations did not contain any prohibitions on transferring members of the population of the occupied territory away from that territory or any prohibitions on discrimination against the population of the occupied territory. Nor were there any provisions on providing medical care for the local population.

In the customary law of war, a belligerent had the right to detain and intern those citizens of the enemy state who fell within its power. Finland had the right to intern even the civilian population of Eastern Karelia. That right, however, also included the corresponding obligation to care for the interned persons – in the spirit of the Martens Clause this means to give them adequate shelter, nourishment and medical care and to treat them in a humane manner.

Before describing and analyzing Finland's occupation of Eastern Karelia, I want to take a brief look at the 1949 Geneva Convention IV on the protection of civilians during war. This Convention takes into account the horrible experiences of the Second World War.

4. 1949 Geneva Convention IV on the Protection of Civilians in Time of War

Geneva Convention IV Relative to the Protection of Civilian Persons in Time of War is a long convention with 159 Articles.[26] Section I of Part III of the Convention contains provisions common to the territories of the belligerents and to occupied territories (Articles 27–34). Article 27 emphasizes that in all circumstances, civilian persons are entitled to respect for their persons and their honour and that they shall be humanely treated and protected against all acts of violence. No adverse distinction based on race, religion and political opinion shall be made. Article 33 prohibits reprisals against civilians and Article 34 prohibits the taking of hostages. Section III is dedicated to occupied territories (Articles 47–78). The very substantial Article 49 deals with and prohibits mass forcible transfers and deportations of civilians from the occupied territory to the territory of the occupying power or to any other country, regardless of their motive. Notwithstanding, evacuation of a given area is permitted if the security of the population or imperative military security so demands. The occupier undertaking such evacuations shall ensure that proper accommodation is provided to civilians and that the transfer is affected under satisfactory conditions of hygiene, health, safety and nutrition. Evacuated persons shall be transferred back to their homes as soon as the hostilities in the area in question have ceased. Similarly, detainment of civilians is also prohibited, unless the security of the population or imperative military reasons demand it. Article 49 finally emphasizes that the occupier shall not transfer parts of its own civilian population into the territory it occupies.

Article 147 of Geneva Convention IV lists the grave breaches of the Convention. The list includes 'unlawful deportation or transfer … of a protected person'. The alleged perpetrators of grave breaches must be brought to criminal justice (Article 146).

The above-described provisions are fundamental demands of humanity for the occupier's treatment of civilians and they concretize the Martens Clause. While Article 49 of 1949 Geneva Convention IV contains welcome new provisions regulating transfers and evacuations of civilians, Article 147 declares unlawful transfers as 'grave breaches' with criminal consequences.

5. Beginning of the Finnish occupation of Eastern Karelia: 1941

One day before the main bulk of the Finnish armed forces began their attack on the Soviet Union, 9 July 1941,[27] Marshal Mannerheim gave a non-public, military order according to which the Russian population of Eastern Karelia would be detained by the Finnish occupying forces and placed in concentration camps.[28] On 15 July, the Military Headquarters ordered the establishment of a provisional military administration of Eastern Karelia and appointed Lt Col. V.A. Kotilainen as its commander. Thus, the Finnish military leadership was not only determined to occupy Eastern Karelia, but it was also convinced that Finland would succeed in occupying the area.

On the day of the attack, 10 July, Mannerheim gave a public military order according to which he would not stop fighting before Karelia, 'the sacred land of our tribe', was free.[29] This order became internationally known and damaged Finland's good reputation. It did, however, fully correspond with the official Finnish intentions and with the actions taken next.

Finland entered the war in July 1941 with massive force. The fighting army had 475,000 soldiers. In addition, some 150,000 persons were engaged in support tasks for the army. Since the Finnish leadership was convinced that the war of aggression fought by Nazi Germany would advance rapidly into the territory of the Soviet Union (something which proved true by the first days and weeks of the attack), a maximum war effort was opted for: first, with the intention to take back the territories lost in the Winter War and then to invade Eastern Karelia – and eventually perhaps go even further. Recovering the territories lost in the Winter War can be regarded as lawful, but extending the invasion to the east to Eastern Karelia could not fit within legitimate self-defence but was rather a case of aggressive war.

The civilian leadership, with President Risto Ryti as its head, supported Mannerheim's policy.[30] Ryti arranged for several studies to be made by Finnish scholars who gathered and developed legal, ethnographic, historical, geographic and economic arguments supporting Finland's right to Eastern Karelia.[31] The leading legal argumentation was made by Professor Rafael Erich who had been a judge at the Permanent Court of International Justice. He referred to the ethnic bond between the Finns and the Karelians, and to the recent population transfers as well as the administrative border changes of the Soviet Union having changed the position of the Karelians from one of majority into becoming a minority in their own territory. Professor Erich also emphasized Finland's right to recover Eastern Karelia as compensation for the poor treatment of Finland by the Russian Empire and the Soviet Union. The argument went that it was only with Finland that the Karelians could survive.[32]

One positive point was that already at an early stage of the occupation, Marshal Mannerheim appointed a qualified legal expert, Professor Veli Merikoski, whose office was in Helsinki, to advise the commander of the Military Administration on legal matters. The first commander, Lt Col. Kotilainen, commented that the appointment was meant to ensure that 'we do nothing stupid'.[33]

It is no surprise that the first months of the occupation of Eastern Karelia were quite chaotic. The local population was transferred from one place to another more than once. The occupier's task, however, was made easier than it could have been by the fact that the overwhelming majority of the population of Eastern Karelia (population: 469,000 in the 1939 census) had been evacuated from the area before the arrival of the Finnish army. The only people left were 85–87,000 inhabitants, mostly women, children under fifteen and the elderly. The Slavic population was somewhat bigger than the Finno-Ugric population.[34] The small number of people remaining in Eastern Karelia was a surprise to the Finns, who had hoped to have a larger and better local labour force to serve the occupying power in the exploitation of the natural resources of Eastern Karelia.

6. Division of the Finnish occupation into two periods

In light of the above, it is clear that the Finnish occupying force entered Eastern Karelia with the intention of making Eastern Karelia a part of Finland. The strong position of the Academic Karelia Society in the military administration and the plan to transfer the Russian population away from Eastern Karelia were factors contributing to the hostility shown towards the Russian population and the negligent treatment they were given.

The attitude of the Finnish occupier remained similar in 1942. This was a difficult year due to the shortage of food in Finland. Finland had concentrated its energy on the summer attack in 1941, believing that the Soviet Union would soon be decisively defeated. At the time of the harvest, an overwhelming proportion of Finnish men (and also many women) between 20–45 years were involved in the military effort. The result was an acute shortage of food and even famine, especially in the camps maintained by Finland.[35] In fact, the situation in camps became unbearable. With the oncoming summer season of 1942, the nourishment situation began to improve, especially during the autumn. In early 1943, as the Finnish leadership's belief in the destruction of the Soviet Union and Russia began to fade, the treatment of the Russian population in Eastern Karelia began to clearly improve. This trend continued in 1944.[36]

When the Finnish occupation of Eastern Karelia has been discussed in subsequent years, the Finns have preferred to focus on the years 1943–1944 and to leave the previous period aside. From the perspective of a critical legal assessment, however, the years 1941–1942 constitute the most important period – the period when the Finns believed that as the new masters of Eastern Karelia, they could afford to treat the ethnically 'alien' population in an arrogant manner.

7. System of differential treatment and segregation

One key tactic applied by the Finnish occupant was to separate the Finno-Ugric population from the ethnically 'alien' population.[37] This was considered to be of great importance, because the plan was to create an ethnically 'fully clean' Finno-Ugric province. The military administration put considerable efforts and energy into identifying the ethnicity of every single inhabitant of the occupied territory. In unclear cases, a person was regarded as Finno-Ugric if he or she agreed.

What did the differential treatment and separation mean in practice? Differential treatment meant that, in many ways, Finno-Ugric persons were given preferential treatment: larger food rations, higher salaries, better medical treatment and educational possibilities, and greater freedom of movement. This demonstrated to the Finno-Ugric population the friendliness of the occupying force. The segregation was intended as a step towards confining the Russian and other 'alien' populations to concentration camps. This was only achieved, however, to a limited extend. A part of the 'alien' population remained free, although they were segregated from the Finno-Ugric population.[38]

All inhabitants of Eastern Karelia were given residence permits: green cards to the Finno-Ugric and red cards to the 'aliens'.[39] This 'apartheid'-like system was formally abolished in the autumn of 1943.[40] Nevertheless, over 15,000 persons considered as 'ethnically alien' remained in camps.

8. Concentration camps (from 1943: transfer camps)[41]

The camp system was established shortly after the Finnish occupation. In February 1942, the number of persons in camps reached over 23,000.[42] During the autumn of 1942, the number decreased quite significantly due to high death tolls among the inmates and releases of inmates. In 1943–1944, the number of persons confined in such camps was between 15–18,000.

The concentration camps in Eastern Karelia were not extermination camps. The purpose was rather to gather 'aliens' in camps in preparation for their transfer away from Eastern Karelia. Another declared explanation for the confinement was the need to transfer civilians away from the theatre of war.

Finnish concentration camps in Eastern Karelia were overcrowded. In the first months, inmates had a limited possibility to move outside the camps, but after that the camps were segregated from the outside world.[43]

The largest groups of inmates in these camps were women (many were mothers), children and the elderly. Nearly half of the inmates were children under the age of fifteen. The fact that there were so many children and elderly in the camps presented a challenge for the camp administration to avoid the spreading of epidemics in the overcrowded camps.

The Finnish occuping power failed severely in its administration of the concentration camps in 1941–1942. Negligence and hostility towards the Russians certainly played a role. Individual acts of violence against inmates occurred without any consequences for the perpetrators. In 1942 in particular, 'alien' persons were discriminated against by being given smaller food rations, with disastrous consequences. In fact, not all inmates received even those food rations which the occupier's rules stated they were entitled to. Furthermore, medical care during the first period was inadequate, because the Finnish Red Cross was not present in the camps. The daily forced labour outside the camps was harsh for the inmates, many of whom were not fit for the work of cutting and transporting wood in the forests.

No Finnish historian has made any study based on interviews with Russian inmates in the camps. Such a book was, however, recently published by Finnish novelist Marja-Leena Mikkola, who had interviewed seventeen Russian persons who had lived in camps in Eastern Karelia as children. They described the conditions in the camp in 1941–1942 as inhuman: there was a complete lack of privacy, and the inmates were forced to cope with, inter alia, cold, hunger, fear, anxiety, inadequate food, and rags as clothes.[44]

Lt Col. Helge Seppälä was a young soldier serving in Eastern Karelia during the occupation. He did not have the right to enter the closed camps, but at one time he was ordered to pick up inmates at the gate of a concentration camp and take them to work in a factory. According to him, the labour brigade was a depressing sight. There were children, women and the elderly dressed in rags. Every morning and especially on Mondays, wagons full of ready-made coffins followed the brigade. There was a terrible smell of death hanging over the gate. This was the summer of famine of 1942.[45]

The mortality rate among the inmates of the camps in Eastern Karelia (excluding prisoner of war camps) was at least 18, perhaps as much as 25 per cent. According to Laine, at least 4,600 persons died in the camps.[46] Seppälä writes that we do not know with any certainty how many inmates died in the camps, because the lists of deceased inmates drawn up by the Military Administration were very carelessly made.[47] Kulomaa regards the lists as incomplete.[48] The main causes of the high mortality were epidemics, overcrowding, hunger and hard work. Many victims were children and the elderly. Most of the deaths occurred in 1942.

In frustration, the head of the camp system in Eastern Karelia, Lt Col. K. E. Levälahti, proposed in August 1942 that the camps should be closed.[49] His proposal was not supported; however, the treatment of inmates began gradually to improve.[50]

When one compares the Finnish authorities' incomplete registration of deaths in the camps (and the high rate of deaths of inmates) with the thoroughness applied in determining whether an inhabitant of Eastern Karelia was ethnically Finno-Ugric or 'alien', it is hard to avoid a cynical conclusion.

9. Role of the Finnish Red Cross

Marshal Mannerheim had been the chair of the Finnish Red Cross Society since the early 1920s, and he continued to maintain that position during the war era.[51] In August 1941, a provisional regional Eastern Karelian branch of the Finnish Red Cross was established. Upon Mannerheim's insistence, the governing board of the Finnish Red Cross nominated the military commander of the provisional Military Administration in Eastern Karelia, Lt Col. Kotilainen, as the chair of the Eastern Karelian branch. This practice continued during the entire period of occupation: every new military commander was also appointed as the chair of the Eastern Karelian branch. This chairperson had the authority to appoint the members of the regional governing board.[52]

Thus in Eastern Karelia, the Finnish Red Cross was subordinated to the power of the Military Administration. It appears that the Finnish Red Cross was made a tool of the Finnish military in its efforts to consolidate the occupation of Eastern Karelia. On the other hand, in practice it became evident that in the course of time, since the second half of 1942, the role of the Finnish Red Cross in Eastern Karelia, with its increasing presence and activities, proved to be positive, especially with regard to medical care.[53]

I have found no documentation proving, or even indicating, that the International Committee of the Red Cross (ICRC) commented on the subordination of the East Karelian Red Cross branch to the power of the Military Administration.[54] This subordination may have been awkward for the ICRC also because of the highly questionable legitimacy of Finland's occupation of Eastern Karelia.

During its war of 1941–1944, Finland did not permit the ICRC to visit its camps. This chapter has examined the situation in camps for civilians in Eastern Karelia, but Finland also maintained prisoner of war camps in this area. The ICRC was especially concerned about the prisoner of war camps and would certainly have wanted to visit Finland's camps. Finland appealed to the Soviet Union's disregard of the Hague Regulations as the reason for forbidding the ICRC to visit its prisoner of war camps.[55] This did not, however, prevent Finland from asking the ICRC for help to deal with famine in its prisoner of war camps.[56]

10. Finnish withdrawal from Eastern Karelia in 1944

The Soviet military forces did not seriously challenge the Finnish occupying forces until June 1944, but at that time they did so with a massive attack. It was directed at the Karelian Isthmus, i.e., clearly south of Eastern Karelia.[57] An attack in the Karelian Isthmus was most dangerous to Finland, because a decisive breakthrough there would enable Soviet forces to move towards Helsinki. The Finnish military leadership decided to quickly move military units from Eastern Karelia to the front on the Karelian Isthmus. It was also decided that even though the Soviet forces did not yet seriously threaten the Finnish presence in Eastern Karelia, it was advisable to withdraw these forces without delay and concentrate on defending the Finnish territory. In military terms, this proved to be the correct decision. By heroic military defence, the Finnish forces warded off the massive Soviet attack and saved Finland from occupation.[58]

When Finland withdrew its forces from Eastern Karelia in late June 1944, fewer Karelians followed the Finns to Finland than expected. This was caused partly by the failure of Finland to fulfil its promises to evacuate Karelians and partly by the decision of many Karelians to stay. Among the reasons for staying was the fact that many Karelians were not impressed by the Finnish performance in Eastern Karelia, and many wanted to stay and wait for their family members' return from the east. Altogether 2,800 inhabitants of Eastern Karelia moved to Finland: 2,200 Finno-Ugric and 600 Russians plus other 'aliens'.

Finland should not be blamed for the unexpectedly low number of emigrants from Eastern Karelia. At the time of their withdrawal, the Finns were already suspecting that in the eventual peace treaty, Finland would be obligated to return all Soviet citizens to the Soviet Union. This suspicion proved to be true. Finland returned to the Soviet Union 1,800 emigrants from Eastern Karelia, whereas the rest 'disappeared', mostly to Sweden.

11. Post-war peace treaties imposed on Finland and their implementation

Finland had lost the war against the Soviet Union, and an Armistice Agreement and a Provisional Peace Treaty were signed in September 1944. The terms of the Treaty were generally quite hard on Finland, but the Soviet Union had given up its initial demand of Finland's unconditional surrender. Finland retained its independence and political system. The terms of peace were sealed in the 1947 Paris Peace Treaty[59] imposed on Finland by the Soviet Union, Britain and eight other Allied states which had declared war on Finland (not including the United States). The Peace

Treaty stated in the Preamble that Finland had been an ally of Hitler's Germany.

According to the Provisional Peace Treaty between the Soviet Union, Britain and Finland,[60] the Allies would send a Control Commission to Finland to supervise Finland's compliance with the terms of the Treaty. Besides having to return all Soviet citizens who were residing in Finland to the Soviet Union, Finland also had to return a considerable amount of property transferred from Eastern Karelia to Finland.[61] Furthermore, Finland had to pay a large sum of war reparations to the Soviet Union. Fascist-minded and anti-Soviet organizations had to be dissolved, *inter alia*, the Academic Karelia Society.

The Allied Powers had agreed that the leaders of all states fighting beside Nazi Germany were to be brought to criminal trial. Article 13 of the Provisional Peace Treaty stipulated 'Finland undertakes to collaborate with Allied Powers in the apprehension of persons accused of war crimes and in their trial'.[62] The Allied Powers demanded that eight leading political figures in Finland had to be put on trial, among them President Risto Ryti and several ministers, but not Marshal Mannerheim. The trial was political, but Finland had its reasons not to obstruct it as it was allowed to arrange the trial within its own judicial system and thus avoid death penalties.[63] In addition, Mannerheim, who as the Supreme Commander of the brave Finnish Army had become a national hero and unifying personality, was saved from trial.[64] A retroactive criminal law was grudgingly enacted by the Finnish Parliament[65] and the eight accused leading figures were sentenced to prison terms. The occupation of Eastern Karelia played only a minor role in the trial.

In addition to the trial of leading figures the Control Commission handed the Finnish Prime Minister a list of sixty-one persons who were to be put on criminal trial as alleged war criminals. This list included many persons who had served in the military administration in Eastern Karelia. The Finnish authorities, however, could identify only forty-five persons from the names on the list and thirty-five of these were approached and detained during the autumn of 1944. Only fifteen of the detained persons were found guilty and had imposed a penalty imposed on them.[66]

The Finnish Military Administration of Eastern Karelia had three commanders during its three years of existence. They were all on the Control Commission's list. One of them escaped to Sweden and another to Argentina, and therefore could not be brought to trial. The third commander, Lt Col. V. Paloheimo, had been the last commander and was in charge at the time when the treatment of Russians in Eastern Karelia had substantially improved. Paloheimo was found not guilty at the trial.

One may conclude that as an ally (or collaborator) of Nazi Germany, Finland could not have avoided the negative sanctions, yet the sanctions imposed were in fact bearable. Finland should be pleased that its unfortunate occupation of Eastern Karelia only received very limited attention in the peace settlement. Moreover, it must be kept in mind that the Soviet leaders fully escaped responsibility for the Soviet Union's aggressive war on Finland in 1939 and forcible annexation of three Baltic states under Soviet sovereignty.

12. Finnish occupation of Eastern Karelia in light of international law

It seems clear that Finland's occupation of Eastern Karelia was an act of war of aggression. Although not successful, the occupation took place with the intention of ultimately annexing Eastern Karelia to Finland and with the belief that this could be done.

The occupying power's treatment of the Russian and other 'alien' inhabitants in 1941–1942 appears to have involved inhuman acts contrary to the 1907 Hague Regulations and the Martens Clause. Article 43 of the Regulations calls upon the occupying state to ensure safety in the territory and Article 46 obliges it to respect family honour and the rights and the lives of persons. Both Articles are of a fundamental character and can be seen as an expression of customary international law. The treatment of the inmates in the concentration camps, such as overcrowding, hard labour for children and the elderly, and poor nourishment and medical care, especially in 1941–1942, definitely violated Article 46.

The discriminatory treatment and segregation of Russian and other 'alien' inhabitants in 1941–1942 must also be seen as inhuman treatment and at least a violation of the Martens Clause, unworthy of a civilized nation.[67]

I am pleased to note that Finland did not realize the plan to transfer the Russian and other 'alien' population away from Eastern Karelia to German-occupied territories in Russia. That would have been ethnic cleansing. Besides, it is evident that a great majority of the transferred persons would have been killed by the German occupier or would have otherwise vanished. The transfer would have resulted in Finland being charged with having collaborated with Nazi Germany in the extermination of tens of thousands of civilians. This would be a moral burden on the Finnish people even today.

So why did Finland not realize the plan of transfer? The reason is not fully clear, but according to Rautala, the Finnish and German troops were not able to create a connection on the southern side of Lake Ladoga as required in the plan.[68] Thus, in geographical terms, the transportation would have been difficult. On a similar note, Laine has argued that the plan of transfer could not be realized due to a lack of suitable transportation equipment.[69] One may thus conclude that transport-related problems of some form prevented the transfer (in 1941–1942). Since early 1943, however, there appears also to have been a legal reason for the plan not being carried out. The Finnish Foreign Ministry requested Erik Castrén, an expert in international law, to present his analysis on the question of the transfer's legality. Castrén's conclusion in March was that the transfer would be contrary to the 1907 Hague Regulations.[70]

13. Attitude of present-day Finland to the Finnish occupation of Eastern Karelia

In the 1950s–1970s, Finland tried to forget its wartime occupation of Eastern Karelia or at least to present it in a positive light as an effort to help the Karelians. This also applied to scholars of political history, many of whom had either been members of the Academic Karelia Society or otherwise supporters of the occupation. Many popular books on Finland's role in the Second World War presented Finland only as a victim of aggressive Soviet policy and as a country caught between two totalitarian powers, the Soviet Union and Nazi Germany.

Since the 1980s, a number of objective and critical monographs have been published in Finland on the Finnish occupation of Eastern Karelia and Finland's collaboration with Nazi Germany.[71] Finnish political leadership and public opinion, however, do not share this critical line of thinking. This is especially true for the post-Cold War years, when the Finns have become free from Soviet (Russian) political dominance and nationalist feelings have been on the increase.[72] Their focus is still on the victim status of Finland and the wartime leaders.

In the Finnish public discussion concerning Finland's role in 1941–1944, the incontestable fact that Finland was guilty of aggression and the statement in the Paris Peace Treaty that Finland was an ally of Nazi Germany, are entirely ignored. True, there is quite a lively discussion as to whether Finland was an ally of Nazi Germany or only a co-belligerent, but that discussion does not include the statement in the Peace Treaty. According to the prevailing view in Finland, it is Finland's exclusive right to determine what kind of role it had in its armed conflicts during the Second World War. This right is seen as extending as far as permitting a complete 'whitewashing' of Finland's wartime record.

I end this chapter by referring to the view of the greatest hero of independent Finland, both during the war and today, namely Marshal Mannerheim, on Finland's occupation of Eastern Karelia as presented in his memoirs after the Second World War. According to Mannerheim, when the Soviets withdrew from Eastern Karelia in 1941, they destroyed nearly all industry in the area and left the remaining population to starve. It fell on the occupier to care for this population. The occupying power had no frictions with the Karelian or Slavic population. Mannerheim concluded that not only could it be justifiably stated that the inhabitants of the territories occupied by Finland were granted all the rights to which they were entitled under international Conventions, but also that their treatment was so good that it remained unique in the history of the Second World War.[73]

Thus, no wrinkles, no stains!

Notes

1 See L. Hannikainen, 'The Finnish Civil War 1918 and its aftermath' in L. Hannikainen, R. Hanski and A. Rosas, *Implementing Humanitarian Law Applicable in Armed Conflicts: The Case of Finland* (Dordrecht: Martinus Nijhoff Publishers, 1992) 8–31. In subsequent studies, the numbers of casualties and victims have proven to be somewhat higher than presented by Hannikainen in 1992.

2 *Ibid.* 32–40, and J. Niinistö, *Heimosotien historia 1918–1922* (Helsinki: SKS, 2005) 10–85 and 148–183.

3 Treaty of Peace between Finland and Russia, 3 LNTS 5.

4 See J. Niinistö, *Bobi Sivén, Karjulan puolesta* (Helsinki: SKS, 2001) 149–65.

5 J. Kallenautio, *Suomi katsoi eteensä – Itsenäisen Suomen ulkopolitiikka 1917*–1955 (Helsinki: Tammi, 1985) 62–6.

6 See Niinistö, *Bobi Sivén*, 16–21, and T. Nygård, *Suur-Suomi vai lähiheimolaisten auttaminen* (Helsinki: Otava, 1978) 21–4.

7 See Niinistö, *Heimosotien*, 214–61, and H. Seppälä, *Suomi miehittäjänä 1941–1944* (Helsinki: SN-kirjat, 1989) 13–14.

8 *Finland v. Russia, Advisory Opinion on the Status of Eastern Karelia*, Advisory Opinion No. 5, 1923,PCIJ, www.worldcourts.com.

9 See Nygård, *Suur-Suomi vai lähiheimolaisten auttaminen*, the English summary at 259–65. The underlying ideology was to unite the kindred people of Finland.

10 Treaty of Peace between Finland and the Union of Soviet Socialist Republics, Finnish Treaty Series no. 3/1940.

11 See M. Jokipii, *Jatkosodan synty – Tutkimus Saksan ja Suomen sotilaallisesta yhteistyöstä 1940–41* (Helsinki: Otava, 1987).

12 See A. Laine, *Suur-Suomen kahdet kasvot – Itä-Karjalan siviiliväestön asema suomalaisessa miehityshallinnossa 1941–1944* (Helsinki: Otava, 1982) 61–91.

13 Ingria was located south of Leningrad. The Ingrians are a Finno-Ugric people like the Karelians.

14 See R. Alapuro, *Akateeminen Karjala-Seura. Ylioppilasliike ja kansa 1920- ja 1930-luvulla* (Helsinki: SKS, 1973).

15 See Laine, *Suur-Suomen kahdet kasvot*, 46–59; O. Hyytiä, '*helmi Suomen maakuntien joukossa*' *– Suomalainen Itä-Karjala 1941–1944* (Helsinki: Edita, 2008) 18–32; and T. Pimiä, *Sotasaalista Itä-Karjalasta – suomalaistutkijat miehitetyillä alueilla 1941–1944* (Helsinki: Gummerus, 2007) 11–18.

16 See Hyytiä, *Itä-Karjala 1941–1944*, 157–60, and Laine, *Suur-Suomen kahdet kasvot*, 219–22. To give an example, Lenin Street became Karjalankatu (Karelia Street).

17 In the census of 1939, the Finno-Ugric inhabitants amounted to only 27 per cent of the population of 469,000.

18 Before the German attack against the Soviet Union, the Finns could hardly be expected to have foreseen that the German war of invasion would develop into a war of extermination of the population of the occupied Soviet territory. This terrifying fact became known to the Finns with the continuation of the German invasion. In their relations with the Finnish ally, the Germans acted fairly decently.

19 See Laine, *Suur-Suomen kahdet kasvot*, 310–14.

20 *Trial of the Major War Criminals before the International Military Tribunal*, Judgment of the Nuremberg Tribunal, 1946, vol. I (Nuremberg 1947) 286 and 220. See also I. Brownlie, *International Law and the Use of Force by States* (Oxford University Press, 1963), Chs. IX and X, 167–213.

21 J. B. Scott (ed.), *The Hague Conventions and Declarations of 1899 and 1907* (New York: Oxford University Press, 1918) 100–27.

22 L. Oppenheim, *International Law*, Vol. *II*, *War* (7th edn, H. Lauterpacht (ed.), London: Longmans, 1952) 440.

23 On the ratification of Hague Convention IV, see R. Hanski, 'The Second World War' in Hannikainen, Hanski and Rosas, *Implementing Humanitarian Law*, 44–6. Was the war of 1941–1944 a bilateral war between Finland and the Soviet Union or was it connected to the broader war? Czechoslovakia had not ratified Hague Convention IV and its government in exile in London had declared war on Germany and its allies, including Finland. Thus, in the strict interpretation of Article 2, Hague Convention IV would not be applicable.

24 See *ibid*. 46.

25 *Ibid*. 47.

26 *Final Record of the Diplomatic Conference of Geneva of 1949* (Bern: Federal Political Department) vol. I, 297–330.

27 See Hyytiä, *Itä-Karjala 1941–1944*, 18–23 and 43–56, and A. Rautala, *Itä-Karjalan valtaus 1941* (Jyväskylä: Gummerus, 2007) 175 and 178.

28 See Laine, *Suur-Suomen kahdet kasvot*, 116.

29 The texts of Mannerheim's military orders can be found at www.mannerheim.fi/pkaskyt/s_paiva.htm (these military orders are in Finnish).

30 See Hyytiä, *Itä-Karjala 1941–1944*, 23–32.

31 I. Jaakkola, *Suomen idänkysymys* (Porvoo-Helsinki: WSOY, 1941), and V. Auer and E. Jutikkala, *Finnlands Lebensraum* (Helsinki, 1941).

32 The Statement (in Finnish) by Rafael Erich on 26 November 1941, Horellin kokoelma PK 1350/5, SA. See Laine, *Suur-Suomen kahdet kasvot*, 56–8.
33 See Laine, *Suur-Suomen kahdet kasvot*, 68.
34 See Hyytiä, *Itä-Karjala 1941–1944*, 63.
35 See G. Rosén, *Sata sodan ja rauhan vuotta – Suomen Punainen Risti 1877–1977* (2nd edn, Helsinki: Suomen Punainen Risti, 2002) 481. One additional factor was also that in 1940, Finland had lost 12 per cent of its territory, and from the lost territory some 400,000 Finns had moved to Finland. An earlier version of Rosén's book is published also in English, *One Hundred Years of War and Peace: Finnish Red Cross 1877–1977* (Helsinki: Finnish Red Cross, 1989).
36 See G. Rosén, *Suomalaisina Itä-Karjalassa – Sotilashallinnon ja Suomen Punaisen Ristin yhteistoiminta 1941–1944* (Helsinki: Suomen Historiallinen Seura, 1998) 164–225, and Hyytiä, *Itä-Karjala 1941–1944*, 250–303.
37 See Laine, *Suur-Suomen kahdet kasvot*, 104–141, and Hyytiä, *Itä-Karjala 1941–1944*, 57–69.
38 See Hanski, 'Second World War', 88–9.
39 Laine, *Suur-Suomen kahdet kasvot*, 297.
40 *Ibid*., 340–50.
41 See *ibid*., 115–27, and Seppälä, *Suomi*, 75–88.
42 At the end of 1941 the number was already about 20,000, see Rautala, *Itä-Karjalan valtaus 1941*, 179.
43 See J. Kulomaa, *Äänislinna – Petroskoin suomalaismiehityksen vuodet 1941–1944* (Helsinki: Suomen Historiallinen Seura, 1989) 86–7 and 105–6.
44 M.-L. Mikkola, *Menetetty lapsuus – suomalaismiehittäjien vankeudessa 1941–1944* (Helsinki: Tammi, 2004).
45 Seppälä, *Suomi*, 83.
46 Laine, *Suur-Suomen kahdet kasvot*, 126, see also 140, 240, 247 and 372. See also Hanski, 'Second World War', 91–4, Hyytiä, *Itä-Karjala 1941–1944*, 63, and Kulomaa, *Äänislinna*, 79–81 and 130–3. Of course, a number of these persons, especially the elderly, would have died in any case in the period of autumn 1941-September 1944.
47 Seppälä, *Suomi*, 84–86. It is especially difficult to discover the mortality rate of the inmates in the turbulent months of November-December 1941.
48 Kulomaa, *Äänislinna*, 79.
49 See Hyytiä, *Itä-Karjala 1941–1944*, 68.
50 See Rosén, *Sata sodan*, 495–6.
51 He was the chair of the Finnish Red Cross for nearly thirty years, from 1922 until his death in 1951.
52 See Rosén, *Sata sodan*, 473–508.
53 The cooperation between the Military Administration and the Finnish Red Cross was, for example, with regard to medical care and social programmes, so close that it is difficult to clearly identify the role of the Red Cross. See Rosén, *Sata sodan*, 476 and 491–500.
54 Rosén's book, *supra* note 36, on the cooperation between the Military Administration and the Finnish Red Cross in Eastern Karelia in 1941–1944 does not refer to any opinions of the ICRC. I have also read through the correspondence between the ICRC and the Finnish Red Cross, and between the League of the Red Cross Societies and the Finnish Red Cross, between June 1941 and the spring of 1944, and found no references to Eastern Karelia. The Finnish Red Cross has placed its historical

papers in the Finnish National Archives (in Helsinki) where the above-mentioned correspondence can be found in files 184 and 191. These files cannot possibly contain the whole correspondence between those Red Cross entities, because I did not find the letter of Marshal Mannerheim which is mentioned *infra* note 56.

55 See Rosén, *Sata sodan*, 510–511 and 520–530.

56 In March 1942, Mannerheim, in the capacity of the chair of the Finnish Red Cross, wrote a request to the ICRC asking for help in order to ensure sufficient nourishment for camps of Soviet prisoners of war (not to Eastern Karelian camps of civilians). The circumstances in prisoner or war camps were even worse than in the Eastern Karelian civilian camps. Several national Red Cross Societies and other associations responded affirmatively and sent food materials to Finland. See Rosén, *Suomalaisina*, 123–6. In the war of 1941–1944 Finland captured about 64–67,000 Soviet soldiers as prisoners of war. Of these, almost 19,000 died, nearly all in 1941–1942; see A. Kujala, *Vankisurmat – neuvostosotavankien laittomat ampumiset jatkosodassa* (Helsinki: WSOY, 2008) 307–11.

57 See Laine, *Suur-Suomen kahdet kasvot*, 350–61; Hyytiä, *Itä-Karjala 1941–1944*, 308–17; and Seppälä, *Suomi*, 143–53.

58 Helsinki was one of the three capitals of war-waging states which was not occupied during the Second World War. The others were London and Moscow. Not a bad performance for a small nation.

59 Treaty of Peace with Finland concluded in 1947 in Paris, 48 UNTS 2003 and Finnish Treaty Series no. 20/1947.

60 Finnish Treaty Series no. 4/1944 and the national implementing act no. 645/1944 in the *Finnish Law Gazette*.

61 On the transferred property, see Pimiä, *Sotasaalista*, esp. 113–17, 162–71 and 182–4.

62 The text of the provisional Peace Treaty can be found in Finnish Treaty Series no. 3/1944 and in *Documents on American Foreign Relations* (Boston, 1947) vol. VII, 879.

63 On the trial and its background, see J. Tarkka, *Hirmuinen asia* (Helsinki: WSOY, 2009).

64 The Soviet Union did not demand that Mannerheim should be put on trial. Mannerheim had been elected as President of Finland during the armistice negotiations. His prosecution would have caused unrest in Finland – perhaps even Finland's preference to continue fighting instead of agreeing to an armistice and the establishment of a strongly anti-Soviet government.

65 Act no. 890/1945 in the *Finnish Law Gazette*.

66 See Laine, *Suur-Suomen kahdet kasvot*, 362–5.

67 See Hanski, 'Second World War', 95–7.

68 Rautala, *Itä-Karjalan valtaus 1941*, 179.

69 Laine, *Suur-Suomen kahdet kasvot*, 121–2.

70 Erik Castrén's memorandum, 'Siviiliväestön siirto vallatulta alueelta kansainvälisoikeudelliselta näkökannalta arvosteltuna', 30 March 1943, Archives of the Finnish Ministry for Foreign Affairs, section 110 D 5 on Eastern Karelia.

71 They have been used as sources above. Regarding the occupation, especially relevant sources are Laine, *Suur-Suomen kahdet kasvot*; Kulomaa, *Äänislinna*; and Hyytiä, *Itä-Karjala 1941–1944*.

72 See M. Jokisipilä, '"Kappas vaan, saksalaisia!" Keskustelu Suomen jatkosodan 1941–1944 luonteesta' in M. Jokisipilä (ed.), *Sodan totuudet – Yksi suomalainen vastaa 5.7 ryssää* (Helsinki: Ajatus kirjat, 2007) 154–6. Jokisipilä reports an inquiry made by a Finnish daily newspaper, *Ilta-Sanomat*, to its readers, as to whether Finland's war was separate from Germany's war. Seventy-two per cent of respondents were of the opinion that Finland's war was separate.

73 G. Mannerheim, *Muistelmat, toinen osa* (Helsinki: Otava, 1952) 392–8. His concluding sentence at 398 was in Finnish as follows: 'Täydellä syyllä voitaneen sanoa, että Suomen miehittämillä alueilla ei väestölle ainoastaan myönnetty niitä oikeuksia, mitkä sille kansainvälisten sopimusten mukaan kuuluivat, vaan se myös sai osakseen huolenpitoa, joka jäi toisen maailmansodan aikakirjoihin ainoaksi laatuaan.'

It is true that Eastern Karelia was in a poor shape when the Finns occupied the territory. The Soviets had applied a scorched earth policy of burnt land, when they had to withdraw from their own territories, in order to hamper the occupying force's accomplishment of its goals. In principle, that was legitimate self-defence.

8

The occupied and the occupier: the case of Norway

SIGRID REDSE JOHANSEN

1. Introduction

During the years of occupation in Norway between 1940 and 1945, the German Third Reich introduced changes in all Norwegian jurisdictional areas – in legislation, and in the executive and adjudicative powers. A new government was also introduced in two subsequent periods: first, a government consisting of temporarily appointed Norwegian ministers subordinated to the German occupier and secondly, from 1942, a 'National Government' under the direct leadership of the Norwegian Nazi collaborator Vidkun Quisling. According to the law of occupation, both in 1940 and today, the interference of an occupier in the internal affairs of the occupied state is restricted to security measures which are strictly necessary. What is considered necessary is weighed against, among other things, humanitarian considerations for the occupied population. The first question of this chapter is thus whether the interference in Norwegian internal affairs during the Second World War can be justified as strictly necessary.

I will also discuss the question of attributability of conduct during occupation. The question of attributability is a part of the question of responsibility of states for international wrongful acts. If the law of occupation were violated, who was actually responsible? A determination of the circumstances in which conduct is to be attributed to the state is a precondition for establishing state responsibility.[1] By the wording 'attribute to' or 'attributability', one usually covers situations where a certain conduct is performed *on behalf of* a state, a state organ or another entity. The conduct may legally be said to have been performed *by* the state; it will be an *act of* state.

To illustrate the relationship between the occupier and the occupied, and in particular the relationship between the occupier and the residents of the occupied country who assist the occupier, I will use the situation in Norway between 1940 and 1945. The occupier may to some extent require the collaboration of the occupied population, in accordance with the law of occupation laid down in the Hague Convention of 1907 and later in Geneva Convention IV of 1949, but only in relation to respecting the security and the basic needs of the occupier, not to promote its military and political aims.[2] The question I will address is thus, at what point does collaboration, notwithstanding its criminality according to national law, progress into becoming an actual act of state on behalf of the occupier? Was the assistance offered to the occupier by Norwegian individuals in reality action performed on behalf of the German state? Was the conduct attributable to Germany?

The question of attributability in the case of Norway should, however, be put in context. I will therefore first present a brief overview of the relevant historical facts (section 2 below). Thereafter I will present how certain fundamental aspects of the law of occupation were viewed from a Norwegian perspective, both during the Second World War and in its aftermath (section 3 below). A particular focus will be placed on the concept of humanity and humanitarian considerations as limits of the law[3] and therefore as limits on what the law of occupation actually permits the occupier to do. In section 4 below, I will then move on to the question of responsibility, thereby introducing the question of attributability of conduct, which is then treated further in section 5 below.

2. Historical background

Norway was invaded by German troops on 9 April 1940. The attack took Norway by surprise, and German troops quite rapidly managed to move into a position which enabled them to gradually take complete control over vital Norwegian governmental functions. On 24 April 1940, Hitler issued a Führererlass (a Fuhrer decree), stating that Josef Terboven as Reichskommissar was the superior civilian leader of Norway, only subordinated to Hitler himself. The Führererlass stated further that the Norwegian legal system should exist only as long as it was compatible with the German occupation.[4] On 10 June 1940, Norwegian forces capitulated and Norway was formally occupied.

After this, Terboven tried to achieve a 'legal solution' in Norway by forcing the Norwegian King to abdicate, something he refused to do by way of a famous denial, the so-called 'King's no'.[5] As of 25 September 1940, Terboven therefore introduced temporarily appointed ministers, so-called 'kommissarische Staatsräte'. This arrangement lasted until

1 February 1942, and implied that Terboven could govern Norway directly, only subordinate to Hitler, and with the use of frontmen. The Norwegian government in exile made it clear that the acceptance of such a post as temporarily appointed minister under the German regime would be considered as an act of treason, in violation of the Norwegian Constitution, Article 1, which states that Norway is a free and independent country.[6] From 1 February 1942 and until the end of occupation, the temporarily appointed ministers were replaced by a 'National Government' with the Norwegian fascist leader Vidkun Quisling as their 'Minister President'. This arrangement was quite peculiar for Norway, and the relationship between the 'National Government' and the occupier will be analysed further, in section 5 below.

As Reichskommissar, Terboven enacted several new laws. Subsequent to September 1940, these were published as so-called Verordnungsblatt, which were issued throughout the years of occupation.[7] Laws were issued regarding delivery of weapons, prohibition of political parties, prohibited activity in favour of the Norwegian Royal Family, protection against English espionage, and on a civilian state of emergency. On 12 October 1942, a decree from the Reichskommissar was issued defining crimes against the occupying forces. According to paragraph 3 of the decree, it was a crime to omit to report information on the resistance movement's actions.

According to the Norwegian Constitution, the Supreme Court has the authority to perform judicial review of enacted laws.[8] The Supreme Court made it clear that the activities of the Norwegian courts not were affected by the occupation and that the occupier, as a consequence, did not have the authority to withhold enacted laws from the review of the Supreme Court.[9] The Supreme Court was not permitted to review laws, however, and consequently it decided to close its offices by 12 December 1940, arguing that it was no longer able to fulfil its constitutional mandate.[10] Josef Terboven considered that it was solely at his discretion to decide what measures were appropriate and proportionate to promote law and order in Norway.

On 25 October 1940, Terboven established by decree 'Folkedomstolen', which directly translated means the People's Court. This court was established to 'protect against hostile activity towards the state and the people'.[11] In reality, the Court considered cases against persons who had violated the prohibition on political parties and activity in favour of the Royal Family. Criminal acts committed against the occupying force were, during the first year of occupation, adjudicated by the German military tribunal, the Reichskriegsgericht, but throughout the years of occupation, the adjudicative system became gradually more arbitrary and deprived of fair trial guarantees. From 1 June 1944, the security police (Sicherheitspolizei) could decide on administrative measures, including death sentences without trial. Throughout the occupation, the Germans also made use of court-martial, in the sense of summarily established courts. The trials took place outside the regular court system and were used whenever it was considered necessary, for example to try civilians taking a direct part in hostilities.

Before moving on to the legal questions, I will briefly present some facts about the Norwegians actively supporting the occupier in various functions. It is mentioned above that the temporarily appointed ministers, and the members of the 'National Government', were all Norwegians, but Norwegians also took positions in several other public functions. Among other things, they acted as members of the reconstituted Supreme Court and especially of the established courts-martial, as front-fighters, as county leaders, and in various police functions, either in the German security police, or in the Norwegian state or border police. A central point with regard to the legal discussion is the extent of the Norwegian contribution to the German occupier's exercise of its powers *as an occupier*. The members of the regular Norwegian police force in particular stand out, as 42 per cent of them joined the national fascist party, 'Nasjonal Samling' (NS); a high percentage compared to other public functions where the average number of persons with NS membership was only 6 per cent.[12] The role of the police is commented on below towards the end of this chapter. I will now proceed to consider certain legal questions relating to the law of occupation and the small state perspective of Norway during the Second World War and its aftermath.

3. Humanity, positivism and Norway

3.1 *Considerations of humanity*

It was clearly stated by prominent legal scholars in Norway that the above-mentioned Führererlass of 24 April 1940 in itself was in accordance with international law.[13] Its wording was similar to that of Hague Convention IV, in that it required the occupier to respect the laws in force in the country 'unless absolutely prevented':

> The authority of the legitimate power having in fact passed into the hands of the occupier, the latter shall take all the measures in his power to restore,

> and ensure, as far as possible, public order and safety, while respecting, unless absolutely prevented, the laws in force in the country.[14]

The law of occupation lays down both *rights* and *obligations* of the occupying power.[15] One of the first issues discussed in the case of Norway was whether the changes in governmental powers and legislation made by the occupier in order to secure its own interests really were necessary. I will come back to this aspect, in particular when it comes to the change of governmental structures, in section 4 below. In the present section, the question will be discussed of how to balance two specific considerations in accordance with the law of occupation: the considerations of security and humanity. It is common to state that the two primary considerations to balance are those of humanity, on the one hand, and military necessity, on the other. In this chapter, I refer more to 'security' than to 'necessity'; this is because I relate the two concepts as follows: security is an aim to achieve, a desired condition. Considerations of necessity refer to the question of what measures are necessary to implement in order to achieve a secure condition. There may be other aims to achieve than security, but in the context of this chapter, the focus will mainly be on security. When reference is made to the balance to be struck between necessity and humanitarian considerations, it would also in broad terms imply a balance between security and humanitarian considerations. Furthermore, I will in particular comment on how humanitarian considerations had an impact on the limits of law, or the relationship between law and morals, before moving on to the more technical issues of attributability of conduct.

The development of international humanitarian law is strongly influenced by the wish to minimize the sufferings caused by war. In its core essence, one may say that humanitarian law contains the lowest degree of legal protection a human life may receive compared to the protection offered by alternative legal frameworks. It is the lowest threshold for protecting the *value* of human life. In peacetime, the value of human life is protected through human rights guarantees on the right to life and the right to liberty. In armed conflict it is not considered a violation of the right to life to direct attacks against persons, provided that the act in question is a lawful act of war. The right to liberty is a so-called derogable right, meaning that exceptions may be made if it is necessary in a democratic society, for example during armed conflict.[16] Humanitarian law, being a form of positive law, therefore accepts the *necessities* of war. The right to perform necessary conduct in armed conflict is, however, not unlimited; it is limited by humanitarian considerations.[17] Humanitarian considerations have exerted huge influence on the development of the modern law of armed conflict, and the balance between obtaining military goals and paying respect to humanitarian considerations can be traced back, for example, to the St Petersburg declaration of 1868.[18] The content of the declaration is considered to be customary international law and illustrates the balance to be struck between considerations of humanity and necessity or security,[19] by referring to the prohibition on causing superfluous injury or unnecessary suffering which would be 'contrary to the laws of humanity'.[20] These 'laws of humanity' have also been referred to in later regulations, most famously in the Martens Clause, first in the Preamble to the Hague Convention of 1899, thereafter in 1907,[21] and later in the four Geneva Conventions of 1949 and the Additional Protocols of 1977. In Geneva Convention IV, the Martens Clause appears in Article 158 in the following way:

> The denunciation shall have effect only in respect of the denouncing Power. It shall in no way impair the obligations which the Parties to the conflict shall remain bound to fulfil by virtue of the principles of the law of nations, as they result from the usages established among civilized peoples, from the laws of humanity and the dictates of the public conscience.

This quoted passage appears in a denunciation Clause and emphasises states' duty to abide by the content of the Martens Clause even if they were to withdraw from the Convention. The Martens Clause can be seen in different ways. In the commentary to Geneva Convention IV, it is referred to as principles that 'exist independently of the Convention and are not limited to it'.[22] The reference to '[general] principles of law' is not in itself necessarily controversial. 'General principles of law' is today explicitly established as a source of law in Article 38 of the Statute of the International Court of Justice (ICJ), and is considered customary international law.[23] What is particular about the Martens Clause is the linkage between 'usages' and the last part of the Clause – the reference to 'laws of humanity' and 'dictates of the public conscience'. The Clause goes quite far in placing 'usages' on the same footing as the two last-mentioned categories. 'Usages' may be understood as a reference to general international customary law, which today is codified in ICJ Statute, Article 38.

So what does this mean? Does it mean that 'laws of humanity' and 'dictates of the public conscience' are independent sources of law? Are they interpretative directions to be applied with the application of other positive regulations? Or are the two categories moral requirements that international humanitarian law must abide by in order to be valid: in other words, are they moral requirements to the content of positive law? This last question is a question of legal philosophy. I will to a certain degree come back to the aspect of legal philosophy towards the end of this section. The alternatives are partly overlapping, and are referred to in theory and practice to a varying degree.

3.2 *Norwegian positivism*

Today, it seems to be a clear understanding that the Martens Clause does not constitute an independent legal source.[24] It has also been argued that there is a tendency for the Martens Clause, in the area of humanitarian law, to contribute to lowering the requirement of state practice for determining whether a customary rule has been established, when the aim of the rule is to protect humanitarian values, as opposed to economic, military or purely political aims.[25] Furthermore, it is argued that the Clause is valid as an interpretative factor if the rule in question is not sufficiently clear.[26] The use of the Martens Clause by the Norwegian Supreme Court[27] in the aftermath of Second World War may illustrate this tendency. In a case against a German judge, who was a member of a court-martial established as a reaction to the killing of police chief Marthinsen by Norwegian resistance, the Supreme Court discussed the procedural guarantees set out in international law. It stated that:

> Even though it can often be difficult to decide what is permissible and what is impermissible according to international law, there cannot be any doubt that it establishes certain minimum requirements which have to be considered as absolute, and which are binding upon an Occupier in the land he has possessed … As far as I can understand, it has to be a clear breach of the principles of human justice, which are expressed in the Preamble to the Hague Convention IV of 1907, when the Court Martial have pronounced death sentences on clearly unsatisfactory evidence …. And when it is the case that International law recognises certain fundamental principles as invariable, these rules, if they are to have any meaning, must be binding notwithstanding whether national law violates them. (author's translation)[28]

What is particular about this judgment is that the Martens Clause at the time was not a part of the treaty itself, but rather a part of the Preamble. Even though the Clause was not a part of the binding treaty and even less a transposed part of the Norwegian Criminal Code, the Norwegian Supreme Court allowed the Clause to serve as an argument *in favour* of criminal liability. This is remarkable in the Norwegian legal tradition. In Norwegian law the principle of legality, often referred to as '*nullum crimen sine lege*', has been given a strict interpretation in criminal law. It is only written, formal law[29] in force at the time of the crime which can generate criminal responsibility. In addition to practising a strict principle of legality, Norway has belonged to a positivistic legal tradition in the period after the Second World War, so-called 'Scandinavian legal realism'. The combination of positivism and legal realism has resulted in a tradition where, for instance, law and morals have been understood as two distinct features. An immoral law is not necessarily legally invalid. Moral arguments may be sound, but they would have no legal effect on the binding force of the law. Against this background, it is interesting to note how the Norwegian Supreme Court argued in favour of criminal responsibility in a criminal case. The Martens Clause was, in 1945, more a moral incentive than a penal provision, and therefore the Court's decision may be said to have accorded poorly a positivistic and strict legality tradition.

In the Supreme Court judgment above, the Martens Clause further serves to draw an absolute line for minimum legal requirements. The Court states that some principles are so fundamental that they must be binding in all circumstances. Because of their fundamental character, the principles are binding even if national law violates them. We may say that they are unconditional principles, or absolutes. The Norwegian Supreme Court used the Martens Clause in a similar matter in the so-called *Klinge* case.[30] In that case, the Clause was also used as an argument *in favour* of criminal liability. Furthermore, it was also applied to legalise the use of a provisional decree from 1945 which gave the death penalty retroactive force. The Court argued that since this form of crime (torture) had been criminalised and considered to be the most serious crime in international law before 1945 as well, the use of the death penalty in Norway was lawful.[31] In the following, I will comment further on the relationship between laws and morals.

3.3 Humanity, positivism and the relationship between law and morals

When discussing humanity, references to morality are often very close by. How this relationship between laws and morals is viewed may differ depending on whether one comes from a positivistic background or not. As stated above, someone representing a positivist view may argue that law and morality are separated. An immoral law may be immoral, but immorality has no weight as an argument of legal critique. Persons with a non-positivistic view, however, may be inclined to argue that there are moral requirements that affect the content of positive law. Moral requirements are considered to be external factors, i.e., outside positive law, which are still legally relevant. We may say that views along this line represent natural law tendencies.

None of the quotations or references above directly express that the Clause contains certain requirements based on natural law or other external factors. At the same time, it is difficult to say that the Clause does anything other than reflect moral conceptions and requirements. Morality is introduced to the legal text by way of a vague and indefinite reference: the Martens Clause. Still, this might not be so peculiar. Quite a few legal norms do in fact reflect moral conceptions; hopefully, most legal norms do. What is peculiar about the Court decisions mentioned above is the following: the Norwegian Supreme Court is clearly making its arguments more *in* law than *about* law.[32] By this I mean that the Court is arguing within the borders of the system, within positive law. But nevertheless the argument seems to incorporate moral considerations which affect the content of law to a great degree. These moral arguments are derived indirectly (or almost directly) from the Martens Clause, which at the time was not a part of binding law. Thus, the moral arguments are used as if they were external requirements on the content of positive law, making the argumentation resemble one of natural law.

Furthermore, even though the Court's argument appears to be expressing positivism,[33] in practice, reference is frequently being made to principles as *universal* and *absolutes*, i.e., not subject to evaluation or consideration. Torture, which was the crime considered in the *Klinge* case, is an example of a crime the prohibition of which is considered universal and absolute. Such references provide the Court's argumentation with a distinctive element of natural law, or at least the impression that objective (external) requirements to the content of law exist. If this observation is sound – that moral requirements are introduced under the umbrella of positive law – the following observation may also be made: it is arguable that the threshold for finding that rules of customary law have been formed is being *lowered* because clearly immoral behaviour quickly gets the status of a crime in customary law, even if it is questionable whether the amount of supporting state practice is sufficient. This is most likely to happen when the rules under development concern the protection of human life – not only the life of the victim, but also of the perpetrator and his/her rights as an accused. A result of this lowering of the threshold for law creation is that the limits of law are expanded; more and more cases are included 'into the law'. This is a symptom of law creation which stems from purely moral incentives. In many cases, this is a sound and good development, precisely because the feeling of justice is satisfied for the persons involved. Still, there may be disadvantages and this is the point which I want to make here. When the legal argumentation includes moral incentives, as was done for example in Norway during the aftermath of Second World War, there is a risk of opening a Pandora's box of arguments, all in the name of morality – or security. It cannot be taken for granted that morality will always be a definite size, graspable and clear for everyone to use when applying the law. It may thus offend the above-mentioned principle of legality and the values it protects.

If we look at the *Klinge* case again, the dissenting minority, who applied the prohibition on retroactive laws strictly, represented a positivistic view on law rather than a natural law[34] point of view. This positivistic view was representing the citizen's rights, the human rights of the accused. Ironically, it was the view of the majority, who referred to the 'laws of humanity', which in this case *deprived* the accused of his protection offered by the Constitution and the human rights guarantee laid down there.

3.4 Preliminary conclusion on law and morals: humanity as a fundamental absolute?

What conclusions can be made from this rather messy picture? Humanitarian law is expanding, and the development of law, in particular customary international law, in certain areas of life seems to be driven by moral incentives more than traditional requirements of state practice and *opinio juris*. Those moral incentives in this connection may be referred to as *fundamental absolutes* shaped as requirements of humanity. By absolutes, here I mean unconditional minimum requirements of behaviour; requirements one might refer to as 'objective standards', irrespective of any national discrepancies in legislation. The use of absolutes may seem to aim at securing a purpose (teleologically founded), for example, to serve justice. May this be seen as 'natural law in a positive law wrapping'? That might be so, though it will not necessarily pose any risk, as long as the protection would be there for those who need it. Nevertheless, references to absolutes do not provide any guarantee for a fair and just result. Absolutes in themselves have no value, and in my opinion, rarely exist. They have a function and in this lies their value.

Absolute minimum guarantees are often referred to in connection with fundamental human rights, frequently represented by procedural guarantees to a fair trial. Where the case concerns violations of humanitarian law, the picture is changed; the absolutes no longer represent the rights of the accused, but the protection of victims. Rightly enough, both cases relate to the protection of the individual, but in international humanitarian law, the balance between the interests of the accused and the victim may be said to have shifted in favour of the latter, in particular with regard to moral protection. The requirements introduced to the law by morality are therefore left unclear, in that the accused's right to fair trial is challenged.

4. The question of responsibility

The Norwegian cases commented on above refer to situations where the occupier, or someone acting in the service of the occupier, had violated minimum requirements according to the law of occupation. This leads us to the central point in this chapter: who (i.e., which legal entity) is actually considered to be the perpetrator? This is the question of attributability of conduct. In Norway, the German occupying force found several persons who were willing and able to collaborate with the occupier to promote the German case. The key question here thus becomes: what actions were actually performed on behalf of the German occupying power, as German acts of state, and what actions were 'only' committed by Norwegian individuals on their own behalf, with an unpatriotic motive? The question is relevant in order to analyse the following: the occupier is accused of having committed grave violations of international law, including violations of so-called minimum requirements and 'absolutes' as discussed above. But what if one concludes that the occupier did not actually commit some or more of these acts? What if they were 'only' individual crimes? It is necessary to address the question of attributability of conduct and, more precisely, the question of attributability in relation to the use of straw men.

As pointed out above in the introduction to section 3, the occupier has rights and duties under the law of occupation which entitle it to implement certain changes to ensure its security. The occupier may also require certain assistance from the occupied population in the sense that they must provide for the 'needs of the army of occupation' (Hague Convention IV, Article 52). In Norway, the requirements of the occupier went far beyond what the Convention allows for demands on the occupied population, although in the initial period of occupation certain measures were discussed, and found to be in accordance with the law of occupation. Assistance of a basic nature rendered to the occupying force would not constitute actions performed on behalf of the occupier. More difficult questions arise in connection with the performance of governmental and administrative functions carried out actually on behalf of the occupier. I will first comment briefly on questions concerning the legality of change of government, before moving on to the specific questions concerning the attributability of conduct related to the changed government.

During the period of occupation, it was discussed whether the occupier, under the protection of international law, could change the government with the use of straw men.[35] In Norway, it was pointed out that the occupying power could replace civil administration with its own organ if it were necessary in order to protect the occupier's interests in the occupied areas. The Norwegian view, however, was that it would *not* be in accordance with international law to change or suspend the constitutional organs of the occupied country nor implement measures in order to pursue *political* goals.[36] Still, it was assumed that objectives other than strictly military ones could lawfully be pursued, provided they were not purely political. Regardless of the objective, any new enactments and appointments had to be temporary.[37] It was also pointed out that Norwegian courts should treat all criminal cases according to Norwegian law, unless the cases concerned the security of the occupying power.[38] This is in line with the law of occupation as it is generally understood today.[39]

When it came to the question of replacing the King and the government, opinions varied as to what international law actually permitted. It was claimed by one prominent author that the removal of the King and the government could be accepted if this were the only way to save the state.[40] This was heavily rejected by others who claimed that this would be 'to break our Constitution apart', notwithstanding arguments of necessity.[41] The question of the legality of the government instituted by the Germans, which consisted of Norwegian straw men, was touched upon in Norwegian case law after the war, but it was not considered necessary to discuss this at length, since the laws and enactments issued by that government were in any case considered unlawful under international law. In the following, I will concentrate on the temporarily appointed ministers and on the so-called 'National Government' that came later.

5. Proxies of the occupier or merely individual collaborators?

It was, and is, a question of international law as to whether the establishment of a government of temporarily appointed ministers (the puppet regime) creates or implies international responsibility for the occupying power. And if it does create such responsibility, to what degree? Or to phrase it differently, how 'national' must a puppet regime be in order to be regarded as acting on its own behalf and not directly on behalf of the occupying power? These questions concern all acts performed by Norwegian civil servants working in support of the occupying enemy. One example is the judges and interrogators taking part in proceedings against other Norwegians at the court especially established by Quisling's regime. Such Norwegians were clearly criminally responsible under national law. The question of whether the acts of these Norwegians created responsibility for the occupier according to international law is, however, a separate one. This question could be of particular interest with regard to Norwegian officials taking posts as temporarily appointed ministers without being members of the Norwegian fascist party, NS (there were three such persons), as their connection to the occupying regime would be less clear.

The relevant point of departure was clearly stated by a well-known Norwegian law professor:

> [T]he German soldiers in Norway mostly showed exemplary behaviour. The same cannot be said of Reichskommisar Terboven and his people, and even less the German security police. According to the Hague Regulations, the occupying power shall respect the laws in force in the country, unless absolutely prevented. *The German support of the 'new arrangement' made by NS was a grave violation of this principle.*[42]

This quotation is only a starting point, but it does illustrate that the connection between the NS party and the occupying power was believed to be close and that the German support of the 'new arrangement' contained a violation of international law on the part of the occupier. The question of whether the support of the NS arrangement was in itself a German act of state is not commented on in particular, but the question has been addressed on different occasions during the past years as a question of whether a specific conduct is attributable to the state, even if it is carried out by private individuals.

From 2001, the International Law Commission's Articles on Responsibility of States for Internationally Wrongful Acts of 10 August 2001 have laid down the following in Article 8:

> The conduct of a person or group of persons shall be considered an act of a state under international law if the person or group of persons is in fact acting on the instructions of, or under the direction or control of, that state in carrying out the conduct.

The question whether a conduct is attributable to the state is relevant to the case of occupied Norway even though the Articles are drafted as late as 2001. These Articles have to a large extent been recognised as customary international law. It is, however, a difficult and formidable task to describe the content of customary law at the time of Second World War, and such a task would go beyond the scope of this chapter. Nevertheless, I deem it fruitful to analyse the application of Article 8 to the case of occupied Norway, despite the uncertainty regarding the status of customary law at the time of the conduct.

In general, conduct of private persons or entities is not attributable to a state, but in certain cases where there exists a specific factual relationship between the private actor and the state in question, the conduct may be attributed to that state. Article 8 (*supra*) describes three such types of factual relationship: if the act in question is performed under the *instruction* of the state, if it is performed under the *direction* of the state, or if it is performed under the *control* of the state. In the commentary to Article 8, the following is stated regarding the first alternative (instruction):

> Most commonly, cases of this kind will arise where State organs supplement their own action by recruiting or instigating private persons or groups who act as 'auxiliaries' while remaining outside the official structure of the State. These include, for example, individuals or groups of private individuals who, though not specifically commissioned by the State and not forming part of its police or armed forces, are employed as auxiliaries or are sent as 'volunteers' to neighbouring countries, or who are instructed to carry out particular missions abroad.[43]

In Norway, the occupying power was itself present and the factual relationship between NS as a private entity and the German state as occupier may have differed depending on the act in question. It could be possible to look at the relationship from the point of view of all three alternatives. In cases where there are evidential facts to support the view that the NS was actually under German instruction or direction, the question of attributability would be uncontroversial – acts committed would have been attributable to the German state. The understanding of the third alternative in Article 8 (control), however, has been subject to some interpretative controversy in the international debate. There are at least two different understandings that may be applied: control may mean *effective control*[44] in the sense that each act in question must be subject to instruction or control; or control may mean *overall control*[45] in the sense that it was not necessary to issue instructions for that specific act in order to make the act attributable to the state. When referring to private individuals rather than organised groups, even the opponents of the doctrine of effective control agree that control over the specific acts is required.[46] The question of controversy therefore only remains with regard to organised groups. In the commentary to Article 8, reference is made to this discussion and the discrepancy between the two different views is summed up as follows:

> In any event it is a matter for appreciation in each case whether particular conduct was or was not carried out under the control of a State, to such an extent that the conduct controlled should be attributed to it.[47]

This last quotation may offer guidance, however vague, on the question of attributability in the case of occupied Norway during the Second World War. The controversy referred to above did not arise in the period from 1940–1945 and the nuances of the interpretation of concept of control were not expressed. The debate can therefore serve as no more than guiding principles when discussing the concrete question of attributability of acts to the German state. Nevertheless, it is this author's opinion that the 'overall control doctrine' is supported by reasonable arguments in the *Tadić* case and later emphasised by Cassese, and that these arguments, at least initially, seem to correspond with the historical perspective taken in this chapter.

I will use this as a point of departure when discussing whether the Norwegian citizens in different posts, who helped the Germans to govern occupied Norway, were auxiliaries under the instruction, direction or control of the occupying power. It is necessary to distinguish between different types of conduct performed by the Norwegians – the functions as temporarily appointed ministers, as judges in the Supreme Court and courts-martial, as members of the police, and as front-fighters – when discussing the character of the support given to the German occupier, whether it be financing, planning, equipping, coordination or cooperation.

First, it may be worthwhile looking at the connection between the Norwegian fascist party, the NS (Nasjonal samling), and the occupying power. Vidkun Quisling was the founder and leader of NS, established in 1933. In the first years of its existence, the party did not have any real influence, but after the German invasion in 1940, the Quisling party gained new hope.[48] Quisling was not a popular man, either in Norway or with the German occupier. But he was a particularly clever man, and he was the leader of the only national party which was genuinely willing to cooperate with the occupier in creating a national 'new government'. Against this background, Terboven announced the new ministers in September 1940.

5.1 Temporarily appointed ministers and the relationship to the occupier

First period: from 25 September 1940–1 February 1942, Terboven's ministers

When Terboven declared the so-called 'new arrangement' on 25 September 1940, he had at the same time declared all parties, except NS, unlawful. Terboven's speech was referred to in the media, stating that:

> for a national, Norwegian future solution of the present situation, in other words a solution appropriate, to a wide extent, for regaining freedom and independence for the Norwegian people, it is now offered one road; and this goes through NS.[49]

Despite this, the new temporary ministers were appointed directly by Terboven and subordinated to him. According to the decree issued on 28 September 1940, the appointed ministers were in charge of one ministry each and responsible to the 'Reichskommissar … for an orderly administration within their area of activity' (my translation).[50] The appointed ministers were also authorised to issue decrees on their own, which could change existing Norwegian laws. If the issuing of a decree necessitated a deviation from the Norwegian Constitution, the decision had to be made by the Reichskommissar.[51]

Even though, after September 1940, the NS was the only permitted party, membership in the NS was not necessary in order to fill a post as a temporarily appointed minister. The Norwegian fascist party had no formal power, but since the majority of the appointed ministers were members of the party, Quisling was able to exert considerable influence on the actual politics. Legally, Terboven's arrangements were under the direction and control of the occupying power, Germany. This seems to have been the view of the Norwegian Supreme Court as well, when it later convicted these ministers for being guilty of treachery. One of the ministers, Hagelin, had acted as minister for 'interior affairs' and contributed through his enactments to the deportation of approximately 1,000 Jews to Germany, where they died. Hagelin argued that he acted under duress from the occupying power. The Court did not take this argument into account, arguing that mitigation of sentence was excluded due to the fact that he 'voluntarily had entered the service of the occupier' (my translation).[52]

It would thus be reasonable to conclude so far that the appointed ministers in reality were under the actual instructions of the occupying state and therefore performing German acts of state. This conclusion would be sound notwithstanding the controversy related to the understanding of the doctrine of 'control'. The appointed ministers were subject to the direct instructions of the German Reichskommissar Terboven and were thus accountable to Germany.

Second period: from 1 February 1942–8 May 1945, Quisling's government

Another, more difficult, question is to consider the status of the next arrangement introduced during the period of occupation, the rule of Quisling's 'National Government', instituted on 1 February 1942. After the 'new arrangement' was instituted in September 1940, Quisling was waiting for a possibility to seize power. He thought that he had been promised by Hitler to take over the government as soon as the NS party was strong enough. Quisling apparently believed this to be scheduled for 1 March 1941, but nothing happened. The actual 'hand over' from the German-led government of temporarily appointed ministers to the 'National Government' was initiated by a request to Quisling as the leader of NS from the ministers already appointed. Quisling was requested to form a national government under his own command as 'Minister President'.[53] The ministers argued that their request was legally correct due to necessity. Josef Terboven accepted their resignation and the institution of the new National Government, but neither initiated it, nor demanded it. The actual 'hand over' or investiture of the new National Government occurred at Akershus fortress on 1 February 1942, in what has been named 'The State Act'. The Norwegian government in exile did not recognise this 'State Act' and issued a leaflet, distributed in Norway by the resistance movement. In the leaflet, one could read that: 'Those who exercise sovereignty on behalf of Norway during this war are the King and his Government, and no one else is authorised to make peace on Norway's behalf' and further on: 'Vidkun Quisling has no other position or authority than the one given to him by the occupying power, and an agreement with him is an agreement with the agent of the Germans' (my translations).[54] The official Norwegian view was, in other words, clear. Quisling's 'National Government' was not national, it was an instrument of the German occupier.

The relationship between Quisling's government and the occupying power was also commented on by the Norwegian Supreme Court in the aftermath of the war. In the subsequent criminal proceedings after the war, Quisling was indicted for violating the Norwegian Criminal Code, article 83, by having 'unlawfully contributed to foreign command over Norway in whole or in part' (my translation).[55] The basis for the indictment was, among other things, that Quisling had:

> assisted the German administration in Norway with the establishment of temporarily appointed ministers from 25 September 1940, appointed by Terboven and responsible to him, and undertook from 1 February 1942 as 'Minister President' the leadership of a government which in reality also was a part of the Occupier's administration of Norway and served its [the occupier's] purpose. (author's translation)[56]

The indictment was not disputed by the Court and illustrates that the 'National Government' was conceived as an instrument under the control of the occupier. Neither the indictment nor the previous statements from the Norwegian exile government differentiate between control over specific acts (effective control) and overall control, but it seems to be implied that the actions were considered to require at least an implicit consent of the occupier, if not directly instructed by it, and hence to be in reality *its* actions. The indictment also included accusations of complicity to murder. Against these counts, Quisling argued that the murder paragraph was not applicable when the lives were taken by governmental authorities. This argument was rejected by the Court, on the basis that Quisling, according to Norwegian law, had no governmental authority, and above all no authority to cause the death of his fellow citizens. The Court further stated that: 'the authority the convicted has had was delegated to him from the organs of the occupying power'. This statement further strengthens the view presented in the indictment and by the Norwegian exile government referred to above. The Court also stressed that the occupying power obviously had no authority to equip Quisling with the competence to take the lives of Norwegian citizens where this had no basis in international law.[57] The point here is not the question of what was within Quisling's competence as head of the 'National Government', but the fact that the Norwegian Supreme Court apparently considered it to be up to the occupier's discretion whether Quisling should exercise *de facto* authority or not. In other words, the exercise of *de facto* governmental authority was in reality under the occupier's control.

The case against Quisling clearly shows that the Norwegian Court (both the Court of Appeal and the Supreme Court) considered the 'National Government' to be acting under the actual control of the occupying power. The same view was laid down in the Court of Appeal (Eidsivating) and not contested by Supreme Court (in Rt. 1946, 1139), in the case against one of the members of the 'new Supreme Court', where the Appeal Court held that: 'Quisling's government of 1 February 1942 must according to the Court, without doubt be seen as an organ instituted by the occupier' (my translation).[58] This statement follows from evidence presented during the trial, namely a telephone call by Terboven from Berlin on 29 January 1942 which had been tapped. In the telephone call, Terboven stated that Quisling 'is of course completely under my command'.[59] Terboven's command over Quisling as the leader of the 'National Government' was, in other words, implicit but still a reality. This command, if understood in the ordinary meaning of the concept, would cover both a possibility to issue specific instructions and to choose to keep a more overall control. Thus, acts not performed on the basis of specific instructions would still necessarily be attributable to the German state, as otherwise the command would not have been complete.

When it comes to the other ministers in Quisling's government, the Supreme Court did not explicitly say that their actions were, in reality, German acts of state. Nonetheless, there was no reason to treat the other members differently from their leader. In the case against ministers Irgens and Stang, the dissenting minority judge Hanssen stated that 'the relationship was mainly the same [before and after the establishment of the "National Government"] as Quisling and his ministers were in reality subordinated to the occupying power' (my translation).[60] (Although the quotation is from a dissenting judge, the quoted passage does not concern the subject matter of the dissent.)

It seems to have been the clear opinion of both the Norwegian government in exile and of the Norwegian Supreme Court that the 'National Government' in reality was acting under the instructions or control of the occupying power. It further seems reasonable to conclude that the actions of the 'National Government' would constitute acts of state under international law, as now laid down in the Articles on State Responsibility, Article 8 (see *supra*). But even though the 'National Government' in an overall perspective could render the occupier responsible under international law, this does not necessarily imply that *all conduct* by that government were German acts of state, but as argued above in relation to Terboven's statements presented during the trial against Quisling, it would probably be exceptional that the actions would not be attributable to the German state. With regard to the German occupying power in Norway during the Second World War, the occupier was soon known precisely for its involvement in matters which, according to the international law of occupation, were inherently internal. One example was the educational system. In the criminal proceedings against the temporarily appointed Minister for Church and Educational Affairs, the following passage can be found:

> Immediately after the accused was temporarily appointed as minister, he learned that the German 'Reichskommissariat' had 'Beratere' [advisors] for the school and educational system, and that these advisors would interfere in his administration and present their demands. He was familiar with the fact that the occupying power – according to international law – did not have the right to interfere in the domestic administration in this way. The accused did not oppose this, but cooperated with the enemy and in this way promoted its interference. (author's translation)[61]

This sort of involvement and interference would, once it was concluded that the leadership of the 'National Government' as such (i.e., Quisling) was acting on behalf of the occupier, also make such conduct an act of state on behalf of the occupier.

Another example of the German involvement in the conduct of the 'National Government' can be found in the criminal proceeding against Quisling (see *supra*). Quisling had contributed to the arrest and deportation of, among others, Jews, teachers, priests and officers. He wanted to arrest and deport a further 250 Norwegian officers, but this was denied by the German Commander-in-Chief.[62] He had also proposed to the German occupier to forcibly enlist 50,000 men into German service, but the proposition was turned down by the Germans.[63] These examples again strengthen the position taken above, namely that even if the command was not exercised at all times, the clear possibility to issue specific instructions would imply that actions which were not performed under the specific instructions of the Germans would nevertheless still normally be attributable to the German state. This not only seems to have been the Norwegian view, as implicitly expressed in the reasoning of the Norwegian Supreme Court, it would also be in accordance with the position claimed by the German state itself, represented by Terboven, namely that the 'National Government' was under the 'complete command' of the German state (see *supra*).

Some exceptions may, of course, be found: an example of actions that could be considered outside of what would be attributable to the occupier is the many counts in the indictment against Quisling for theft from the Norwegian population. He had made use of the Royal Castle, and during the period of his use, he had, among other things, removed valuable pieces of art and used them for his private purpose. He had also confiscated huge sums from the political parties when these were prohibited after September 1940 and used the money for his own benefit.[64]

The question of attribution of conduct may, as suggested above in the introduction to this section, cover other functions fulfilled by Norwegian collaborators as well. I will only comment on these groups briefly. The Norwegian police were, as previously mentioned, heavily burdened with NS members. The police department was made into its own ministry from September 1940 and thereby separated from the Ministry of Justice. In this way, the police were under the direct command of Josef Terboven and the occupying force. At least with regard to the leadership and the strategic decisions made, their conduct would be attributable to the occupier. The same can be said about the acts of the other ministers and their direct subordinates in the two 'governments'. Throughout 1941, the police department was reorganised and divided into two subdivisions, the security police and the order police. The security police were again divided into three further subdivisions: the state police (Stapo), the border police (Grepo) and the crime police (Kripo). The Norwegian Stapo closely coordinated with the German security police (Sipo). The Grepo also closely coordinated its activities with the German border police, but subordinated to the police department. One of the focal points to discuss in this regard is the line to be drawn between, on the one hand, upholding law and order which is a regular function under the law of occupation, and, on the other hand, illegal (according to national law) assistance to the enemy and conduct actually attributable to the occupier. This would have to be done on a case-by-case basis, along the same line of argumentation as for the ministers. Functions in the German security police or the Norwegian state police attracted the harshest penalties after the war. Altogether, approximately 1,300 persons were convicted for such activities in the aftermath of the war.[65]

The so-called 'front-fighters' were constituted by Norwegian volunteers enlisted in the German armed forces and were as such directly under German command.[66] Their conduct was therefore not distinguishable as anything other than attributable to Germany. The same was the case for the prison guards. The SS guard battalion was under German command and its acts were therefore clearly acts of state. About 360 Norwegians served in the SS guard battalion.[67]

A particular question may be raised with regard to the Norwegian judges appointed to the reconstituted Supreme Court and courts-martial. In the criminal proceedings against the temporarily appointed Supreme Court Justice, the (regular) Supreme Court stated after the war that he had performed as a 'willing tool in the hands of the Germans' (my translation).[68] When evaluating whether the Supreme Court actually was under the direction or control of the occupier, the background for the reconstituted Supreme Court must be examined. Before the establishment of the reconstituted Supreme Court, the judges of the (regular) Supreme Court had laid down their services in protest against the new enactments issued by the temporarily appointed ministers subsequent to 25 September 1940 (see section 2 above), which stated that legal review of enacted laws was no longer permitted. At the same time, the temporarily appointed ministers issued enactments which gave the new ministers full authority to appoint new judges – or dismiss them.[69] In reality, this meant full control, and conduct of the reconstituted Supreme Court could hence be seen as constituting acts of state on behalf of the occupier.

6. Conclusions

Norway has since the Second World War had a positivist legal tradition, which may be detected from the arguments of the courts. The tradition is positivistic, inter alia, in that legal validity is exhaustively to be determined by the internal criteria of the legal system. During the judicial settlement after the war, the role of this positivism may have met a litmus test in relation to the barbaric Nazi regime, since in a situation such as this, morality might challenge a strict positivist position. The Nazi regime made laws and tried to camouflage its actions in a 'lawful wrapping' or what may be called 'legal solutions'. The solutions were obviously immoral, and needed to be treated accordingly. How was this accomplished by the Norwegian courts? It can be detected in the Norwegian arguments that morality was the incentive for introducing what in reality could be seen as natural law positions in positivist clothing. A certain desired result was the driving force. And there is not really anything new or *necessarily* wrong in that, although a potential warning could be given with regard to the use of so-called absolutes: I do not dispute that it is possible in law to draw an (absolute) line, but one should show considerable care in giving 'absolutes' a value of their own – they exist to perform a function, and in this lies their value. The absolutes could protect the same person one day as it convicts the next day. Humanitarianism must not become too independent, it must always have the appropriate relative position to real human life.

During the same legal settlement after the war, Norway showed a consistent harshness towards its own citizens who had committed treason. One could detect a clear attitude that collaborators were acting at their own risk and at the mercy and control of the occupier, as its tool. Without commenting directly on the question of attributability in international law when it comes to the question of state responsibility (in this case Nazi Germany), the Norwegian case law after the war was consistently clear, in the charges made by the prosecution, in the statements by the government in exile, and in the actual decisions on the merits of the courts: both the temporarily appointed ministers and the Quisling regime were in fact under the control of the occupier, thus making their actions acts of state on behalf of the occupier. The *possibility* to exercise real command by the German occupier seems to have been as decisive for the question of control over acts performed by the NS government and the judicial sector as those examples where actual instructions in fact were given. The argumentation of Norwegian courts and by the Norwegian government in exile may be compared with the current debate concerning 'effective control' or 'overall control'. It seems to have been the Norwegian opinion that the examples of specific instructions given (exercise of 'effective control') were only symptoms of an underlying factual relationship making the NS government and administrative functions dependent upon the consent of the occupier to such a degree that it would make their actions attributable to the German state. In other words, the approach adopted in Norway on the question of attributability of conduct to a given state seems to be a combination of the doctrines of 'effective' and 'overall' control.

Notes

1 See e.g. the 'Commentary to the Draft Articles on Responsibility for States for International Wrongful Acts' in (2001) *Yearbook of the International Law Commission*, vol. II, part 2, 3, available at http://untreaty.un.org/ilc/publications/yearbooks/yearbooks.htm.

2 See Hague Convention IV respecting the Laws and Customs of War on Land, and its annex, Regulations concerning the Laws and Customs of War on Land, The Hague, 18 October 1907, in particular Articles 42–56, and Geneva Convention IV Relative to the Protection of Civilian Persons in Time of War, 12 August 1949, in particular Articles 47–78. The Rights and duties of the occupier are further commented on later in this chapter.

3 By limits of the law, I primarily refer to limitations on the legal system, not on a particular rule, see further below.

4 The Erlass (decree) may be found in F. Castberg, *Norge under okkupasjonen: rettslige utredninger 1940–1945* (Oslo: Cappelen, 1945) 14–15: 'Das bisher geltende Recht bleibt in Kraft, soweit es mit der Besetzung vereingbar ist. Der Reichskommisar kann durch Verordnung Recht setzen. Die Verordnungen werden im Verordnungsblatt für die besetzen norwegischen Gebiete verkündet.' (Author's translation: 'The existing law will stay in force, as far as it is reconcilable with the occupation. The Reichskommisar may through enactments make law. The enactments will be announced in a Proclamation letter for the Norwegian Occupied Territory'.) The same author, Castberg, who was highly recognised in Constitutional law at the time, found the Erlass to be in accordance with international law.

5 In June 1940, the Norwegian King was asked to abdicate by the Presidency of the Norwegian Parliament. The Presidency was under German pressure and saw no other solution, but the King replied with a strong 'no' over London radio, 8 July 1940. He stated that he would not be acting in the interest of his country if he were to accept an arrangement in violation of the Norwegian Constitution which was forced upon the Norwegian people. This radio speech has later become known as 'The King's no'.

6 This was stated by referring to the Norwegian Constitution, 17 May 1814, art. 1. See also M. Skodvin (ed.), *Norge i krig*, (Oslo: Aschehoug & Co., 1986) vol. II, 54 with further references to the statement given from the Norwegian government in exile in London, 26 September 1940, given over London radio.

7 The 'Verordnungsblatt' was a publication distributing newly enacted legislative decrees for occupied Norway. Its full German title was: 'Verordnungsblatt für die besetzten norwegischen Gebiete' (author's translation: 'Decree news for the Occupied Norwegian territory').

8 The right for courts to perform judicial review is in Norway not explicitly stated in the Norwegian Constitution, but it follows from Constitutional customary law, see e.g., J. Andenæs, *Statsforfatningen i Norge* (Oslo: Tanum, 1994) 348.

9 F. Schjelderup, *Fra Norges kamp for retten: 1940 i Høyesterett* (Oslo: Grøndahl, 1945) 206, referring to a letter to the temporarily established Ministry of Legal Affairs, dated 19 November 1940.

10 Norwegian Constitution, 17 May 1814 art. 88 and Schjelderup, *Fra Norges kamp for retten*, 218–219.

11 See Skodvin, *Norge i krig*, vol. II, 80.

12 Ibid. 65.

13 See e.g., Castberg, *Norge under okkupasjonen*, 28.

14 Hague Convention IV, Article 43. This Article refers to 'safety', an English word which may not be found in the French and authentic version of the same Article, which directly translated uses the word (public order and) 'life'. The word 'life' may cover a broader spectrum than the word 'safety' (the French quotation reads: 'l'ordre et la vie publics'). For a more thorough discussion of the differences between the French text and the English translation, see Y. Dinstein, *The International Law of Belligerent Occupation* (New York: Cambridge University Press, 2009) 89–90. This will in turn place a greater obligation on the occupier, which is worth remembering when balancing the duties and authorisations of the occupier. I will not discuss further in this chapter the semantic differences, but rather focus on the concept of security, more precisely, on the security of the occupier.

15 See e.g., E. Benvenisti, *The International Law of Occupation* (New Jersey: Princeton University Press, 2004) 9.

16 See ICCPR, Articles 6 and 9 and ECHR, Articles 2, 5 and 15(2).

17 Today this limitation is laid down, among others, in the basic rule in Protocol Additional to the Geneva Conventions of 12 August 1949, and relating to the Protection of Victims of International Armed Conflicts, 8 June 1977 (AP 1), in Article 35(1): 'In any armed conflict, the right of the Parties to the conflict to choose methods or means of warfare is not unlimited.'

18 The declaration states: 'That the only legitimate object which States should endeavour to accomplish during war is to weaken the military forces of the enemy; That for this purpose it is sufficient to disable the greatest possible number of men; That this

object would be exceeded by the employment of arms which uselessly aggravate the sufferings of disabled men, or render their death inevitable; That the employment of such arms would, therefore, be contrary to the laws of humanity', Declaration Renouncing the Use, in Time of War, of Explosive Projectiles under 400 Grammes Weight (abstract), St Petersburg, 29 November/11 December 1868.

19 See *supra* for my comments on the relationship between security and necessity.

20 See e.g., J.-M. Henckaerts and L. Doswald-Beck, *Customary International Humanitarian Law,* Vol. 1, *Rules*, ICRC Study on Customary Law (Cambridge University Press, 2005) 237. The ICRC Study on Customary Law may have attracted criticism on a number of points, but the prohibition on causing unnecessary suffering is not in itself considered controversial as a rule of customary international law.

21 See Hague Convention II with respect to the Laws and Customs of War on Land, and its annex, Regulations concerning the Laws and Customs of War on Land, The Hague, 29 July 1899, Preamble and Hague Convention IV, Preamble.

22 See J. Pictet (ed.), *Commentary on the IV Geneva Convention Relative to the Protection of Civilian Persons in Time of War* (Geneva: ICRC, 1958) 625. The quotation from the Commentary reads: 'the value and permanence of the lofty principles underlying the Convention. Those principles exist independently of the Convention and are not limited to it. The clause shows clearly that a Power which denounced the Convention would nevertheless remain bound by the principles contained in it in so far as they are the expression of the imprescriptible and universal rules of customary international law.'

23 Statute of the International Court of Justice, 26 June 1945. See also e.g., I. Brownlie, *Principles of Public International Law* (6th edn, Oxford/New York: Oxford University Press, 2003) 5, who states that: 'Article 38 is generally regarded as a complete statement of the sources of international law.'

24 See e.g., practice of the International Criminal Tribunal for the Former Yugoslavia (ICTY) in *Zoran Kupreskić et al.* (IT-95–16-T), ICTY Trial Chamber Judgment, 14 January 2000, para. 525: 'More specifically, recourse might be had to the celebrated Martens Clause which, in the authoritative view of the International Court of Justice, has by now become part of customary international law. True, this Clause may not be taken to mean that the "principles of humanity" and the "dictates of public conscience" have been elevated to the rank of independent sources of international law, for this conclusion is belied by international practice. Nevertheless, this Clause enjoins, as a minimum, reference to those principles and dictates any time a rule of international humanitarian law is not sufficiently rigorous or precise: in those instances the scope and purport of the rule must be defined with reference to those principles and dictates. In the case under discussion, this would entail that the prescriptions of Articles 57 and 58 [rules regulating precautions in attack] (and of the corresponding customary rules) must be interpreted so as to construe as narrowly as possible the discretionary power to attack belligerents and, by the same token, so as to expand the protection accorded to civilians.'

25 The requirements for creation of customary international law are according to ICJ Statute Article 38(1)(b), twofold: there must be widespread and uniform state practice as evidence of a general practice 'accepted as law', the last criteria being usually referred to as '*opinio juris*'. When it comes to the Martens Clause, see A. Cassese, *International Law,* (2nd edn, New York: Oxford, 2005) 161 and the *Kupreskić* case, *supra* note 24, para 527.

26 *Kupreskić* case, *supra* note 24, para 525.
27 This is the regular Supreme Court re-established after the war. Where decisions by the Commissary 'Supreme Court' established by the occupier are referred to, this is done explicitly.
28 Norwegian Supreme Court Judgment Publications: Retstidende (Rt.). 1947, 468.
29 This means laws enacted by Parliament in accordance with the procedures in the Norwegian Constitution of 17 May 1814, arts. 76–80.
30 The case is published in Riksadvokatens meddelelsesblad (Ram)-15–23 at 35, where the court stated: 'The accused has been sentenced for several acts of grave torture. Torture is not only explicitly prohibited according to Norwegian law, the Constitution Article 96, second paragraph. It is also a breach of "laws of humanity" and the "dictates of the public conscience".'
31 *Ibid.* 25.
32 The reference to law in this context meaning positive law.
33 If one holds that the validity of positive law can be exhaustively evaluated according to the internal criteria of the legal system (norms of validity), one will rarely take the position that the binding force of the law is created by a metaphysical 'something', given by God or by reason itself. This position is an expression of legal positivism.
34 If one holds that there are criteria outside the internal norms of validity in the legal system, which may be another basis for legal validity, one may also hold that the binding force of the law can be explained by reference to external criteria. This kind of position will be compatible with different natural law theories and other ethical theories.
35 The question is also raised by Dinstein, *Belligerent Occupation*, 123.
36 This was, among others, stated by the Norwegian Supreme Court in a Memorandum issued 15 June 1940 stating that: 'It would not be in accordance with general principles of international law (Hague Convention of 1907 Article 43) if the occupying forces required that the Parliament should make decisions that according to Norwegian Constitutional law it was not authorised to make' (my translation). From Schjelderup, *Norges kamp*, 118. The Norwegian text: 'Det vil ikke stemme med alminnelige folkerettslige grunnsetninger (jfr. landkrigsreglementet av 1907 Art. 43) om det av okkupasjonsmyndighetene skulle bli stilt krav om at Stortinget skal fatte beslutninger som det etter norsk statsrett ikke har myndighet til.' See also Schjelderup, *Norges kamp*, 159.
37 See also Rt. 1954, 232, stating this view in a case concerning tax exemptions issued under the period of occupation.
38 See Schjelderup, *Norges kamp*, 184–9 and Rt. 1940, 343. The case concerned a young boy (17 years old) who had pointed at Norwegian girls sitting with German soldiers. The boy had made gesticulations that he would cut the girls' hair off and pretended he had a revolver in his hand when being asked to remove himself by the soldiers. In this case, the Norwegian Supreme Court held that this was obviously not a case regarding the security of the occupying power and also that German soldiers were protected in accordance with Norwegian criminal law and criminal proceedings against criminal actions not of a military nature. In another case, the Supreme Court held that acting as prosecutor for a German special court was in principle in accordance with the law of occupation, even though the prosecutor was Norwegian. To uphold law and order when faced with serious crimes was not seen as assistance to the enemy, according to Rt. 1950, 11.

39 See e.g., Dinstein, *Belligerent Occupation*, 112 and 123.
40 Castberg, *Norge under okkupasjonen*, 55.
41 Schjelderup, *Norges kamp*, 165.
42 J. Andenæs, *Det vanskelige oppgjøret* (Oslo: Tanum-Norli, 1979) 207–8. Emphasis added, author's translation from Norwegian.
43 Commentary on the (Draft) Articles on Responsibility for States for International Wrongful Acts, 47.
44 This position is taken by the ICJ in its Judgment in the *Case Concerning Military and Paramilitary Activities in and against Nicaragua* (*Nicaragua* v. *United States*), 27 June 1986, see in particular paras. 110–15 and followed up in the *Case Concerning the Application of the Prevention and Punishment of the Crime of Genocide* (*Bosnia and Herzegovina* v. *Serbia and Montenegro*), 26 February 2007.
45 This position is taken by the International Tribunal for the Former Yugoslavia (ICTY) in *Dusko Tadić* (IT-94-1-A), ICTY Appeals Chamber Judgment, 15 July 1999, see in particular para. 95 ff. and upheld by Cassese, *International Law*, 248–9.
46 *Ibid.* and A. Cassese, 'The *Nicaragua* and *Tadić* tests revisited in light of the ICJ Judgment on Genocide in Bosnia', (2007)18 *European Journal of International Law* 649 at 657.
47 Commentary to the Draft Articles on Responsibility for States for International Wrongful Acts, 48.
48 Skodvin, *Norge i krig*, vol. II, 45.
49 Author's translation. From a propaganda paper for NS, quoted from Skodvin, *Norge i krig*, vol. II, 43.
50 Skodvin, *Norge i krig*, vol. II, 43, from the decree of 28 September 1940.
51 *Ibid.* para 3(2).
52 Rt.1946, 449, at 450.
53 Skodvin, *Norge i krig*, vol. II, 240.
54 Skodvin, *Norge i krig*, vol. IV, 12, with further references.
55 Norwegian Criminal Code of 10 May 1902, no. 22, art. 83.
56 Rt. 1945, 109 at 119–20 (from the Appeal Court Judgement).
57 Rt. 1945, 109 at 114.
58 Rt. 1946, 1139, from the Appeal Court Judgment, at 1160.
59 *Ibid.*, 1160.
60 Ram-13–55, 71, the minority dissenting opinion of Judge Hanssen.
61 Rt. 1947, 165 at 177.
62 Rt. 1945, 109 at 141.
63 Andenæs, *Det vanskelige oppgjøret*, 38.
64 Rt. 1945, 109, at 137.
65 Andenæs, *Det vanskelige oppgjøret*, 194.
66 The term 'front-fighter' has in Norwegian history been given this specific meaning, and is thus not to be confused with a generic reference to a person fighting at the front.
67 Andenæs, *Det vanskelige oppgjøret*, 193.
68 Rt. 1946, 1139 at 1141. The Norwegian text is as follows: 'Ved å motta utnevnelse til og ved å fungere som høyesterettsdommer var domfelte med på å erstatte den lovlige Høyesterett som var fratrådt av konstitusjonelle og folkerettslige grunner med et kollegium som var et villig redskap i tyskernes og N.S.'s hender.'
69 See e.g., in Rt. 1946, 1139 at 1151.

9

Multinational peace operations forces involved in armed conflict: who are the parties?

OLA ENGDAHL

1. Introduction

The involvement of multinational peace operation forces in armed conflicts is often accompanied by national debate within the troop contributing nations (TCNs). Many states may show reluctance to admitting involvement in an armed conflict. With regard to the ISAF (International Security Assistance Force) operation, arguments have been advanced claiming that an armed conflict exists only in some parts of Afghanistan, while some states deny that there is an armed conflict at all in that country. In Sweden, the discussion has gone so far as to involve the question of whether or not the nation, for the first time in 200 years, actually is at war. Such political considerations naturally have legal implications. Does international humanitarian law (IHL) apply? If so, which entity is responsible for its application? Who in actual fact, in the case of an armed conflict, are the parties to such a conflict?

The precise role played by the parties concerned is of the utmost importance in cases of both international and non-international armed conflict. The parties to an armed conflict have a responsibility to ensure that their actions comply with IHL and they are responsible for the acts of their forces. Applicable law is moreover partly dependent on the types of treaty the different parties to the conflict are bound to apply. In its oft-quoted decision in the *Tadić* case, the International Criminal Tribunal for Former Yugoslavia (ICTY) stated, in relation to the existence of an armed conflict, that until a general conclusion of peace was reached, or a peaceful settlement achieved, then 'international humanitarian law continues to apply in the whole territory of the warring states or, in the case of internal conflicts, the whole territory under the control of a *party*, whether or not actual combat takes place there'.[1] The identification of the parties in relation to an armed conflict is thus also of interest with regard to the geographical scope of IHL.

It is apparent that different levels of control over armed forces are of importance in order to identify which entity is a party to an armed conflict. This chapter therefore makes a brief assessment of the different levels of control of the armed forces in multinational peace operations. It goes on to discuss those criteria under international humanitarian law, which govern and define the existence of an armed conflict and inquires into the criteria that constitute being a party to such a conflict. A brief case study of the ISAF operation will be presented, discussing whether or not an armed conflict exists in Afghanistan and, if so, who exactly under international law could be regarded as being a party to such an armed conflict. On these matters, a survey conducted by the Swedish Armed Forces has disclosed different positions among the TCNs in the ISAF operation. The chapter initially presents the result of this survey. Lastly, Operation Unified Protector in Libya is briefly examined.

It must be acknowledged that there is a dearth of literature on this specific topic. There seems to be an understanding that a party to an armed conflict is a known concept and basically easy to identify.[2] This chapter has been based upon analogies from closely related areas of international law in order to examine how various levels of control over armed forces could be used to identify parties to an armed conflict. These include the practice of the ICTY on the applicable legal framework for deciding individual criminal responsibility (in international or non-international armed conflict), state responsibility and responsibility for international organisations under the approach adopted by the International Law Commission (ILC) and the International Court of Justice (ICJ). Against this background, this chapter does not purport to reach an ultimate conclusion on identifying particular parties to an armed conflict involving multinational peace operation forces, but rather to provide the reader with arguments for different positions.

2. Positions by some states and NGOs in relation to the ISAF operation in Afghanistan

The Swedish Armed Forces Headquarters has struggled with the question of the legal status of the ISAF operation and the related issue of the applicability of IHL.On this issue, the following questions were put to the Swedish Defence Attachés in Denmark, Norway, Finland, Germany and Hungary: (i) Is the situation in Afghanistan regarded as an armed conflict? (ii) Are ISAF and the state's contingent participating in the armed conflict? (iii) Does the national contingent apply the laws of war? (iv) How has that affected the Rules of Engagement (ROE)/national restrictions?[3] The different positions of these states, discussed below, are thus based upon the reports of the Swedish Defence Attachés in those respective states.

Denmark regards the conflict as a non-international armed conflict and is of the view that Denmark participates in that conflict. According to the Attaché, this means that ISAF also participates in the armed conflict. According to parliamentary decision, the Danish forces should apply the Geneva Conventions, even though Denmark is of the opinion that they are not formally applicable in all aspects.[4] The Danish forces apply the NATO ROE applicable for the ISAF forces, which has also been adjusted to national ROEs.

Norway is of the opinion that a non-international armed conflict exists in Afghanistan, where the Afghan government has requested support from the United Nations to maintain security. Norwegian forces are in Afghanistan based upon a clear mandate from the UN Security Council and the ISAF presence is furthermore founded upon consent from the legitimate representatives of Afghanistan. Norway participates in the non-international armed conflict in Afghanistan,[5] applying the international law applicable in this type of armed conflict. The international humanitarian law applicable in this type of conflict, however, is only the outer framework for ISAF's offensive operations. Within this legal framework there can be other limitations, such as the United Nations Security Council (UNSC) mandate, the Operation Plan (OPLAN), ROE and other political considerations.

Hungary views the state of affairs in Afghanistan as representing a non-international armed conflict, with Hungarian troops accordingly applying the laws of war in all areas where they are deployed. It appears that Hungarian troops, owing to national restrictions, are not permitted to participate in offensive operations, but there are no limitations on the defensive use of force.

Germany does not consider that the situation in Afghanistan constitutes an armed conflict, based primarily on national political considerations. Certain representatives of the Ministry of Foreign Affairs, however, have claimed that the position in Afghanistan is partly an armed conflict but not in most of the regions in the north. Consequently, the laws of war are not applicable for German forces in Afghanistan. German officers consider that they are participating in an armed conflict, including combat situations, against a militant and criminal attacker, and accordingly desire that the operation in Afghanistan should be correctly so described. Since the report of the Defence Attaché, however, Germany has changed its position and now considers the situation in Afghanistan to be 'an armed conflict within the parameters of international law'.[6]

The Swedish government has not been clear on the matter. In its governmental propositions on future Swedish participation in ISAF, it has described the situation in Afghanistan as one where there indeed exists an armed conflict, but not in all parts of the country. The armed conflict exists in the south and in the east, but not in the northern parts where Swedish forces are deployed. It is considered that occurrences in Afghanistan certainly differ between various regions, and that the fighting has *de facto* been carried out in the southern parts.[7] In its latest declaration on the continued participation in ISAF, the language has slightly changed. It now says that the non-international armed conflict in Afghanistan between the Afghan government with the support of the international military presence and the Taliban and other groups hostile towards the government is still most apparent in the southern and eastern parts of the country.[8] The government now recognises that an armed conflict exists in the whole of the territory of Afghanistan. It should also be noted that the security situation in the area where Swedish forces are deployed has deteriorated. The government has pointed out that insurgent groups have shown a capability for conducting coordinated attacks with firearms, improvised explosive devices and suicide attacks. The capability of these groups, however, is limited compared with such groups in the south, but active Taliban groups have established themselves in the north.

The Armed Conflict Database of the International Institute for Strategic Studies characterises the conflict as that of an internal armed conflict involving Taliban forces and NATO-ISAF forces as non-state parties and the Afghan government as the only state party.[9]

Even among such like-minded states as the Nordic ones, positions nevertheless differ on the applicability of IHL to the peace operation forces in Afghanistan. Such differences, however, should not be over-estimated. They are due partly to the actual conditions on the ground where particular forces are deployed. The more hesitant approach by Sweden regarding the application of IHL probably arises from the experiences of Swedish troops in a (so far) calmer area of Afghanistan compared with those of Danish and Norwegian forces.[10] Until recently, the actions of Swedish troops have been guided exclusively by human rights law. Owing to the deteriorating security situation, Swedish troops have increasingly become involved in the actual fighting. Human rights law is still the guide in this more insecure environment, and when troops participate in the armed conflict and conduct combat-related operations, they apply IHL. The varying positions among the Nordic states seem to be primarily based upon different perceptions of how one identifies a party to an armed conflict, and less on the applicable law itself.

3. Levels of control in multinational peace operations

For the purpose of this chapter, a peace operation is defined as that which supports the maintenance of international peace and security based upon a mandate from the UNSC, but not necessarily conducted under UN command and control.[11] The question under this heading centres on attribution and responsibility under international law and might not necessarily be decisive in identifying a party to an armed conflict. Nevertheless, it is important to broadly outline different perceptions on the control of those armed forces involved in a multinational peace operation.

Given the fact that the United Nations does not maintain military forces of its own, it is dependent on voluntary troop contributions from member states for each individual operation. In UN-led operations, the TCNs transfer authority over their contributing troops to the United Nations, which then exercises command over the operation as a whole. The TCNs do not transfer full command of their troops but retain some influence, such as disciplinary powers, exclusive criminal jurisdiction over their military personnel and the right to withdraw from the operation in question. TCNs may furthermore issue so-called caveats for their troops, which are basically restrictions on the Force Commander on the use of troops from that state. Despite these restrictions, the position of the United Nations is that in principle it assumes exclusive control over those forces engaged in a UN peace operation. Such operations are regarded as subsidiary organs of the United Nations, so that 'an act of a peacekeeping force is, in principle, imputable to the Organization'.[12]

The question of control is more complicated in operations where the UN Security Council authorises a particular operation and another international organisation executes it. In certain cases, there could also be a single state leading the operation.[13] Such was the initial position in Afghanistan where the UK-led ISAF was then followed by Turkey, and thereafter came under the combined leadership of Germany and the Netherlands.[14] Since August 2003, NATO has commanded ISAF.

In the military context, the terms 'operational command' and 'operational control' are central to the overall question of control in military operations.[15] NATO defines 'operational command' as 'the authority granted to a commander to assign missions or tasks to subordinate commanders, to deploy units, to reassign forces, and to retain or delegate operational and/or tactical control as the commander deems necessary'.[16] The term 'operational control' is defined as 'the authority delegated to a commander to direct forces assigned so that the commander may accomplish specific missions or tasks which are usually limited by function, time, or location; to deploy units concerned, and to retain or assign tactical control of those units'.[17] A glossary of UN peace-keeping terms prepared by the DPKO Training Unit largely coincides with the NATO definitions.[18]

Control of military forces is of critical importance in relation to the question of responsibility for the use of force. In multinational peace operations, TCNs usually place their military forces at the disposal of an international organisation, which assumes responsibility for implementing the Security Council mandate. The practice of the United Nations has to a large extent formed the basis for the work of the ILC on the responsibility of international organisations in situations where a state organ is placed at their disposal. Article 7 of the Draft Articles on Responsibility of International Organizations reads: 'The conduct of an organ of a State or an organ or agent of an international organization that is placed at the disposal of another international organization shall be considered under international law an act of the latter organization if the organization exercises effective control over that conduct.'[19]

According to the Commentary to Article 7, it deals with the:

> situation in which the lent organ or agent still acts to a certain extent as organ of the lending State or as organ or agent of the lending organization. This occurs for instance in the case of military contingents that a State placed at the disposal of the United Nations for a peacekeeping operation, since the State retains disciplinary powers and criminal jurisdiction over the members of the national contingent. In this situation the problem arises whether a specific conduct of the lent organ or agent has to be attributed to the receiving organization or to the lending State or organization.[20]

It is apparent that the important condition for determining responsibility is the exercise of effective control, explained as 'the factual control that is exercised over the specific conduct taken by the organ or agent placed at the receiving organization's disposal'.[21] With regard to responsibility of states, the question of effective control is largely discussed in relation to such control over persons or groups of persons and whether the conduct of those groups is at all attributable to a state. In the context regulated by Article 7, control plays a different part. It seeks to answer the following question: to which entity is a certain course of conduct attributable, the state organ or the international organisation?[22]

The Venice Commission, with regard to the NATO-led peace operation in Kosovo, discussed levels of control in such operations and stated:

> When States contribute troops to a NATO-led operation they usually transfer only the limited powers of 'operational control' and/or 'operational command'. These powers give the NATO commander the right to give orders of an operational nature to the commanders of the respective national units. The national commanders must implement such orders on the basis of their own national authority.[23]

In relation to the application of the European Convention on Human Rights, the Venice Commission found that the conduct of KFOR was not attributable to the United Nations, since KFOR was not one of its subsidiary organs. The Commission found that acts committed by KFOR troops were either attributable to NATO or to the TCNs and had to be assessed on a case-by-case basis.[24]

The criterion of effective control did not guide the European Court of Human Rights (ECtHR) in the *Behrami and Saramati* case.[25] It was the first case where the responsibility for alleged violations of human rights law within a multinational peace operation was tested in an international court. Mr Saramati held that his right to freedom and security (Article 5 of the ECHR) had been violated due to the fact that he had been detained between 13 July 2001 and 26 January 2002.[26] His right to a fair trial had also been breached since he had not had access to a court of law. According to the claimant, France, Germany and Norway, which in different ways had been involved in the detention, failed to guarantee the rights to individuals provided by the ECHR in Kosovo.[27]

The key question, according to the ECtHR, was whether or not the UNSC retained ultimate authority and control, with the operational command only being delegated. The Court listed the following factors as being crucial to establishing whether or not the UNSC retained authority and control: (1) Chapter VII of the UN Charter allowed the UNSC to delegate in accordance with UNSC Resolution 1244 (1999); (2) the power was a delegable power; (3) the delegation was prior and explicit in the Resolution itself; (4) the Resolution put sufficiently defined limits on the delegation. The mandate was adequately precise 'as it set out the objectives to be attained, the roles and responsibilities accorded as well as the means to be employed'. It was recognised that some provisions were broad, but this was in the nature of such an instrument as its role was not to interfere with the detail of operational implementation and choice; and (5) the leadership of the military presence was required to report to the UNSC, thereby allowing the UNSC to exercise its overall authority and control. According to the Court, the UNSC exercised ultimate authority and control (or overall control) while NATO, through the KFOR Commander down to the multinational brigades and to the TCNs, exercised operational command.[28]

The claimants had argued that the influence of TCNs undermined operational command. Such TCN influence included, inter alia, their exclusive retention of criminal jurisdiction over the military forces as well as disciplinary powers. Their contributions were voluntary and they could decide at any time to withdraw from the operation in question. The ECtHR recognised the TCN influence, but stated that the important question was not whether NATO exercised *exclusive* command but rather as to whether it was *effective*. The Court also held that it did 'not find any suggestion or evidence of any actual TCN orders concerning, or interference in, the present operational (detention) matter'.[29] It continued by declaring that despite TCN influence, NATO did in fact exercise effective command over relevant operational matters and that the United Nations retained ultimate authority and control. KFOR thus exercised power lawfully delegated by the UNSC, under Chapter VII, and the action in question was in principle to be attributed to the United Nations.

The position of the ECtHR has in fact been upheld in subsequent decisions,[30] but has been subject to criticism in the legal literature, mainly based on the condition employed by the Court regarding attribution of conduct.[31] The Special Rapporteur to the ILC on the responsibility of international organisations did not accept the approach taken by the ECtHR.[32] The majority of states, in commenting on draft Article 6 (now Article 7), endorsed the condition of effective control proposed in the Article.[33]

4. What is an armed conflict?

4.1 International armed conflict

The term 'armed conflict' was introduced in the Geneva Conventions of 1949 for the purpose of avoiding endless discussions on the legal definition of the term 'war'.[34] Common Article 2 to the four Geneva Conventions reads in part: 'In addition to the provisions which shall be implemented in peacetime, the present Convention shall apply to all cases of declared war or of any other armed conflict which may arise between two or more of the High Contracting Parties, even if the state of war is not recognized by one of them.' The term 'armed conflict' denotes a lower threshold than 'war' and does not admit the same room for manoeuvre in debating the legal definition of this term in comparison with the term 'war'. The Commentaries explain it in the following way: 'Any difference arising between two States and leading to the intervention of members of the armed forces is an armed conflict within the meaning of Article 2, even if one of the Parties denies the existence of a state of war. It makes no difference how long the conflict lasts, or how much slaughter takes place.'[35]

The ICTY defines an international armed conflict as 'whenever there is a resort to armed force between States'.[36] In its Opinion Paper on the term 'Armed Conflict' in international humanitarian law, the ICRC proposes the following definition, based upon prevailing legal opinion: 'International armed conflicts exist whenever there is *resort to armed force between two or more States.*'[37] Schindler finds that an international armed conflict 'can always be assumed when parts of the armed forces of two States clash with each other ... Any kind of use of arms between two States brings the Conventions into effect.'[38]

4.2 Non-international armed conflicts

Common Article 2 relates to international armed conflicts between two or more states. Current armed conflicts, however, are more often of a non-international character between a state and an armed group or between such armed groups. Common Article 3 to the four Geneva Conventions applies: 'In the case of armed conflict not of an international character occurring in the territory of one of the High Contracting Parties'. According to the Commentaries to Common Article 3, the definition of an 'armed conflict not of an international character' was the subject of considerable debate during the diplomatic conference and it was clear that states feared that it might include *any* form of armed force. A number of conditions in this regard were discussed, but in the end did not find their way into the final text.[39] These conditions, however, were regarded as 'useful as a means of distinguishing a genuine armed conflict from a mere act of banditry or an unorganized and short-lived insurrection'.[40]

In its first case (the *Tadić* case), the ICTY was faced with the question of defining an armed conflict.[41] According to the Tribunal:

> an armed conflict exists whenever there is a resort to armed force between States or protracted armed violence between governmental authorities and organized armed groups or between such groups within a state. International humanitarian law applies from the initiation of such armed conflicts and extends beyond the cessation of hostilities until a general conclusion of peace is reached; or, in the case of internal conflicts, a peaceful settlement is achieved. Until that moment, international humanitarian law continues to apply in the whole territory of the warring states or, in the case of internal conflicts, the whole territory under the control of a party, whether or not actual combat takes place there.[42]

The Tribunal dealt both with international and non-international armed conflicts. In its later practice, the Tribunal has identified criteria for establishing the existence of a non-international armed conflict. Given the nature of current armed conflicts and the environment in which multinational peace operation forces are most often deployed, this chapter is intended to largely focus on non-international armed conflicts.[43]

A non-international armed conflict is thus defined as a situation where there is protracted armed violence between governmental authorities and organised armed groups or between such groups within a state. The ICTY has thereafter had the opportunity to further explore the nature of these criteria. Regarding the criterion of 'protracted armed violence', it has in later practice placed greater emphasis on the intensity of armed violence and less on its duration.[44]

In subsequent cases concerning the existence of armed conflict, the ICTY identified a number of indicative factors, although none of them in themselves are essential to establish the existence of protracted armed violence. The Trial Chamber referred to the following indicative factors including:

> the number, duration and intensity of individual confrontations; the type of weapons and other military equipment used; the number and calibre of munitions fired; the number of persons and type of forces partaking in the fighting; the number of casualties; the extent of material destruction; and the number of civilians fleeing combat zones. The involvement of the UN Security Council may also be a reflection of the intensity of a conflict.[45]

On 'organisation', the Tribunal identified the following indicative factors, although none of them are essential to establishing whether or not the criterion of 'organisation' is met. These indicative factors include:

> the existence of a command structure and disciplinary rules and mechanisms within the group; the existence of a headquarters; the fact that the

> group controls a certain territory; the ability of the group to gain access to weapons, other military equipment, recruits and military training; its ability to plan, coordinate and carry out military operations, including troop movements and logistics; its ability to define a unified military strategy and use military tactics; and its ability to speak with one voice and negotiate and conclude agreements such as cease-fire or peace accords.[46]

It should also be noted that even though Common Article 3 makes reference to a non-international armed conflict occurring in the territory of one of the High Contracting Parties, this should not be interpreted so as to exclude cross-border conflicts. A non-international armed conflict is distinguished from an international armed conflict 'by the parties involved rather than by the territorial scope of the conflict'.[47]

The current ICRC definition states:

> Non-international armed conflicts are *protracted armed confrontations* occurring between governmental armed forces and the forces of one or more armed groups, or between such groups arising on the territory of a State [party to the Geneva Conventions]. The armed confrontation must reach *a minimum level of intensity* and the parties involved in the conflict must show *a minimum of organisation*.[48]

The intensity of the fighting and the organisation of the non-state actors are of particular importance in establishing the situation of a non-international armed conflict from that of internal disturbance. It is true that the existence of an armed conflict is dependent on the facts on the ground, and it is indeed difficult to provide a set of pre-existing criteria for defining exactly when IHL becomes applicable.[49]

4.3 *Internationalised armed conflicts*

The term internationalised armed conflicts does not, at least in this chapter, denote a third category of armed conflict, but rather accounts for the reality of armed conflicts today where both an international and non-international armed conflict may exist simultaneously on a state's territory, or be transformed from one to the other depending on the parties involved.[50] Such transformations, however, may be difficult to fix in time. Regarding the latter situation, a non-international armed conflict may evolve into an international one if a foreign state exercises control over an armed group fighting against government forces. The level of control in this respect has been disputed. In its practice, the ICJ has referred to a criterion of 'effective control' over a non-state actor on the question of attribution of conduct, while the ICTY has employed a condition of 'overall control' over such armed groups in order to characterise the armed conflict as international.[51] The exercise of the necessary level of control by a state over rebel forces not only has the potential for changing the nature of the armed conflict, but will in such cases also affect the standing of the rebel forces as a party to the conflict. The new party to the conflict will instead be the state which exercises some level of control over the rebel forces.

5. Who can be a party to an armed conflict under international humanitarian law?

After discussing the criteria governing the existence of an armed conflict, it is now necessary to analyse how a party to an armed conflict is defined under international humanitarian law.

5.1 International armed conflicts

The High Contracting Parties to the Geneva Conventions and their Additional Protocols are naturally competent in relation to becoming a party to an armed conflict. Entities other than states may also become parties to an armed conflict. This is natural, given the fact that non-international armed conflicts involve parties other than member states to the Geneva Conventions and the Additional Protocols. Even in international armed conflicts there has been a scope for other subjects to become a party to an armed conflict by way of the reference in Article 1(4) of Additional Protocol (AP) I which speaks of 'armed conflicts in which peoples are fighting against colonial domination and alien occupation and against racist regimes in the exercise of their right of self-determination'.

In international armed conflicts, there are specific requirements for the armed forces of a party to the conflict. Article 43(1) in AP I regarding armed forces reads as follows:

> The armed forces of a Party to a conflict consist of all organized armed forces, groups and units which are under a command responsible to that Party for the conduct of its subordinates, even if that Party is represented by a government or an authority not recognized by an adverse Party. Such armed forces shall be subject to an internal disciplinary system which, *inter alia*, shall enforce compliance with the rules of international law applicable in armed conflict.

From the way this paragraph is drafted, it is apparent that subjects other than states may also be regarded as parties to the conflict in question.[52] In summary of the conditions applicable to armed forces, the Commentaries indirectly define a party to a conflict when it is stated that such forces must meet the following conditions:

(a) subordination to a 'party to the conflict' which represents a collective entity which is, at least in part, a subject of international law;
(b) an organisation of a military character;
(c) a responsible command exercising effective control over the members of the organisation;
(d) respect for the rules of international law applicable in armed conflict.

These four conditions should be fulfilled effectively and in combination in the field.[53]

Being a party to an international armed conflict thus appears to require a collective entity, which at least partly is considered to be a subject of international law. The fact that the United Nations (and possibly other international organisations, such as NATO) can become a party to an armed conflict is at least implicitly supported in the literature and by recent international instruments.[54] Seyersted and Glick explicitly link the exercise of command and control to the party to an armed conflict and therefore exclude the TCNs as parties to an armed conflict in UN operations.[55]

A state may also support an organised group fighting the government in another state. Depending on the level of control over the armed group, the character of the armed conflict may change from that of a non-international armed conflict to one of an international armed conflict between the two states.[56] This also means that the parties to the particular armed conflict change. To be a party to an armed conflict therefore requires a certain level of independence from the other actors involved. The level of control, however, is disputed. The Appeals Chamber in the *Tadić* case was faced with the question of finding criteria establishing the point at which armed groups could be regarded as acting on behalf of a state, thereby rendering a *prima facie* non-international armed conflict an armed conflict between states. It was necessary to answer this question for the purpose of deciding whether or not the acts of Tadić had been committed in a situation governed by international humanitarian law applicable in an international armed conflict, or in a non-international armed conflict. As a point of departure, it referred to the criteria in Article 4 of Geneva Convention III. According to Article 4(A)(2), militias and organised armed groups were to be regarded as legitimate combatants if they belonged to a party to an armed conflict. The Tribunal recognised that this particular provision established the criteria of becoming a combatant but found that, as a logical consequence, if armed groups belonged to a state party (other than the state against which they were fighting) the conflict would become international.[57] The Appeals Chamber further held that the requirement of 'belonging to a Party to the conflict' implicitly referred to a test of control.[58]

The Appeals Chamber recognised that the ICJ, in the *Nicaragua* case, had employed a condition of 'effective control' in order to establish whether or not the United States was responsible for the acts of the rebel forces in Nicaragua (the Contras) by training, financing, equipping, organising and planning the operations of those paramilitary forces.[59] The 'effective control' test required not only that operations by private individuals acting as *de facto* organs of the state be financed, coordinated and supervised by a particular state, but also required issuance of specific instructions for the commission of the unlawful acts under consideration by the ICJ.[60]

The Appeals Chamber in this regard stated that in respect of armed groups, as opposed to individuals or a group of persons not military organised, it was not necessary to require 'the issuing of specific orders by the State, or its direction of each individual operation' but rather that the control 'may be of an overall character (and must comprise more than the mere provision of financial assistance or military equipment or training)'.[61] The Tribunal explained the condition of 'overall control' in these terms:

> The control required by international law may be deemed to exist when a State (or, in the context of an armed conflict, the Party to the conflict) has a role in organising, coordinating or planning the military actions of the military group, in addition to financing, training and equipping or providing operational support to that group. Acts performed by the group or members thereof may be regarded as acts of *de facto* State organs regardless of any specific instruction by the controlling State concerning the commission of each of those acts.[62]

The ICJ employed a test of 'effective control' when deciding the responsibility of states for the actions of armed groups. Yet in the *Genocide* case, the ICJ did not rule out that the test of 'overall control' could be used in order to determine the nature of the armed conflict.[63] The court was not convinced, however, that the test of overall control could be used to determine state responsibility.[64]

Article 8 of the Articles on State Responsibility reads: 'The conduct of a person or group of persons shall be considered an act of a State under international law if the person or group of persons is in fact acting on the instructions of, or under the direction or control of, that State in carrying out the conduct.'[65] The ILC did not find the reasoning of the Appeals Chamber in the *Tadić* case convincing in relation to the law of state responsibility, but pointed out that 'the question in that case concerned not responsibility but the applicable rules of international humanitarian law'.[66]

Cassese has advanced an argument in favour of the 'overall control' condition. He argues that the 'overall control' test is valid for attributing conduct of organised armed groups to a state, while the stricter test of effective control is relevant for attribution of conduct to single individuals.[67] Moreover, he recognises its validity in identifying responsibility in multinational peace operations, based upon the *Behrami and Saramati* judgment, where the ECtHR employed a test of 'ultimate authority and control' – or as the Court also described it, 'overall control'.[68]

The different levels of control employed by the ICJ, ICTY, ILC and the ECtHR may have implications for both questions of responsibility and the nature of armed conflict, and there is indeed a difference of opinion as to how to apply those conditions and for what purposes – not least regarding the difference between individual criminal responsibility and state responsibility.[69] Its validity for identifying the parties to an armed conflict involving armed forces of a multinational peace operation will be considered below.

5.2 *Non-international armed conflict*

The four Geneva Conventions refer mainly to the High Contracting Parties to the Conventions, which is limited to states parties. Common Article 3, which applies in non-international armed conflicts, however, obligates each party to the conflict to apply the provisions of that Article. According to the Commentaries to Article 3, the words 'each party' marked major progress in international law. It enabled non-signatory parties to the Conventions to be bound by the Conventions – in fact, even parties not yet in existence.[70] The characteristics of a party to an armed conflict also appear to be closely tied to the criteria governing the existence of an armed conflict. The Commentaries to Common Article 3 are adamant on the point that an armed conflict cannot possibly be clearly defined, but rather one must identify relevant criteria for establishing the existence of such a conflict. This is, of course, the way in which institutions have subsequently approached this question. As is evident from the identification of such criteria, there is a line to be drawn between mere banditry and armed conflict. Apart from the criterion concerning the intensity of the conflict in question, the most significant condition is that of the organisation of non-state actors. In short, a party to an armed conflict, in order to distinguish it from that of common criminals, must be properly organised. This includes the ability to negotiate and conclude agreements. It should be noted that if the armed group were properly organised, it would not necessarily follow that it must have a political objective.[71] The ICTY has confirmed this position in a case concerning the fighting between Serbian forces and the Kosovo Liberation Army, where the defence argued that the purpose of the Serbian forces was to perform so-called ethnic cleansing rather than the defeat of the enemy. The ICTY clearly rejected this argument and stated that 'the determination of the existence of an armed conflict was based solely on two criteria: the intensity of the conflict and organization of the parties, the purpose of the armed forces to engage in acts of violence or also achieve some further objective is, therefore, irrelevant'.[72]

To be a party to a non-international armed conflict requires, as seen above on the characterisation of an armed conflict, that the parties involved have reached a certain level of organisation. The indicative factors have been accounted for. The discussion on the required level of control of a state over an armed group, for the sake of establishing state responsibility or determining the nature of the armed conflict, will in relation to the armed groups be a question of independence, mirroring the same arguments referred to above.

5.3 *Summary*

As described above, the required level of control is dependent on which test the specific question is subjected to: should the stricter test of 'effective control' or the more relaxed criterion of 'overall control', or the condition of 'ultimate authority and control' referred to by the ECtHR, be employed? For the purpose of this chapter, it is interesting to see if any of these tests could be applied in order to identify the parties to an armed conflict involving multinational forces. Does the chain of command running from the operation on the ground to the UNSC establish the United Nations as a party to the armed conflict, or would some other entity in the chain be regarded as being a party to it?

Levels of control are also of importance with regard to general questions of responsibility for states and international organisations. As discussed above, the different levels of control are referred to with reference to attribution of conduct. In this respect, however, IHL regulation is quite clear. According to Article 91 of AP I, a party to an international armed conflict 'shall be responsible for all acts committed by persons forming part of its armed forces'. This rule, according to the ICRC Study, has also developed into a rule of customary law applicable in non-international armed conflicts.[73] The responsibility of parties to an international armed conflict is thus subject to the *lex specialis* regulation of IHL in relation to all acts committed by its armed forces.[74]

In conclusion, whether or not someone is a party to an international armed conflict is open to wide interpretation. It includes not only states, but also any collective entity which, at least in part, is subject to international law – encompassing, for example, international governmental organisations.[75] A party to a non-international armed conflict needs to be sufficiently organised, but need not have a specific political agenda. Where such rebel forces or armed groups act with independence, they may be regarded as being a party to an armed conflict. If they come under some level of control of a state (or any other collective entity which, at least in part, is subject to international law), however, the armed groups may lose its position as a party to the armed conflict and the conflict as such may change in character.

6. The case of ISAF

6.1 The mandate

In December 2001, the UNSC authorised the establishment of an International Security Assistance Force (ISAF) to support the Afghan Interim Authority in maintaining security in Kabul and the surrounding areas.[76] The UNSC called upon member states to contribute personnel to ISAF and authorised participating member states to take all necessary measures to fulfil its mandate. In October 2003, the mandate was expanded to support the Afghan Transitional Authority in the maintenance of security in areas of Afghanistan outside Kabul and its environs.[77] It was reiterated that member states were authorised to take all necessary measures to accomplish the terms of the ISAF mandate. There was an obligation on the part of the ISAF leadership to provide quarterly progress reports on the implementation of the mandate to the UNSC through the Secretary-General. The Security Council further recognised 'that the responsibility for providing security and law and order throughout the country resides with the Afghans themselves' and reaffirmed 'its strong commitment to the sovereignty, independence, territorial integrity and national unity of Afghanistan'.[78]

The mandate appears to be particularly broad. What does it mean to support Afghan authorities in the maintenance of security in the country? Who makes the decision that something is considered to be 'necessary measures'? The ISAF forces were invited to Afghanistan, and if this constituted the only legal grounds for the presence of foreign forces on Afghan territory, it would be possible for the Afghan authorities simply to withdraw their consent if and when they regarded ISAF measures to go beyond what was necessary for the maintenance of security. Notwithstanding, the UNSC has also declared that the situation in Afghanistan represented a threat to international peace and security and the presence of ISAF forces was therefore also based upon UNSC authority under Chapter VII of the UN Charter. While in practical terms one could assume that supporting the Afghan authorities in the maintenance of security would require cooperation between ISAF and the Afghan forces, it must also be acknowledged that ISAF derives its presence and task from the UNSC, and thereby the international community, and that the decision on what is considered to be necessary measures ultimately lies with ISAF and the chain of command leading to the UNSC. Given the requirement of quarterly reports to the UNSC, the Security Council thereby retains some insight into the operation, with the possibility open to it to make adjustments in the ISAF mandate.

The mandate provides ISAF with a right to take all necessary measures in supporting the Afghan authorities in maintaining security in that country. There is thus no limitation on these forces' ability to operate in an armed conflict against hostile forces. Can the current conflict in Afghanistan be described as an armed conflict?

6.2 *Armed conflict*

Apart from more publicised actions such as the bombing of two fuel tankers by ISAF in September 2009,[79] even the briefest perusal of ISAF news releases on the operational updates makes it clear that the intensity of the fighting has reached such a level that it leaves no doubt that the conflict must be regarded as an armed conflict, provided that the armed group concerned has reached the necessary level of organisation.[80]

Indicative factors for establishing the intensity of the conflict (duration and intensity of individual confrontations, types of weapon and other military equipment used, the quantity and calibre of munitions discharged, the number of persons and type of forces taking part in the fighting, and the amount of casualties) have certainly been met. Are, then, the Taliban considered to be sufficiently organised so as to fulfil the second condition of an armed conflict? Again, the indicative factors referred to above, such as command structure, control of certain territory, the ability to gain access to weapons, to plan, coordinate and carry out military operations, together with the ability to define a unified military strategy and employ military tactics, are surely fulfilled. In conclusion, there can be no doubt that there exists today an armed conflict on the territory of Afghanistan. Since this armed conflict is not one *between states*, it should accordingly be characterised as that of a non-international armed conflict.

Furthermore, it must be beyond doubt that some of the ISAF national contingents are involved in this armed conflict. British, Danish and Canadian forces, for example, in the south of Afghanistan have clearly been involved in armed conflict, while other contingents in the north, for example, Swedish forces, up until now have not been involved in similar fighting. It is, moreover, beyond doubt that the Afghan forces are involved in an armed conflict with Taliban forces in Afghanistan. This scenario leads to the question of how the particular *parties* to this armed conflict are to be characterised.

Legally, IHL is applicable in the whole territory under the control of the parties to the conflict.[81] Depending on how the parties to this particular armed conflict are characterised, IHL may also apply outside the territory of Afghanistan. This raises the question whether the Taliban forces are entitled to attack targets outside Afghanistan. There would not seem to be any explicit prohibitions under IHL to attack the adverse party outside the current area of operations.[82] Even if Taliban forces would have the capacity to attack targets beyond the Afghan territory, however, the individuals involved would still be committing a crime under the national law of the target state.[83]

It has furthermore been held that the right of the parties to international armed conflicts to expand the area of military operations is not unlimited. In such conflicts, the area of operations will be dependent on limitations of the right of self-defence. A state cannot be expected to only defend itself in the areas where an aggressor chooses to attack, but an expansion of the area of operations may not go beyond necessary and proportionate measures of self-defence.[84] This argument draws support from the concept of *jus ad bellum* and would not formally apply to non-state actors.

6.3 *Possible parties*

Against this background, the following propositions become topics for consideration: (i) the Afghan government is a party to the conflict, while ISAF forces should be regarded as supporting forces; (ii) the TCNs are parties to the conflict, alternatively only those particular TCNs whose contingents *de facto* are involved in the armed conflict are parties to the conflict; (iii) ISAF, which exercises effective control over the ISAF forces, should be regarded as a party to the armed conflict; (iv) NATO, which exercises effective control over the ISAF forces, should be regarded as a party to the armed conflict; (v) the United Nations, which exercises overall authority and control over ISAF forces, should be considered a party to the conflict.

The Afghan government is a party to the conflict, while ISAF forces should be regarded as supporting forces

The position of the Afghan government as a party to the armed conflict with the Taliban is here taken for granted. The question is, does that exclude the international forces from being parties to the armed conflict as well? One argument for this position is that the mandate of ISAF is limited to supporting the Afghan authorities and it would not include measures lacking the expressed or tacit consent of the Afghan government. The UNSC takes note of the fact that the Afghan authorities welcome the deployment to Afghanistan of the UN-authorised international security force and, moreover, it is determined to ensure the full implementation of the mandate in consultation with the Afghan Interim Authority.[85]

The lead role of the Afghan government recognised by the UNSC, as well as the Council's commitment to the sovereignty and independence of Afghanistan, has the effect, the argument goes, that it is only the Afghan government that could be regarded as being a party to the armed conflict while the ISAF forces cannot be considered to be an independent party to the conflict. ISAF should instead be regarded as comprising military forces that the Afghan authorities are permitted to use in fighting its war against Taliban forces. The need for the Afghan government's consent in order to act within the territory of the sovereign state of Afghanistan is thus the overall limiting factor for regarding ISAF forces as an independent party to the armed conflict.

There is certainly extensive cooperation between the Afghan authorities and ISAF forces. Furthermore, a major part of ISAF support is to train Afghan National Army (ANA) forces to become more professional. ISAF forces nevertheless retain a high level of independence. One could hardly claim that ISAF forces have been placed under the control of the forces of the Afghan authorities. The mandate to support the Afghan government in maintaining security throughout Afghanistan does not mean that ISAF is under the authority of the Afghan government, but rather that ISAF forces act in cooperation, one could assume, with ANA forces which participate in the armed conflict against the Taliban. The independent position of ISAF forces suggests that they should be considered to form a separate party to the conflict, albeit with the same objective as the Afghan government. The situation would have been quite different had ISAF forces been integrated into ANA forces and then acted under its command and control. According to the Supreme Allied Commander Europe (SACEUR) OPLAN, the Joint Force Commander 'is authorised to conduct combined operations with Afghan national security forces. In such operations, ISAF will retain primacy for its own operational decision-making and ROE.'[86] From an IHL perspective, the independent manner in which ISAF plans and conducts its operations suggests that ISAF forces could not be regarded as forces belonging to the ANA.

The TCNs are parties to the conflict, or alternatively, only those TCNs with contingents *de facto* involved in the armed conflict are parties to the conflict

The military personnel of certain TCNs are *de facto* involved in armed conflict. Does that mean that the TCNs in question are at war with the Taliban? This has become a highly politicised issue in some TCNs. In Sweden, for instance, many voices are raised against the Swedish participation in ISAF, based to a large extent upon the view that Sweden is at war in Afghanistan. One could initially argue that the Swedish forces have so far not been involved in any serious combat against the Taliban and that Sweden therefore cannot be regarded as constituting a party to the armed conflict. It is true that the law follows the facts, and not the reverse. In the case of a particular TCN not being involved in any fighting, there may thus be an argument in favour of that TCN not being regarded as a party to the armed conflict. ISAF forces are made up of forty-eight independent military forces, and in order to follow this line of reasoning, there must necessarily be an individual assessment of every TCN to decide whether or not each particular force is involved in the armed conflict.[87] ISAF, however, is a multinational force under a unified command and it may in fact not be possible to compartmentalise such a force into participating and non-participating forces. Even if that were possible, would it be true that the TCNs were parties to the armed conflict, in view of the fact that the authority of the troops contributed was transferred from the TCNs to NATO? A tentative conclusion is that the transfer of authority indicates that the different TCNs should not be regarded as independent parties to the armed conflict.

A common state practice in this area is difficult to identify. Denmark and Norway regard themselves as being parties to the armed conflict in Afghanistan, while Germany and Sweden do not. A policy argument in support of finding the different TCNs to be parties to the armed conflict is that it is the states, not NATO or ISAF, that are parties to the central IHL instruments. The argument would then go as follows: if the states themselves are not acknowledging being parties to the armed conflict, the compliance with IHL could be negatively affected. While this line of argument is commendable, it fails to recognise the fact that states cannot evade their obligations under IHL when their military forces participate in an armed conflict, irrespective of whether they are under the command of another state or an international organisation.[88] The point is that it does not seem to be a necessary requirement that TCNs declare themselves to be parties to an armed conflict in order to secure compliance with IHL. The duty to respect IHL – and to ensure its respect – applies in all circumstances.[89]

ISAF, which exercises effective control over ISAF forces, should be regarded as a party to the armed conflict

ISAF fulfils the necessary criteria of being an organised armed group and could therefore on that basis be regarded as an independent party to the armed conflict. ISAF, however, is under NATO command and control where the chain of command runs from SACEUR to Commander ISAF (COMISAF). It is therefore difficult to recognise ISAF as an independent party to the armed conflict.

NATO should be regarded as a party to the armed conflict

Since 2003, NATO has taken the lead in the ISAF operation. The chain of command in the operation suggests that NATO exercises effective control over ISAF forces. The TCNs transfer the authority of their troop contributions to NATO, with certain caveats relating to such things as limitations in geographical positions of the forces and restrictions on the use of force. As stated above, the TCNs do not transfer full command over their troops.[90] They still retain, for example, exclusive criminal jurisdiction over their forces and as their contributions are voluntary, they also retain the right to withdraw their troops. Nevertheless, given these considerations, the authority to *use* the troops in military operations is transferred to NATO. Unified command over the troops lies with NATO, which develops the ROEs for the operation and has the authority to order the troops under its command.[91] NATO thus appears to exercise effective control over the ISAF troops as it is understood in the ILC Draft Articles on responsibility for international organisations.

What amounts to effective control seems to be based upon a factual criterion. Conduct by forces in an operation conducted under unified command would *prima facie* be attributable to the entity exercising such command. If the particular conduct is in fact based upon instructions from the TCN, however, it might be attributable to that state. The important criterion here is to identify which entity exercises effective control over the particular conduct in question.

The role of NATO is clearly one of 'organising, coordinating or planning the military actions' of ISAF forces and it will from that perspective certainly exercise 'overall control' over the troops.[92] A *prima facie* case can undoubtedly also be made in favour of effective control. The influence of the TCNs, however, may in a given case have the result of attributing certain conduct of ISAF troops to a particular TCN. In the case of troops of a particular TCN committing a war crime, that act may be attributed to the TCN if the influence of the TCN was of such character that NATO did not exercise effective control over its conduct. It has been pointed out by the above-mentioned Venice Commission that the attribution may change depending on the control over a certain conduct between TCNs and NATO during an operation. This may in fact prove that the 'effective control' test is less suitable for identifying the parties to an armed conflict if the identity of those parties changes dependent on the control of a particular conduct in light of the armed conflict as a whole. A condition of 'overall control' may therefore be more appropriate, as it is less likely to change depending on the degree of control over specific conduct. A condition of 'overall control' retains a higher degree of stability over time, which not only fulfils a functional purpose, but also, in the cases where the identity of the parties to an armed conflict affects the character of the conflict, meets the need for foreseeability in terms of applicable law.

One needs also to consider the fact that NATO acts on behalf of the United Nations and implements the mandate of the UNSC. The ISAF force acts under a unified command of NATO and acts as an instrument for the UNSC in the implementation of its power and authority. Nonetheless, the decision to engage in armed conflict may not necessarily be attributed to the United Nations. The overall mandate is to assist the Afghan authorities in maintaining security in Afghanistan. It is the decision of the UNSC, representing the collectivity of UN member states, to assist the Afghan authorities in the maintenance of security in that country. The authority to use all necessary measures is derived from the powers of the UNSC, but the decision as to what measures are deemed necessary seems to lie with NATO, which the TCNs have put in command of the operation. The measures chosen have engaged the ISAF forces in an armed conflict and the party to the armed conflict could therefore, based upon this line of argument, be NATO.

The United Nations should be considered a party to the conflict

As made clear from the discussions so far, the United Nations will *prima facie* not exercise 'effective control' over military forces in a UN-authorised operation where command and control is vested elsewhere. The position of the ECtHR in the *Behrami and Saramati* case, however, was that the conduct of KFOR forces was in fact attributable to the United Nations, but subject to a condition of 'ultimate authority and control'.[93]

If one accepts the reasoning of the ECtHR, that the important condition is that of ultimate authority and control, the acts and omissions of ISAF forces could be attributable to the United Nations. The five factors listed by the Court for the purpose of identifying whether or not the UNSC retained ultimate authority and control are largely met in the case of ISAF. The fourth condition, that the mandate should be adequately precise, however, is potentially not met with regard to the ISAF operation when one considers the very broad mandate given to ISAF to support the Afghan Transitional Authority in the maintenance of security in areas of Afghanistan outside Kabul and its environs.

If the criterion of 'overall control' of armed forces, as used by the ICTY, is indeed used in respect of the ISAF forces in Afghanistan, then the United Nations might be regarded as being a party to the non-international armed conflict existing there. The UNSC does exercise some control through the authorisation to member states participating in ISAF to use all necessary measures to implement the mandate, and in that it may at any time withdraw its authorisation. The quarterly reports from ISAF provide some insights into the progress of the mission. Nonetheless, the UNSC is not 'organising, coordinating or planning the military actions' as envisaged by the ICTY. The influence of the UNSC is more likely to be described in terms of 'ultimate authority and control', as employed by the ECtHR. The latter position, however, must be regarded in the context of human rights law and may not necessarily have an impact on identifying the parties to an armed conflict.

7. Case of Operation Unified Protector in Libya

UN Security Council Resolution 1973 authorised member states, acting nationally or through regional organisations, to take all necessary measures to protect civilians and civilian populated areas under attack in Libya.[94] Initially the operation was headed by France, the United Kingdom and the United States. The operation was thereafter conducted under the command of NATO. According to its homepage, 'NATO has been in full command and control of enforcing UNSCR 1973 since 31 March.'[95] NATO forces have attacked several objects on the territory of Libya and these forces are clearly involved in an armed conflict with Libyan governmental forces. Who, then, could be regarded as being a party to the armed conflict against the state of Libya?

Given the fact that the command structure in the Afghan context appears similar to that of Operation Unified Protector (OUP), regarding the relationship between the United Nations, NATO and the Task Force, it seems that much of the reasoning on ISAF in Afghanistan is transferrable to the Libyan context. Nordic state practice, however, is inconsistent. In the Swedish declaration from the government, later approved by Parliament, the legal situation is described in the following terms:

> The right of the participating states to use force is ultimately based on the mandate from the UN Security Council in accordance with Chapter VII of the UN Charter, which provides the international operation with an exceptional position, according to international law, in relation to the parties to the conflict. The state or the organisation that exercises the factual control over the operation may become a party to the armed conflict if the operation is involved in hostilities with governmental forces. All use of force must be in accordance with the international humanitarian law and human rights law. It is ultimately the Security Council which is responsible for the international military operation.[96]

Sweden apparently adopts the position that it is the state or organisation that exercises factual control over the operation that may become a party to the conflict. As discussed above, the condition of factual control, which has been used by the ILC to explain the meaning of effective control, is a more rigid condition than that of overall control, referred to by the ICTY when establishing the nature of armed conflict. The Swedish declaration, however, maintains furthermore that it is the Security Council that is ultimately responsible for the operation. International responsibility for international organisations, according to the ILC Draft Articles, rests on a condition of effective control (or factual control). The Security Council does not, however, exercise effective control over the operation, as has been explained by the ILC. One would need to apply the condition suggested by the ECtHR, of ultimate authority and control, in order to conclude that the conduct of the OUP is attributable to the Security Council, and hence has the potential of being ultimately responsible under international law. Not even the ECtHR claimed that the UNSC exercised effective control over KFOR, which it recognised was exercised by NATO, but rather introduced the new condition of ultimate authority and control. It would thus seem that the Swedish position, at least as it has been expressed in the governmental declaration, is that factual control over military forces is the condition for becoming a party to an armed conflict, while possibly the condition of ultimate authority and control would determine international responsibility.

The Norwegian Ministry of Defence (MoD) explained in a memorandum its view on its country's role in the armed conflict.[97] The memorandum concerns the situation before NATO assumed command over the operation. It is dated 24 March 2011 and refers to the Joint Task Force – Operation Odyssey Dawn. The memorandum refers to UNSC Resolution 1973, and the right to use military power in order to protect civilians and civilian populated areas. It is stated that there is no doubt that the situation is, according to the laws of war, defined as an international armed conflict where coalition forces participate on behalf of their respective states, which according to the laws of war, must be regarded as parties to the armed conflict with the state of Libya.[98] According to this memorandum, Norway is considered to be a party to the international armed conflict in Libya. The MoD found no reason to change its position when the operation changed into Operation Unified Protector, in which the forces came under the command of NATO.

Thus, the view of the Norwegian MoD is that when states act in coalition warfare, the military forces act on behalf of the respective states, and hence the respective states are to be regarded as parties to the armed conflict. A key to this analysis could be that the authority of the military forces is retained by the participating states and that their forces act as state forces. The effective control of forces still rests with the respective states. If one were to employ the criteria of ultimate authority and control, however, it could possibly be argued that the UNSC is in control of the forces, and hence is the only party to the armed conflict against Libya (notwithstanding the rebels on the ground, who must be regarded as being involved in a non-international armed conflict with the governmental forces). Nevertheless, the fact that the MoD did not alter its position when NATO took command of the operation requires another explanation. It may be founded on a presumption that international organisations are not capable of becoming parties to an armed conflict and, furthermore, that being a party to an armed conflict is in fact a requirement for the application of international humanitarian law. Therefore, Norway would of necessity regard itself as a party to the armed conflict in order to be able to respect its international obligations. It could mean that the Norwegian MoD is of the opinion that whenever its forces participate in an armed conflict, Norway as a state is ultimately considered to be a party to that conflict.

These issues are complex and politically sensitive. This is aptly illustrated by the comments of Norwegian Prime Minister Stoltenberg in a parliamentary debate (after the issuance of the MoD memorandum). The Prime Minister stated that Norway was, in terms of international law, not participating in war. If that had been the case, Norwegian soldiers would have been legitimate targets. Norwegian soldiers executed a UN mission and were therefore not legitimate targets for the soldiers of the regime in Libya. But, Stoltenberg continued, Norwegian soldiers did, of course, participate in combat, which are acts of war. That meant that those soldiers participated in military operations that people in common terms described as war.[99] While one should not draw too strong a conclusion of *opinio juris* from the statements of a Prime Minister when involved in political debate in Parliament, it nevertheless illustrates the complexity and political sensitivity of such matters.

No official Danish documentation on these issues has been identified. Prime Minister Lars Løkke Rasmussen indicated in interviews, however, that Denmark was in a state of war by participating in the Libyan conflict.[100] In a similar vein (outside the Nordic context), Prime Minister David Cameron, during a parliamentary debate, stated that the United Kingdom was at war in Libya.[101] The United States did not consider itself to be at war with Libya for the purposes of its Constitution. This was partly due to the fact that its limited involvement in the military operations was not sufficiently extensive, especially after the operation's transfer to NATO command.[102]

8. Conclusions

The multinational nature of peace operations raises many important issues, not least pertaining to responsibility under international law. In cases where military elements of such operations are involved in an armed conflict, the question of who should be regarded as being a party to the conflict is also of importance, including the issue of responsibility under IHL.

This chapter has assessed those factors that indicate the existence of an armed conflict, based primarily upon practice from the ICTY. The focus has largely been on non-international armed conflicts. IHL, however, is not particularly clear on how one identifies the parties to an armed conflict. Based upon the criteria governing the existence of a non-international armed conflict, it is clear that non-governmental actors need to meet a condition of organisation to distinguish the situations of armed conflict from those merely involving law enforcement in relation to common criminals. To be party to a non-international armed conflict, it is thus necessary to be properly organised. It does not appear to be a requirement for armed groups to fight for the realisation of political objectives. A non-international armed conflict, however, may change in character to become an international armed conflict if the armed group fighting the government concerned is in fact controlled by another state. According to the practice of the ICTY, a state which exercises 'overall control' over the armed group in question is in fact considered to be a party to the conflict, and that conflict is thus between states. One could therefore assume that being a party to an armed conflict requires a certain amount of independence from other actors who may be involved in different capacities. The Libyan example has also raised the question of the characterisation of an armed conflict between a state and an international governmental organisation. A formal reading of international humanitarian law could lead to the conclusion that such a conflict should be characterised as a non-international armed conflict since it is not an armed conflict between states. Notwithstanding, an international organisation made up of states could not reasonably be regarded as a non-state actor for the purpose of international humanitarian law. An armed conflict between a state and an international governmental organisation must therefore be regarded as an international armed conflict.

In relation to multinational peace operations, the question of independence pertains to questions of command and control. The relevance of these issues has been addressed by the ILC in its work on responsibility for international organisations. The identification of the party to an armed conflict involving multinational forces, however, is not the same as identifying the responsible actor in such operations. Nevertheless, such identification makes it possible to draw assessments and conclusions on the levels of control over such forces. The TCNs put their troops at the disposal of an international organisation acting upon a mandate from the UNSC. TCNs transfer authority over their armed forces to the organisation leading the operation. In UN-led operations, the United Nations in principle claims exclusive control over the troops. The UN peace operation is in fact considered to be a subsidiary organ of the United Nations. The question of control over the troops, however, is more complicated in cases where the operation also involves another organisation commanding the troops in the field. The work of the ILC refers to a condition of 'effective control' in order to identify to whom a certain conduct should be attributed. The United Nations claims only that it exercises effective control over those troops in UN-led operations, but not where another organisation undertakes the operational planning and controls the conduct of operations.

In the ISAF operation, NATO exercises command and control and is thus responsible for operational planning and manages such matters on the ground. It acts within the limits of the UNSC mandate, but NATO issues ROEs and decides how the UNSC mandate should be implemented. The duty of NATO to report to the United Nations every three months provides the United Nations with some insight into the daily work of ISAF and provides it with the practical possibility of intervening and changing the mandate if it disagrees with how it is being executed.

The 'effective control' test seems *prima facie* to lead to the conclusion that the conduct of ISAF forces is attributable to NATO. Given the possibility of TCN influence over specific conduct, however, such attribution will depend on case-by-case evaluation. This test, therefore, may not be the most suited to identify those parties considered to be involved in an armed conflict. The overall control test, employed by the ICTY to characterise the nature of armed conflict, may be more appropriate for identifying the parties to an armed conflict. In the case of ISAF, it would mean that NATO is capable of becoming a party to the armed conflict in Afghanistan. If, however, the United Nations were recognised as exercising overall control over ISAF forces, the United Nations could potentially be identified as a party to the armed conflict. It should also be noted that the ECtHR used the term 'overall control' interchangeably with the notion of 'ultimate authority and control' in the *Behrami and Saramati* case, but seemingly not with the intention of placing it on a par with the 'overall control' term used by the ICTY.

In applying these criteria, it may also be argued that NATO was a party to the armed conflict with the Libyan government. This analysis, however, rests on the presumption that NATO in real terms exercised at least overall control over the military forces. If, despite the command and control arrangements accounted for above in the Afghan and Libyan operations, this was not the case, then the particular states may be regarded as parties to the armed conflict. There is thus a rebuttable presumption that NATO in these operations was regarded as a party to the armed conflicts, which can be judged differently depending on the facts.

It should in this regard be noted that there is a tendency among states to be more involved in the decision-making process when it comes to the use of aircraft compared with regular armed forces. Possibly this involvement is of such a nature that, in this context, it is difficult to compare the ISAF operation with Operation Unified Protector. The factual TCN involvement in the latter operation may be of such a character that the TCNs indeed should be regarded as parties to the armed conflict with Libya.

State practice is not consistent, and the positions of TCNs in ISAF range from those states that do not recognise the existence of an armed conflict in Afghanistan at all, to those who see themselves as individual parties to a non-international armed conflict. We have also observed different positions on the part of the Nordic TCNs with regard to the OUP. These differences may be influenced by national political considerations, or different perceptions on the requirements for the applicability of international humanitarian law. Some states may take the position that it is necessary for the state to be a party to the armed conflict in which its forces participate so as to apply international humanitarian law, notwithstanding that such forces are commanded by an international organisation. Some states may also demonstrate hesitance in recognising that international organisations have the capacity to become parties to an armed conflict at all. States' approach may, of course, also be founded on a realisation of how the operations function in practice and the real influence of TCNs.

Notes

1 *Prosecutor* v. *Tadić*, (IT-94–1-AR72), ICTY, Appeal on Jurisdiction, 2 October 1995, para. 70. Emphasis added.

2 See e.g., R.D. Glick, 'Lip service to the laws of war: humanitarian law and United Nations Armed Forces'(1995) 53 *Michigan Journal of International Law* 74.

3 MUST UNDK PM 2009–05–08. No reply was received from the Attaché in Finland.

4 See also the Danish government's answer to a question on how the government perceived the war in Afghanistan: 'Spørgsmål 37: "Hvordan opfatter den danske regering krigen i Afghanistan; som en international væbnet konflikt, som en ikke-international væbnet konflikt eller som omfattet af fredstidsregulering og hvilke folkeretslige konsekvenser følger af regeringens opfattelse?"' '[Question 37: "How does the Danish government view the war in Afghanistan: as an international armed conflict, as a non-international armed conflict, or as a situation governed by peacetime regulations, and what are the consequences under international law of the government's view?"'

'Svar: "Det er regeringens opfattelse, at der i Afghanistan pågår en ikke-international væbnet konflikt, som defineret i Artikel 1 Tilægsprotokol II af 18. juni 1977 til Genève-konventionerne af 12. August 1949 vedrørende beskyttelsen af ofre i ikke internationale væbnede konflikter, mellem på den ene side den legitime afghanske regering og dens internationale allierede, herunder Danmark, og på den anden side en eller flere fjendtlige organiserede væbnede grupper. Det følger heraf, at konflikten er underlagt de konventionsbestemte og sædvaneretlige folkeretlige regler for ikke-internationale væbnede konflikter, herunder fælles artikel 3 dl Geneve-konventionerne. Denne forståelse deles blandt andet af Den Internationale Røde Kors Komité (ICRC) og Amnesty International samt af vores nærmeste alliancepartnere i Afghanistan."' ['Response: "The government's view is that there is a non-international armed conflict in Afghanistan, as defined in Article 1 of Additional Protocol II of 18 June 1977 to the Geneva Conventions of 12 August 1949 relating to the protection of victims of non-international armed conflicts, between, on the one hand, the legitimate Afghan government and its international allies, including Denmark, and, on the other hand, one or more hostile organised armed groups. As a consequence, the conflict is governed by conventions and customary international law pertaining to non-international armed conflict, including Common Article 3 of the Geneva Conventions. This view is shared, inter alia, by the International Committee of the Red Cross (ICRC) and Amnesty International, as well as by our closest allied partners in Afghanistan."' Udenrigsudvalget (2. samling) URU alm. del – Svar på Spørgsmål 37 Offentligt, Bilag 1, Journalnummer 6.B.28.a. Folkeretskontoret 7 March 2008.

5 See article by the Norwegian Minister of Defence in *Dagens Næringsliv*, 26 August 2009, where the Minister clearly spells out that Norway is a party to the non-international armed conflict in Afghanistan, available at www.regjeringen.no/nb/dep/fd/aktuelt/taler_artikler/ministeren/forsvarsminister-stroem-erichsen/2009/krigsbegrepet-og-afghanistan.html?id=574474.

6 German Foreign Minister Guido Westerwelle in a speech to the German Parliament on 10 February 2010, available at www.dw-world.de/dw/article/0,5234588,00.html.

7 Regeringens proposition om Fortsatt svenskt deltagande i den internationella säkerhetsstyrkan i Afghanistan, Prop. 2008/09:69 (2008), 8.

8 Regeringens proposition om Fortsatt svenskt deltagande i den internationella säkerhetsstyrkan i Afghanistan, Prop. 2009/10:38 (2009), 8.

9 See www.iiss.org/publications/armed-conflict-database/.

10 The deterioration of the security situation is evidenced by the tragic deaths of two Swedish officers and a local interpreter on 7 February 2010, see www.svd.se/nyheter/utrikes/svenska-officerare-dodade-i-afghanistan_4225291.svd.

11 See, e.g., the UN Secretary-General, *An Agenda for Peace: Preventive Diplomacy, Peacemaking and Peacekeeping*, UN doc. A/47/277 – S/24111 (1992), and the Report of the Panel on United Nations Peace Operations, para. 10. Both state that these

reports 'reflect a practice of operations, in the new terminology "peace operations", of a much more complex character than the initial peacekeeping operations'. M. Bothe, 'Peacekeeping' in B. Simma *et al.* (eds.), *The Charter of the United Nations: A Commentary* (2nd edn, Oxford University Press, 2002) vol. 1, 648, 663.

12 ILC, Report on the work of its fifty-sixth session, UN doc. A/59/10 (Suppl. No. 10) 111–12 (footnote omitted).

13 See the Australia-led International Force in East Timor (INTERFET), SC Res. 1264, UN SCOR, 4045th mtg, UN doc. S/RES/1264 (1999).

14 See SC Res. 1386, UN SCOR 4443rd mtg, UN doc. S/RES/1386 (2001); SC Res. 1413, UN SCOR 4541st mtg, UN doc. S/RES/1413 (2002); and SC Res. 1444, UN SCOR 4651st mtg, UN doc. S/RES/1444 (2003).

15 See the position of the UN Secretary-General with regard to levels of control in joint operations: 'In joint operations, international responsibility for the conduct of the troops lies where operational command and control is vested according to the arrangements establishing the modalities of cooperation between the State or States providing the troops and the United Nations. In the absence of formal arrangements between the United Nations and the State or States providing troops, responsibility would be determined in each and every case according to the degree of effective control exercised by either party in the conduct of the operation.' Report of the Secretary-General on Financing of United Nations Peacekeeping Operations, UN doc. A/51/389/6, paras. 17–18.

16 NATO Glossary of Terms and Definitions, AAP-6 (2010), 2-O-3.

17 Operational Control does not include 'authority to assign separate employment of components of the units concerned. Neither does it, of itself, include administrative or logistic control.' See NATO Glossary of Terms and Definitions, *ibid.*

18 Glossary of UN Peacekeeping Terms, available at www.un.org/en/peacekeeping/sites/glossary/index.html. The index is not an official UN document. See also United Nations Peacekeeping Operations, *Principles and Guidelines (Capstone Doctrine)* (2008), and on Report of the Secretary-General, *Command and Control of United Nations Peacekeeping Operations*, UN doc. A/49/681 (1994).

19 ILC, Sixty-third session, responsibility of international organizations, Texts and titles of draft articles 1 to 67 adopted by the Drafting Committee on second reading in 2011, UN doc. A/CN.4/L.778 (30 May 2011), 3.

20 ILC, Report on the work of its fifty-sixth session, UN doc. A/59/10 (Suppl. No. 10) 110 (The Article was at that time numbered 5, thereafter numbered 6, and after the second reading became Article 7) (footnote omitted).

21 *Ibid.* 111.

22 *Ibid.*

23 European Commission for Democracy Through Law (Venice Commission), Opinion on Human Rights in Kosovo, Opinion no. 280/2004 CDL-AD (2004) 033, para. 14 (2004).

24 The Commission gave the following example: it is clear, for example, that if the KFOR Commander orders different national contingents to establish a certain number of roadblocks at certain locations this measure, in itself, must be attributed to NATO. This is because the individual troop-contributing states do not have a possibility to influence such a decision by the KFOR Commander, except perhaps by expressly prohibiting their soldiers to follow the order of the KFOR Commander. Therefore, should the roadblocks have been ordered for no valid reason and, as such, have caused foreseeable damage, responsibility for any such damage would have to

be borne by NATO and not by the state whose soldiers happened to maintain one particular roadblock. If, on the other hand, a person who happens to be searched at one of the roadblocks is mistreated by one of the soldiers, it is, in principle, more plausible to attribute this act to the state of origin of the misbehaving soldiers, because in that situation they acted under the supervision and the responsibility of their national commander. European Commission for Democracy Through Law (Venice Commission), Opinion on Human Rights in Kosovo, Opinion no. 280/2004 CDL-AD (2004) 033, para. 79 (2004).

25 *Behrami and Behrami v. France*, appl. no. 71412/01 and *Saramati* v. *France, Germany and Norway*, appl. no. 78166/01.

26 The case of *Behrami* mainly concerned UNMIK. The fact that UNMIK was a subsidiary organ of the United Nations meant that in principle the acts and omissions of UNMIK were attributable to the United Nations. The judgment of the ECtHR would not seem to have caused debate in this respect.

27 The case against Germany was withdrawn as it had not been possible to establish any involvement of German officers in the arrest of Mr Saramati. See Saramati, *supra* note 25, para. 64.

28 *Ibid.* paras. 134–5.

29 *Ibid.* para 139. This can be interpreted to mean that if TCNs had interfered, the acts could have been attributed to those states instead of the United Nations.

30 *Ilaz Kasumaj* v. *Greece*, appl. No. 6974/05; Decision of 5 July 2007, *Slavisa Gajić* v. *Germany*, appl. No. 31446/02; Decision of 28 August 2007, *Dusan Berić et al.* v. *Bosnia and Herzegovina*, appl. nos. 36357/04, 36360/04, 38346/04, 41705/04, 45190/04, 45578/04, 45579/04, 45580/04, 91/05, 97/05, 100/05, 101/05, 1121/05, 1123/05, 1125/05, 1129/05, 1132/05, 1133/05, 1169/05, 1172/05, 1175/05, 1177/05, 1180/ 05, 1185/05, 20793/05 and 25496/05, Decision of 16 October 2007.

31 See e.g., K.M. Larsen, 'Attribution of conduct in peace operations: the "ultimate authority and control" test' (2008), 19 *EJIL* 509; H. Krieger, 'A credibility gap: the *Behrami and Saramati* decision of the European Court of Human Rights' (2009), 13 *International Peacekeeping* 159; A. Sari, 'Jurisdiction and international responsibility in peace support operations: the *Behrami* and *Saramati* cases' (2008), 8 *Human Rights Law Review*, 151.

32 'Without denying the importance of this jurisprudence, it would be difficult to accept, simply on the strength of the judgment in *Behrami and Saramati*, the criterion there applied as a potentially universal rule. Also as a matter of policy, the approach taken by the European Court of Human Rights is unconvincing. It would lead to attributing to the United Nations conduct which the organization has not specifically authorized and of which it may have little knowledge or no knowledge at all. It is therefore not surprising that in his report of June 2008 on the United Nations Interim Administration Mission in Kosovo, the United Nations Secretary-General distanced himself from that criterion and stated: "it is understood that the international responsibility of the United Nations will be limited to the extent of its effective operational control"' *Seventh Report on Responsibility of International Organizations*, UN doc., A/CN.4/610 (27 March 2009) para. 30. See also UNSG Report on United Nations Interim Administration Mission in Kosovo, UN doc., S/2008/354 (June 2008) para. 16.

33 United Kingdom, Germany and the Nordic countries all supported the effective control test. Cf. Greece. *Eighth Report on Responsibility of International Organizations*, UN doc. A/CN.4/640 (14 March 2011) para. 33.

34 Historically, states had claimed that the hostilities they were involved in could not be characterised as war and it was believed that the term 'armed conflict' would make such an argument more difficult to entertain. See J.S. Pictet *et al.* (eds.), *Commentary on the Geneva Conventions of 12 August 1949* (Geneva: ICRC, 1958) ('Commentaries') Article 2 GC IV, available at www.icrc.org/ihl.nsf/CONVPRES?OpenView.

35 *Ibid.* Regarding a requirement of intensity see e.g., C. Greenwood, 'Scope of application of humanitarian law' in D. Fleck (ed.), *The Handbook of International Humanitarian Law* (2nd edn, Oxford, 2008) 48.

36 *Tadić*, *supra* note 1, para. 70.

37 'How is the term "Armed Conflict" defined in international humanitarian law?', International Committee of the Red Cross (ICRC) Opinion Paper, (March 2008) available at www.icrc.org/eng/resources/documents/article/other/armed-conflict-article-170308.htm.

38 D. Schindler, 'The different types of armed conflicts according to the Geneva Conventions and Protocols' (1979), 163 *RCADI*, 131.

39 These conditions are listed in the Commentaries to Common Article 3, *supra* note 34.

40 *Ibid.*

41 *Tadić*, *supra* note 1, para. 70.

42 *Ibid.*

43 This author does not agree with the position claiming that the involvement of a UN-mandated multinational force in an armed conflict automatically makes the conflict international in character, irrespective of the status of other parties. See O. Engdahl, 'The status of peace operation personnel under international humanitarian law' (2008), 11 *YIHL* 109.

44 That the intensity of a conflict is of greater importance than its duration is further supported by the Inter-American Commission on Human Rights in the so-called *Tablada* case. An attack on a military compound lasted approximately thirty hours. Owing to the intensity of the fighting, the Commission found that it could not be regarded merely as an internal disturbance but rather an internal armed conflict triggering Common Article 3 to the four Geneva Conventions. The Commission found the following criteria decisive to its conclusion: 'the concerted nature of the hostile acts undertaken by the attackers, the direct involvement of governmental armed forces, and the nature and level of the violence attending the events in question. More particularly, the attackers involved carefully planned, coordinated and executed an armed attack, i.e., a military operation, against a quintessential military objective – a military base'. *Juan Carlos Abella* v. *Argentina*, Case 11.137, Inter-American Commission on Human Rights, 18 November 1997, OEA/Ser.L/V/II.98 doc. 6 rev., 13 April 1998, para. 154. See also, L. Zegveld, 'The Inter-American Commission on Human Rights and international humanitarian law: a comment on the *Tablada* case' (1998) 324, *IRRC* 505.

45 *Prosecutor* v. *Haradinaj et al.*, (IT-04–84), ICTY Trial Chamber I, Judgment, 3 April 2008, para. 49. In later judgments, the ICTY referred to even more indicators in order to assess the intensity of the conflict. These indicative factors included 'seriousness of attacks and whether there has been an increase in armed clashes; the spread of clashes over territory and over a period of time; any increase in the number of government forces and mobilisation and the distribution of weapons among both parties to the conflict; as well as whether the conflict has attracted the attention

of the United Nations Security Council, and whether any resolutions on the matter have been passed. Trial Chambers have also taken into account in this respect the number of civilians forced to flee from the combat zones; the type of weapons used, in particular the use of heavy weapons, and other military equipment, such as tanks and other heavy vehicles; the blocking or besieging of towns and the heavy shelling of these towns; the extent of destruction and the number of casualties caused by shelling or fighting; the quantity of troops and units deployed; existence and change of front lines between the parties; the occupation of territory, and towns and villages; the deployment of government forces to the crisis area; the closure of roads'. *Prosecutor* v. *Ljube Boskoski, Johan Tarculovski*, (IT-04-82-T), ICTY, Judgment, 10 July 2008, para. 177 (footnotes omitted).

46 *Haradinaj, supra* note 45, para. 60 (2008). In the *Boskoski and Tarculovski* case, the Tribunal found a number of indicative factors for assessing the organisation of armed groups. They fell into the following five broad groups: command structure and organisation and structure of the armed group; ability to carry out operations in an organised manner; the level of logistic capacity; necessary level of discipline; and ability to speak with one voice and to act on behalf of the group. *Prosecutor* v. *Ljube Boskoski, Johan Tarculovski, supra* note 45, para. 177.

47 L. Zegveld, *The Accountability of Armed Opposition Groups in International Law* (Cambridge University Press, 2002) 136.

48 ICRC Opinion Paper, *supra* note 37, 5.

49 UK Ministry of Defence, *Manual of the Law of Armed Conflict* (2004), 29.

50 ICRC Opinion Paper, 5, *supra* note 37, 5.

51 *Military and Paramilitary Activities in and against Nicaragua (Nicaragua* v. *United States*), Merits, Judgment, [1986] ICJ. Reports 14, paras. 105–15. See also *Case Concerning the Application of the Convention on the Prevention and Punishment of the Crime of Genocide (Bosnia and Herzegovina* v. *Serbia and Montenegro*), Judgment, 2007 paras. 309–401. See *Prosecutor* v. *Tadić*, (IT-94-1-A), (ICTY Appeals Chamber Judgment, 15 July 1999, para. 137.

52 The Commentaries to this Article state that 'it is perfectly clear that the Protocol has extended its field of application to entities which are not States .... If they conform to the requirements of the present article, liberation movements fighting against colonial domination ..., paragraph 3, and resistance movements representing a pre-existing subject of international law may be "Parties to the conflict" within the meaning of the Conventions and the Protocol. However, the authority which represents them must have certain characteristics of a government, at least in relation to its armed forces. Nor is it out of the question that the United Nations could be a "Party to an armed conflict" in the material sense, although the problem of the accession of the United Nations to the Geneva Conventions and the Protocol remains a delicate question which has not yet been resolved ... Theoretically at least, the notion of "Party to the conflict", within the meaning of the Protocol, is fairly wide, involving not only resistance movements representing a pre-existing subject of international law and governments in exile, but also those fighting for conflicts of "self-determination" or "national liberation".' Y. Sandoz, C. Swinarski and B. Zimmerman (eds.), *Commentary on the Additional Protocols of 8 June 1977 to the Geneva Conventions of 12 August 1949* (Geneva: ICRC, 1987). Article 43 AP I (footnote omitted).

53 *Ibid.*

54 See e.g., D.W. Bowett, *United Nations Forces: A Legal Study of United Nations Practice* (London: 1964) 493–516; F. Seyersted, *United Nations Forces in the Law of Peace and War* (1966) 197–220; C. Greenwood, 'International humanitarian law and United Nations military operations' (1998) 1 *YIHL* 23; L. Green, *The Contemporary Law of Armed Conflict* (3rd edn, Manchester University Press, 2008) 376–7; D. Shraga, 'The applicability of international humanitarian law to United Nations operations' in C. Emanuelli (ed.), *Blue Helmets: Policemen or Combatants?* (Montreal: Wilson & Lafleur, 1997) 17, 30; B. D. Tittemore, 'Belligerents in Blue Helmets: applying international humanitarian law to United Nations peace operations' (1997) 33 *Stanford Journal of International Law* 61 at 109. See also UK Ministry of Defence, *The Manual of the Law of Armed Conflict* (2004), ch.14; Convention on the Safety of United Nations and Associated Personnel, 9 December 1994, 2051 UNTS 363, Article 2; Statute of the International Criminal Court, 17 July 1998, 37 ILM 999, Article 8(2)(b)(iii), (e)(iii); UN Secretariat, Observance by United Nations forces of international humanitarian law, Secretary-General's Bulletin, UN doc. ST/SGB/1999/13 (1999).

55 Seyersted declares that: 'When the action is carried out by a Force under United Nations command and responsibility, the States providing contingents … are not internationally responsible for the conduct of the operation and are not parties to the conflict …. They are only responsible *vis-à-vis* the United Nations for ensuring that their contingents obey United Nations' orders and for prosecuting the members thereof for any offences in accordance with the internal agreements concluded by these States with the Organization. It is the United Nations which, although it does not itself have disciplinary and criminal jurisdiction over the members of the Force, is externally responsible and which alone is a party to the conflict and to any external agreement.' Seyersted, *United Nations Forces*, 204–5 (footnotes omitted). Glick argues: 'As a consequence of its command and control, the United Nations is deemed a party to armed conflict and thereby subject to the obligations of IHL. In contrast, as a consequence of their lack of control, troop contributing states are neither parties to the armed conflict nor directly responsible for the actions of UN armed forces.' Glick, 'Lip service', 98. Van Hegelsom refers to a classified document on EU policy on the use of force, which states that if the EU becomes party to an armed conflict, which according to van Hegelsom has not yet been the case, it will apply the laws of armed conflict to the full extent. G.-J. van Hegelsom, 'Coalition warfare: who is a party to armed conflict in joint missions?' in *Armed Conflicts and Parties to Armed Conflicts under IHL: Confronting Legal Categories to Contemporary Realities*, Proceedings of the 10th Bruges Colloquium, 22–23 October 2009.

56 See S. Vité, 'Typology of armed conflicts in international humanitarian law: legal concepts and actual situations' (2009) 91 (873) *IRRC* 71.

57 *Tadić* (1999), *supra* note 51, para. 92.

58 *Ibid*. para. 95.

59 *Ibid*. para. 100.

60 *Ibid*, para. 114. Cf. Talmon who explains that the ICJ in the *Nicaragua* case employed a 'strict control' test requiring complete dependence on the part of the secessionist movement (the Contras) equated with *de facto* organs of the foreign state. The 'effective control' test is a subsidiary test and relates to effective control over specific conduct. S. Talmon, *The Various Control Tests in the Law of State Responsibility and the Responsibility of Outside Powers for Acts of Secessionists*, Legal Research Paper Series,

Paper No. 16/2009 (Oxford 2009) 5–9. See also ICJ in the *Genocide* case, *supra* note 51, paras. 385–400.

61 *Tadić* (1999), *supra* note 51, para. 137.

62 *Ibid.*

63 *Genocide* case, *supra* note 51, para. 404. The ICJ held that '[i]nsofar as the "overall control" test is employed to determine whether or not an armed conflict is international, which was the sole question which the Appeals Chamber was called upon to decide, it may well be that the test is applicable and suitable; the Court does not however think it appropriate to take a position on the point in the present case, as there is no need to resolve it for purposes of the present Judgment'.

64 It found that the test of 'overall control' in this regard was unsuitable since 'it stretches too far, almost to breaking point, the connection which must exist between the conduct of a State's organs and its international responsibility'. *Ibid.* para. 406. The ICJ recognised that: 'logic does not require the same test to be adopted in resolving the two issues, which are very different in nature: the degree and nature of a State's involvement in an armed conflict on another State's territory which is required for the conflict to be characterized as international, can very well, and without logical inconsistency, differ from the degree and nature of involvement required to give rise to that State's responsibility for a specific act committed in the course of the conflict.' *Ibid.* para. 405.

65 (2001) *Yearbook of the ILC*, UN doc. A/CN.4/SER.A/2001/Add.1 (Part 2), 47.

66 *Ibid.* 48.

67 A. Cassese, 'The *Nicaragua* and *Tadić* tests revisited in the light of the ICJ Judgment on *Genocide in Bosnia*, (2007) 18(4) *EJIL* 649.

68 *Behrami* and *Saramati* cases, *supra* note 25, para. 135.

69 See also, T. Meron, 'Classification of armed conflict in the former Yugoslavia: *Nicaragua's* fallout' (1998) 92 *AJIL* 236 and J. G. Stewart, 'Towards a single definition of armed conflict in international humanitarian law: a critique of internationalized armed conflict' (2203) 85 (850) *IRRC* 323. The reasoning of the ICTY in the *Tadić* case has also been criticised by the ILC which claims the need to differentiate between the identification of individual responsibility and that of state responsibility, see Report of the International Law Commission, General Assembly, Official Records, Fifty-sixth session, Supp. 10 (A/56/10) (2001) 106–7. Cf. M. Sassòli, 'State responsibility for violations of international humanitarian law' 2002 (84) 846 *IRRC* 408.

70 Commentary to Common Article 3, *supra* note 34, 37.

71 See Vité, 'Typology', 78.

72 *Prosecutor* v. *Limaj*, (IT-03-66-T), ICTY Trial Chamber Judgment, 30 November 2005, para. 170.

73 J.-M. Henckaerts and L. Doswald-Beck (eds.), *Customary International Humanitarian Law* (Cambridge University Press, 2005) Rule 149, 530.

74 Sassòli, 'State responsibility', 405–406. See also *Tadić* (1999), *supra* note 51, note 117.

75 Naert briefly discusses whether the EU could become a party to an armed conflict. He finds that '[t]he position of the EU as a distinct international legal person theoretically means it might be a party to an armed conflict without its Member States being a party to that conflict'. F. Naert, *International Law Aspects of the EU's Security and Defence Policy, with a Particular Focus on the Law of Armed Conflict* (Antwerp: Intersertia, 2009) 534. In the context of an international armed conflict he finds that

an analogy with the condition of belonging to a party to an armed conflict is complex and he questions if it is possible to shield from attack the armed forces of Member States not yet under EU command but which may subsequently be transferred to that command. This would, according to Naert, not only pose practical problems but also seem unfair towards the opponent and he finds that a condition based on the voting procedure could possibly be used to identify which states are parties to the armed conflict.

76 SC Res. 1386, UN SCOR 4443rd mtg, UN doc., S/RES/1386 (2001).

77 SC Res. 1510, UN SCOR 4840th mtg, UN doc., S/RES/1510 (2003).

78 SC Res. 1386, UN SCOR 4443rd mtg, UN doc., S/RES/1386 (2001) Preamble, 1–2.

79 See www.cnn.com/2009/WORLD/asiapcf/09/04/afghanistan.airstrike/index.html.

80 See http://www.isaf.nato.int/article/isaf-releases/index.php

81 *Tadić*, *supra* note 1, para. 70. The principle of unity of territory means that IHL applies in the whole territory of the state engaged in conflict. R. Kolb and R. Hyde, *An Introduction to International Humanitarian Law* (Oxford: Hart, 2008) 95.

82 It cannot be ruled out, however, that an attack against a target outside the territory of Afghanistan might be regarded as an attack separated from the armed conflict in Afghanistan and the applicability of IHL in relation to that attack would depend on the relevant criteria governing the existence of a non-international armed conflict.

83 On the relation between national criminal law and IHL, see Engdahl, 'Status'.

84 Greenwood, 'Scope of Application', 61–2.

85 In later Resolutions it recognises 'that the responsibility for providing security and law and order throughout the country resides with the Afghan Authorities, stressing the role of the International Security Assistance Force (ISAF) in assisting the Afghan Government to improve the security situation and *welcoming* the cooperation of the Afghan Government with ISAF'. SC Res. 1833, UN SCOR 5977th mtg, UN doc. S/RES/ 1833 (2008).

86 SACEUR OPLAN 10302 (Revise 1) ISAF Unclassified, para. 3 (i)(7)(a).

87 See www.isaf.nato.int/images/stories/File/Placemats/110606-isaf-placemat.pdf.

88 Greenwood, 'International Humanitarian Law', 18. Greenwood states in this respect that 'the attribution of responsibility should not be confused with the existence of the obligation'. UK Ministry of Defence, *Manual of the Law of Armed Conflict*, (2004) 376.

89 See Common Article 1 of the four Geneva Conventions.

90 NATO defines 'full command' in the following way: 'The military authority and responsibility of a commander to issue orders to subordinates. It covers every aspect of military operations and administration and exists only within national services. Note: the term "command" as used internationally, implies a lesser degree of authority than when it is used in a purely national sense. No NATO or coalition commander has full command over the forces assigned to him since, in assigning forces to NATO, nations will delegate only operational command or operational control.' See NATO Glossary of Terms and Definitions, AAP-6 (2009), 2-F-7.

91 The ISAF command structure, as presented on the NATO Homepage, is as follows: 'Based on the 16 April 2003 North Atlantic Council's decision, NATO has assumed responsibility, from the United Nations, for command, control and coordination of the International Security Assistance Force in Afghanistan since 11 August 2003. NATO's Allied Command Operations (ACO), based at the Supreme Headquarters Allied Powers in Europe (SHAPE), in Mons (Belgium), has the overall command

of the operation. ACO's subordinate headquarters, Allied Joint Force Command (JFC) Headquarters Brunssum (The Netherlands) runs the operation, including the planning and command of the force, as well as the provision of a force commander and headquarters'. See www.isaf.nato.int/isaf-command-structure.html Based in Kabul, the ISAF Headquarters serves as the operational command for the NATO-led mission. See www.nato.int/isaf/structure/hq/index.html.

92 The ICTY furthermore held the above requirement 'to be in addition to financing, training and equipping or providing operational support to that group'. The latter set of conditions is generally the responsibility of TCNs. While these conditions are significant, they may be of less importance in multinational peace operations as these conditions need not necessarily generate particular influence over the operation as a whole.

93 *Behrami and Saramati*, *supra* note 25, para. 141.

94 SC Res. 1973, UN SCOR 6498th mtg,. UN doc. S/RES/1973 (2011) para. 4.

95 See www.jfcnaples.nato.int/Unified_Protector/Mission.aspx. See also, www.nato.int/nato_static/assets/pdf/pdf_2011_03/20110325_110325-unified-protector-command-control.pdf.

96 Svenskt deltagande i den internationella militära insatsen i Libyen, Prop. 2010/11:111 (2011), 8 (author's translation).

97 Overordnede Rettslige Rammebetingelser for den Norske Deltakelsen i JTF Odyssey Dawn, Ref.2011/00761-1/FDII 5/ANW, 24 March 2011.

98 *Ibid.*, 1.

99 See www.stortinget.no/no/Saker-og-publikasjoner/Publikasjoner/Referater/Stortinget/2010-2011/110329/1/ (author's translation)

100 See https://mail.fhs.se/owa/redir.aspx?C=14d002e8458c4003a0f3c211741b3744&URL=http%3a%2f%2fnyhederne-dyn.tv2.dk%2farticle.php%2fid-38270444%3al%25C3%25B8kke-vi-skal-tage-del-i-krig.html%3fss; and https://mail.fhs.se/owa/redir.aspx?C=14d002e8458c4003a0f3c211741b3744&URL=http%3a%2f%2fmobil.eb.dk%2fnyheder%2fkrigogkatastrofer_article.pml%3farticleid%3d1521501

101 House of Commons Official Report, vol. 530 no. 175 (22 June 2011), 315.

102 Testimony by Legal Adviser Harold Hongju Koh, US Department of State on Libya and War Powers Before the Senate Foreign Relations Committee, 28 June 28 2011, 13.

10

Security detention in UN peace operations

PETER VEDEL KESSING

1. Introduction

The question of which detention standards are applicable in times of armed conflict, particularly non-international armed conflict, is controversial and has been much debated in recent years. Is detention governed by international humanitarian law (IHL), international human rights law (IHRL) or national law, or a combination thereof?

In 2011, following an internal two-year study on the current state of IHL, the ICRC concluded that the existing legal framework on detention in armed conflict is unsatisfactory, and recommended after consultations with states that the legal framework should be strengthened in order to provide greater protection for detainees.[1]

Even more complex and unclear practical and legal questions arise when it is UN forces with a UN mandate that are carrying out the detention during a UN peace operation. Such operations are often performed in blurred and complex situations involving both peacetime and situations of armed conflict, with an often ambiguous legal mandate from the UN Security Council and in cooperation with a number of different troop contributing nations with different detention standards.[2]

This question of when UN forces may detain individuals has become pertinent in recent years in line with the change in international peace operations after the end of the Cold War.[3] The spectrum of contemporary UN peace operations has become increasingly broad and includes both UN-led peace operations and operations conducted by other actors with the authorisation of the UN Security Council.[4]

It is possible to distinguish between three different types of UN peace operations: *UN peacekeeping operations* consist of forces under the command and control of the United Nations. They operate with the consent of the parties to the conflict to observe a cease-fire or peace agreement in a situation where the fighting has ceased. The forces are only allowed to use force in self-defence. *UN-controlled enforcement operations* are forces operating under UN command and control. They are authorised by the UN Security Council to engage in enforcement and are permitted to use armed force. Finally, *UN-authorised enforcement operations* consist of forces with a mandate from the UN Security Council to use armed force.[5] Such forces are not operating under UN control but under national or alliance command and control. Some examples are the multinational stabilisation operations authorised by the UN Security Council pursuant to Chapter VII of the UN Charter in Afghanistan and Iraq.[6]

The term 'UN forces' is used in a broad sense in this chapter, covering both forces operating under UN control and forces operating with a UN mandate under national or alliance control, and both forces operating in a peacetime context and in an armed conflict context.

As of November 2009, the deployment of UN peace-keepers (operating in peace-keeping operations and UN-controlled enforcement operations) is at a record high, with more than 113,000 personnel serving in eighteen operations on four continents.[7] Furthermore, the UN Security Council has in recent years authorised enforcement operations under national or alliance control in a number of countries, e.g., in Afghanistan, Iraq and Libya.

In practice, it is common for UN forces to detain individuals during peace operations.[8] But there is no common agreement on which grounds and procedures determine the extent to which UN forces may detain individuals during international peace operations.

This uncertainty about applicable detention standards constitutes an operational problem, as it might lead forces operating on the ground in certain situations to tend to avoid detaining individuals, who from a strict military and operational point of view should have been detained. Moreover, the uncertainty might be of concern from a humanitarian perspective, which is the overall theme for this volume. Unclear and disputed detention standards will without doubt increase the risk of innocent civilians being arbitrarily detained for prolonged periods of time.

All conflicts can be said to consist of a pre-conflict phase, a conflict phase and a post-conflict phase. While there are well-developed rules in international law governing the pre-conflict phase (*jus ad bellum*) and the conflict phase (*jus in bello*), there are no well-established and clear rules in international law concerning the post-conflict phase. Therefore, some researchers argue that there is a need to develop a *jus post bellum*.[9] The current uncertainty regarding what rules to apply for detention in peace operations, which usually takes place in a post-conflict phase, can be seen as a concrete example of the need for regulating or at least clarifying and reaching agreement on applicable detention standards in the post-conflict phase – or in other words, to develop a *jus post bellum*.

This chapter will discuss when and under which procedures UN forces may detain individuals during international peace operations and explore if it is possible to identify common minimum detention standards for UN peace operations. There will be a particular focus as to whether UN forces may detain individuals simply for security reasons (hereinafter 'preventive detention').[10]

In section 2 below, the question of whether UN forces on a general basis are bound by standards in international humanitarian law and international human rights law, including when detaining individuals in peace operations, will be explored. It is argued that due to their special protective and humanitarian mandate, UN peace operations should respect IHL and IHRL standards when detaining individuals.

Section 3 below goes on to give an overview of the detention standards in IHL and IHRL applicable in *international armed conflicts*. Similarities and main differences between these legal regimes will be identified.

Section 4 below focuses on detention standards in times of *non-international armed conflict*, this being the form of conflict where most problems arise. Four different ways in which the IHL and IHRL detention standards may interrelate are examined and assessed.

Finally, in section 5 below, it is discussed whether it is possible, based on the existing standards in IHL and IHRL, to identify common minimum detention standards applicable for all UN forces in all situations and all types of operations.

2. Are UN forces bound by IHL and IHRL detention standards?

2.1 To what extent is the United Nations bound by international law?

From a legal perspective, it is disputed whether the United Nations as an international organisation is bound by international law, including IHL and IHRL. The International Court of Justice (ICJ) established in the *WHO Headquarters Agreement* case from 1980 that:

> International organizations are subjects of international law and, as such, are bound by any obligations incumbent upon them under general rules of international law, under their constitutions or under international agreements to which they are parties.[11]

Thus, an international organisation may in principle be bound by international law in three ways: (i) through 'general rules of international law' – this concept is not clearly defined in international law, but it must include 'general principles of law recognized by civilized nations' (cf. Article 38(1)(c) in the Statute of the International Court of Justice) and arguably also 'customary international law' (cf. Article 38(1)(b));[12] (ii) through the terms of the international organisation's constituent instrument, e.g., the UN Charter in relation to the United Nations; and (iii) if the organisation has become party to an international convention.

Likewise, the International Law Association stated in its final report from 2004 on the *Accountability of International Organizations* with regard to the applicability of human rights that:

> Human rights obligations, which are increasingly becoming an expression of the common constitutional traditions of States, can become binding upon IOs [international organizations] in different ways: through the terms of their constituent instruments; as customary international law; or as general principles of law or if an IO is authorised to become a party to a human rights treaty. The consistent practice of IOs points to a recognition of this.[13]

The United Nations is not a party to IHRL conventions or to IHL conventions and is thus not directly bound by these conventions.

With regard to IHRL, it is set out in Article 1 of the UN Charter that one of the purposes of the United Nations is 'promoting and encouraging respect for human rights and fundamental freedoms for all'.[14] In a similar line, it is prescribed in the Preamble to the Charter that one of the aims of the United Nations is to 'establish conditions under which justice and respect for obligations arising from treaties and other sources of international law can be maintained'. It is, however, not directly prescribed that the United Nations is bound by IHRL.

Nevertheless, it is widely held that the United Nations must respect IHRL and IHL standards which hold the status of *jus cogens* and arguably also IHRL and IHL standards which are a codification of general principles of law and customary international law.[15]

Thus, from a strictly legal point of view, it is a controversial question to what extent the United Nations and UN bodies are bound by international law, including IHRL and IHL.

If we are looking particularly at UN peace operations, however, a number of statements of a more political nature indicate that forces in such operations must comply with IHL and IHRL standards.

2.2. *Must UN forces comply with IHL and IHRL detention standards in peace operations?*

When assessing this question, it is necessary to distinguish between forces under UN command and control, and forces under national/alliance command and control.[16]

UN-controlled operations

With regard to IHL, it is stipulated in Article 1 of the UN *Secretary-General's Bulletin on Observance of International Humanitarian Law* from 1999[17] that UN forces shall comply with (some) IHL rules and principles when they are actively participating in an armed conflict as combatants. IHL rules and principles are (as prescribed in Article 1.1 in the Bulletin) '*accordingly* applicable in enforcement actions, or in peace-keeping operations when the use of force is permitted in self-defence' (emphasis added).[18] The *Bulletin* is only applicable for UN forces operating under UN command and control, i.e., in UN peace-keeping operations and in UN-controlled enforcement operations.

With regard to detention, it is specifically stated in Article 8 in the *Bulletin* that detained members of the armed forces and other persons who no longer take part in military operations by reason of detention shall be treated with humanity and respect and in accordance with the relevant provisions of Geneva Convention III. In particular, their capture and detention shall be notified without delay to the party on which they depend and the Central Tracing Agency (*litra* a) and the ICRC is given the right to visit detained persons (*litra* g). No other form of supervision or review of the detention is provided for here.

Concerning IHRL, it is directly stated in the principles and guidelines for UN Peacekeeping Operations from 2008 (elaborated by the UN Department of Peacekeeping Operations and the UN Department of Field Support) that IHRL is an integral part of the normative framework for UN peace-keeping operations and that such operations 'should be conducted in full respect of human rights and … seek to advance human rights through the implementation of their mandates'.[19]

UN-authorised operations under national/alliance control

Such forces, operating under national or alliance command and control, are not bound by the UN *Bulletin* on IHL from 1999 or by the UN principles and guidelines for UN peace-keeping operations from 2008.

Nevertheless, it is common in UN Security Council resolutions authorising enforcement operations to lay down that such forces shall act in accordance with IHL and IHRL standards. For instance, with regard to Afghanistan, such a statement is included in the Preamble to the UN Security Council Resolution from 2009, which extends the mandate of the ISAF forces for one more year:

> Expressing its serious concern with the high number of civilian casualties, and calling for compliance with international humanitarian and human rights law and for all appropriate measures to be taken to ensure the protection of civilians.[20]

Even in situations where there is no explicit reference to IHL or IHRL in Security Council Resolutions authorising enforcement operations, it is to be expected, due to the UN's role in promoting and respecting human rights, that forces under national/alliance control and command will comply with IHL and IHRL obligations when implementing the Resolution. See, for example, the Grand Chamber judgment of the European Court of Human Rights (ECtHR) in the *Al-Jedda* case:

> [T]he Court considers that, in interpreting its resolutions, there must be a presumption that the Security Council does not intend to impose any obligation on Member States to breach fundamental principles of human rights. In the event of any ambiguity in the terms of a Security Council Resolution, the Court must therefore choose the interpretation which is most in harmony with the requirements of [the European Convention on Human Rights] and which avoids any conflict of obligations. In the light of the United Nations' important role in promoting and encouraging respect for human rights, it is to be expected that clear and explicit language would be used were the Security Council to intend States to take particular measures which would conflict with their obligations under international human rights law.[21]

Against this background, it is concluded for the purpose of this chapter that UN forces operating under UN control as well as under national/alliance control (at least from an overall policy consideration) must respect standards of international humanitarian law and international human rights law during peace operations. Therefore, when trying to identify under which grounds and procedures UN forces can detain individuals in peace operations, the point of departure must be applicable detention standards in IHL and IHRL.

IHL and IHRL detention standards are discussed in international armed conflicts in section 3 below and in non-international armed conflicts in section 4 below.

3. International standards on detention in international armed conflict and occupation

3.1 *International humanitarian law*

Interpreting ambiguous detention standards in the context of standards on targeting

When establishing whether and pursuant to which procedures an individual may be detained for preventive reasons of security in times of international armed conflict and occupation (IAC), the Geneva Conventions distinguish between three categories of individuals, namely: prisoners of wars; civilians who pose an imperative security threat; and other civilians.

It is well established in IHL that prisoners of war (POW) may be detained for security reasons for the duration of hostilities. Likewise, it is clear that 'other civilians' cannot be detained for reasons of security, see e.g., Article 79 of the Geneva Convention (GC) IV. They may, however, possibly be detained pursuant to national law for committing ordinary crimes.

To the contrary, it is unclear in which situations a *civilian who poses an imperative security threat* can be detained. GC IV only regulates two situations: first, protected civilian aliens in the territory of a party to the conflict can be detained if the 'security of the detaining power makes it absolutely necessary', see Article 42 GC IV; secondly, an occupying power can detain civilians on the occupied territory for imperative reasons of security, see Article 78 GC IV. But what about civilians who are not aliens in enemy territory or civilians in occupied territory, e.g., civilians captured by invading forces during active hostilities in an international armed conflict on enemy territory? Under which circumstances can they be detained?

This is not regulated in GC IV. The ICRC Commentary proposes (arguably to avoid a norm vacuum) a broad interpretation of the term 'occupation' to include situations of active hostilities with the consequence that civilians in these situations could be detained according to detention standards applicable under occupation, i.e., Article 78.[22] This interpretation is, however, controversial.[23]

Particularly in certain situations where there is doubt about the interpretation as to the applicable detention standard, it is relevant to take into consideration the corresponding standards on targeting in international armed conflict. See also Article 31(1) in the Vienna Convention on the

Law of Treaties which stipulates that a treaty shall be interpreted in good faith in accordance with the ordinary meaning to be given to the terms of the treaty in their context, comprising the text of the treaty (see Article 31(2)), and in the light of its object and purpose.

The rules on targeting and detention may in principle relate to each other in four different ways: there may be (i) a situation where an individual can both be targeted and be detained; (ii) a situation where an individual can neither be targeted nor detained; (iii) a situation where an individual cannot be targeted but can be detained; and finally (iv) a situation where an individual can be targeted but not detained.

In the first three situations, the rules on targeting and detention correspond and fit well with each other. However, the contrary is true with regard to situation (iv). It must be a basic precondition that if an individual can be lawfully targeted in IAC without restrictions, it must also be lawful to detain the individual for the duration of hostilities without further restrictions. States could otherwise have an incentive to kill individuals instead of detaining them in situations where it is not necessary due to military necessity. Such a situation would be in clear conflict with the fundamental principle of humanity in international humanitarian law.

When deciding whether an individual can be targeted, IHL distinguishes between three categories of individuals, namely: combatants; civilians who are taking direct part in hostilities; and other civilians who are not participating directly in hostilities. While combatants and civilians taking direct part in hostilities can lawfully be targeted, civilians who are not participating in hostilities are immune against attacks.

The three categories of individuals specified in relation to targeting are not identical with the categories of individuals specified in relation to detention, as described above. Thus, in order to secure that the rules on targeting correspond and fit with the rules on detention (i.e., if an individual can be lawfully targeted, it should also be lawful to detain the individual), it is necessary to assess how the three categories of individuals specified in relation to targeting relate and fit with the three categories of individuals specified in relation to detention. This relationship may be expressed as shown in table 10.1.[24] Table 10.1 also includes IHRL detention standards which will be discussed in section 3.2 below.

Table 10.1 *Overview of targeting and detention standards in IHL (IAC) and IHRL*

		Targeting under IHL	Preventive detention	Review of detention
Row A POW/combatants, i.e. regular and irregular armed forces, who have been captured (GC III and AP I)		*Cell 1* Yes	*Cell 2* IHL: Yes IHRL: Yes	*Cell 3* IHL: No IHRL: Yes
Row B Civilians who pose an imperative security threat (GC IV Arts. 46, 78)	**B.1** Civilians taking direct part in hostilities	*Cell 4* Yes	*Cell 5* IHL: Yes IHRL: Yes	*Cell 6* IHL: No (?) IHRL: Yes
	B.2 Civilians taking indirect part in hostilities	*Cell 7* No	*Cell 8* IHL: Yes IHRL: Yes	*Cell 9* IHL: Yes, adm. IHRL: Yes, court
Row C Other civilians Non-participation in hostilities, including ordinary criminals		*Cell 10* No	*Cell 11* IHL: No IHRL: Yes	*Cell 12* IHL: No IHRL: Yes, court

Row A consists of POWs. POWs are simply combatants who have been captured. Thus, this group consists of individuals who can either be targeted or detained without restrictions as POWs for the duration of hostilities and thus there is no conflict between detaining or targeting (situation (i)).

Row C consists of 'other civilians' who can neither be preventively detained nor deliberately targeted. Consequently, there is no conflict between standards on detention and targeting (situation (ii)).

Row B consists of civilians who pose an imperative security threat who can be preventively detained for security purposes. In relation to targeting, that group must be split up into civilians taking direct and indirect part in hostilities. *Row B.2* consists of civilians taking indirect part in hostilities, e.g., in terms of financing and other indirect support to the fighting (see definition). This category of individuals can be detained but not targeted and consequently there is no risk of conflict between standards on detaining and targeting (situation (iii)).

Problems may arise in relation to civilians taking direct part in hostilities (see definition) in *row B.1*. They may undoubtedly be targeted as combatants, but the question is, if they are going to be detained, whether they should be detained as combatants or as civilians. Civilians may be detained in more restrictive circumstances than combatants. Whereas combatants may be detained for the duration of hostilities without restrictions and review, civilians may only be detained if it is established that they pose an imperative security threat and with access to review by an administrative body. Thus, if civilians in *row B.1* may 'only' be detained as civilians posing an imperative security threat, that could lead to a situation (which must be avoided) where a civilian can be detained under more restrictive conditions than killed (situation (iv)). This question and the content of the applicable detention standard for the various categories of individuals are discussed in further detail below.

IHL standards on preventive detention/internment

POW/combatants. It is well known (Article 21 GC III, see Table 10.1, cells (2) and (3)), that POW/combatants may be detained as prisoners of war for the duration of hostilities without any form of review. They may be detained simply for reasons of military necessity because they are combatants and would take part in hostilities if released. The detaining power must inform the protecting power when detaining a combatant and the ICRC must be given access to visit detained combatants (Article 126 GC III).

There are only two reasons why a detaining power would have to release a POW. First, if the POW is seriously wounded or sick, he must be repatriated for medical reasons (Article 109 GC III). Secondly, after the cessation of active hostilities, a POW must be repatriated without delay (Article 118 GC III).

Civilians who only indirectly participate in hostilities. Civilians who only indirectly take part in hostilities (see Table 10.1, cells (8) and (9)), can be defined as civilians who offer general support to war activities, e.g., in the form of financial support as opposed to direct participation (defined below).[25]

They can be detained 'if the security of the Detaining Power makes it absolutely necessary' or for 'imperative reasons of security'. 'Imperative reasons of security' is not defined in GC IV, but it is highlighted in the ICRC Commentary to GC IV that 'Detention is an exceptionally severe measure which may be applied only if it is absolutely necessary for the security of the State'.[26]

The detainee must pose an individual threat to the security of the detaining state. Preventive detention cannot be used to punish someone for acts that have already been committed or to deter others from committing them. The purpose is to prevent the tangible risk presented by the acts of the detainee to the security of the state.[27]

Furthermore, the International Criminal Tribunal for the Former Yugoslavia (ICTY) has found (quoting from the ICRC Commentary to GC IV) that:

> [T]he mere fact that a person is a national of … an enemy party [is not] a valid reason for [detaining] him. To justify [detention] the party must have good reason to think that the person … by his activities, knowledge or qualifications, represents a real threat to its … security. The fact that an individual is male and of military age should not necessarily be considered as justifying [detention].[28]

GC IV lays down procedures for reviewing the detention of such civilians (Article 43 and 78(2) GC IV). The detention must be 'reconsidered as soon as possible by an appropriate court or administrative board' and thereafter periodically, and at least twice yearly. Also, there is a right to appeal in occupied territories (Article 78 GC IV). According to the ICRC Commentary to GC IV, the review must be 'absolutely objective and impartial', and it is further stated that where the decision is an 'administrative one, it must be made not by one official but by an administrative board offering the necessary guarantees of independence and impartiality'.[29]

The ICTY Appeals Chamber has further in the *Delalić* judgment defined the requirements that the court or board must meet under Article 43 GC IV:

(a) it must have the necessary power to decide finally on the release of prisoners whose detention is unjustified; and
(b) the onus of justifying detention of civilians is upon the detaining power – if the detaining power cannot establish that the civilians pose an imperative security threat, then they must be released.[30]

If these procedural requirements (on independence, impartiality, power to release and burden of proof) are met, there might in essence not be a major difference between a review by a court, as required by human right instruments, or by an administrative board, as required by GC IV. This will be addressed later.

Civilians taking direct part in hostilities. With regard to the category of civilians taking direct part in hostilities (see Table 10.1, cells (5) and (6)), it is strongly debated what actually amounts to direct participation and for what length of time civilians are to be considered as taking direct part in hostilities. A recent contribution to this debate is the ICRC's 'Interpretive Guidance on the notion of direct participation in hostilities', published in May 2009.[31] Direct participation is defined in the Guidance as 'specific acts carried out by individuals as part of the conduct of hostilities between parties to an armed conflict'.[32]

In relation to targeting – and only targeting – it is evident that civilians taking direct part in hostilities lose their protection against direct attack for the period that they are taking part in hostilities. It is debated, however, as to the length of time that civilians actually lose this protection. Is it only while taking direct part in hostilities or is it more permanent? Is it possible to be a 'fighter by night and a farmer by day' – and continue to be protected as a civilian during the daytime (the so-called 'revolving door' problem)?

This is a particularly contentious question in non-international armed conflicts (NIAC). In the ICRC's Interpretative Guidance, it is argued that civilians only lose protection against direct attack while taking part in hostilities. By contrast, members of organised armed groups belonging to a non-state party are considered to cease to be civilians, and thereby more permanently lose their protection against direct attack, as long as they are members of the armed group.[33]

Thus, civilians taking direct part in hostilities because of their individual acts, or because of their membership of an armed group, lose protection against targeting. But what about detention? Should civilians taking direct part in hostilities be treated as combatants, not only in relation to targeting, but also in relation to detention? Or in other words, can civilians taking direct part in hostilities be detained for security reasons for the duration of hostilities without the need to establish that they pose, and continues to pose, an imperative security threat and without any form of review? – Just like combatants!

In my view, it is as mentioned a strong argument that if states have the right under IHL (as they do) to target and kill civilians taking direct part in hostilities just as if they were combatants (Additional Protocol (AP) I, Article 51(3)), then they must also be able to detain those civilians just as if they were combatants as a less severe measure. It is, as explained above, of utmost importance to avoid a situation (situation (iv) above) where a civilian can be targeted under less restrictive conditions than he/she can be detained.

It might not in practice make a big difference in relation to the legal basis for detention (See Table 10.1, cell (5)), whether a civilian taking direct part in hostilities is perceived as a combatant or a civilian. This is because it is possible under IHL to detain civilians who pose an imperative security threat, and civilians taking direct part in hostilities may undoubtedly also be qualified as an imperative security threat in relation to detention. Nevertheless, if an individual were detained as a civilian posing an imperative security threat, then the detaining power would have to establish on the basis on an individual assessment that the person does in fact pose an imperative security threat to the detaining power. That is not required in relation to detention of combatants, who can be detained simply for belonging to the group of combatants.

More importantly, in relation to review of detention (see Table 10.1, cell (6)), it does make a significant difference whether a civilian who participates in hostilities is perceived as a combatant, with no right to review of detention, or a civilian. If the civilian protection were only lost while taking direct part in hostilities, then civilians who have ceased participating in hostilities would regain their protection. A consequence of this view would be that civilians taking direct part in hostilities would have the right to have their detention reviewed, as any other civilian, as they obviously have ceased to take part in hostilities when being detained.

It is a contentious question whether a civilian taking direct part in hostilities should be perceived as a combatant or a civilian in relation to detention. That is why a question mark has been placed in Table 10.1, cell (6). I would argue that situations where civilians are taking direct part in hostilities (most often) will be situations where there are ongoing hostilities and thus exist in ongoing international armed conflict. In such situations, which are not covered directly by Article 42 GC IV ('aliens in the territory of a party') or Article 78 GC IV ('protected civilians in occupied territory'), there are, as discussed above, no explicit standards in GC IV as to whether and pursuant to which procedures civilians may be detained. Thus, it seems particularly relevant to interpret detention standards in GC IV in the context of targeting standards and thus to hold that civilians taking direct part in hostilities may also be detained as combatants, i.e., without restrictions and review for the duration of hostilities.

In addition to arguing that POW standards on detention should be analogically applied to the detention of civilians who pose an imperative security threat by taking direct part in hostilities in times of active hostilities, it could also be argued that state practice probably indicates that civilians taking direct part in hostilities in practice are detained as combatants and therefore this is arguably customary international law (state practice and *opinio juris*).

Civilians who do not participate (directly or indirectly) in hostilities. Finally, with regard to civilians who do not participate either directly or indirectly in hostilities, (see Table 10.1 cells (11) and (12)), it follows from Article 79 GC IV that such civilians cannot be preventively detained for reasons of security. But they can be detained pursuant to national law if charged with a criminal offence.

To sum up, it is clear that combatants may be detained without review (Table 10.1, cells (2) and (3)). It is also clear that civilians who do not in any way participate in hostilities (Table 10.1, cells (11) and (12)) cannot be preventively detained pursuant to IHL standards and accordingly do not have a need for any review. Also, with regard to Table 10.1, cells (8) and (9), it is evident that civilians taking indirect part in hostilities and who constitute an 'imperative security threat' to a party to the conflict may be detained for preventive reasons and they have a right to review by a court or an administrative board.

Contentious questions arise in regard to Table 10.1, cells (5) and (6). Should civilians taking direct part in hostilities be perceived as combatant also in relation to detention with the consequence that they could be detained for the duration of hostilities without any review? Or should they be perceived as civilians in relation to detention with the consequence that they can only be detained if it can be established that they pose an imperative security threat and with regular administrative review of the detention?

Let us now turn to international human rights standards on detention.

3.2 *IHRL standards on detention*

The International Covenant on Civil and Political Rights (ICCPR) prohibits in Article 9 'arbitrary arrest and detention'. The provision does not rule out preventive detention. The Human Rights Committee (HRC) stated in its General Comment No. 8 that if preventive detention is used, it must not be *arbitrary*. In a concrete case, the HRC has further clarified that detention is arbitrary if it is 'indefinite and prolonged' and continues 'beyond the period for which the State can provide appropriate justification'.[34]

Accordingly, it is possible under the ICCPR to detain individuals merely for security reasons. In Europe, however, the situation is much more difficult because Article 5 of the European Convention on Human Rights (ECHR) explicitly lists the grounds on which persons may be detained, and preventive detention for security reasons is not included and has been firmly ruled out by the European Court of Human Rights (ECtHR).[35]

Furthermore, the Human Rights Committee has stressed that detention must be based on *grounds and procedures established by law;* that anyone arrested must be informed of the *reasons for arrest*; and that there must be a *court review* of the detention, in accordance with the right to *habeas corpus*.[36] With regard to the final requirement of a court, this may be a special court in the form of an administrative or a constitutional court, and the HRC has also accepted a military court; however, review carried out by a purely administrative body would *not* suffice.[37]

3.3 *Interaction between IHL and IHRL detention standards in IAC*

If we compare standards in IHL with IHRL standards on detention, we can see in Table 10.1, column 3 (cells 2, 5, 8 and 11) that preventive detention for security reasons is possible under both IHL and IHRL standards.[38]

The divergence between IHL and IHRL detention standards relates to review of detention in column 4 (cells 3, 6, 9 and 12). Two main differences can be identified.

First, combatants (Table 10.1, cell (2)) and possibly also civilians taking direct part in hostilities (cell (4)) do not have a right to review under IHL, but they do under the ICCPR and other IHRL instruments.

Secondly, civilians taking indirect part in hostilities (Table 10.1, cell (6)) have, according to IHL, a right to review by an *administrative body*, whereas they have a right to *court* review under the ICCPR.

How could these differences be overcome? It is argued by many – with reference to the analogous reasoning of the International Court of Justice in cases concerning the right to life – that standards on detention in IHL take precedence as *lex specialis* over human rights standards on detention in international armed conflicts and in times of occupation, with the consequence that POWs would have no right to review of detention and civilians only the right to review by an administrative body. It is, in my view, reasonable to argue that IHL standards on review of detention as a general rule must be *lex specialis* in times of international armed conflict and occupation.[39]

Notwithstanding, it should be remembered, as stated by the International Law Commission, that the relationship between *lex specialis* and other norms of interpretation or conflict solution – e.g., the *lex posterior* rule – cannot be determined in a general way, but should be decided contextually.[40]

It must be decided on a case-by-case basis. Against this background, it may be discussed if it is possible to maintain that IHL standards on review of detention can continue to supersede IHRL standards on review in situations where there is severe doubt as to whether there continues to exist an international armed conflict and also in times of protracted occupation. In uncertain and protracted armed conflicts, it could reasonably be argued that at some point in time, human rights standards on review of detention must be taken into consideration.

Likewise, the Inter-American Commission on Human Rights has found that IHL standards on detention are *lex specialis* in times of international armed conflict and occupation. They, however, also observed that:

> Notwithstanding the specific rules and mechanisms governing the detention of persons in situations of armed conflict, there may be circumstances in which the continued existence of active hostilities becomes uncertain, or where a belligerent occupation continues over a prolonged period of time. Where this occurs, the regulations and procedures under international humanitarian law may prove inadequate to properly safeguard the minimum human rights standards of detainees.

Accordingly, where detainees find themselves in uncertain or protracted situations of armed conflict or occupation, the Commission considers that the supervisory mechanisms as well as judicial guarantees under international human rights law and domestic law, including *habeas corpus* and amparo remedies, may necessarily supersede international humanitarian law where this is necessary to safeguard the fundamental rights of those detainees.[41]

4. Detention in times of non-international armed conflict

The problem in NIAC is that neither Common Article 3 nor AP II clarifies for which reasons and by which procedures a person may be detained.

It is complicated to argue that standards in IHL on detention take precedence as *lex specialis* over human rights detention standards in NIAC, when IHL is silent on grounds and procedures for detention in non-international armed conflict.

This problem can hardly be remedied by reference to customary international law, as there is no general agreement as to which detention and review standards form part of customary international law applicable in NIAC. In this regard, it may be noted that the ICRC Study on Customary International Law from 2005, to a large extent, seems to perceive IHRL standards of detention as an expression of customary international law in NIAC.[42] This is, however, a view that is probably not shared by all commentators. Furthermore, many states have traditionally denied the existence of a NIAC on its territory, something which makes it difficult to argue in favour of applying IHL standards as *lex specials* or just as a complementary source to the applicable human rights standards.

Four possible options for remedying this situation and filling the lack of international detention and review standards in NIAC may be identified.

1. First, could HRL detention standards be perceived as *lex specialis* in NIAC? It could furthermore be discussed whether the detention standards known from IAC should be applied in NIAC by analogy or

as part of customary international law. This could in principle happen in two ways (b) and (c).

2. Detention standards from Geneva Convention III concerning POWs could be applied. When discussing the application of IAC standards in NIAC, reference is most often made to the standards in Geneva Convention III for combatants. If applied to NIAC, this would have as a consequence that persons participating in the hostilities could be detained for security reasons for the duration of the hostilities without any right to review. As there is no distinction between combatants and civilians in NIAC, however, it could just as well be argued that the relevant standards from IAC that should be applied in NIAC are the detention standards from Geneva Convention IV.
3. Detention standards from Geneva Convention IV concerning civilians could be applied.
4. And finally, it may be discussed if one should apply detention standards from IHL and IHRL in parallel.

Let us take a brief look at these four possible options.

4.1 *Human rights detention standards?*

From a strictly formal legal point of view, it seems logical to argue that IHRL standards on review of detention must function as *lex specialis* in NIAC since IHL is silent on reasons for and review of detention. This view has apparently been adopted by a number of national courts which have applied IHRL detention standards, and not standards from IHL, during NIAC. For example, the UK House of Lords in the *Al-Jedda* case from 2007 only assessed the British forces' detention of Al-Jedda in Iraq, during periods undoubtedly amounting to a NIAC, on the basis of the review standards in Article 5 of the ECHR, and not on the basis of the detention standards in IHL.[43] The ECtHR has likewise, in a number of cases where there undoubtedly existed a NIAC, applied the detention review standards from Article 5 of the ECHR, and has not taken IHL detention standards into consideration.[44]

Finally, as a last example of applying human rights detention review standards during times of NIAC, the Danish force' detention of persons in Afghanistan may be mentioned. Danish forces in Afghanistan are authorised to arrest and detain persons in Afghanistan if it is necessary, inter alia, for self-defence or for the protection of ISAF forces. When Danish forces detain a person in Afghanistan, the detainee is first photographed and informed of the reasons for arrest and his rights. As Danish forces have no prison or holding facilities in Afghanistan, the person must be transferred within twenty-four hours to the British holding facility for further questioning and interrogation. Within ninety-six hours, the detained person must be either be released or transferred by Danish forces to Afghan authorities and brought before a court. If there is sufficient evidence to raise charges against the person, he is detained on remand. If there is not enough evidence to start a criminal case against the person, he will be released.[45]

Thus, security detention, as possible according to standards in international humanitarian law, is not used. The detained person is offered a court review, as required by human rights instruments (and national law), and released if there is no basis for starting a criminal case against the person.

Applying HRL detention review standards in NIAC, however, is not without problems. First, it can be questioned if it is realistic to expect that states in the midst of an armed conflict will be able – and willing – to bring detained person before a court without delay. Secondly, there is no general consensus among states as to whether states are bound by human rights obligations when they are acting outside their own territory.[46] Thirdly, it must be kept in mind that human rights standards, including detention review standards, only bind state actors. Non-state actors are not bound by human rights obligations. On the contrary, IHL standards bind both state actors and non-state actors in NIAC.

The consequence of applying HRL detention review standards could lead to an imbalance between the parties to the NIAC – between state actors and non-state actors.[47] Detention by non-state armed groups would be unregulated. If a soldier from a state's armed forces were detained by a non-state armed group, he would *not* have the right under international law to a court review of the detention; whereas a detained fighter from a non-state armed group would have the right to such a review. To remedy this situation, it has been proposed to apply IHRL and IHL standards on detention in parallel, which I will come back to later.

To sum up, it is not unproblematic to apply HRL detention standards as *lex specialis* in NIAC. Another option could be to apply the detention standards from GC III.

4.2 Detention standards from Geneva Convention III concerning combatants

The consequence of applying GC III detention standards would be that participants in hostilities could be detained without any form of review for the duration of the non-international armed conflict. This may also give rise to certain problems.

First, as is well known, there is no distinction between combatants and civilians in NIAC, and consequently there are also no criteria (as there are in IAC) for determining who is a combatant. Thus, it is particularly difficult in NIAC to determine who is a fighter and thus who may be detained. Such a determination must be based on an individual assessment.

Secondly, it is difficult in NIAC to determine when the armed conflict begins and ends. It is easier in IAC where there are two states parties to the conflict and where the conflict may end with a cease-fire or surrender.

Thirdly, it could also be mentioned that in IAC, another state party would have a direct interest in protecting, and therefore make a greater effort to protect both combatants from its own armed forces and civilians who have been detained by the enemy power. But in NIAC, no other state would have a direct interest in protecting detained fighters. All in all, there is a risk that this might lead to a misuse of power and to protracted detention of innocent civilians without any form of review.

Another possibility could be to apply review standards from GC IV applicable to civilians.

4.3 Detention standards from Geneva Convention IV concerning civilians

If we apply detention standards from GC IV, the consequence would be that participants in hostilities in a NIAC could only be detained if it can be established by the detaining power that they pose an imperative security threat and they would have a right to review of their detention. The detention must be reconsidered as soon as possible by an appropriate court or administrative board and thereafter periodically, and at least twice yearly. Also, there should be a right to appeal the decision on detention.

An example of this approach seems to be the detention standards applied by the multinational force in Iraq. In 2003, the Coalition Provisional Authority (CPA) in Iraq established the procedures under which the multinational force could detain individuals for security reasons:

> *Section 7: Coalition Force Security Internee Process*
>
> (1) Consistent with the Fourth Geneva Convention, the following standards will apply to all persons who are detained by Coalition Forces where necessary for imperative reasons of security (hereinafter 'security internees'):

(a) In accordance with Article 78 of the Fourth Geneva Convention, Coalition Forces shall, with the least possible delay, afford persons held as security internees the right of appeal against the decision to intern them.
(b) The decision to intern a person shall be reviewed not later than six months from the date of induction into an internment facility by a competent body established for the purpose by Coalition Forces.
(c) The operation, condition and standards of any internment facility established by Coalition Forces shall be in accordance with Section IV of the Fourth Geneva Convention.
(d) Access to internees shall be granted to official delegates of the International Committee of the Red Cross (ICRC).[48]

The security detention standard applicable for the multinational force in Iraq, including in situations of NIAC, appears to be based on detention standards from GC IV. The following possible problems could be mentioned. First, that it is unrealistic to require states to carry out review, even by an administrative body, in the midst of the fighting. Furthermore, it might be argued that such an administrative review, as required by GC IV, would undermine the clear standards in HRL which undoubtedly require court review without delay.

4.4 *Detention standards from IHL and IHRL*

It has been argued by some that IHL and IHRL detention standards should be applied in parallel in NIAC.[49] The consequence of this proposal would be that the review standards in GC IV requiring detention review by an administrative board would be applicable to non-state actors (and also to state actors), while HRL detention standard requiring court review would be applicable to state actors.

It is clearly an advantage that detention and review standards would be regulated not only for states who are bound by IHRL obligations, but also for non-state actors bound by IHL standards in NIAC, as there would then be no imbalance between the obligations of state and non-state actors. It must be questioned, however, whether the traditional reciprocity approach of IHL is workable in NIAC. There is a natural imbalance between a state party to an armed conflict and a non-state party, because the non-state party is accountable under criminal law for acts carried out against government forces.[50] Also, it can be questioned if such an approach is realistic; as already mentioned, it can be doubted whether it is realistic to expect states to be able, and willing, to provide court review for all detainees in NIAC. It may further be doubted whether it is realistic to expect non-state actors to be able and willing to establish a reliable administrative review of detained combatants from a state's armed forces.

To sum up, the detention standards in international armed conflicts and occupation are rather clear. Should there be a conflict between standards in IHL and IHRL, e.g., if the detention review should be undertaken by a proper court or an administrative body, then IHL standards will arguably in many situations be the applicable *lex specialis*, thereby taking precedence over IHRL standards. In non-international armed conflicts, the question is much more complicated because IHL is silent on the grounds and procedures for detention in NIAC. Four possible options for regulating detention in NIAC can be identified.

With regard to applicable detention standards in UN peace operations, such standards must be based on standards in IHL and IHRL, as argued in section 2 above. It must, however, be appreciated that UN forces often will operate in mixed and blurred situations ranging from IAC, occupation, NIAC, to peacetime situations, and a combination thereof. In addition, peace operations will often include troops from various nations with different detention standards and they will often operate under a vague and imprecise mandate from the UN Security Council.

Therefore, it must be questioned whether it is realistic to expect UN forces in UN peace operations to clarify and decide applicable detention standards on a case-by-case basis in each given operation and context.

5. Common minimum detention standards for UN peace forces

5.1 Context specific grounds and procedures for detention by UN forces

The traditional UN peace operations from the first operation in 1956[51] until the end of the Cold War are characterised as traditional peacekeeping operations, often establishing a buffer zone between the parties to the conflict and monitoring cease-fires. From the perspective of international law, these peace operations took place in a peacetime context, after the end of active hostilities in an international armed conflict – in a context regulated by international human rights law and national law. International humanitarian law, only being applicable in times of armed conflict, was thus not of major relevance to these missions.

After the end of the Cold War, the contexts in which UN peace operations are employed have changed. Now peace operations are often employed in internal rather than international conflicts, and they are often employed in situations where there is an ongoing armed conflict on the territory or on part of the territory. In parallel with this, the mandate of UN peace operations has been changed and broadened. Peace operations have been authorised by the UN Security Council under Chapter VII of the UN Charter to use a range of coercive measures, including the use of military force. There has been a change from traditional peacekeeping to *peace enforcement operations* with a more robust and muscular mandate.[52]

As a consequence of these changes in context and mandate of UN peace operations, such operations are today often carried out in complex and blurred situations, where there might be an ongoing NIAC on the territory where the peace support operation is being undertaken, or on certain parts of the territory, and where both IHL and IHRL standards are applicable and relevant.

Based on the discussion above, it can be argued that UN peace forces in contemporary UN peace operations, when detaining individuals, will need to assess each given concrete operation and the context and situation in which it is carried out in order first to clarify the applicable detention framework: IHL, IHRL, national law or a combination thereof, depending on whether the detention is carried out in an international armed conflict, an occupation, a non-international armed conflict or in a peacetime context. Furthermore, it must be clarified how an authorisation from the Security Council to the UN peace operation to use 'all necessary measures' will influence applicable detention standards in IHL, IHRL and national law.

If IHL is applicable to the situation, the UN force will then need to assess whether the detainee should be qualified as a combatant, a civilian taking direct part in hostilities or as a genuine civilian, and finally it must be assessed how the applicable standards interrelate, e.g., whether detention standards in IHL or IHRL should be perceived as *lex specialis* in the given situation.

It must be questioned if this is a satisfactory situation. First, it might be difficult to qualify the given conflict. Is it an IAC, occupation, NIAC or peacetime situation? In addition, states often disagree as to how to qualify a given conflict, and this is particularly problematic in UN peace operations comprising of a number of different states.

Secondly, there is no common agreement between states on which detention standards are applicable, particularly in NIACs, as discussed above.

Thirdly, UN forces might operate under a mandate from the UN Security Council authorising the use of 'all necessary measures'. This phrase is understood to imply that states may use military force in the given operation and, as a less severe measure, that states have the authority to detain individuals.[53] Nevertheless, the extent to which the authorisation to use force and detention from the UN Security Council will supersede other international obligations in IHL and IHRL, e.g., in relation to detention, is strongly debated, cf. Article 103 of the UN Charter.[54]

In my view, it is not tenable to argue, in particular in relation to UN peace operations assisting the state concerned with establishing security, rule of law, etc., that all international detention standards in IHL and IHRL are superseded by the UNSC mandate pursuant to Article 103 of the UN Charter, and that UN forces may detain individuals in peace operations for prolonged periods of time without any form of review, simply by referring to the authorisation from the Security Council to use 'all necessary measures'. The question has been discussed in a European context. In the UK House of Lords decision from 2007 in the *Al-Jedda* case, the majority of judges pragmatically argued that ECHR Article 5 detention rights could be 'qualified but not displaced' by a Security Council authorisation to 'use all necessary measures'.[55]

This pragmatic approach was, however, rejected by the Grand Chamber in the ECtHR decision in the *Al-Jedda* case from 2011. The Court clearly ruled out that an authorisation to use all necessary means from the Security Council could overrule (or even qualify) detention standards in Article 5 ECHR. Article 5 detention standards must be fully complied with.

Consequently, if a given UN peace force wants to detain an individual for security reasons, it is complicated to determine the precise grounds and procedures on which the individual may be detained. It is hardly feasible to expect that a given peace operation can decide applicable detention standards on an individualised case-by-case basis in each given operation and context. This is, for humanitarian and operation reasons, a clearly unsatisfactory situation, as discussed in section 1 above.

Against this background, it is relevant and pertinent to discuss whether it is possible to elaborate common minimum standards for detention by UN forces in peace operations. In 2007, the Danish Ministry of Foreign Affairs launched the so-called 'Copenhagen Process' together with a number of states and international organisations discussing and trying to elaborate a common detention framework in UN peace operations.[56]

5.2 *Establishment of common minimum standards on security detention in UN peace operations*

Common minimum standards or guidelines for detention by UN forces in peace operations should in principle be applicable in all situations, both during armed conflict and in peacetime situations.[57] The minimum standards should only apply to preventive security detention carried out by UN forces. Criminal detention authorised by courts in the troop-receiving state would normally be carried out in line with grounds and procedures established by national law.

It must be acknowledged, however, that it seems difficult to elaborate common detention standards that may be applicable in IAC, NIAC and peacetime situations. Preventive detention of combatants without any review is firmly established in times of IAC. However, for reasons discussed in section 4 above, prolonged detention without any form of review cannot be accepted in NIAC – particularly not by UN forces which often have a specific humanitarian and protective mandate – and is firmly ruled out in peacetime. As UN peace operations most often take place in NIAC and peacetime situations and only rarely in the context of an IAC (with Afghanistan, Iraq and Libya as significant exceptions) the best solution would probably be to exclude IAC from the scope of application of the common detention guidelines. Also one must take into consideration that there is no strong need for common detention standards in IAC, as detention standards in times of IAC are rather clear in IHL (except in relation to 'civilians taking direct part in hostilities' as discussed in section 3.1 above) and IHRL can only play a minor role (if any) in IAC in times of active hostilities.

Common minimum detention standards could possibly be annexed to Security Council resolutions authorising the use of 'all necessary measures', including detention by UN forces. This would provide guidance on security detention standards for states participating in UN peace operations.

As a point of departure, the minimum standards should establish, in line with Article 8(g) in the UN *Secretary-General's Bulletin on Observance of International Humanitarian Law* from 1999 (see section 2.2 above) that the ICRC and, if the states in question have ratified the UN Convention Against Torture, possibly also the so-called National Preventive Mechanism established under its Optional Protocol, should be promptly informed when UN forces detain a person in a peace operation and be allowed to visit the detained person.

Table 10.2 *Overview of detention review standards in IHL and IHRL*

	IHL (GC IV)	IHRL
Review body must be independent	Yes	Yes
Impartial	Yes	Yes
Power to release	Yes	Yes
Burden of proof on detaining power	Yes	Yes
Appeal	Yes	No
Timing first review	'Soon as possible'	'Without delay', 3 months too long
Timing subsequent review	At least every 6 months	Not specified

But this in itself is not sufficient protection. Some form of review of detention must be established in order to avoid prolonged and unjustified detention of 'innocent civilians'. This is, as discussed, particularly important and necessary in relation to multinational UN peace operations because states disagree on the applicable detention standards.

The minimum standards for detention by UN forces in peace operations must be established on the basis of existing detention standards in IHL and IHRL.

Both IHL and IHRL (although the latter in a more limited way) are open for preventive detention in certain emergency situations.[58] There are, however, differences, particularly with regard to the requirements for review of detention.

As outlined, the main difference between detention review standards in IHL (GC IV) and human rights instruments is whether the review is to be undertaken by an administrative body or by a court. But instead of focusing on whether it formally is a court or an administrative board that will undertake the review, it seems more constructive and relevant to focus on the content and scope of the various forms of review.

Table 10.2 provides an overview of applicable standards for review of detention in GC IV and in IHRL.

If we compare the requirements of review in IHL and IHRL instruments, there is not a major difference. And in some respects, the standards in IHL provide a better protection than the corresponding IHRL standard. This may be the situation in relation to the timing of the review. Just because a review is carried out by a court of law it is not necessarily a more properly conducted and better review than a review carried out by an administrative review board. It is no secret that in many parts of the world, the independence and efficiency of the judiciary can be seriously questioned.

Thus, it might be argued that the pertinent issue should not necessarily be whether the review is undertaken by a court or by an administrative board, but whether basic minimum procedural guarantees are complied with. In addition, it must be acknowledged from a practical point of view that it is probably more realistic to require UN peace forces to establish an administrative review of security detention in peace operations than a proper court review.

6. Conclusion

By way of conclusion, it is to be hoped that the so-called Copenhagen Process initiated by the Danish Ministry of Foreign Affairs will succeed in establishing some form of common minimum standards on detention for UN forces.[59] It is needed and necessary due to the uncertainty surrounding the applicable detention standards in UN peace operations, especially when considering the special protective and humanitarian mandate of UN peace forces. Also, from a humanitarian perspective it seems to be of utmost importance in order to avoid prolonged arbitrary detention that states reach agreement on when and under which procedures individuals may be detained in UN peace operations.

Common minimum standards could potentially establish that UN forces may detain individuals for security reasons as long as the detention is not arbitrary and that the ICRC and possibly the relevant National Protective Mechanism under the Optional Protocol to the UN Convention Against Torture should be promptly informed about the detention. Security detainees should have the right to review of their detention. The review should be carried out as soon as possible and thereafter on a regular basis. The review body must be independent and impartial; it should have the power to release detainees; the burden of proof must be on the detaining power; and, finally, appeal should be possible.

Notes

1 For more information on the ICRC initiative see www.icrc.org/eng/resources/documents/interview/2011/ihl-development-interview-2011-05-12.htm.

2 See section 5 below for further elaboration.

3 See, inter alia, B. Oswald, 'The law on military occupation: answering the challenges of detention during contemporary peace operations?'(2007) 8 *Melbourne*

Journal of International Law 311; see also B. Oswald, 'The treatment of detainees by peacekeepers: applying principles and standards at the point of detention' in R. Arnold (ed.), *Law Enforcement within the Framework of Peace Support Operations* (Martinus Nijhoff, 2008) 197–220; M. Sassòli, 'The international legal framework for stability operations: when may international forces attack and detain someone in Afghanistan' (2009) 39 *Israel Yearbook on Human Rights* 177; M.C. Waxman, 'United Nations detention operations in Afghanistan and the law of armed conflict' (2009) 39 *Israel Yearbook on Human Rights* 161; F. Naert, *Detention in Peace Operations: The Legal Framework and Main Categories of Detainees*, Institute for International Law Working Paper No. 94 (May 2006).

4 See discussion in section 5 below. For an overview of different types of peace operations see UN Department of Peacekeeping Operations/Department of Field Support, *United Nations Peacekeeping Operations, Principles and Guidelines*, 2008, available: http://pbpu.unlb.org/pbps/Library/Capstone_Doctrine_ENG.pdf.

5 See also A. Roberts and R. Guelff, *Documents of the Laws of War* (3rd ed, Oxford University Press, 2000) 721–5.

6 With regard to Afghanistan see UN SC Res. 1386 (2001), 20 December 2001, establishing an International Security Assistance Force to assist the Afghan Interim Authority in the maintenance of security, and a number of subsequent SC Resolutions extending the mandate of the Security Assistance Force. Concerning Iraq see UN SC Res. 1511 (2003), 16 October 2003, authorising a multinational force under unified command to contribute to the maintenance of security and stability in Iraq, and subsequent SC Resolutions extending the mandate of the multinational force.

7 See UN Press Release, 5 November 2009, available at www.un.org/apps/news/story.asp?NewsID=32857&Cr=peacekeeping&Cr1.

8 For examples of UN peace support operations that have detained individuals see Oswald, 'Treatment of detainees'.

9 See, inter alia, I. Österdahl and E. van Zadel, 'What will jus post bellum mean? Of new wine and old bottles' (2009) 14 *Journal of Conflict and Security Law* 175.

10 Criminal detention by UN peace forces authorised by the troop-receiving state should take place pursuant to grounds and procedures for detention established in national law.

11 *WHO Headquarters Agreement* [1980] ICJ Reports 73, para. 37.

12 It should be noted that it is disputed to what extent international organisations are bound by international customary law. See e.g., B. Fassbinder, *Targeted Sanctions and Due Process*, Study commissioned by the UN Office of Legal Affairs (20 March 2006) 19: 'At present, customary international law does not provide for sufficiently clear rules which would oblige international (intergovernmental) organizations to observe standards of due process *vis-à-vis* individuals. To the extent that rules of customary law exist with respect to such standards, they address obligations of States in the sphere of domestic law, and not obligations of international organizations.' To the contrary, see e.g., A. Reinisch, 'Developing human rights and humanitarian law accountability of the Security Council for the imposition of economic sanctions' (2001) 95 *AJIL* 858: 'The assumption that the UN member states could have succeeded in collectively "opting out" of customary international law and general principles of law by creating an international organization that would cease to be bound by those very obligations appears rather unconvincing.'

13 International Law Association, *Accountability of International Organisations*, Final Report, Berlin Conference (2004), 22.

14 UN Charter, Article 1(3). Likewise in Article 55 of the UN Charter.

15 See references *supra* note 12 and for further discussions C. Olivier, 'Human rights law and the international fight against terrorism: how do Security Council Resolutions impact on states' obligations under international human rights law? (revisiting Security Council Resolution 1373)' (2004) 73 *Nordic Journal of International Law* 399; G. Nystuen, 'Terrorbekjempelse og folkerettslige normkonflikter' (2003) 21 *Mennesker og Rettigheder* 2; M. Darrow and L. Arbour, 'The pillar of glass: human rights in the development operations of the United Nations' (2009) 103 *AJIL* 446 at 463; P.V. Kessing, 'Terrorbekæmpelse og menneskeret' (2009) *DJØF* 244.

16 It falls outside the scope of this chapter to discuss the question of attribution. See e.g., the much discussed and criticised judgment of the ECtHR in *Behrami* v. *France*, appl. no. 71412/01, *Saramati* v. *France*, appl. no. 78166/011, ECHR, Grand Chamber, Admissibility Decision, 2 May 2007. Nevertheless, it must be presumed that acts of UN forces in UN-controlled operations to a larger extent can be attributed to the United Nations, compared to acts of UN forces in UN-authorised but national/or alliance controlled operations.

17 *Secretary-General's Bulletin on Observance by United Nations Forces of International Humanitarian Law*, ST/SGB/1999/13, 6 August 1999, available at www.un.org/peace/st_sgb_1999_13.pdf.

18 The wording of Article 1 is ambiguous. First, the Article and the *Bulletin* cover both international and non-international armed conflicts, but the term 'combatant' is not used in non-international armed conflicts. Secondly, it is misleading that the word 'accordingly' is used. Peace-keeping forces using force in self-defence do not necessarily establish an armed conflict situation. For further discussion of the *Bulletin* see Naert, *Detention*. See also D. Shraga, 'The Secretary-General's Bulletin on the Observance by UN Forces of International Humanitarian Law, a decade later' (2009) *Israel Yearbook on Human Rights* 357.

19 *UN Peacekeeping Operations, Principles and Guidelines*, *supra* note 4, 14.

20 See UN Security Council Res., S/Res/1890 (2009), 8 October 2009. Likewise, although only explicitly mentioning IHL, in UN SC Resolutions authorising operations in Iraq, e.g., SC Res. 1723 (2006): '*Affirming* the importance for all forces promoting the maintenance of security and stability in Iraq to act in accordance with international law, including obligations under international humanitarian law, and to cooperate with the relevant international organizations, and *welcoming* their commitments in this regard'

21 *Al-Jedda* v. *United Kingdom*, ECtHR 7 July 2011, para. 102.

22 See J.S. Pictet, *Commentary to the IV Geneva Convention* (ICRC, 1958) commentary to Article 6, 60: 'The word "occupation", as used in the Article, has a wider meaning than it has in Article 42 of the Regulations annexed to the Fourth Hague Convention of 1907. So far as individuals are concerned, the application of the Fourth Geneva Convention does not depend upon the existence of a state of occupation within the meaning of the Article 42 referred to above. The relations between the civilian population of a territory and troops advancing into that territory, whether fighting or not, are governed by the present Convention. There is no intermediate period between what might be termed the invasion phase and the inauguration of a stable regime of occupation. Even a patrol which penetrates into enemy territory without

any intention of staying there must respect the Conventions in its dealings with the civilians it meets.'

23 See e.g., K. Dörmann, *Expert Meeting on the Supervision of the Lawfulness of Detention During Armed Conflict* (24–25 June 2004) 11, where it is stated that such a broad interpretation of 'occupation' is not supported in most national military manuals.

24 See, for a similar distinction, R. Goodman, 'The detention of civilians in armed conflict' (2009) 103 *AJIL* 1 at 5.

25 On the definition of indirect participation, see also ICRC *Interpretative Guidance on the Notion of Direct Participation in Hostilities* (May 2009) in which it is stated at p. 53: 'Therefore, individual conduct that merely builds up or maintains the capacity of a party to harm its adversary, or which otherwise only indirectly causes harm, is excluded from the concept of direct participation in hostilities. For example, ... providing [a party] with supplies and services (such as electricity, fuel, construction material, finances and financial services) would have a potentially important, but still indirect, impact on the military capacity or operations of that party.' See also at 54: 'For example, the financing or production of weapons and the provision of food to the armed forces may be indispensable, but not directly causal, to the subsequent infliction of harm.'

26 *ICRC Commentary to GC IV*, 258.

27 See likewise *A and B* v. *State of Israel*, Supreme Court of Israel, 11 June 2008, para. 18.

28 ICTY, *Prosecutor v. Mucić* (IT-96–21), ICTY Trial Chamber II, 16 November 1998, para. 577.

29 *ICRC Commentary to GC IV*, 260.

30 *Prosecutor v. Delalić et al.* (IT-96–21-T), ICTY, 16 November 1998, 329.

31 ICRC, *Interpretative Guidance on the Notion of Direct Participation in Hostilities* (May 2009). It should be noted that some states have expressed reservations about certain aspects of the interpretive guidance. For a discussion of the guidance paper, see D. Akande, 'Clearing the fog of war? The ICRC's Interpretive Guidance on Direct Participation in Hostilities' (2010) 59 *ICLQ* 180.

32 ICRC, *Intrepretative Guidance*, 16, where it is further stated that 'In order to qualify as direct participation in hostilities, a specific act must meet the following cumulative criteria: (1) The act must be likely to adversely affect the military operations or military capacity of a party to an armed conflict or, alternatively, to inflict death, injury, or destruction on persons or objects protected against direct attack (threshold of harm), and (2) There must be a direct causal link between the act and the harm likely to result either from that act, or from a coordinated military operation of which that act constitutes an integral part (direct causation), and (3) The act must be specifically designed to directly cause the required threshold of harm in support of a party to the conflict and to the detriment of another (belligerent nexus).'

33 *Ibid.* 70.

34 UN Human Rights Committee, General Comment No. 08, *Right to Liberty and Security of Persons (Art. 9)*, (30 June 1982) para. 4.

35 See e.g., the ECtHR Grand Chamber decision in the *Al-Jedda* case from 2011, *supra* note 21, paras. 99–100: 'The text of Article 5 makes it clear that the guarantees it contains apply to "everyone". Sub-paragraphs (a) to (f) of Article 5 § 1 contain an exhaustive list of permissible grounds on which persons may be deprived of their liberty. No deprivation of liberty will be compatible with Article 5 § 1 unless it falls

within one of those grounds … It has long been established that the list of grounds of permissible detention in Article 5 § 1 does not include internment or preventive detention where there is no intention to bring criminal charges within a reasonable time.'

36 *Supra* note 34.

37 *Antti Vuolanne* v. *Finland*, Communication No. 265/1987, UN Human Rights Committee, UN doc. supp. no. 40 A/44/40 (2 May 1989) 311, para. 9.6.

38 A problem arises, as mentioned, in relation to the European Convention on Human Rights, which does not provide for preventive detention for security reasons.

39 Contrary in the ECtHR's judgment in the *Al-Jedda* case. The case concerned the United Kingdom's detention of an individual in Iraq from October 2004 until December 2007 in a period where the United Kingdom first was an occupying power and later became involved in a NIAC. Regrettably, the ECtHR did not take IHL detention standards (which permit preventive detention as described in section 3.1 above) into consideration or interpreted Article 5 of the ECHR in the context of exigencies of the situation and the more liberal and undoubtedly applicable detention standards in IHL. The Court strictly assessed the case on the basis of ECHR Article 5 which rules out preventive detention. The Court found that the United Kingdom had violated Article 5 and awarded the detainee EUR 25,000 in compensation.

40 ILC Report, 58th session, 2006, UN doc. A/61/10, para. 2S1(6).

41 IACHR, *Report on Terrorism and Human Rights*, OEA/Ser. L/VII.116, Doc. 5 rev. 1. corr (22 October 2002) para. 146. See also more recently IACHR, *Inter-State Petition, Ecuador–Colombia*, Report No. 112/10 (21 October 2010) para. 113–126, where the Commission in a situation of international armed conflict interpreted standards in the American Convention on Human Rights in the light of applicable standards in IHL.

42 J.-M. Henckaerts and L. Doswald-Beck (eds.) *Customary International Humanitarian Law* (Cambridge University Press, 2005) 428–57.

43 *R (on the application of Al-Jedda) (FC)* v. *Secretary of State for Defence (Respondent)*, Session 2007–08 [2007] UKHL 58, 12 December 2007.

44 See e.g., *Bazorkina* v. *Russia*, appl. no. 69481/01, ECtHR, 27 July 2006.

45 Danish Defence Command, Power point description of detention by Danish forces operating in Afghanistan, on file with the author.

46 There seems to be an emerging consensus that states are bound by IHRL obligations when they are acting extra-territorially, to the extent that they exercise effective control over territory or authority and control over persons. This view, however, is not shared by all states. The United States and Israel have consistently held that IHRL obligations only bind states on their own territory and not when they are acting extra-territorially.

47 See M. Sassòli and L.M. Olson, 'The relationship between international humanitarian and human rights law where it matters: admissible killing and internment of fighters in non-international armed conflicts' (2009) 871 *International Review of the Red Cross* 599.

48 From CPA Memorandum No. 3 of 18 June 2003 entitled 'Criminal Procedures'. Article 6 in the Memorandum contains a provision on criminal detention authorised by Iraqi courts. The Memorandum and the Articles are reproduced in ECtHR, *Al-Saadoon and Mufdhi* v. *United Kingdom*, appl. no. 61498/08, ECHR, 30 June 2009, para. 5.

49 Sassòli and Olson, 'Relationship', 599–627. See also L.M. Olson, 'Practical challenges of implementing the complimentarity between international humanitarian law and human rights law – demonstrated by the Procedural Regulation of Internment in Non-International Armed Conflict' (2007) 40 *Case W Res J Int'l L* 437.

50 Human Rights Council, *Report of the OHCHR on the Outcome of the Expert Consultation on the Issue of Protecting the Human Rights of Civilians in Armed Conflict*, A/HRC/11/31, 2 June 2009, para. 24: 'In non-international armed conflicts, the traditional reciprocity approach of international humanitarian law was unworkable. It was underscored that there was a natural imbalance between a State party to an armed conflict and a non-State party, because the latter was accountable under criminal law for acts carried out against Government forces. Thus, since the reciprocity approach would be hardly acceptable in the context of non-international armed conflicts, the better paradigm to apply was that of human rights law.'

51 UNEF, the First United Nations Emergency Force, November 1956. UNEF I was established to secure and supervise the cessation of hostilities, including the withdrawal of the armed forces of France, Israel and the United Kingdom from Egyptian territory and, after the withdrawal, to serve as a buffer between the Egyptian and Israeli forces and to provide impartial supervision of the cease-fire. See www.un.org/Depts/dpko/dpko/co_mission/unefi.htm.

52 See B. Kondoch, 'Human rights law and the UN peace operations in post-conflict situations' in N.D. White and D. Klassen (eds.), *The UN, Human Rights and Post-conflict Situations* (Manchester University Press, 2005) 19–41.

53 See e.g., UNSC Res. 1546 (2006) on Iraq and UNSC Res. 1890 (2009) on Afghanistan, both authorising the use of 'all necessary measures'.

54 See references *supra* note 15 and P.V. Kessing, 'Terrorbekæmpelse', 252–278 with further references.

55 *Al-Jedda* case, *supra* note 21. Lord Bingham (supported by all other judges except Lord Roger of Earlsferry) proposed to reconcile the conflict in the following way, para. 39: 'The UK may lawfully, where it is necessary for imperative reasons of security, exercise the power to detain authorized by UNSC Res. 1546 and successive resolutions, but must ensure that the detainee's rights under Article 5 [in the ECHR] are *not infringed to any greater extent than is inherent in such detention*' (emphasis added). See also Baroness Hale of Richmond, para. 126: 'The right is qualified but not displaced. The right is qualified only to the extent required or authorised by the resolution. What remains of it thereafter must be observed. This may have both substantive and procedural consequences.'

56 For more information, see T. Winkler, '*The Copenhagen Process on the Handling of Detainees in International Military Operations*', Presentation at XXXIst San Remo Roundtable Meeting, September 2008; Ministry of Foreign Affairs of Denmark, Legal Department, '*The Copenhagen Process on the Handling of Detainees in International Military Operations*', *Military Law Review*, December 2007; T. Winkler, 'The Copenhagen Process on Detainees: a necessity' (2010) 78 *Nordic Journal of International Law* 489.

57 For the establishment of common detention standards in armed conflict and peacetime not only applicable for UN peace operations, see J. Pejić, 'Procedural principles and safeguards for internment/administrative detention in armed conflict and other situations of violence', (2005) 87(858) *International Review of the Red Cross* 375.

58 Problems arise as discussed previously in relation to ECHR Article 5. In the ECtHR Grand Chamber judgment in the *Al-Jedda* case from 2011, the Court declined to interpret Article 5 in the context of Article 103 or applicable IHL standards allowing preventive detention, but squarely ruled out that preventive detention is possible under Article 5. This might make it difficult for European states to participate in UN peace operations where they need to be able to detain individuals for preventive reasons.

59 See *supra* note 56 for a description of the initiative.

11

Humanity and the discourse of legality

RIKKE ISHØY

Denmark takes pride in being a society based on the rule of law; a country which supports the development of the international legal system, and works internationally to further respect for human rights and international humanitarian law (IHL). In the Danish political discourse, as well as that of the armed forces, support for IHL features prominently. But have we, when war becomes a question of law, removed ourselves from the political responsibility and moral implications of killing?

This chapter discusses recent Danish responses to questions of IHL, and whether our good intentions to respect the law have changed the way we discuss war.

1. War and law

In November 2008, David Kennedy, Professor of Law at Harvard Law School and Director of the Institute for Global Law and Policy, visited Denmark to participate in a Conference on War and Law arranged by the Danish Institute for Military Studies.[1] In an interview with Danish national radio, he commented on the relationship between the two:

> In the Iraq war, there were many accounts of soldiers who would come back from the battlefield quite upset that they had killed civilians, or that they felt that civilian deaths were part of what they were responsible for. And then, whether they talked to their religious leaders, to their military officers or to their psychological counsellors they were very often counselled that what they had done was proportional, was within the legal fabric and that they therefore should not feel responsible for those deaths.
>
> There is something valuable also in the human experience of experiencing remorse when you've killed; of understanding the weight of the decision to take another life and the legal vocabulary can be a way of reducing that experience.[2]

To demonstrate Kennedy's argument, the interviewer quoted an exchange between a member of the parliamentary opposition, Rune Lund, and the

Danish Minister of Foreign Affairs. Rune Lund had asked whether the Minster could confirm 'that the fact that Taliban members were hiding amongst civilians did not justify putting civilian lives at risk by using air bombardments in civilian areas'. In the brief written response, the Minister stated:

> IHL contains rules whereby a concrete military operation, which results in civilian casualties, can be legal.
>
> Whether this is the case in relation to a given military operation will depend on a concrete assessment. It follows from the fundamental IHL rule on military necessity that a precondition for the legality of such a military operation is that the expected concrete and direct military advantage of an operation must be considerably larger than the expected civilian casualties. Furthermore, if it is possible to choose between several military means to have the same military advantage, the means which can be expected to cause the least civilian casualties must be chosen.[3]

It is difficult to disagree with the Minster and his staff on legal grounds, quoting almost verbatim as he does Additional Protocol I to the Geneva Conventions;[4] but with the chosen wording, in its sobriety and correctness, the moral consequences or political responsibility for the acts committed are left unaddressed. Arguably, the exchange illustrates a political consensus that, where it is possible to argue that something is lawful, it is also morally right. To quote Kennedy further:

> We have often thought that [adopting legal rules] would be a way of limiting the kinds of means that the military would bring to bear in the conduct of warfare, and that sometimes does happen. But what we find more often is that people imagine that the conduct of their enemy was not proportional, but that whatever it was they did, was. So we get a situation where, rather than judging their own conduct, they judge that of the enemies, and experience themselves as legitimate in their activity. And when that happens, people on both sides of the battlefield lose the sense of scrutinising their own tactics to ensure that they are ethically or politically justified and use the legal terminology as a substitute.[5]

2. Limiting rules of engagement

In the mid-1990s, when Denmark first launched its current international political doctrine and its newfound willingness to use armed force as a means in its international engagements, only the most ardent internationalists were aware of the Geneva Conventions, the core IHL treaties. Now IHL has become, if not a household subject, then at least regularly referenced in national discussions of Denmark's military engagements abroad. How does this legalisation relate to military engagements?

For years, the armed forces have (as they must according to the Conventions) taught IHL to their troops, and with deployments in the Balkans, Iraq and Afghanistan, theory has been being put to practical use. In operational terms, IHL is translated into rules of engagement (ROE) that are adapted to the specific context and determine when, where, and how force shall be used. ROE combine legal, political and tactical considerations. ROE, in turn, are condensed into 'soldier's cards' or 'officer's cards', which are handed out to each soldier. This is where fundamental humanitarian law rules of distinction, proportionality and military necessity are translated into the reality experienced by the individual on the ground.

At least judging from the general ROE in Iraq and Afghanistan, Danish armed forces have limited themselves beyond what legal doctrine strictly speaking requires. In Iraq, for example, according to the Danish armed forces officer's card, force could be used in the following instances:

> You can use necessary and proportional force, including lethal force to defend yourself, your unit and coalition forces against an attack or immediately impending attack. ...
>
> In a situation where you can legally use force, you are in any event only allowed to use the minimum force necessary to achieve your immediate objective, the execution of the task or in self-defence. Ensure, to the extent possible, that collateral damage is minimised.[6]

When considered against IHL's rules on conduct of hostility, it transpires that in the quoted ROE, based as they are on self-defence, the threshold for the use of armed force may in some situations be higher than what is permissible under IHL:

> As far as objects are concerned, IHL defines legitimate military objectives as: those objects which by their nature, location, purpose or use make an effective contribution to military action and whose total or partial destruction, capture or neutralization, in the circumstances ruling at the time, offers a definite military advantage.[7]

Accordingly, objects become legitimate military objectives as a consequence of the use made of them, whereas persons may be legitimate targets as a consequence of their status: a civilian is anyone who is not a combatant, and the civilian population as such, as well as individual civilians, may not be made the object of attack.[8] The protection afforded to civilians is only lost when and for so long as he or she decides to engage directly in hostilities.

The officer's card cited above, however, does not distinguish between situations where a soldier is faced with a combatant, a civilian engaging directly in hostilities, or an otherwise armed civilian. Obviously, unarmed civilians and other civilians taking no part in hostilities may never be directly attacked and supposedly would not pose a threat.[9] Conversely, there is no prohibition in IHL against attacking combatants, even if they are not directly engaged in hostilities at the time of the attack, and thus in the immediate situation do not pose a threat. There is furthermore no obligation to use minimum force against legitimate military targets beyond what is required to limit damage to civilian objects and individuals.

In Afghanistan, Danish armed forces are bound by ISAF (International Security Assisstance Force) rules of engagement, and similarly to Iraq, the general rule is that armed force can only be used in self-defence.[10] Besides that, ISAF troops operate with a set of offensive rules of engagement that allow for the use of armed force beside what is strictly required in self-defence. Nonetheless, the option to do so is strictly regulated and any use of force under the offensive rules of engagement must be previously approved at a higher level. It has been limited over the duration of the mission.

According to Nicholas Brace Olsen, Chief of Operations of Team Four of the Danish ISAF contingent in Afghanistan, Danish forces in Afghanistan will always be present during deliberate operations when they are involved in the execution.[11] According to Olsen: 'self-defence is a very good and flexible ROE. The self-defence ROE allow the soldiers to react in direct response to a given situation.' As an example, he mentions an occasion when a soldier called him from the field to ask if he could attack a person who he had been observing for some time and who he was convinced was a Taliban fighter. 'I told him that I couldn't tell him. The assessment has to be made by the soldier on the ground in the actual situation. He has to assess the threat and act accordingly.'

According to Olsen, the emphasis given to the protection of civilians is also viewed in terms of the consequences of the operation:

> In Afghanistan, operations are influence driven and non-kinetic operations – operations that do not depend on the use of firepower are extremely important. We are very focussed on the consequences our acts will have on the civilian population, and on what messages people, who we come into contact with, will pass on. In our military analysis, we work with what we call a centre of gravity. In Afghanistan, the civilian population is the centre of gravity.

Contrary to Kennedy's point that legal vocabulary has substituted ethical and political scrutiny, it appears that, in their adopted normative framework, the Danish armed forces attempt to tackle the consequences of their actions by limiting themselves beyond what is strictly required legally speaking. Thereby, they try to foresee the political consequences and ultimately boost their military impact, an acknowledgement of the basic lesson of counter-insurgency: military action must provide human security to the population rather than destroy the enemy.[12] In its wording, ISAF's tactical directive similarly reflects the shortcomings of a traditional definition of military victory:

> We must fight the insurgents, and will use the tools at our disposal to both defeat the enemy and protect our forces. But we will not win based on the amount of Taliban we kill, but instead on our ability to separate insurgents from the centre of gravity – the people. That means we must respect and protect the population from coercion and violence – and operate in a manner, which will win their support.
>
> This is different from conventional combat, and how we operate will determine the outcome more than traditional measures, like capture of terrain or attrition of enemy forces. We must avoid the trap of winning tactical victories – but suffering strategic defeats – by causing civilian casualties or excessive damage and thus alienating the people.
>
> While this is also a legal and a moral issue, it is an overarching operational issue – clear-eyed recognition that loss of popular support will be decisive to either side in this struggle. The Taliban cannot militarily defeat us – but we can defeat ourselves.[13]

Judging from public discussion, the Danish conscience struggles with the harsh realities of war, too. In April 2009, news that Danish soldiers had ambushed a group of Afghans who were in the process of recovering unexploded roadside bombs, which they allegedly wanted to use in new attacks, made headlines.[14] The Danish Minister of Defence commented:

> Ambushes by Danish soldiers contribute to saving lives and demoralise the enemy. Of course, it comes across as incredibly violent when I say this, and it may sound cynical. But war is violent, and part of being in an armed conflict is that you get shot at and that you will shoot at the enemy.[15]

As described in the news, the ambush was legitimate under IHL, but to Danish sentiments, it was evidently disturbing. Contrary to the Minister of Foreign Affairs, whose response to a parliamentary question was quoted above, the assessment of the Minister of Defence seemed to be that of a response aimed at the general public – he could not get away with a purely legalistic response.

The discussion of the reality and purpose of the Danish presence in Afghanistan arose again in 2010 after the release of the documentary 'Armadillo'. The documentary is based on Danish filmmaker Janus Metz Pedersen and photographer Lars Skree's six-month stay with the Danish forces at forward operating base Armadillo in Helmand. Its graphic description of battle scenes provoked both shock and furious debate: shock that this was the lethal reality of what had largely been explained by politicians as a reconstruction, peace-keeping mission, as well as a debate as to the meaningfulness of the military presence. In an opinion piece published in the newspaper *Jyllandsposten*, Minister of Defence Gitte Lillelund Bech responded by focusing on the 'illegal' methods used by the enemy and the results achieved by the Danish contingent – again with little mention of the brutality of the war, but a discourse of reconstruction and rebuilding.[16]

The Danes' fortunate remoteness from violence definitely shapes the way war is discussed and the tolerance towards its reality. On an anecdotal level, back in 2006 I was teaching an IHL course to members of the Danish Ministry of Foreign Affairs' International Humanitarian Service roster. During a discussion on direct participation in hostilities, a few participants had rather vocally objected to the fundamental rule protecting civilians against being attacked except where directly engaging in hostilities, arguing that in many countries, for example Afghanistan and Iraq, many males were armed at any given time, and therefore, it was to be understood, posed a threat, which made them military objectives. For the final lecture, I had invited a Danish army officer recently returned from Iraq. I urged the participants to ask him about the practicalities of implementing the discussed rule. No one 'took the bait' – with the young man in front of them, still sunburned from the field, they were acutely aware that they could not ask him to kill indiscriminately. The way we see 'the other' clashed with our perception of ourselves as peace-builders.

3. Bosnian crimes

Another place where IHL comes into contact with reality is in court. Danish courts have had three noticeable opportunities to examine IHL. The first was in 1995, when a Bosnian man was accused of twenty-five counts of serious violence, acquitted on twelve counts and ultimately sentenced to eight years in prison for the remaining thirteen counts, two of which had led to the death of the victims.[17] The acts of violence had been carried out against co-detainees at Dretelj Camp in Bosnia, where the accused, himself a detainee, had acted as guard.

The Geneva Conventions have not been directly implemented in Danish law and the Bosnian was not accused of war crimes or similar breaches of international law. Instead, he was accused of serious violence under the Danish Penal Code, articles 245 and 246. In its sentencing comments, the Supreme Court referred to the Geneva Conventions only with regard to the question of jurisdiction. The Danish Penal Code prescribes jurisdiction in Danish courts for crimes committed outside of Denmark, no matter the nationality of the perpetrator, if Denmark under international treaties *has an obligation to have jurisdiction*; hence the Court's reference to the Conventions and their Articles on universal jurisdiction.[18]

The Supreme Court noted first that most of the counts on which the Bosnian was accused were very serious acts of violence that had been committed under similar circumstances. Accordingly, the Court found that all counts fulfilled the Conventions' definition of grave breaches and it did not have to examine each count individually. This subsumption of all counts under the Conventions' Articles on grave breaches, because of the similar circumstances under which they were committed rather than the nature of the acts, may well be correct, but deserved more than just a cursory note.

The Court did not discuss whether the war in Bosnia was an international armed conflict according to Common Article 2 of the Geneva Conventions, nor whether the victims were protected under Article 4 of either Geneva Conventions III or IV.[19] These are issues that were not obvious, as is evident from the International Criminal Tribunal for the Former Yugoslavia's *Tadić* judgment, where in the appeal judgment, the Tribunal meticulously established that the war was international and the individuals concerned – also detainees (were protected persons) a landmark ruling which came to define the work of the Tribunal in the cases that followed.[20]

4. Handling detainees

It took a long time before Danish courts eased into applying the European Convention on Human Rights, and references to other international instruments are still rare in Danish jurisprudence. During the ten years that followed the ruling discussed above, however, the courts seem to have become more comfortable with international law.[21] In 2006, in a case concerning the treatment of individuals captured by Danish forces in Iraq, a Danish captain and four sergeants were sentenced at Copenhagen City Court for serious neglect of their duty to treat persons deprived of liberty humanely, as specified under the Geneva Conventions and relevant Danish military regulations. The ruling was appealed, and five months later, the five were acquitted by the High Court. In particular, the City Court made reference to the Geneva Conventions and examined both its application and the status of protected persons.

The ruling reflects on the extent to which the armed forces, by the beginning of 2004, had prepared – or not prepared – for detainee handling. Notwithstanding the fact that it could have been foreseen that Danish troops in Iraq would end up holding individuals captive, even if only for a limited amount of time, it became obvious during the trial that training as well as the applicable regulations were outdated, in that both had been prepared during the Cold War, to cover the possibility of a take-over of Danish territory.[22] But perhaps it was first of all a lack of preparedness for the role we had taken upon ourselves in Iraq: that of the occupying power, 'the other', who could legitimately be opposed.

As for the other allied forces, detainee handling has presented Danish troops in Iraq and Afghanistan with a thorny dilemma. On the one hand, there is little interest in holding detainees for longer than strictly necessary, not least given the practical and political problems involved. On the other hand, handing over detainees to either local or coalition partners has presented its own difficulties and the Danish government has faced questioning and criticism for doing so, either because of outright allegations of ill-treatment by other parties or because of what can kindly be referred to as diverging interpretations of the law.[23]

In Afghanistan, it took years before Danish forces began handing over detainees to Afghan authorities, primarily because they were operating under British command and detainee handling was a British responsibility. Danish forces began their current mission in Helmand in spring 2006, but, according to the Ministry of Defence, the first time Denmark handed over detainees to Afghan authorities was on 5 June 2008, when two men were handed over to the National Directorate of Security in Lashkar Gar, the provincial capital of Helmand.[24]

A newspaper article from April 2009, with the attention-grabbing headline 'Danish soldiers take no prisoners in Afghanistan', argued that there is a tendency in Afghanistan to either kill the enemy or let him get away rather than to take prisoners due to the intensity of the hostilities and the dangers involved in doing so.[25] It also indicated that the Danish soldiers were reluctant to take prisoners because of the demanding procedures for detainee handling. This was (naturally, one might say) denied by a Danish colonel interviewed by another newspaper.[26] Danish forces have, however, been criticised for letting local partners, either the Iraqi or Afghan armed forces, arrest rather than have the trouble themselves, and implicitly ignoring allegations of ill-treatment by these troops. Moreover, following a report by Amnesty International on detainees transferred to Afghan detention by ISAF, the Danish Amnesty International chapter stressed Denmark's moral responsibility as a coalition partner for other ISAF forces' handling of detainees.[27]

In 2005, prior to ISAF taking over responsibility for the south of Afghanistan and the Danish troop deployment to Helmand, Danish and Afghan authorities signed a Memorandum of Understanding concerning the transfer of persons withheld by the Danish troops in Afghanistan to the Afghan authorities.[28] The agreement specifies that persons transferred by Danish forces may not be made subject to the death penalty and must be treated humanely. Similar agreements have been signed by other states in Afghanistan in other contexts, and have been duly criticised for having failed to prevent ill-treatment – rather, they have been referred to as legalistic talk with little basis in reality.[29] An obvious problematic issue is how to monitor compliance. In the case of the Danish-Afghan memorandum, it specifies that the Afghan Independent Human Rights Commission, as well as Danish forces, must have full access to detainees, and the International Committee of the Red Cross (ICRC) must be allowed to visit. Whether the Afghan Independent Human Rights Commission has the capacity to follow up individual cases in the hands of Afghan security forces is doubtful. Danish armed forces will also have difficulties in following up cases outside of their area of responsibility, and they have little experience with this type of rights monitoring. As for the ICRC, it operates under confidentiality and would only be able to share its findings with the detaining authorities, that is, the Afghans, not the Danes.

In the end, Danish authorities decided to 'do something' about what they perceived as an unclear legal framework and launched the Copenhagen Process, an international consultative process on the handling of detainees led by the Danish Ministry of Foreign Affairs.[30] Four years down the road, it is difficult to say where it is headed.

Detainee transfers raise the general question of what to do in situations where allies use legal terminology differently. In relation to the handing over of persons deprived of liberty to US forces by Danish special forces, the debate has been heated. Questions from the parliamentary opposition focused in on what they saw as divergences between Danish and US interpretations of the Geneva Conventions, which led the Danish government to respond with the following statement:

> The American legal interpretation first of all meant that the US would apply IHL, including the third Geneva Convention, in Afghanistan. As far as concerns the fact that the American legal interpretation meant that Al Qaida and Taliban fighters would not be given status as prisoners of war, it is noted that this interpretation of the Convention – *regardless that it could give rise to some uncertainty* – did not lead to infringement of the detainees' rights of such a character that from the Danish side it would be a reason not to hand over detainees to American forces.[31] (emphasis added)

David Kennedy, when interviewed in connection with his participation in the Danish Conference on War and Law, also had something to say about divergent interpretations of international treaties and the danger in thinking that they express a universal agreement:

> It can certainly make a difference to specify the rules of warfare very clearly and decide as a nation whether you sign up for this or sign up for that. It is important as a tool of communication not only to your enemies and to your allies but also to yourself and to your own troops about what is possible and permitted. But we shouldn't mistake that as a universal vocabulary of virtue.

In a ruling from 26 April 2011, the High Court concluded that the Afghan citizen Ghousoullah Tarin, who together with thirty other individuals was held by Danish special forces in Afghanistan in March 2002 and handed over to American forces, by whom he alleged that he was ill-treated, was not entitled to compensation by the Danish Ministry of Defence.[32] The Court did not challenge the claimant's allegations of ill-treatment, but found that at the time neither Danish soldiers nor the Ministry of Defence had knowledge or reasons to believe that prisoners handed over to American forces would not be treated humanely. Neither did the Court find that a lack of supervision of handed-over prisoners could lead to responsibility. The Court referred to a statement given by one of the soldiers involved in the hand-over, that it was presumed that the prisoners would be held only for a short time, and concludes that had it been known that the concerned would be held for longer, supervision would have been carried out. The ruling has been appealed to the Supreme Court.

5. *Fighters and Lovers*

In March 2009, the Danish Supreme Court issued its judgment in the *Fighters and Lovers* case.[33] The case concerned six persons, who had been accused of attempt to support groups that commit or intend to commit terrorist acts.[34] Via the company Fighters and Lovers, the six had participated in the sale of T-shirts allegedly with the intent to send some of the profits to PFLP (Popular Front for the Liberation of Palestine) and FARC (Fuerzas Armadas Revolucionarias de Colombia). All six were found guilty and given suspended sentences of between sixty days and six months.

In its judgment, the Court did not directly refer to IHL, let alone the Geneva Conventions, but the article on terrorism in the Danish Penal Code, which is based on the European Council Framework Decision on Combating Terrorism, is based on definitions of terrorism in times of armed conflict as well as peace:

> Any person who, by acting with the intent to frighten a population to a serious degree or to unlawfully coerce Danish or foreign public authorities or an international organisation to carry out or omit to carry out an act or to destabilise or destroy a country's or an international organisation's fundamental political, constitutional, financial or social structures, commits one or more of the following acts, when the act due to its nature or the context in which it is committed, can inflict on a country or an international organisation serious damage, shall be guilty of terrorism and liable to imprisonment for any term extending to life imprisonment.[35]

The first part, committing any of the acts that the article proceeds to list 'with the intent to frighten a population to a serious degree', makes reference to terrorism as defined in IHL.[36] Furthermore, the acts which the Court referred to in its argumentation for defining the PFLP and FARC as terrorist groups, such as killings of civilians and serious violence committed against civilians, or indiscriminate firing of grenades into civilians areas leading to the death of civilians, are violations of IHL when committed during armed conflict.

The defence of the accused submitted that FARC and PFLP had to be viewed as equivalent to state actors and that their acts therefore had to be judged based on the rules on war crimes. This is an interesting submission: if the acts were war crimes, it would mean that they were not necessarily terrorist acts – terrorism, when committed during armed conflict, is one amongst a number of war crimes and requires that the perpetrator had the specific intent to spread terror. It is also to some extent an incorrect submission: under international law, state actors as well as non-state actors can be guilty of war crimes, and the comparison of FARC and PFLP to state actors is therefore unnecessary.

In response, the Supreme Court simply stated that it did not find reason 'to compare the acts of FARC and PFLP with the use of force by States, ref. Article 11 of the European Council Framework Decision on Combating Terrorism'. This is a second mistake. According to Article 11:

> Actions by armed forces during periods of armed conflict, which are governed by international humanitarian law within the meaning of these terms under that law, and, inasmuch as they are governed by other rules of international law, actions by the armed forces of a State in the exercise of their official duties are not governed by this Framework Decision.

The omission of reference to *state* armed forces in the first part of the paragraph is intentional: IHL governs the acts of state actors as well as non-state actors during armed conflict, and according to Article 11, IHL, not the Framework Decision, governs their acts during armed conflict. Consequently, if the Supreme Court wanted to make reference to Article 11 of the Framework Decision, it should first have examined whether the situation in Colombia or Israel and the Occupied Territories were armed conflicts. If so, it should have examined whether PFLP and FARC were 'armed forces'. If the Court had found that to be the case, their acts would have been governed not by the Framework Decision, but IHL. The Court failed to make the distinction between the law applicable in peacetime and that applicable in times of armed conflict, and therefore wrongly applied Article 11 of the Framework Decision. Once again, the Court showed reluctance to directly apply international law.

6. Concluding remarks

Although Denmark has been an active contributor to peace-keeping missions across the world since the end of the Second World War, it is only since the Balkan Wars that Danish armed forces have engaged actively in hostilities. This willingness to engage militarily abroad came to define Denmark's response to the so-called global war on terror.

In recent decades, Danes have had the good fortune to live lives mostly removed from violence, and in public discourse Danish politicians have had to balance their audience's understandable abhorrence of violence with the military realities faced by Danish troops abroad. Sometimes it seems that this has led them to take the 'easy' way out – by choosing a legalistic response rife with references to international humanitarian law. Arguably, and somewhat self-contradictory, when this happens, the human dimension of the wars in which we have engaged is often left unaddressed.

The courts soldier on. Written judgments by Danish courts are notoriously short, with judges reluctant to apply international law. Copenhagen City Court seems to have been the boldest in this regard, whereas the higher courts largely prefer to avoid the subject. The Supreme Court seems to have been affected by the tunnel vision induced by the 'global war on terror', and moved swiftly to its conclusion in the *Fighters and Lovers* terror support case. Whether or not its conclusion is right, the argumentation certainly deserved a little more consideration.

The armed forces seem to have acknowledged the fact that in their counter-insurgency and anti-terrorist campaigns, a legalistic analysis of consequences cannot stand alone: that just because something can be designated as lawful does not mean that it is a good idea. Nonetheless, and not wanting to disregard the humanitarian considerations, it would be wrong to ignore the fact that the armed forces' decisions are ultimately guided by military considerations and objectives.

Notes

1 The Conference on Legal Arguments in Debates on War and Peace took place in Copenhagen on 6 November 2008 and was arranged by the Danish Institute for Military Studies, www.difms.dk.

2 Danish National Radio, P1, orienteering, 7 November 2008, www.dr.dk/P1/orientering/indslag/2008/11/07/153659.htm.

3 Response to s. 20 question: On civilian casualties in Helmand, author's translation, not quoted in full. The original response in Danish, 'Svar på § 20-spørgsmål: Om civile tab i Helmand', is available at www.ft.dk/dokumenter/tingdok.aspx?/samling/20061/spoergsmaal/S5738/index.htm.

4 See in particular Article 57 of Additional Protocol I to the Geneva Conventions.

5 See www.dr.dk/P1/orientering/indslag/2008/11/07/153659.htm.

6 Author's translation, quoted from the judgment U.2006.2927Ø, where the Danish High Court found a captain and four sergeants not guilty of charges of abuse of Iraqi detainees. For operational and security reasons, ROEs are usually confidential.

7 Article 52(2) of Additional Protocol I to the Geneva Conventions.

8 Article 50(1), and Article 51(2) of Additional Protocol I to the Geneva Conventions.

9 The discussion on when attacks against individuals, who do not qualify for combatant status under IHL but still participate in hostilities, are legal, i.e., what constitutes direct participation, is extensive. It is not the purpose of this chapter to discuss this issue, reference is made to Nils Meltzer, *Interpretative Guidance on the Notion of Direct Participation in Hostilities* (ICRC, 2009).

10 International Security Assistance Force (ISAF), the NATO commanded coalition in Afghanistan.

11 R. Ishøy, 'It should never be questioned' (interview with Nicholas Brace Olsen) (2009) 78 *Nordic Journal of International Law* 481.

12 Literature on counter-insurgency is prolific, see e.g., D. Kilcullen, *The Accidental Guerrilla: Fighting Small Wars in the Midst of a Big One* (C. Hurst & Co. Publishers Ltd, 2009).

13 ISAF tactical directive, 6 July 2009, available at www.nato.int/isaf/docu/official_texts/Tactical_Directive_090706.pdf.

14 'Soldater Skyder Taliban Uden Varsel [Soldiers shoot taliban without warning]', *Politiken*, 23 April 2009, (author's translation).

15 *Ibid.* Author's translation.

16 'En vigtig indsats og en vigtig film [An important mission and an important movie]', Gitte Lillelund Bech, Minister of Defence, *Jyllandsposten*, 1 June 2006, available at http://jp.dk/opinion/breve/article2084220.ece.

17 Danish Supreme Court judgment U.1995.838H.

18 Articles 129 and 130 of Geneva Convention III and Articles 146 and 147 of Geneva Conventions IV.

19 Article 4 of Geneva Convention III Relative to the Treatment of Prisoners of War defines who will be a prisoner of war; Article 4 of Geneva Convention IV Relative to the Protection of Civilian Persons in Time of War defines who will be 'protected persons' under the Convention.

20 IT-94-1-A, ICTY Appeals Chamber Judgment, 15 July 1999.

21 This budding willingness to consider international law as actionable in Danish courts, as well as the very real political consideration that a number of individuals who had sought asylum in Denmark were excluded from refugee status because of suspicion of involvement in international crimes, eventually led to the establishment of a special public prosecutor office for serious international crime.

22 After he stepped down in 2008, the Chief of Staff at the time came as close as one can to apologising to the captain, Annemette Hommel, for the armed forces' treatment of her, when in an interview he said that he regretted the case against her. 'Forsvarschefen fortryder sin behandling af Hommel [Chief of Staff regrets his treatment of Hommel]', *Berlingske Tidende*, 14 June 2008. Hommel was granted DKK 100,000 in damages in a civil case against the army command for having been sent home from Iraq because of the allegations without having been heard first. 'Hommel får 100.000 kroner i erstatning [Hommel gets 100,000 in compensation]', Danish Radio, 16 February 2007.

23 See e.g., 'Danmark vil føre tilsyn med afghanske fanger [Denmark will monitor Afghans detainees]', *Information*, 20 November 2007.

24 'Danmark overdrager afghanske fanger trods risiko for tortur [Denmark hands over Afghan detainees despite the risk of torture]', *Information*, 12 June 2008.

25 'Danske soldater tager ingen fanger i Afghanistan', *Politiken*, 24 April 2009.

26 'Danskerne tager ingen fanger i Helmand [The Danes Take no Prisoners in Helmand]', *Berlingske Tidende*, 23 April 2008.

27 'Detainees Transferred to Torture: ISAF Complicity?' (Amnesty International, 2007), available at www.amnesty.org/en/library/info/ASA11/011/2007. In response, the Danish Minister of Defence commented: 'I have met [Afghan President] Karzai and feel completely confident in that he has initiated an investigation and declared that

such behaviour will not be tolerated', 'Danmark vil føre tilsyn med afghanske fanger [Denmark will monitor Afghans detainees]', *Information*, 20 November 2007.

28 Memorandum of Understanding between the Ministry of Defence of the Islamic Republic of Afghanistan and the Ministry of Defense of the Kingdom of Denmark concerning the transfer of persons between the Danish contingent of the International Security Assistance Force and Afghan authorities, signed in Kabul on 8 June 2005, available at www.afghanistan.um.dk/NR/rdonlyres/97DB19DB-2A1D-4C6E-92A1–742671501049/0/DKAFGoverdragelsesaftale.pdf.

29 See e.g., the report 'Still at Risk', *Human Rights Watch*, 14 April 2005, available at www.hrw.org/en/reports/2005/04/14/still-risk.

30 See more at www.afghanistan.um.dk/NR/rdonlyres/E13E6FCF-C0D0–48E8-BC5C-BD172BA44786/0/CopenhagenProcess.pdf.

31 Redegørelse for faktuelle og retlige spørgsmål i tilknytning til danske styrkers tilbageholdelse og overladelse af personer i Afghanistan i 1. halvår 2002, Forsvarsministeriet, 13 December 2006 [Clarification of factual and legal questions related to the detention and hand over of persons in Afghanistan in the first six months of 2002, Ministry of Defence, 13 December 2006]. The original response in Danish is available at www.dr.dk/forbrug/portal/cms-assets/hemmeligkrig/Redegørelse_13122006.pdf.

32 'Afghaner-sag – afghansk statsborgers erstatningssag mod Forsvarsministeriet, [Afghan-case: Afghan citizen's compensation claims against the Ministry of Defence]', Eastern High Court Press Release, 26 April 2011, available at www.domstol.dk/oestrelandsret/nyheder/Pressemeddelelser/Pages/Afghaner-sag'-afghanskstatsborgerserstatningssagmodForsvarsministeriet.aspx. The complete ruling has not yet been released as the Supreme Court is still to examine whether documents and statements provided by authorities and witnesses can be made public. The reasoning behind the ruling, however, was quoted in its entirety in the press release.

33 Danish Supreme Court, U2009.1453.H.

34 Danish Penal Code, art. 114b.

35 Danish Penal Code, art. 114. Financing of terrorism, which is what the *Fighters and Lovers* case dealt with, is found in art. 114b.

36 See the ICTY's *Galić* judgment (IT-98–29-T), 5 December 2003.

12

Implementation in practice: 60 years of dissemination and other implementation efforts from a Norwegian perspective

ARNE WILLY DAHL AND CAMILLA GULDAHL COOPER

1. Introduction

This chapter intends to give an overview of the efforts made to implement and disseminate the law of armed conflict in Norway, from the ratification of the four 1949 Geneva Conventions to the present. While the chapter aims to give a general overview of implementation efforts, a particular emphasis will be placed on the extent to which references are made, or not made, to a 'principle of humanity' or humanitarian considerations, in order to see whether the perception or application of this principle has changed over time. By way of introduction, and to set the scene, an overview of the situation in Norway before the ratification of the 1949 Geneva Conventions will be included, before going on to examine what was done by way of implementation and dissemination of the Geneva Conventions in the period up until the 1970s when the Additional Protocols were negotiated and eventually adopted. We will then present the relevant aspects of the Norwegian participation at the conferences leading up to the adoption of the Protocols and how these Protocols were dealt with in the subsequent years. An overview of the current measures of implementation will also be presented, as will certain challenges. An emphasis will be placed on the training within the Norwegian armed forces, the group most likely to be in a position where they need to apply the law of armed conflict. Finally, we will attempt to draw some general conclusions on implementation efforts in Norway, and the influence a 'principle of humanity' may seem to have had on this.

2. Law of armed conflict in Norway before the 1949 Geneva Conventions

Although the focus of this chapter will be on the efforts made in Norway to implement the 1949 Geneva Conventions and later instruments, earlier implementation efforts will also briefly be considered in order to provide a historical perspective. As has been seen in some of the previous chapters, such as those of Lauri Hannikainen, Chapter 7 and Sigrid Redse Johansen, Chapter 8, there is no doubt that certain implementation efforts had been taking place even before the 1949 Geneva Conventions entered into force, both in Norway and other countries. As an example of Norwegian practice during this period, we would refer to the *Norwegian Soldier's Handbook* (*Norges soldathåndbok*) published in 1920.[1] Having been published so shortly after the 1907 Hague Convention IV respecting the Laws and Customs of War on Land and its annex, the Regulations concerning the Laws and Customs of War on Land, one would perhaps expect that a reference similar to that of the Martens Clause to a 'principle of humanity' would be included in the Handbook. However, no such reference could be found, nor were there any appeals to compassion. What was appealed to, however, was the soldier's own sense of dignity. For instance, after having called on the soldier to show bravery and provided good advice on how to defeat the enemy, the book provides some instructions on how to behave towards a beaten enemy:

> For a soldier it is dishonourable to show cruelty against enemy soldiers or to exercise violence against a defenceless enemy. It is for this reason also forbidden.
>
> When an enemy throws away his weapons and by words or signs indicates that he surrenders, he shall be spared and taken prisoner.
>
> An enemy who is taken by surprise while sleeping, must not be killed, but shall be taken prisoner.
>
> Violence must not be exercised against prisoners of war; they shall be treated with the respect they are entitled to according to rank. As soon as possible they shall be handed over to the officer in charge. Until then, the captive is obliged to obey his captor.

There were also some instructions on how a soldier should behave towards the wounded and sick, which again focused on the soldier's honour rather than humanitarian constraints:

> To shoot at sick and wounded persons who are not carrying or using weapons, is dishonourable for a soldier and is therefore forbidden. Likewise, it is prohibited to shoot at, harm or disturb the enemy's medical personnel, marked with the distinctive sign of Geneva, his hospitals or dressing stations (marked with the flag of Geneva).

Finally, with regard to civilians, the Handbook simply states that:

> Peaceful citizens, as well as public or private property in the homeland or in enemy territory, shall be respected.

As these examples illustrate, even though there is no explicit reference to a 'principle of humanity' or even humanitarian considerations, it is clear that the result sought undoubtedly was that the soldiers should treat prisoners, wounded and sick, and civilians humanely. By stressing that '[a]n enemy who is taken by surprise while sleeping, must not be killed, but shall be taken prisoner', it may even be argued that the Handbook goes further than what would be demanded by a 'principle of humanity' today: a soldier is a lawful target even when he sleeps, although many would hold that he should be given an opportunity to surrender, if practicable. It is therefore clear that the Handbook reflects the humanitarian considerations implicit in the law of armed conflict, even if it does not refer to a 'principle of humanity' as such.

Another example of the influence of humanitarian considerations and the Martens Clause can be found in the trials from the aftermath of the Second World War. As was presented in the previous chapter by Johansen, the Norwegian Supreme Court used the Martens Clause as a basis for their decision to find the suspects criminally liable. As the Court normally adhered to a strict positivistic approach in its interpretation of law, it is interesting to see that 'the laws of humanity and dictates of public conscience' referred to in the Clause were considered to be of such fundamental importance that criminal responsibility could be inferred; especially when taking into consideration that the result of this finding was that the law was given retroactive effect, thereby violating another central, yet in this case, seemingly less important, principle, '*nullum crimen sine lege*'.

Finally, it should be mentioned that in the very year of the adoption of the four Geneva Conventions of 1949, the Army had issued printed translations of the 1907 Hague Convention IV respecting the Laws and Customs of War on Land and its annex, the Regulations concerning the Laws and Customs of War on Land, the 1929 Geneva Convention for the Amelioration of the Condition of Wounded and Sick in Armies in the Field and the 1929 Geneva Convention Relative to the Treatment of Prisoners of War,[2] thereby supplementing what could be found as regards instructions on basic principles for soldiers in Handbooks. This translation effort naturally made the rules and principles set out in those treaties and regulations more accessible for the soldiers, and is thus an important aspect in the general process of implementation of the law of armed conflict.

3. Implementation and dissemination 1949–1977

3.1 Legislation

The completion of the 1949 Geneva Conventions was a landmark event, and Norway was among the fifteen countries that signed the treaty at the end of the Conference on 12 August 1949.[3] Once the Conventions were ratified on the 3 August 1951, legislation was passed to make violations of the Conventions punishable. With the exception of this introduction of provisions making the violation of the Conventions a crime, however, it was not considered necessary to enact new legislation.[4]

The main provision to be introduced in order to make violations of the Conventions punishable was the Military Penal Code (Militær straffelov), section 108. According to this provision, a person may be sentenced to up to four years' imprisonment if he or she:

> violates or contributes to violate provisions given for the protection of persons or property by the Geneva Conventions of 12 August 1949 for the Amelioration of the Condition of the Wounded and Sick in Armed Forces in the Field; for the Amelioration of the Condition of Wounded, Sick and Shipwrecked Members of the Armed Forces at Sea; Relative to the Treatment of Prisoners of War, and Relative to the Protection of Civilian Persons in the Event of an Armed Conflict, unless the matter is covered by a more severe penal provision. (authors' translation)

The maximum sentence that can be given under section 108 is four years. According to the *travaux préparatoires*, this is because the provision is only intended to be subsidiary; the acts covered by section 108 were to a large extent already covered by pre-existing provisions, permitting harsher sentences to be given, and a new provision was thus not strictly necessary. For instance, the killing of prisoners of war would be sentenced under the provision of murder, and the taking of food from the civilian population could be punished as theft. It was still considered beneficial to include the provision in order to comply with the obligations under the Conventions to enact such legislation, thereby ensuring that no violations of the Conventions could go unpunished. Other factors were that the Norwegian Red Cross and the Judge Advocate General's office strongly encouraged the introduction of such provisions, and the fact that Norway's close neighbour Sweden had already introduced a similar provision.[5]

In addition to section 108, certain violations of the Geneva Conventions would also be covered by the pre-existing section 107. This provision made it punishable to use poison or any means of warfare prohibited by any international agreement which Norway had ratified against the enemy; to kill an enemy who has surrendered or is wounded, or to mutilate the dead.[6] It would thus be applicable to violations of the rules in the Geneva Conventions relating to these matters.

The implementation of the Conventions also resulted in another alteration to the Military Penal Code. The Conventions oblige states to punish those who violate the Conventions, regardless of nationality. The Military Penal Code, however, was only applicable to a defined group of persons, mainly persons connected to the armed forces. It was thus added that 'anyone' violating section 108 could be tried by a Norwegian court.[7] With regard to the place where the crime was committed, the law already included a provision stating that the law would apply extra-territorially, i.e., 'anywhere'.[8] In this way, by departing from the traditional requirements of nationality, country of residence, or any other relation with the prosecuting country, the legislation enabled Norway to apply a form of universal jurisdiction for violations of the Geneva Conventions.

3.2 Dissemination and training

In addition to penalising violations of the Conventions, efforts were made to translate the Conventions, thereby making them more accessible to Norwegian citizens. The Ministry of Foreign Affairs produced a Norwegian translation of the Conventions in 1951, included in the White Paper proposing their ratification.[9] The translation was later made available to the general public by the Norwegian Red Cross and the Armed Forces Medical Services. This was followed in 1962 by a comprehensive collection of treaties in Norwegian and original language (English or French) relevant to the Law of War, issued by the Ministry of Foreign Affairs and aimed at academic users.

Information about the Geneva Conventions was also included in military publications such as the *Army Soldier's Handbook* (*Håndbok for soldaten*). The 1957 version, for instance, includes a short synopsis of GC I, GC III and GC IV, and also the 1907 Hague Regulations concerning the Laws and Customs of War on Land.[10] The focus here is on the practical implications of the treaties for the soldiers, such as what information a prisoner of war is required to give, and acts which it is prohibited to carry out against civilians. Perhaps not surprisingly, considering that the book is a practical book for soldiers, no explicit reference is made to any of the principles, including the 'principle of humanity'.

Another implementation effort was the practical training given to officers and soldiers, particularly in the military police and the medical services. It seems, however, that the emphasis here was on the treatment of prisoners of war. From 1974, the training of officers was based on a book on the Law of War issued by the Armed Forces Medical Services.[11] The author, High Court Judge Odd Blomdal, served at that time as lecturer at the Military Academy in Oslo and later became Judge Advocate General. Judge Blomdal also developed a military correspondence course in 1977, with a supplementary course based on the Additional Protocols in 1979.

Blomdal's book was aimed at the soldiers and their use of the book in practice. Still, in his introduction, Blomdal argues that '[m]ore important than the concrete prohibitions are perhaps the general provisions which in wide terms prescribe or prohibit certain courses of actions'.[12] He then goes on to list what may be referred to as general principles of the laws of war:

> The inhabitants and the belligerents remain under the protection and the rule of the principles of the law of nations, the laws of humanity, and the dictates of the public conscience.
>
> The right of belligerents to adopt means of injuring the enemy is not unlimited.
>
> It is prohibited to make the civilian population the object of attack.
>
> Distinction must always be made between persons participating in the hostilities and the civilian population.[13]

Nevertheless, after making this reference to the importance of among others the laws of humanity, he goes on to argue that the weakness of such wide formulations is the lack of international organs which may determine whether these laws have been violated.[14] The remainder of the book is thus focused on the more specific rules set out in the relevant Conventions, although with the emphasis that in cases where no specific rule applies, the Martens Clause will prevent there being a so-called *lacuna*.

Finally, implementation is not only a matter of legislation and training, but also a matter of introducing regulations and administrative routines at lower levels, such as the management of postal services for prisoners of war. In 1959, the Norwegian Red Cross Society entered into an agreement with the Norwegian government on providing an official Information Bureau for prisoners of war and other protected persons who are in its power, pursuant to Article 122 GC III and Article 136 GC IV. This agreement was renewed in 2007. It should be mentioned that during the Second World War, the Norwegian Red Cross Society maintained such services on its own account.

3.3 Summary

In the period from the adoption of the four 1949 Geneva Conventions until the start of the negotiations of the 1977 Additional Protocols, the Norwegian implementation efforts with regard to the law of armed conflict are arguably characterised by pragmatism rather than idealism. The Conventions were translated, some new penal provisions were included, and the military introduced new books and training, but the focus was on the practical implications of the Conventions, not the underlying principles or values. References to humanitarian considerations or even a 'principle of humanity' are thus hard to find.

4. 1977 Additional Protocols and their aftermath

4.1 Negotiation and adoption of the Additional Protocols

In the Norwegian proposals at the conferences leading up to the adoption of the two Additional Protocols (APs) to the Geneva Conventions and in the report sent to the Norwegian Parliament,[15] perhaps the clearest references so far to an influence of humanitarian considerations may be found. The report argues that there are several aspects of modern warfare which have contributed to undermine the Geneva Conventions, therefore creating the need for new regulations. For instance, the combined effects of the development of guerrilla warfare and new technology, including aerial bombardment, have resulted in armed conflicts no longer being fought in certain geographical areas only; warfare has become increasingly mobile, with an element of surprise and thus unpredictability. As a result, civilians are increasingly affected. And when states participate in conflicts far from their own territory, thereby making the risk of harm to their own civilian population very small, the technologically superior states fighting guerrilla forces abroad may be inclined to show less respect to the local civilian population. An important consideration for states when agreeing to restrict their own freedom of action is the principle of reciprocity; but in this case the risk of the guerrilla forces being able to attack the opposing state's population is limited, and if it occurs, it will be seen as international terrorism – a crime, rather than an act of war.[16] Thus, the Norwegian representatives argued that there is a risk of the humanitarian considerations in the law of armed conflict being given less weight than they ought to, as there is little risk of retaliation. In their view, there was thus a need to strengthen the rules ensuring such humanitarian considerations. For instance, Norway proposed a prohibition on the use of certain weapons and weapon systems which may cause unnecessary suffering or indiscriminate effects, such as cluster bomb units, flechettes, small calibre high velocity ammunition, fuel-air explosives, booby traps, mines, and incendiary weapons. The Norwegian view was that there were 'particularly strong humanitarian objections to the use of such weapons and weapon systems' and that 'these humanitarian objections could not easily be ignored by reference to strategic considerations'.[17] The proposal did not, however, attract sufficient support,[18] although as current readers may be aware, many such prohibitions have now been introduced in separate regulations. What was achieved in 1977, on the other hand, was the inclusion of a reference to the Martens Clause – in Article 1(2) of AP I. The humanitarian considerations underlying the proposal to ban such weapons are therefore still included, even if it is in more general terms.

Another development after the Second World War is that armed conflicts increasingly take place within the territory of a state and are non-international. As the legal framework existing at the time mainly applied in international armed conflicts, there was a need to develop rules for such non-international armed conflicts as well. The ICRC proposal was to deal with these types of conflicts separately; however, Norway argued that only one new Protocol should be made, dealing with both types – 'the victims of war's need for protection would be identical regardless of the legal and political classifications'.[19] It would also ease the training of military personnel if the same rules applied in all conflicts. Furthermore, there was a concern that a Protocol on non-international armed conflicts would provide less protection for the victims of war than an international Protocol because states consider their treatment of own citizens to be a part of a state's internal affairs. Again, Norway did not manage to attract sufficient support for the position that all types of conflicts should be covered by the same Protocol, and hence two separate Protocols were made. In an attempt to secure the protection of as many victims of armed conflicts as possible, Norway then went on to propose that the definition of international armed conflicts should be as wide as possible, thereby making it more difficult to argue that certain groups are owed less protection because the conflict is not international. It was thus proposed that 'wars of liberation fought by national liberation movements demanding a right to self-determination, freedom and independence' ought to be considered international armed conflicts, even though they take place within one state.[20] A similar wording can now be found in Article 1(4) AP I. Again, the Norwegian argument was expressly based on humanitarian concerns.

It is clear then that Norway based its standpoint on the development of the law of armed conflict, not only on the potential strategic needs Norway may face, but also to a great extent on considerations of humanity; this, in some cases, even to the detriment of potential military and strategic needs. The main focus was on the widest possible protection of victims of war. A similar position is also reflected in later acts by Norway. For instance, Norway was among the first states to abolish anti-personnel mines and a diplomatic conference on an international ban on such weapons was organised in Norway in September 1997.[21] Similarly, with regard to the international ban on certain cluster munitions, Norway also played a considerable role.[22] It is not within the scope of this chapter to provide a detailed overview of the Norwegian role in the development of all Conventions prohibiting certain weapons. It suffices to say here that the total ban on such weapons is based clearly on humanitarian considerations; the strategic and operational needs are not considered sufficiently important to permit the weapons being used under any circumstances.

The ratification by Norway of the 1977 Additional Protocols on 14 December 1981 gave a new boost to the Norwegian implementation and dissemination activities. In addition to updating the penal legislation, the ratification of AP I meant, among other things that legal advisers must be made available to military commanders (Article 82 AP I).

4.2 *Legislative measures*

As mentioned above, section 108 of the Military Penal Code allows those who violate or contribute to violating the Geneva Conventions of 1949 to be sentenced up to four years' imprisonment. After the adoption of the Additional Protocols, this provision was merely expanded to cover the Additional Protocols as well, on the same terms. However, as the introductory provisions of the Code stipulate that its provisions apply 'in times of war',[23] it was also considered necessary to alter that provision by specifying that section 108 would apply when the conditions for the application of the Conventions and the Protocols respectively were met. This was considered particularly important with regard to violations of Additional Protocol II applicable to non-international armed conflicts.[24]

The above-mentioned section 107 was also altered as a result of the ratification of the two Protocols. The first half of the provision, regarding poison and unlawful means of warfare, was amended to refer to 'weapons or means of warfare which are prohibited by any of the international agreements Norway has entered, or who contributes thereto' (authors' translation). The second part of the old section 107, dealing, among other things with killing surrendered or wounded enemies, was repealed on the basis of the adoption of AP I, which deals with those issues, together with the expansion of section 108 to include violations of the Protocols, making that part of the provision superfluous.[25]

4.3 Legal advisers

It was initially decided that legal advice on the laws of war should be provided by the Judge Advocates, whose main role was to prosecute violations of the Military Penal Code. It was later found that the role of legal adviser should be separated from the role of military prosecutor, whose office is subordinate to the Ministry of Justice rather than the Ministry of Defence. This led to a new organisation of legal advisers from about 1992. Initially, they were mainly reservists, to be called upon on in the event of a mobilisation of the Armed Forces. Since around 2002, they have been supplanted by permanently employed lawyers in operational law in various parts of the armed forces, most of whom are trained officers. Furthermore, the Home Guard, which is based on a militia concept, has in the same period established a corps of legal advisers for the various Home Guard districts. These are barristers and other practising lawyers in peacetime who are being trained for Home Guard duties in the event of war or any other critical situation.

4.4 Literature

As is well known, the 1977 Additional Protocols were not just an update of the Geneva Conventions, but also contained a considerable amount of new treaty law. This led to the production of a new textbook in 1980 by Morten Ruud,[26] who had participated in the diplomatic conference and until recently was the Permanent Secretary of the Ministry of Justice. In his book, Ruud included a separate chapter on the Martens Clause. He stressed that the Clause 'must guide any interpretation of the international treaties on the laws of war'.[27] Furthermore, he went on to argue that:

> This is not, as is commonly the case in international preambles, an example of purely oratorical, but meaningless, formulations. The Clause makes it clear that the Conventions in themselves are not exhaustive, and equally important, it creates a binding principle of interpretation for applying the written rules: the Convention must not be interpreted

> antithetically … The texts must be interpreted in such a way that they fulfil the requirements of the public conscience. (authors' translation)[28]

In other words, the Martens Clause and the principles referred to in it are not important for what they say, but rather the impact they have on the interpretation of the existing rules. The vagueness of these principles therefore does not undermine their importance. Furthermore, Ruud argues, 'it is clear that the application of these principles may result in rules with a clear and defined content'.[29] The focus of the remainder of the book is thus on these clearly defined rules, resulting from the principles, rather than the principles themselves.

Ruud's book was for many years the backbone of military education in Norway, but in 2003, it was supplemented by a Handbook[30] written by one of the current authors, Arne Willy Dahl, who is the present Judge Advocate General. A second edition appeared in 2008.[31] The Handbook covers a wide range of topics relevant to the use of military power, including both *jus ad bellum* and *jus in bello,* peace operations, multinational operations, operational law, and implementation aspects. This book also makes a brief reference to the principles of the law of armed conflicts, but as in the book by Ruud, emphasis is placed on the rules themselves. In addition to emphasising that the rules are a more detailed expression of the principles, Dahl also stresses the importance of the principles in areas not covered by the law, or where the rules are less clear.[32]

4.5 Training

Training in the law of armed conflict has varied for different levels of education and for different branches. At the lower levels, it was intended that the law of armed conflict was to be taught by the soldier's closest superiors, however, in many cases these were assisted by the local military chaplains or by contracted lawyers. At the Military Academies, however, the training was carried out by permanently employed lawyers, in the case of the Navy and Army, or by contracted lawyers, in the case of the Air Force. Other training in the law of armed conflicts would be provided in accordance with needs, by available personnel. In addition, annual training courses in the law of armed conflict have been organised from 1983. Initially they were run at the Army's Military Academy, with the Judge Advocates as the main target audience, although it was increasingly offered to other members of the Armed Forces as well. The course was inspired by the courses held at the International Institute of Humanitarian Law in San Remo, Italy. Short theoretical sessions alternated with discussion in small groups of practical problems related to a scenario where Norway was invaded by an unspecified enemy. The courses have later been developed to reflect current operations.

4.6 *Summary*

After having focused mainly on the practical implications of the Geneva Conventions in the period after 1949, the negotiations for the Additional Protocols and the role played in later efforts to restrict the use of weapons illustrates that Norway increasingly emphasised the humanitarian values underlying the law of armed conflict. In an effort to ensure the greatest possible protection for the victims of war, Norway was willing to go further than many other states in sacrificing the ability to use certain means or methods, which in many circumstances could be seen as militarily or strategically beneficial. The scale balancing the humanitarian considerations and military necessity seems to have shifted somewhat, so as to make the former weigh more than was perhaps the case before. Although it is not possible to provide a definite explanation for this development, the fact that Norway has not seen an armed conflict on its territory, nor to any significant extent participated in any armed conflicts elsewhere, must clearly be taken into account. It is perhaps easier to restrict what the military may do if the prospect of their actually having to fight for survival is remote.

5. Current implementation of the laws of war

The Geneva Conventions and their Protocols require that their rules are disseminated and made known to all those who may be affected by them. Perhaps the most important aspect of this is the training of soldiers and officers within the armed forces. Nonetheless, other parts of society should also have knowledge of the rules, and to an increasing degree, are offered information and training in the law of armed conflict. This section aims to present a general overview of the relevant current activities, with an emphasis on the armed forces.

5.1 *Training and implementation within the armed forces*[33]

Norway practises compulsory military service for men over the age of eighteen, and voluntary service for women. Presently, approximately 10,000 persons are called in every year. During their compulsory year, the soldiers are given four hours of instruction in the law of armed conflict, and they must complete an electronic course, which includes a two-hour test.[34] This basic training focuses on the more practical application of the law of armed conflict and is limited to what is necessary to know at a lower level in the military system. For instance, it includes the basic principles, protected persons and objects, protective emblems, and means and methods of warfare. Those who choose to join the officer candidate school will be required to complete a second electronic course and will also be given further training in the subject. In addition to repeating what they have already learned, they are also taught, among other things, about the application of the law of armed conflict in complex systems, rules of engagement, the responsibility of the commander, enforcement of the rules, and repression of crimes. Again, the focus is mainly practical and on aspects that are most relevant to the soldiers' area of service, and the training therefore does not cover the principal questions of the law of armed conflict to a great degree.

At the Military Academies and at the Command and Staff College, officers are given further training in the practical application of the law of armed conflict suitable for their level of rank. In addition, they study the ethical dimensions of the law of armed conflict, the application of human rights law, and dilemmas relating to the application of the law of armed conflict. There is thus scope for discussion concerning the basic principles of the law of armed conflict, including humanity, although experience shows that in reality, the focus remains to a large extent on the operationalisation of these principles.

In addition to this, there are various forms of voluntary or ad hoc training. From 2008, all conscripts are offered a bachelor module in law, tailored for their needs. A textbook[35] has been written for this purpose, and a considerable part of this is the law of armed conflict. Parts of this textbook are also being used as curriculum, among other things, for the compulsory education of conscripts and for the teaching at the Command and Staff College. Although this voluntary module offered to conscripts requires a better understanding of the subject than the obligatory training at this level, and the module does specifically cover the basic principles, the focus remains on the practical application of these, as expressed in the rules set out in the relevant treaties. Personnel due to participate in international operations are also given extra training. In addition to redoing the two electronic courses and having a repetition of the basic rules, they are given a refresher of the basic principles of the applicable law of armed conflict, mission-specific training in rules of engagement and cases to illustrate the practical application of the law.

Finally, responsibility for the above-mentioned annual courses on the law of armed conflict now rests with the Command and Staff College. In recent years, this annual course has been aimed more towards the lower level officers who teach basic training in the law of armed conflicts for conscripts, civilians working with related areas, and officers in need of a repetition of the rules. As a result, and due to demand, the course has thus been supplemented with a more in-depth version for military lawyers.

A survey conducted by the Norwegian Red Cross Society in 2004 showed that the level of knowledge on the law of armed conflict among soldiers was not too impressive. As a result, several measures were introduced to improve the training in the armed forces. A follow-up survey in 2009 shows a clear improvement. There is, however, still need for further improvements.

As Norwegian forces are increasingly exposed to situations where an understanding of the law of armed conflict is required, through the participation in peace support operations both above and below the threshold of armed conflict, there has been an increased need to clarify how Norway interprets these rules. For instance, the Chief of Defence has created directives on acquisition and use of less lethal weapons and the international legal obligations relating to the medical services.[36] For similar reasons, it has been decided that Norway is to have a Manual of the law of armed conflict.[37] The project started in August 2009 after having been granted funding by the Ministry of Defence, and completion is expected within three years. The Manual will be aimed at the tactical and operational levels, and will thus mainly have a practical and operational perspective on the law of armed conflict. The basic principles, including the 'principle of humanity' or humanitarian considerations, will thus mainly be reflected through the concrete rules.

5.2 *Teaching outside the armed forces*

In addition to training and teaching within the armed forces, other groups of society are also taught about the law of armed conflict. For instance, the Police Academy introduced this subject as part of the curriculum for its students in the fall of 1992. The Norwegian Red Cross and its regional offices also play a significant role in educating the public about the Geneva Conventions and their Protocols. The society runs courses for its own members, and offers courses for other interested groups as well. A particular focus has been given to youth, with a textbook and exercise book on the topic having been distributed to all secondary schools in the country,[38] and youth from the Red Cross societies, in particular in Oslo, offering to teach about the law of armed conflict at schools and as part of the preparation for confirmation. Perhaps curiously, there is no focus on a 'principle of humanity' – again, the emphasis is on the practical application and implications of the rules.

5.3 *Translations of treaties*

The Norwegian Red Cross has continued to make an effort to ensure the distribution of the Conventions after the ratification of the 1977 Additional Protocols, issuing a translation of the Protocols together with the 1949 Geneva Conventions and the 1980 Conventional Weapons Convention in 1984.[39] A more comprehensive treaty collection in Norwegian (on CD-ROM) was issued by the Chief of Defence Headquarters in 2001.[40] In 2007, the Norwegian Red Cross published a new translation of the Geneva Conventions and Additional Protocols, correcting some errors in the previous translation, introducing more consistent terminology, as well as including certain human rights documents.[41]

5.4 *Committees*

In 1989, a Consultative Committee for International Law of War was tasked with coordinating the various implementations and disseminations. One of the first tasks was to provide answers to a questionnaire from the ICRC on national implementation measures. The Committee was very active until 1994, when it issued a report on its activities, but has been less visible since.

In 1998, the Ministry of Defence established an advisory committee for the review of new weapons, means or methods of warfare to fulfil its obligations under Article 36 AP I. The work of this committee is not public.

5.5 *Dealing with violations of the law of armed conflict*

Implementation of the law of IHL also has international aspects related to investigation and prosecution of war crimes committed by foreigners abroad when such persons take residence in Norway. Following an example set by Denmark, the office of the Director of Public Prosecutions conducted a study on how such matters should be handled and proposed a recommendation in September 2004. Following the recommendation, a war crimes investigation unit was established at the KRIPOS

(National Criminal Investigation Service) in January 2005, and a National Prosecution Service (Det nasjonale statsadvokatembetet) was set up as of August 2005.

New legislation on war crimes, crimes against humanity and genocide was passed on the 7 March 2008. Shortly thereafter, the first indictment since the aftermath of the Second World War was issued for war crimes and crimes against humanity committed by a Bosnian against Serbian civilians. The main focus of the case was on the unlawful internment of civilians. The sentence in the lower court was passed on 2 December 2008,[42] finding the accused guilty of war crimes, but not of crimes against humanity, but the case was appealed. Part of the appeal concerned the reluctance of the judge to apply the provisions regarding crimes against humanity to crimes perpetrated before the new legislation came into force, a decision which questioned the legality of the legislator's retroactive application of the law.[43] In its decision of 12 April 2010, the High Court also came to the conclusion that the retroactivity of the law was in breach of the principle of *nullum crimen sine lege* set out in section 97 of the Norwegian Constitution.[44] The Court stressed that the act in question had to have been a crime under Norwegian law at the time it was committed, not just under international law. The Court thus made it very clear that the decision in the much criticised *Klinge* case[45] from 1946, that being a crime under international law was sufficient, is no longer considered accurate.[46] While the relevant Norwegian crime of unlawful internment seeks to protect individuals' right to freedom of movement, the crime against humanity of unlawful internment is aimed at protecting the civilian population from widespread or systematic attacks. The object and purpose of the crimes are thus different, and as there was no crime in Norway at the time penalising such attacks on humanity, the crime against humanity provision of the new Penal Code could not be applied in this case.[47] The same acts were, however, considered to be war crimes. As the war crime of unlawful detention is very similar to the same crime in the Norwegian Penal Code, and the war crime issue in any case would have to be included in the consideration of seriousness of the crime under national law, the application of the new war crime article was not considered to violate the prohibition of retroactivity.[48]

In the final appeal to the Norwegian Supreme Court, the prohibition of retroactivity was interpreted in a more absolute manner. The majority of the Supreme Court concluded that the international crimes, i.e., war crimes, crimes against humanity and genocide, are equally stigmatising as they are all 'serious violations of international humanitarian law'.

Furthermore, being punished for these crimes is to such an extent more stigmatising and incriminating than the alternatives in the old Penal Code that they must be considered to be new crimes rather than a reformulation of existing crimes. Thus, their retrospective application violates the absolute prohibition on retroactivity in the Norwegian Constitution. The fact that the International Criminal Tribunal for Rwanda refused to transfer the *Bagragaza* case to Norway on the basis that he would only be prosecuted for 'ordinary crimes' was considered by the Court to support the conclusion that the international crimes are considerably more stigmatising, and that their application thus would be detrimental for the accused. The correct law to be applied was thus section 223 of the Penal Code of 1902 and not that on the international crimes introduced in the 2005 Penal Code.[49]

As for the sentence, this was initially set at five years, but was reduced to four years six months by the High Court. Interestingly, despite having concluded that applying the new law on international crimes retrospectively was a violation of the Constitution, the Supreme Court allowed the prosecution's claim that the sentence be increased. Nonetheless, while the prosecution asked for six years, the Supreme Court concluded that taking the seriousness of the acts into account, eight years was more appropriate, despite the fact that the crimes had been committed nineteen years before.[50]

On the face of it, the trial went some way to undermine the attempt by the Norwegian Parliament to make serious violations of the law of armed conflict and similarly serious crimes punishable under Norwegian law. From this point on, the new penal provisions can only be applied to acts committed after the law came into force in 2008. Nevertheless, the Supreme Court has proved that the system is both willing and able to punish such acts under the ordinary Penal Code, and that the seriousness of the crimes will be reflected in the sentencing. It also underlined the Supreme Court's role as a protector of the principle of legality. As Judge Møse points out, '[i]n our country, section 97 of the Constitution provides absolute protection in the area of criminal law, and this protection must be provided to all'[51] – even persons suspected of having committed war crimes and crimes against humanity.

In the context of dealing with violations of the law of armed conflict, it should finally be mentioned that the Norwegian Centre for Human Rights at the University of Oslo has been running a 'Legal Tools' programme since 2007. This programme is in support of the International Criminal Court (ICC) and other courts that have cases on war crimes, genocide or crimes against humanity. The programme is developing a database of legal sources relevant to such work, including both international and national legislation, as well as cases from all over the world. The programme has also played a role in developing a digital tool for organising the investigation and prosecution of persons accused of such crimes, called the 'Case Matrix'.[52]

5.6 *Academia*

Following many years of consideration and deliberations, an academic post for International Humanitarian Law was established at the University of Oslo's Institute for Human Rights (today, Norwegian Centre for Human Rights). University courses in International Humanitarian Law have been run regularly since 2004 and are available at both bachelor and masters level. In accordance with a special agreement between the armed forces and the University of Oslo, these modules are available to students at the Military Academies and the Command and Staff College as well. From around the same time, the Institute for Public Law at Oslo University has been running regular courses in International Criminal Law. Both courses are offered in English and attract considerable numbers of students from abroad, in addition to Norwegians. The University has thus increased their attention to both the law of armed conflict and international criminal law, both of which have humanitarian considerations or a 'principle of humanity' as part of their fundamental principles and understandings.

5.7 *Media and civil society*

Although not strictly a matter of implementation, it is interesting to note the increased attention given in recent years to the law of armed conflict and especially violations of these rules, both in the media and by representatives of civil society. This increased attention may be seen as an indication that the general knowledge of the existence of the law of armed conflict has improved. For instance, the media covers the Norwegian contribution to the ISAF mission in Afghanistan rather extensively, and any incidents where Norwegian forces wound or kill anyone are closely scrutinised. For example, after Norwegian forces killed a motorbike driver who failed to stop when repeatedly told to do so, *Dagbladet*, one of the larger national papers in the country, ran the following headline: 'Norwegian soldiers killed Kahl's dad'.[53] The headline was accompanied by the photo of a sad-looking young boy. The focus of the media attention surrounding this incident was whether the man killed was a civilian or an insurgent – in other words, was he a lawful target? Or had the Norwegian forces committed an unlawful act? In the end, this question was not answered, but based on an investigation, the Judge Advocate concluded that the soldiers had acted lawfully as they acted in self-defence.[54]

The media focus on the Norwegian participation in the bombing of Libya, first as part of the US Operation Odyssey Dawn and then NATO's Operation Unified Protector, was intense from the start. The focus can be divided into two categories. First, the media and commentators have discussed the role of the Norwegian contribution and whether the UN Security Council mandate actually permits the bombing of Libyan forces as a way to protect the civilian population. A part of this debate has been who and what are lawful targets, and the perhaps unsurprising debate concerning the legality and legitimacy of collateral damage to civilians. The other focus has been on the decision made by the Norwegian Air Force not to release detailed information concerning the operations Norwegian pilots have been involved in. As the number of fighter pilots in Norway is relatively small, it was feared that the media would link individual pilots to the attacks they had been ordered to carry out, and it was considered that this would impose an unacceptable strain on the pilots and their families. Nevertheless, the public criticised the armed forces for being unnecessarily secretive and stressed that they had a right to know what the forces were involved in.[55] As the pressure to release more information increased, the compromise solution was reached that the armed forces would release a weekly summary of Norwegian F-16 operations.[56]

The media is not exclusively critical of the activities of the armed forces. When commenting on allegations made that Norwegian forces had committed war crimes and may have witnessed torture without doing anything to prevent it, the media offered some defence of the role of the armed forces. The allegations were set out in a book by Erling Borgen in 2009, *Fredsnasjonens hemmeligheter*,[57] which roughly translates as *The Secrets of the Peace Nation*. In this case, the media was quick to point out the many mistakes they had found in the book, and it became clear that the media considered the allegations to be unfounded.[58] Borgen was even given an invitation, through the media, to present his information to the Judge Advocate General's office in order for them to look into the need for an investigation,[59] but he did not respond to the offer. The debate about the book was over after a short while.

The critical scrutiny of acts carried out during armed conflicts is not only aimed at the acts of the Norwegian armed forces. In the fighting between Israel and Palestinians in Gaza 2008–2009, the media paid considerable attention to the extent of compliance with the law of armed conflicts. For instance, the Israeli use of white phosphorus was much criticised,[60] but it was also pointed out that Israel gave the civilian population warning that areas would be attacked.[61] Perhaps more interesting evidence of the increased knowledge of the law of armed conflict is the demand by a group of Norwegian lawyers for charges to be brought against a list of Israeli politicians, including current ministers, and high-level officers,[62] although it should be pointed out that the lawyers to some extent mix the *jus in bello*, and the consequences of violations of these rules, together with aspects of *jus ad bellum*. The Public Prosecutor decided not to investigate the matter, among other things due to the lack of connection between Norway and the persons accused.[63]

5.8 *Summary*

Recent years have seen an increase in the focus and attention given to the law of armed conflict, within the armed forces, among politicians, and in the media. The training in the armed forces has been expanded and improved, new treaties have been signed and national legislation adopted; the first Norwegian trial concerning war crimes since the Second World War has been completed, and the media does not seem to miss any opportunity to comment on the legality of acts carried out by the armed forces. During the same period, Norwegian participation in armed conflicts has also increased, especially through troop contribution to the ISAF mission in Afghanistan, and more recently to operations Odyssey Dawn and Unified Protector in Libya. This may explain the increased attention to the rules governing what the armed forces actually do in such operations, i.e., the law of armed conflict in general; however, does it explain the increased focus on the humanitarian aspects of the rules seen among members of the general public and the media in particular? As mentioned in the summary in Section 4.6 above, the lack of threats to Norway as a state is probably an influential factor in this development. Most people will agree that it is desirable to limit the brutalities of war; the question is how much should be permitted under the justification that it is militarily necessary in order to win. If the latter becomes less important, more weight will be given to humanitarian considerations. Another aspect is the fact that this development may form part of a bigger picture in international relations, where the period in question has seen an increased emphasis on human rights and attempts to justify interventions into other states on the basis of humanitarian considerations or a responsibility to protect civilians.[64] These matters are, however, far beyond the scope of this chapter.

6. Some reflections

6.1 Delay in implementation

Although considerable efforts have been made in order to implement the obligations under the law of armed conflict, their implementation has sometimes been slower than desirable. In many cases, as much as ten to twenty years might elapse from when the Judge Advocate General or someone else drew attention to the fact that there was an obligation that had not been fulfilled, or otherwise forwarded some proposal, until it was implemented in practice. Examples of such cases are the introduction of a university-level course on the law of armed conflict, the establishment of the body responsible for the review of new weapons, the creation of a military Manual of the law of armed conflict, and an upgrade of the training given to soldiers. All of these have, however, now been implemented. Furthermore, there has been considerable delay in organising the armed forces' legal advisers on operational law into some form of a corps. This group plays a vital role in ensuring implementation and understanding of the law of armed conflict in the armed forces, and the lack of formal organisation has meant that training to some extent has become fragmented and less coordinated. Although the creation of a corps presently seems unlikely, efforts are being made to better coordinate and support the military legal advisers (as of May 2012).

6.2 Present challenges

Article 58(b) of the Additional Protocol requires that the parties to the conflict 'to the maximum extent feasible … [shall] avoid locating military objectives within or near densely populated areas'. This means that measures should be taken in peacetime to ensure that objects which may become lawful targets in the event of an armed conflict occurring in Norway are not located in areas where there are many civilians. With the exception of civil defence, this has arguably not been given sufficient attention. Although several military bases or other objects are located in fairly isolated areas, there are also some located in or near city centres. Three examples may illustrate this. First, the Joint Operational Headquarters at Jåttå, near Stavanger, became over the years surrounded by residential areas. The Headquarters have now been moved to Reitan outside Bodø. A second example is the air transport museum which was established in 1998 in Bodø. The museum, which is a protected object, was located close to the runway of one of the main military airbases in the country. This is, however, a minor problem compared to the fact that the town of Bodø is close to the airbase as well. Finally, the Headquarters of the Chief of Defence was in 2003 moved from the outskirts of Oslo to be co-located with the Ministry of Defence in the vicinity of the ancient castle of Akershus, in central Oslo. It was argued that modern precision weapons were able to distinguish sufficiently between the buildings in question. This argument, however, is valid only as long as the guidance system of the weapon does not malfunction or the weapon is not deflected by successful counter-measures by the party under attack. In case of such malfunction or counter-measures, it is likely to hit something else, for instance, the ancient castle mentioned. Although the prospect of Norway becoming involved in an armed conflict on Norwegian territory thankfully seems fairly unlikely today, the implications of the location of certain military objects would perhaps benefit from renewed attention.

As long as the risk of an armed conflict affecting Norwegian territory seems remote for the time being, the most immediate challenges are related to peace support operations. Nonetheless, as Norwegian participation in such operations is increasing, military personnel are increasingly exposed to situations requiring an application of the law of armed conflict, and there may be an increased risk of these rules being violated by Norwegian citizens. Certain areas where there has been debate concerning the Norwegian application of the law of armed conflict can be mentioned. First, the question of treatment of detainees that are handed over to the Afghan national security forces has in principle been resolved by agreement with the Afghan authorities, with the aim of ensuring that detainees receive proper treatment and are guaranteed not to be given a death penalty. It seems, however, that some ISAF partners are experiencing problems in their corresponding arrangements. Although this has not been a problem for Norway to date, it is important to follow this development closely.

Another question which has been subjected to debate is the anti-personnel use of certain explosive bullets. Experiments carried out by Norwegian researchers in 2002–2003 concluded that the relevant type of ammunition will deflagrate 35 to 70 centimetres after hitting the target, which means that in most cases, it will have passed through a person, leaving a wound similar to that produced by a non-explosive bullet of similar calibre. Similar test results had been achieved in Switzerland in 1999. The ammunition is thus not considered to be covered by the prohibition in the 1868 St Petersburg Declaration,[65] a conclusion reached, among others, by the United States, Australia and Belgium as well. This view is, however, questioned by the ICRC who in their film 'Wound ballistics'[66] show an experiment where a round explodes in a soap-block shortly after entry. There is thus still some debate surrounding the anti-personnel use of such ammunition, but there are no indications that Norway intends to depart from the previous research-based conclusions and change the official position.

7. Conclusions

Implementation is not accomplished over night; in practice it is a long-term task. The situation in Norway is no doubt better today than sixty years ago. The circumstances are, on the other hand, more complicated, for several reasons. In contemporary operations, it is not always clear what rules are applicable. Is it an international armed conflict or a non-international one? Who are lawful combatants? Who are protected civilians? Who are just looking like civilians but are in fact persons participating directly in hostilities and are thus lawful targets? Who may be detained, and for how long? The nature of modern conflicts, combined with increased expectations of the soldiers' knowledge of law, require that those who fight are well trained in the laws applicable to their operations. Furthermore, it is not sufficient to apply the law of armed conflict; other areas of international law must be taken into consideration as well. One of the most important of these is international human rights law, the application of which is contested both in the extra-territorial dimension and in relation to the law of armed conflict as *lex specialis*. This debate has been touched upon by other contributions in this book, and has not been covered further here.

So is it possible to draw some general conclusions on the process of implementing the Geneva Conventions and their Protocols, and other agreements relating to the conduct of warfare? Is it possible to find a 'Norwegian approach' to dealing with these rules that indicates an altered attitude towards the weight that should be given to the underlying humanitarian considerations? It is impossible to find a clear answer to these questions, but a few observations may be presented.

In the first years after the ratification of the 1949 Geneva Conventions, the focus in Norway was on enabling those who violate the rules to be punished – perhaps not surprising when considering the many violations of the laws of war that were committed by the Nazi occupying forces. Post-war trials, however, show that it was accepted that the German occupying power had the right to implement several measures to ensure their security, something which indicates a somewhat pragmatic approach to the rules. Still, when the occupying force and those working with them went beyond what was permitted by the rules or considered acceptable in light of the Martens Clause, the courts were willing to depart from their usual positivistic approach, sentencing those responsible for violating the laws of humanity and the dictates of the public conscience.[67] Thus, despite the pragmatism, the underlying values and considerations of the laws were also given considerable weight.

The next question then is whether this has changed in recent years. At the conference leading up to the adoption of the Additional Protocols, Norway suggested a ban on certain weapons. As already discussed, these proposals show a prioritisation of the humanitarian consideration above military needs. In the years after, Norway has continued to work for such bans, for instance of anti-personnel mines and cluster munitions. Although the training and teaching in the law of armed conflict has retained its practical focus, it has expanded in scope, reflecting the increased emphasis placed on this area. The main reason for this is probably the increased Norwegian participation in situations requiring an application of the law of armed conflict, such as the international operations in Kosovo and Afghanistan. However, it is not entirely clear whether there is a relative increase in the emphasis on humanitarian consideration, to the detriment of other considerations such as military necessity, or whether there is just an increased emphasis on the law of armed conflict in general, including the humanitarian considerations.

An improved awareness of the law of armed conflict can also be found among civilian actors and the general public. The establishment of tribunals for war crimes and other core international crimes has probably contributed to this heightened awareness, which has led to political and administrative attention. Such awareness is, however, in many cases directed more towards issues with the potential for drama, such as war crimes investigations and international operations, while the more mundane tasks of preparing the civil society for a war that hopefully never will come, receives less attention.

It may also be argued that the expectations of the general public have changed. The 'public conscience' seems to dictate that no losses should be made, neither among Norwegian soldiers nor others. Mistakes, even if considered acceptable under the law of armed conflict, are less tolerated. If the media reflects public opinion, it seems that soldiers are expected to do even more to ensure that no mistakes are made, even if it is not required by law and it puts them at considerable risk. This gives the impression that humanitarian considerations weigh more, thereby shifting the balance between military necessity and humanity. However, one might speculate as to whether this may merely be caused by a confusion of the elements of the law of armed conflict with elements of human rights law. It may also be speculated on whether humanitarian considerations will always weigh relatively more than military necessity, thereby restricting the military acts more than the laws require, as long as this military necessity is not dictated by one's own country's struggle for survival.

Notes

1 Norwegian Ministry of Defence, *Norsk soldathåndbok* (Fredrikshald: E. Sem, 1920) (authors' translation).
2 Chief of Army, D9 Offprint of Regulations concerning the Laws and Customs of War on Land: Agreement (the revised Geneva Convention) for the Amelioration of the Condition of Wounded and Sick in Armies in the Field; Geneva Convention Relative to the Treatment of Prisoners of War (authors' translation, original title: D9 Særtrykk Reglement angående Landkrigens Lover og Sedvaner – Overenskomst (den reviderte Genève-konvensjon) om forbedring av såredes og sykes skjebne i arméer i felten – Overenskomst om behandling av krigsfanger), Oslo, 7 June 1949.
3 Parliamentary proposition (St.prp.) no. 28 (1951) 3. The other states were: Chile, Colombia, Cuba, Denmark, Ecuador, Guatemala, Liechtenstein, Monaco, Nicaragua, Pakistan, Peru, Switzerland, Syria, Turkey and Uruguay. All signatures were made subject to ratification.
4 Parliamentary proposition (St.prp.) no. 28 (1951) 17.
5 Parliamentary proposition (Ot.prp.) no. 30 (1954) 2.
6 Section 107 was later amended (see below), and has now been repealed by the introduction of the new civil Penal Code 2005.
7 Military Penal Code (Mil.strl.), s. 9(5).
8 Military Penal Code (Mil.strl.), s. 11.
9 Parliamentary proposition (St.prp.) no. 28 (1951) 25 ff.
10 *Håndbok for soldaten* (Stavanger: Dreyer Aksjeselskap, 1957) 224–31.
11 O.E. Blomdal, *Krigens rett* (Oslo: Forsvarets Sanitet, 1974).
12 *Ibid.* 3 (authors' translation).
13 *Ibid.* 3 (authors' translation).
14 *Ibid.* 4.

15 Parliamentary report (St.meld.) no. 109 (1972–1973).
16 *Ibid.* 11–12.
17 *Ibid.* 16.
18 *Ibid.* 16–17; Parliamentary report (St.meld.) no. 102 (1978–1979) 36–8.
19 Parliamentary report (St.meld.) no. 109 (1972–1973) 12.
20 *Ibid.* 13–14.
21 See Parliamentary proposition (St.prp.) no. 73 (1997–1998) para 2.2.
22 See e.g., Parliamentary proposition (Ot.prp.) no. 7 (2008–2009) para 2.1.
23 Military Penal Code (Mil.strl.), s. 3.
24 Parliamentary proposition (Ot.prp.) no. 80 (1980–1981) 6.
25 *Ibid.* 8.
26 M. Ruud, *Innføring i krigens folkerett* (Oslo: Tanum-Norli, 1980).
27 *Ibid.* 97.
28 *Ibid.* 97.
29 *Ibid.* 99.
30 A.-W. Dahl, *Håndbok i militær folkerett* (Oslo: Cappelen Akademisk forlag, 2003).
31 A.-W. Dahl, *Håndbok i militær folkerett* (2nd ed, Oslo: Cappelen Akademisk forlag, 2008).
32 Dahl, *Håndbok* (1st ed), 40–1; *Hanbook* (2nd ed), 45.
33 The Norwegian armed forces' training in the law of armed conflict was modernised in the period 2004–2006, in accordance with the Standard NATO Agreement (NATO STANAG) 2449, introduced 29 March 2004, and the standards set for the law of armed conflict training programme for the various levels of military personnel.
34 This electronic course was based on the teaching material produced by Associate Professor at the Military Academy, the late Judge Advocate Terje Lund, in 1987.
35 S.R. Johansen and J.T. Staib, *Jus og militærmakt* (Oslo: Gyldendal akademisk, 2009).
36 Chief of Defence, Direktiv for anskaffelse og bruk av mindre dødelige våpen (Directive on acquisition and use of less lethal weapons), Oslo, 6 December 2007, and Direktiv om etterlevelse av enkelte folkerettsforpliktelser vedrørende saniteten (Directive on the compliance with certain international legal obligations relating to the medical services), Oslo, 22 January 2008, updated 01 May 2009.
37 Parliamentary proposition (St.prp.) no.1 (2008–2009) 63.
38 Norwegian Red Cross, *Når krigen raser – regler, dilemmaer og konsekvenser* (Oslo, 2006).
39 Norwegian Red Cross, *Menneskerettigheter i krig* (Oslo: Grøndahl, 1984).
40 *Traktat og Konvensjonssamling i Krigens folkerett*, version 1.0, published by FO/VI (legal department) and produced by the Military Police, February 2001.
41 Norwegian Red Cross, *Genevekonvensjonene av 12. august 1949: med tilleggsprotokoller samt sentrale menneskerettigheter* (Oslo, 2007).
42 Oslo District Court (Oslo tingrett), 2 December 2008, case no. 08–018985MED-OTIR/08.
43 The argument of the legislator is that the new term 'crime against humanity' may be applied to all acts which were both an international crime at the time and a crime in Norway, even if under a different name. See Parliamentary proposition (Ot.prp.) no. 8 (2007–2008).
44 Section 97 of the Norwegian Constitution: 'No law must be given retroactive effect.'
45 This case is further discussed by Sigrid Redse Johansen, Chapter 8.

46 LB-2009–24039, 10–11. The same comment is made by the Supreme Court, HR 2010–2057-P, 84
47 LB-2009–24039, 63–4.
48 LB-2009–24039, 14–16.
49 HR-2010–2057-P, 62–127.
50 HR-2010–808-A.
51 HR-2010–2057-P, 119, authors' translation.
52 For more information, see www.jus.uio.no/smr/english/about/programmes/icc/.
53 See www.dagbladet.no/2009/07/30/nyheter/innenriks/afghanistan/forsvaret/7426325/.
54 See e.g., www.nrk.no/nyheter/1.6780657.
55 See e.g., www.vg.no/nyheter/utenriks/libya/artikkel.php?artid=10086318.
56 See e.g., www.tv2.no/nyheter/utenriks/faremo-lover-mer-aapenhet-rundt-libyabombing-3511479.html. The weekly updates are availabe at http://forsvaret.no/om-forsvaret/forsvaret-i-utlandet/libya/Sider/Ukesoppdatering.aspx.
57 E. Borgen, *Fredsnasjonens hemmeligheter* (Oslo: Manifest, 2009).
58 See e.g., www.dagbladet.no/2009/11/21/nyheter/erling_borgen/innenriks/forsvaret/afghanistan/9133163/.
59 See www.dagbladet.no/2009/11/11/nyheter/erling_borgen/innenriks/afghanistan/utenriks/8977084/.
60 See e.g., www.dagsavisen.no/utenriks/article407172.ece.
61 See e.g., www.vg.no/nyheter/utenriks/midtosten/artikkel.php?artid=539617.
62 See www.ntbinfo.no/pressrelease/detail.do?pressId=13509&type=thisweek&searchKey=14cbbe63-2f1c-11de-a5a4-67a16b818523&languageId=NO&pageIndex=1.
63 See www.vg.no/nyheter/utenriks/midtosten/artikkel.php?artid=594368.
64 UN Security Council Resolution 1973 authorising under Chapter VII the use of force against Libya may be seen as an example of this trend to define the international society's responsibility to protect civilians everywhere from atrocities as a permissible ground to use armed force against another state, at least if the situation can be argued to threaten international peace and security.
65 1868 St Petersburg Declaration Renouncing the Use, in Time of War, of Explosive Projectiles under 400 Grammes Weight.
66 International Committee of the Red Cross, *Wound Ballistics* (Geneva, 2008).
67 See Sigrid Redse Johansen, Chapter 8.

PART III

Conclusions

13

Conclusions: is there a 'principle of humanity' in international humanitarian law?

KJETIL MUJEZINOVIĆ LARSEN AND CAMILLA GULDAHL COOPER

The introductory chapter to this book asked three separate, but related, questions. Does a 'principle of humanity' exist in contemporary international humanitarian law, or is such a principle at least emerging? Is a shift taking place in the relationship between humanitarian considerations and considerations of military necessity? Are regional or national differences emerging with regard to the import and emphasis placed on humanitarian considerations in international humanitarian law? At this final stage, it is appropriate to recapitulate how the different chapters have addressed these issues, in order to consider whether general conclusions may be drawn.

Robert Kolb has identified four different phases in the evolution of international humanitarian law from 1864 onwards, and he argues that each phase is 'characterised by a set of common fundamental understandings, problems and operational principles'. His approach serves as a reminder of an obvious, but important, fact and a premise for the present book, namely that international humanitarian law is not a static body of law. New positive norms are continuously being adopted, new norms acquire the status of international customary law, and military developments and other changes in the factual context lead to new practice or to new interpretations of existing norms. For the present book, this leads to the observation that even if one considers that a 'principle of humanity' has traditionally not existed in international humanitarian law, or even that it does not exist today, this does not in itself mean that such a principle may not emerge in the future, or that a process of emergence is not taking place. Kolb's chapter is silent on this matter, leaving room for the reader to make his or her own reflections. He does, however, refer to his fourth phase (the current phase, from 1993 onwards) as a phase of 'progressive "humanisation"' of international humanitarian law. He argues that international humanitarian law is becoming more homo-centric rather than state-centred through developments such as individual criminal responsibility for violations of international humanitarian law, the incorporation of human rights concerns, the development of minimum humanitarian standards for situations of internal disturbances, and an extended applicability of international humanitarian law to ensure increased protection of individuals. He also argues that '"absolute" prohibitions' are being postulated, referring to the tendency that 'any attempts of evasion [of obligations under international humanitarian law] tend to be eschewed by legal constructions guaranteeing the applicability of the protections'. Can a 'principle of humanity' emerge as a consequence of the 'humanisation' of international humanitarian law? Can such a principle be invoked as a 'legal construction' that prevents evasions of obligations under international humanitarian law?

Yoram Dinstein would answer these questions in the negative. After Kolb's historic approach, Dinstein's chapter is the natural starting point for an assessment of the contemporary legal situation. In his view, '[t]here is no overarching, binding, norm of humanity that tells us what we must do (or not do) in wartime'. In his chapter, he makes the argument that 'the principles of humanity should be viewed not as legal norms but as extra-legal considerations'. Humanitarian considerations, which is the term Dinstein prefers, 'pave the road to the creation of legal norms', but they 'do not by themselves amount to law'. As will be elaborated upon below, this is perhaps the closest we can get to a concise 'conclusion' to this book insofar as the *lex lata* is concerned. Dinstein's chapter focuses instead on the principle of proportionality, which in his view is 'the key to the effective protection of civilians and civilian objects from the consequences of attack in warfare'. Dinstein describes how this principle offers no protection to combatants, but he continues to describe how the principle of unnecessary suffering prohibits the use of weapons which uselessly aggravates the suffering of combatants. Since he even concludes by referring to the 'non-existence of a normative "principle of humanity"', the reader should be in no doubt as to his view. By combining Dinstein's presentation of the principles of proportionality and of unnecessary suffering, the reader may also be convinced that there is no particular *need* for a supplementary 'principle of humanity'. Nevertheless, Dinstein makes a number of arguments that may cause the reader some concern. He concludes, for example, that it may be legal to attack a munitions factory even if this creates a hazard for thousands of civilian employees, and that the principle of proportionality may be relaxed in situations where involuntary human shields are involved. These conclusions may be legally well-founded, but they may – if nothing else – spur some reflections concerning the relationship between law and morality.

Cecilie Hellestveit does not purport either to support or contest Dinstein's conclusions; her chapter lies on a different level. The chapter introduces a factual premise that must be kept in mind throughout the book, namely the fundamental distinction between international and non-international armed conflicts. For this reason it has been included at the earlier stage of the book. Could, or does, a 'principle of humanity' play a different role in non-international armed conflicts than in international armed conflicts? The rudimentary rules applicable in non-international armed conflicts could suggest that there is more room for a 'principle of humanity' that could offer elementary protection to victims of armed conflicts to the extent that no positive norms exist. While Hellestveit does not make this argument, her conclusion that humanitarian purposes may be best served by upholding the dichotomy between international and non-international armed conflicts, may provide a basis for the reader to consider this option further.

One of the editors, Kjetil Mujezinović Larsen, builds, in one sense, on one of Hellestveit's arguments. Hellestveit argues that '[t]he more unsettled and flexible set of rules applicable to [non-international armed conflicts] … opens the door for an increased role for other regimes of international law in such conflicts, notably human rights law', and that this is to the benefit of the victims of non-international armed conflicts. Larsen explores the current impact of international human rights law on the conduct of hostilities and poses the question as to whether human rights law 'impact[s] on the conduct of hostilities to such an extent that one can say that IHL must now nevertheless be interpreted in light of a set of purely humanitarian norms'. Larsen's assumption is that human rights law now fills the role that could have been played by a 'principle of humanity'. He also addresses, however, the fact that there are important counter-arguments to the application of human rights law to the conduct of hostilities. He discusses whether the emergence of a 'principle of humanity' in international humanitarian law in reality could achieve the same aim as the application of human rights law to the conduct of hostilities sets out to achieve. This could, he argues, 'contribute to a more coherent relationship between IHL and HRL, since a "principle of humanity" could function as a "humanitarian exception" entirely within the framework of IHL and thereby reduce the need to turn to external rules'.

In the final chapter on the theoretical basis for a principle of humanity, Katarina Månsson has also focused on the interrelationship, and what she sees as interdependence, between international human rights law and international humanitarian law. She concludes, based on her thorough study of the protection of children in armed conflict, that '[t]he legal standing of the principle of humanity may be more diffuse, but is still implicit in the principle's status as the normative foundation of both international humanitarian law and human rights law'. She further argues that such a principle must be seen to exist in customary international humanitarian law. Nevertheless, even if such a principle exists, Månsson points out that there remain considerable challenges with the practical application of the protection this principle provides. The question of whether this poor record of state practice in fact serves to undermine the finding that a customary law rule exists today is not discussed, but perhaps it is an element to consider with regard to whether the norm is emerging or already in existence.

In the first presentation of a Nordic perspective, Lauri Hannikainen provides another example of state practice, which is arguably not in total compliance with a principle of humanity. As his title suggests, it seems more like an example of international regulation being 'pushed aside'. As part of the plan 'to create an ethnically "fully clean" Finno-Ugric province' in Eastern Karelia, people considered to be 'alien' were placed in camps where the conditions, according to survivors, were inhumane: 'there was a complete lack of privacy, and the inmates were forced to cope with, inter alia, cold, hunger, fear, anxiety, inadequate food, and rags as clothes'. Hannikainen concludes that this is a clear violation of both the 1907 Hague Regulations and of the Martens Clause. In contrast to the more current trends of Nordic states, this perhaps provides an example of how states attach less weight to humanitarian considerations when they are more directly affected by armed conflicts than is the case with participation in international operations. Furthermore, the practice of Finland, especially in 1941–1942, does not exactly provide support for the existence of a customary law principle of humanity at that time.

In contrast, Sigrid Redse Johansen provides insight into an example of humanitarian considerations being given substantive weight, despite the fact that the conflict in question was the Nazi occupation of Norway. Norway has a tradition of positivism and legal realism, and the principle of legality has been given a strict interpretation in criminal law. Still, in the post-war settlement, the Norwegian Supreme Court made reference to the Martens Clause and the fundamental principles intrinsic in the Clause as a legal basis for penal prosecution. They argued that such fundamental principles must be seen as binding, even if national law violates them. This is thus a clear argument in favour of humanitarian considerations having a legally binding effect, although perhaps more as an element of interpretation rather than an independent legal basis. In other words, it does not support the assertion that humanity can be seen as a principle, but it still confirms its importance. In fact, Johansen concludes that 'it is arguable that the threshold for finding that rules of customary law have been formed is being lowered because clearly immoral behaviour quickly gets the status of a crime in customary law, even if it is questionable whether the amount of supporting state practice is sufficient'.

In the next chapter, Ola Engdahl brings us back to the current situation, being the first of three chapters focusing on international peace and security operations. Engdahl's chapter addresses one initial problem with this book's question concerning a 'Nordic perspective' on international humanitarian law. When the armed forces of a state are deployed to international operations, the troop contributing nation does not (necessarily) become a party to an armed conflict. And if a state is not a party to an armed conflict, it may not be the entity that is responsible for adherence to international humanitarian law in the conflict, and it may then be methodically difficult to use the practice of that state as an indication of a particular 'perspective' on international humanitarian law. Engdahl uses the ISAF operation in Afghanistan as a prime example, and demonstrates that even among the Nordic countries there are quite different views as to how the situation in Afghanistan should be classified and what the formal status of the troop contributing nation is; he observes, inter alia, that 'Denmark and Norway regard themselves as being parties to the armed conflict in Afghanistan, while … Sweden do[es] not', and that the position of the states 'differ on the applicability of IHL to the peace operation forces in Afghanistan'. He stresses, however, that none of the observations should be over-estimated. But if one stretches the observation further, it suggests that it may be difficult to identify a common 'Nordic perspective' on international humanitarian law.

Peter Vedel Kessing discusses the legal framework in peace operations in a narrower context, namely with regard to the norms and procedures concerning detention of individuals for security reasons. He examines the relevant norms in international humanitarian law and human rights law, and their application in peace operations. After reaching an intermediary conclusion that it is 'complicated to determine the precise grounds and procedures on which the individual may be detained' in such operations, he continues to discuss whether it is possible to establish 'common minimum standards' for detention in peace operations.

Here he builds on the so-called Copenhagen Process on the Handling of Detainees in International Military Operations, and expresses the hope that this process will succeed, because this 'is needed and necessary due to the uncertainty surrounding the applicable detention standards in UN peace operations, especially when considering the special protective and humanitarian mandate of UN peace forces'. The main point to be underlined now is that this process was initiated by the Danish government. While this process may not have been driven (only) by a desire to improve the humanitarian standards applicable to detainees, it is an example of an initiative taken by a Nordic country to clarify and/or strengthen the position of vulnerable groups in conflicts.

Rikke Ishøy also addresses the Danish responses to its increased foreign military engagement. Focusing on different examples of such responses, such as Danish participation in ISAF and a war crimes case arising from the former Yugoslavia, she makes the argument that the focus often is too legalistic, at the cost of the more human dimensions: 'the moral consequences or political responsibility for the acts committed are left unaddressed'. According to Ishøy, this approach is the result of their remoteness from violence: 'Danes have had the good fortune to live lives mostly removed from violence, and in public discourse Danish politicians have had to balance their audience's understandable abhorrence of violence with the military realities faced by Danish troops abroad. Sometimes it seems that this has led them to take the "easy" way out – by choosing a legalistic response rife with references to international humanitarian law.' Furthermore, she argues that there is a tendency to say that because something is lawful it is also morally right. Still, Danish armed forces do in fact limit themselves beyond what is strictly required by law, that 'just because something can be designated as lawful does not mean that it is a good idea'. Nonetheless, Ishøy concludes that the decisions of the Danish armed forces are ultimately guided by military considerations and objectives, rather than humanitarian considerations. This chapter thereby provides support for the thesis that countries further removed from violence have a different approach to war. Although the argument is made that, rather than focusing more on the humanitarian considerations, the approach in Denmark has been not to give this sufficient weight, this chapter may in itself be seen as an example of how the expectations in such countries are that humanitarian considerations should play a more important role than is perhaps the case today.

The final chapter of the book, written by Arne Willy Dahl and Camilla Guldahl Cooper, provides an overview of how international humanitarian law has been implemented in Norway, in an attempt to discover whether there is a tendency to focus more on humanity than on military necessity. Norway has long played a role in the prohibition of certain weapons, something which arguably demonstrates a prioritisation of humanitarian consideration above military needs. More interestingly, perhaps, are the views presented in the public debates arising from Norway's contribution to ISAF, which is the first armed conflict Norwegian forces have been involved in since the Second World War. According to the authors, '[t]he "public conscience" seems to dictate that no losses should be made, neither among Norwegian soldiers nor others. Mistakes, even if considered acceptable under the law of armed conflict, are less tolerated.' This gives the impression that humanitarian considerations weigh more, thereby shifting the balance between military necessity and humanity. Dahl and Cooper conclude that '[i]t may also be speculated on whether humanitarian considerations will always weigh relatively more than military necessity, thereby restricting the military acts more than the laws require, as long as this military necessity is not dictated by one's own country's struggle for survival'.

Does this provide any guidance on the meaning and existence of a 'principle of humanity'? One of the conclusions to be made is that it depends on how the term 'principle' is understood. If by principle one means a legal norm, legally binding as such, it seems safe to conclude that such a principle of humanity does not exist, and there are limited grounds for even arguing that such a principle is emerging. The closest one can find in international humanitarian law is the principle of unnecessary suffering, which is of more limited application.

Moreover, if by principle one is in fact referring to a wider understanding of the term, enhancing extra-legal considerations rather than legal norms, then such a principle could be argued to exist today. Its legal role, however, will be more limited than in the previous interpretations, being more an element of norm creation than an individual legal basis. It may thus be more appropriate to refer to humanitarian considerations rather than a principle of humanity. It could also be debated as to whether there is a need for such a principle or legal norm. International humanitarian law provides protection for civilians and other persons *hors de combat*, both through the principles of distinction and military necessity, requiring that civilians shall never be the object of an attack and that only those objects which are making an effective contribution to military operations may be considered to be lawful targets. Furthermore, the principle of proportionality ensures that operations which cause harm to civilians that is disproportionate to the military advantage expected are unlawful to carry out. Protection is also awarded to combatants through the principle of unnecessary suffering, which prohibits harm that is greater than that unavoidable to achieve legitimate military objectives.

This does not mean that humanitarian considerations play a limited role. As the authors of this book have shown, humanitarian considerations have always played an important role in international humanitarian law, and will continue to do so – both as an element of interpretation and as a moral test which ensures that the applicability of the law is not too far removed from the expectations of the general public. As some of these chapters have shown, however, the expectations of the general public may change depending on the proximity of the armed conflict to their own lives and the survival of their state, thereby affecting the extent to which the public expect the troops to operate with a standard which is higher than what is required by law.

In many cases, humanitarian considerations are incorporated into the rules of international humanitarian law, thereby leaving limited need for a separate principle of humanity. The potential for such a principle is thus most significant in those cases where the rules of international humanitarian law are inadequate or non-existent, as we have seen may in particular be the case in non-international armed conflicts. In such cases there are arguably two alternative solutions: either further development of international humanitarian law through treaty or custom, or widening the application of international human rights law. It seems that the latter is the current trend; however, if this is to be the solution, some agreement ought to be reached with regard to where the limits of the *lex specialis* applicability of international humanitarian law are and where international human rights law begins. There is also a need to decide under which of these areas new rules should be developed, i.e., whether the development of new rules should be used to enhance and strengthen the position of international humanitarian law as *lex specialis*, or to expand the application of human rights law to areas where the human element of war is seen as not being given sufficient attention. In situations of unrest and disturbances, where the level of violence does not reach the threshold of application of international humanitarian law, it appears that considerations of military necessity are not an issue. In situations of armed conflict, the challenge is of course whether human rights law has the ability to take military necessity into account and make it possible to carry out operations within the applicable legal framework, or whether it becomes in practice impossible to operate within applicable rules, thereby risking undermining the system as a whole. If human rights do gain such a role in armed conflicts, it is clear that there has been a shift in the relationship between humanitarian considerations and considerations of military necessity.

INDEX

Note: The page numbers in italics refer to a table.

www.ingramcontent.com/pod-product-compliance
Lightning Source LLC
LaVergne TN
LVHW011529200926
848484LV00001B/202
9781107021846